CONSTABLE AND BRIGHTON

'something out of nothing'

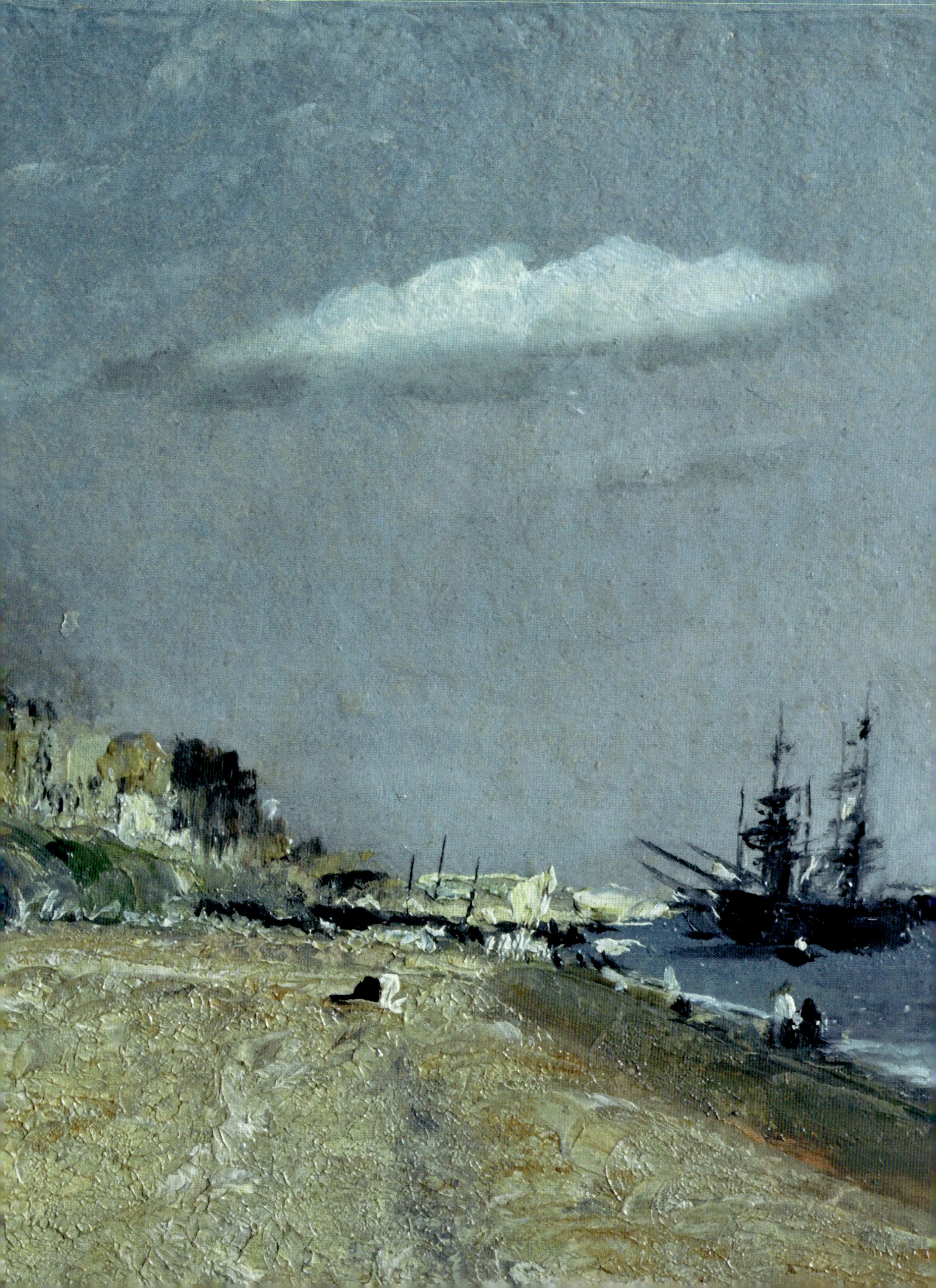

CONSTABLE AND BRIGHTON

'something out of nothing'

EDITED BY SHÂN LANCASTER

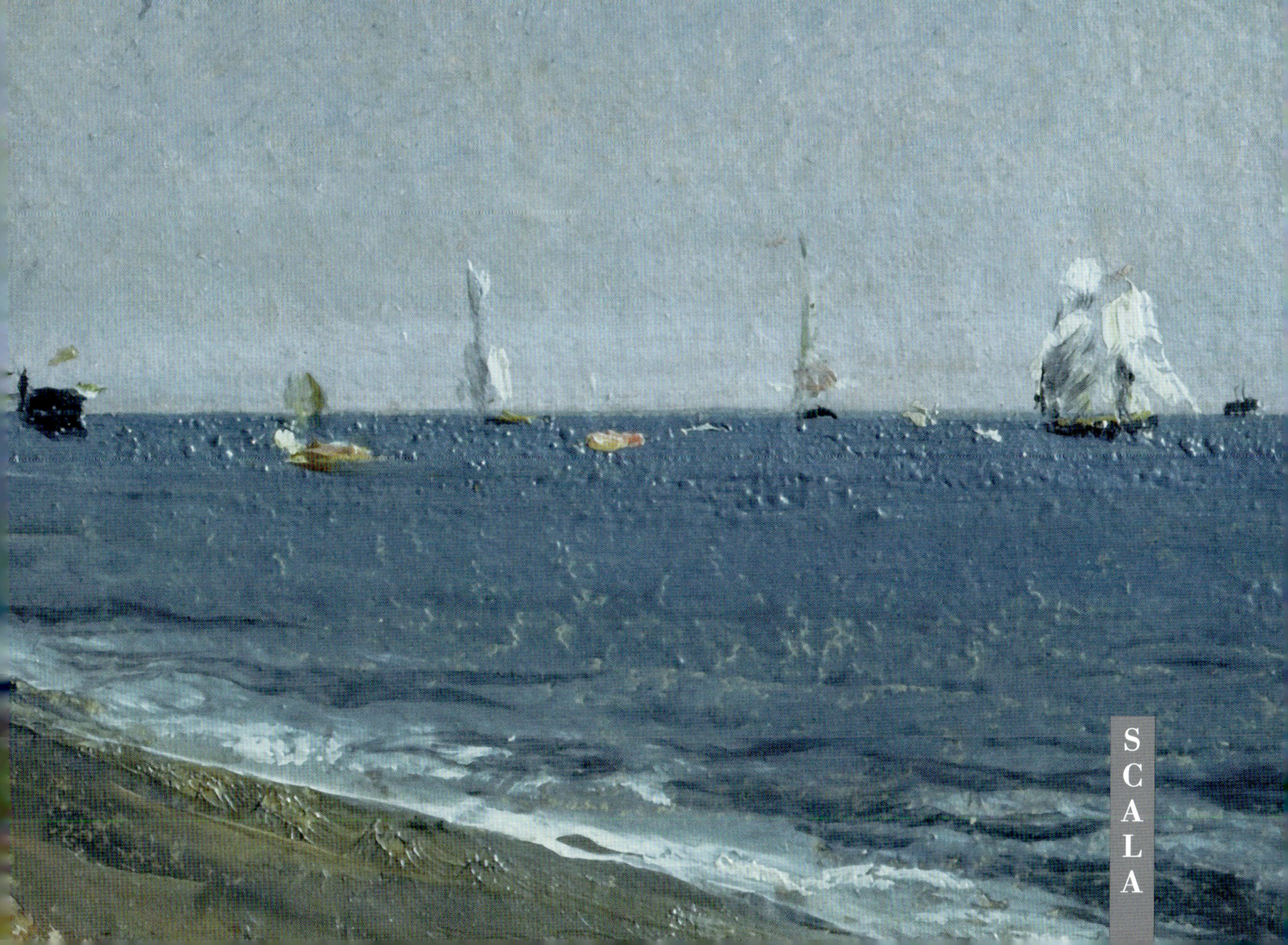

SCALA

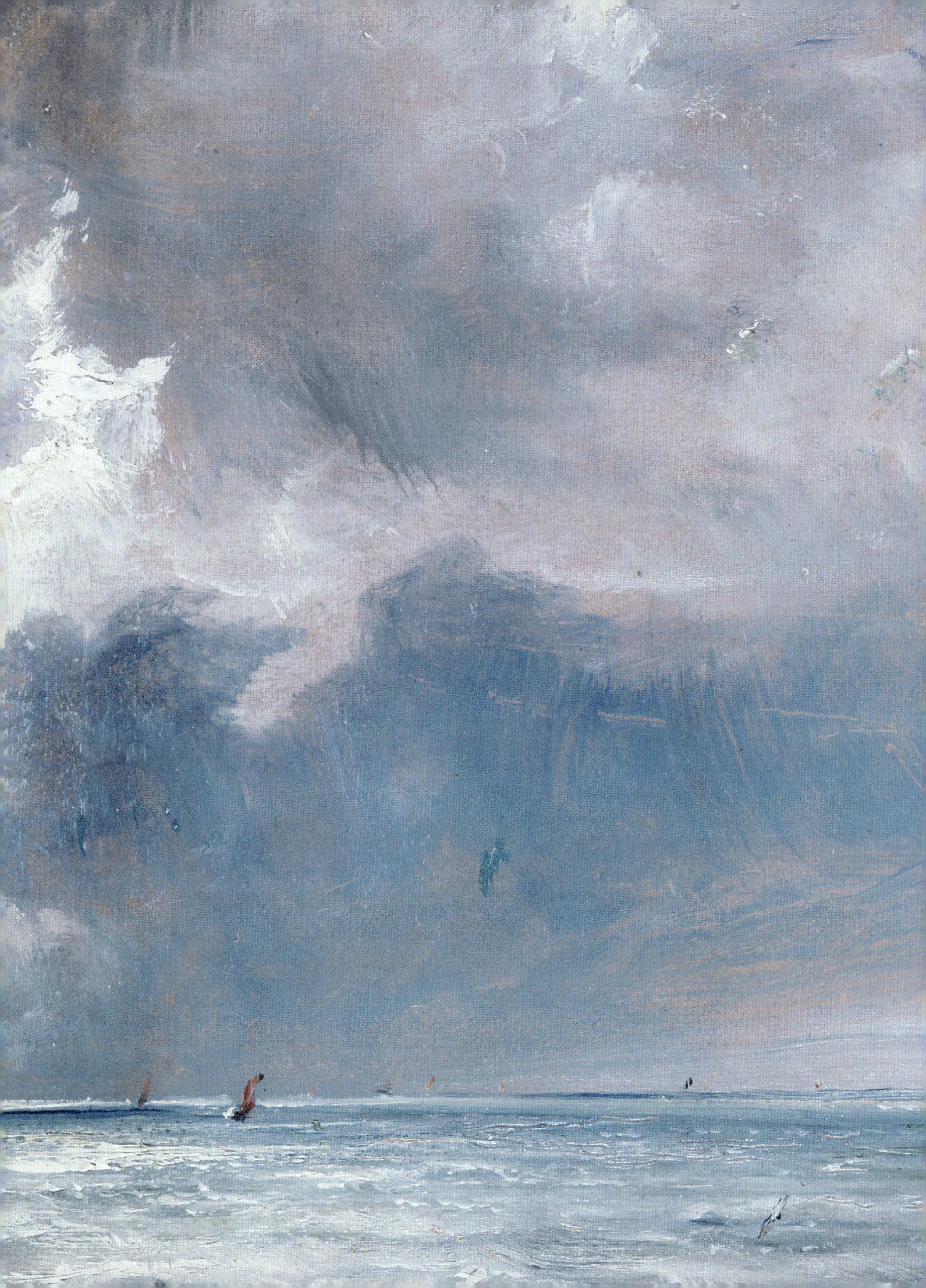

Contents

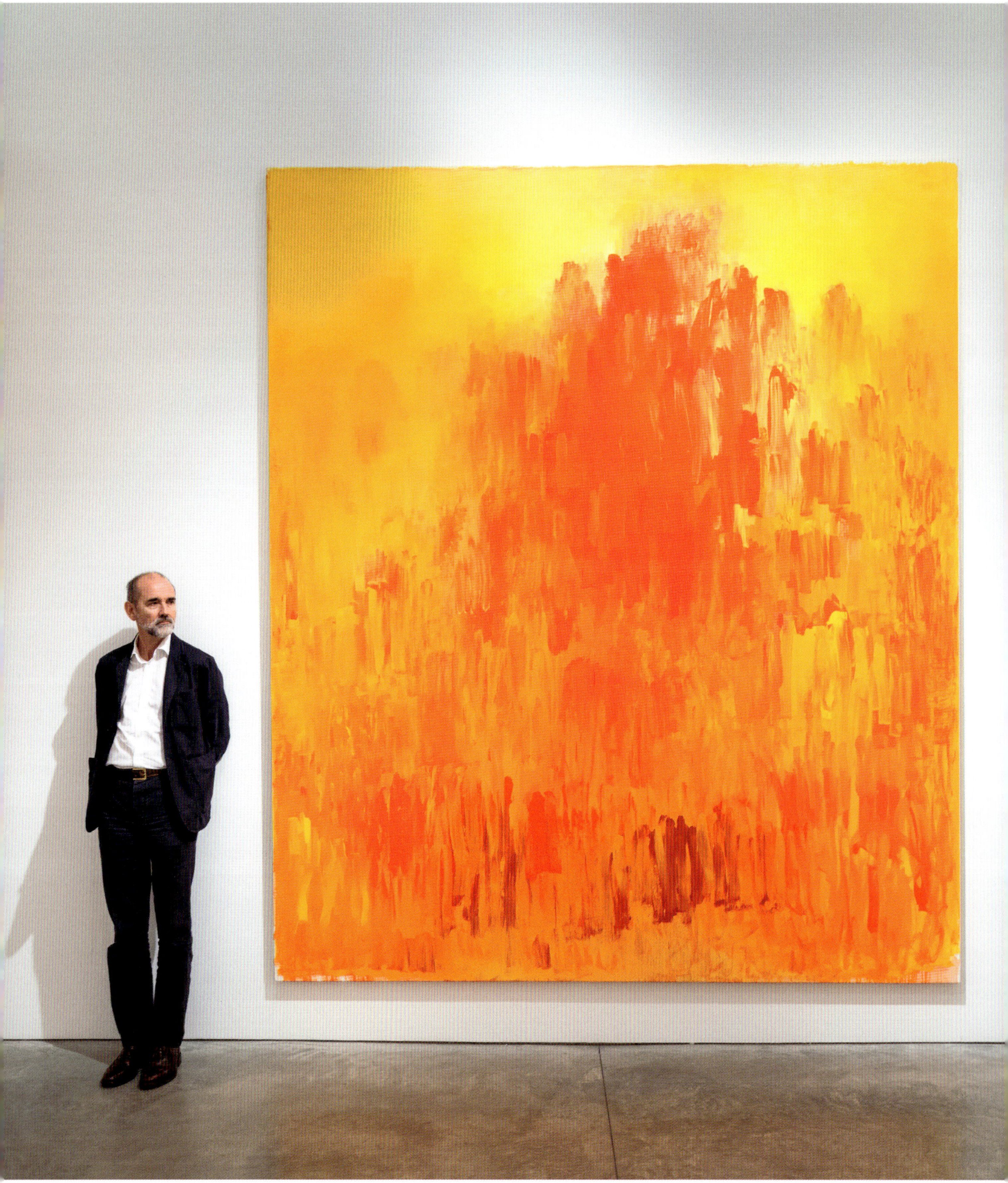

Foreword

Christopher Le Brun,

President, Royal Academy

My very first teaching job was at Brighton Art School. It brought with it the prospect of a little security of income as a young painter and the chance to test and share ideas. I taught there for one day a week from 1976 to 1983, until I became able to support myself from my work alone. Although Gwyther Irwin, the Head of Fine Art, had assembled a distinguished fine art faculty, my first, no doubt mistaken, impression of the staff-room was mostly tweed and pipe smoke (or was that just Raymond Briggs?) and serious poker (Gwyther himself), so I preferred to go down to the beach at lunchtime.

Here I experienced the atmosphere you can still feel in the works Constable and Turner, two of the greatest Royal Academicians of their day, were both inspired to make in the early 1820s during the period covered by this exhibition. Both were drawn to work prolifically by that vast glittering prospect.

The view at Brighton beach is barely altered since Constable's time. Here is the sharp tang of salt, the wash-sound of the surf and the crunch and rattle of pebbles. This is for the foreground, but then the distant horizon – where we search for a sail, possibly an island – is something purely for the eye, an apprehension as pale as thought itself, no sound or smell or touch, unreachable and compelling. Painting itself is a borderland. Its very reliance on imagination to convert one thing to another, material paint into air, to bring it to life, puts it at an edge.

Recently I was in the picture gallery of nearby Petworth House in Sussex. I was listening to a description of a famous artist visitor who stayed for two weeks with the third Earl of Egremont, drawn there by the great collection of paintings and the geniality of his host, but a socially awkward figure, not entirely at ease. Surely the description belongs to Turner? It was a surprise to hear it was John Constable, and a further surprise to learn that none of his paintings was acquired. Turner's identity is clear – the cockney prodigy is magnificently self-sufficient. But Constable, the middle son of a wealthy rural corn merchant, is somehow less comfortable and more in-between, and this is how I see him: in Brighton, at the borderland of sky and sea and England.

Any trip to the sea has something of cheerfulness and hope about it. I was brought up in Southsea, just along the coast to the west, so walking down to its very similar shingle beach was a regular part of my life. In England that comes with a wry glance at the weather but also implies freedom, play, physical well being, pleasure … none of these is very far from what we might wish for art.

My belief in the importance of this Brighton period for Constable is reflected in the Royal Academy's willingness to lend three paintings to this exhibition. The poetry of these works comes from his ability to take a tiny observed fact, a detail of what he sees, and from that point expand into imagination and utterly convincing painterly invention.

Constable's intense relationship with Brighton and its landscapes ended in 1828. A new era for him, both personally and professionally, began just months later, when, on 10 February 1829, he became a Royal Academician. We will be continuing that story as part of our 250th anniversary celebrations at the Royal Academy in 2018.

Christopher Le Brun, President of the Royal Academy of Arts
Image courtesy of Albertz Benda and the Artist
Photo by Adam Reich

9 Sober's Gardens, Brighton

My dear Fisher,

I am living here but I dislike the place – & miss in this my solitude any letter from you... I am however getting on with my french jobs. one of the largest is quite complete and is my best. in freshness and sparkle – with repose – which is my struggle just now...

Brighton is the receptacle of the fashion and offscouring of London. The magnificence of the sea, and its (to use your... beautiful expression) everlasting voice. is drowned in the din & lost in the tumult of stage coaches – gigs – "flys" – etc. – and the beach is only piccadilly (that part of it where we dined) by the sea-side. Ladies dressed & undressed – Gentlemen in morning gowns & slippers on or without them altogether about knee deep in the breakers – footmen – children – nursery maids. dogs. boys. fishermen – preventative service men (with hangers & pistols). rotten fish & those hideous amphibious animals the old bathing women, whose language both in oaths & voice resembles men – all are mixed up together in endless & indecent confusion – the genteeler part the marine parade is still more unnatural – with its trimed and neat appearance & the dandy jetty or chain pier – with its long & elegant strids into the sea a full 1/4 of a mile (small sketch of the Chain pier).

In short there is nothing here for a painter but the breakers – & sky – which have been lovely indeed and always varying. the fishing boats are picturesque. but not so much as the Hastings boats. which are luggers...

But these subjects are so hackneyed in the Exhibition and are in fact so little capable of that beautifull sentiment that Landscape is capable of or which rather belongs to Landscape that they have done a great deal of harm to the art – they form a class of art much easier than Landscape & have in consequence almost suplanted it. and have drawn off many who would have encouraged the groth of a pastoral feel in their own minds – & paid others for pursuing it.

While in the fields (for I am at the west of the city – and quite out of it) I met with a most intelligent and elegant man Mr. Phillips – we are become intimate & he contributes much to our pleasure here. he is a botanist – and all his works on natural history are instructive and entertaining – calculated for children of all ages – his history of trees is delightfull – I shall buy them – & I think you would if you saw them –

Our next door neighbour is Mr & Mrs Masquerier, a portrait painter – retired from business with a fortune – she is a Scotch woman a niece of Ld. Buchan's – vulgar – & clever – with the assurance of the devil – Masquerier & I have no one feeling in common on the Art. – On the score of the Academy the grapes are sour. & although he has made a fortune in the Art. he enjoys it only as a thief enjoys the fruits of his robbery – while he is not found out. he would (I see) give half his fortune for half my reputation

No 9. Mrs Sober's Gardens – so called from Mrs Sober the Lady of the Manor – & rich in estates here – which are more so now by their new building. she is of the <u>good</u>, and has built a Chapple in which she preaches herself. I have heard this story – a man was taken before the Magistrates quite drunk – when asked what he was – he said he was one of Mrs Sober's congregation.

Last Tuesday the finest day that ever was we went to the Dyke – which is in fact a Roman remains of an embankment. overlooking – perhaps the most grand & affecting natural landscape in the world – and consequently a scene the most unfit for a picture. it is the business of a painter not to contend with nature & put this scene (a Valley filled with imagery 50 miles long) on a canvas of a few inches. but to make something out of nothing. in attempting which he must almost of necessity become poetical. But you understand this better than me.

My wife & children are delightfully well. Ever yrs. most truly

John Constable.[1]

Facsimile of a missing letter, dated 29 August 1824, written by Constable and reproduced here by calligrapher Ewan Clayton, as part of a project researching the handwriting of Romantic poets and artists.

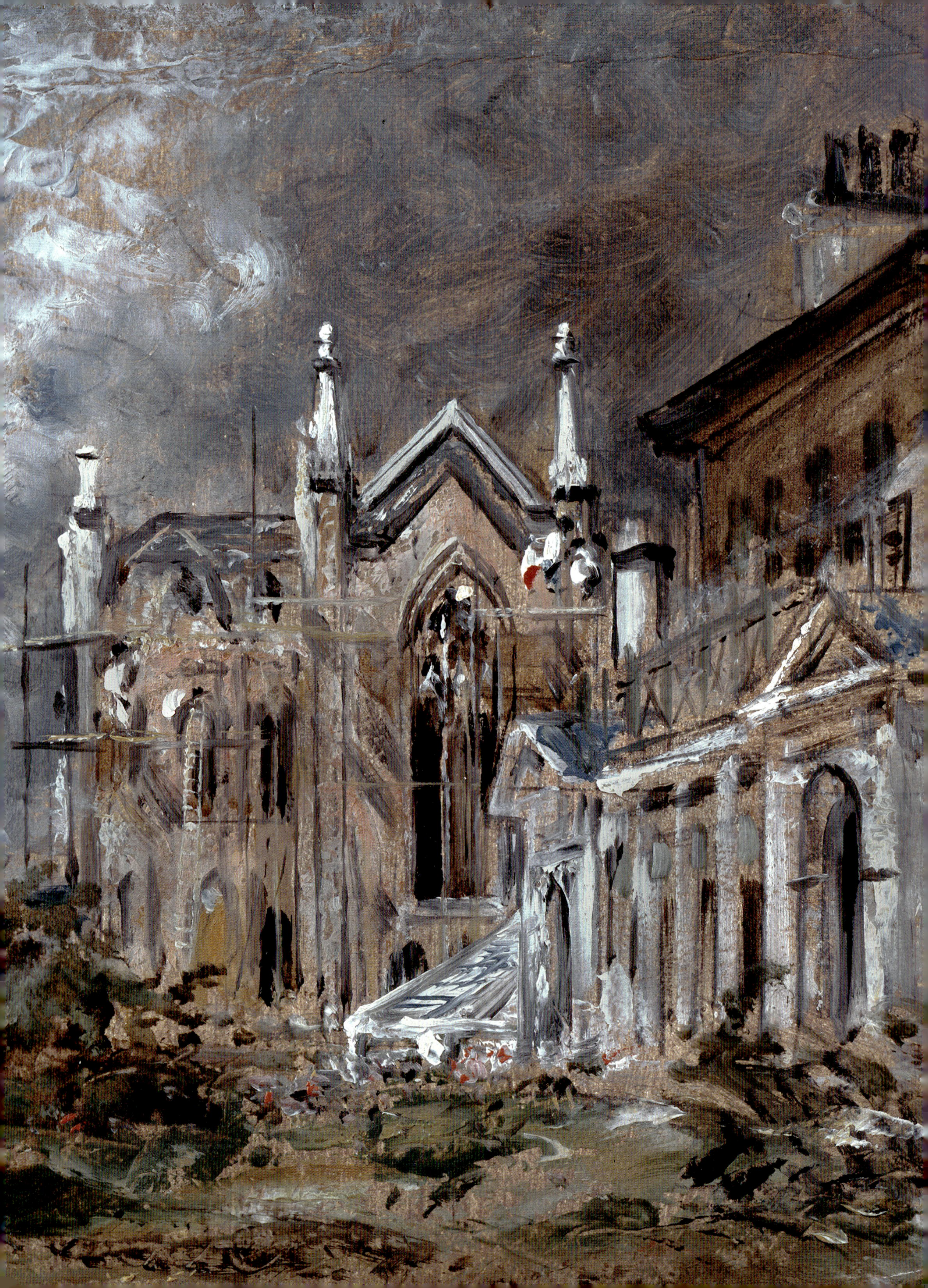

Introduction

'I now want the sea air as much as you'[1]

Shân Lancaster

THIS BOOK and its associated exhibition, *Constable and Brighton*, are based on a charming coincidence. An artist, on moving to Brighton, is told that he is living in the very house where a great landscape painter he reveres once lodged, 186 years ago. From that chance remark has grown a wealth of new insights into Constable's Brighton period.

When Peter Harrap and his young family moved to Brighton in 2010, he and his wife, Natasha Kissell, set up a painting studio on the top floor of their new seaside home, in a light filled space that seemed tailor-made for the purpose. A neighbour, admiring the painterly chaos of easels, brushes, sketches and splashes of paint, casually told them that many years ago John Constable himself was believed to have done exactly the same thing when visiting Brighton on holiday. From that that happy discovery and the joyous response of 'Is there any actual proof of that?' grew a body of research[2] that firmly established that the house was indeed once 9 Sober's Gardens, the address used by Constable in 1824 when he wrote his famous denunciation of the resort as 'Piccadilly … by the sea-side'.[3] His scathing description of the overcrowded town with its 'indecent confusion' of every class of society, cheerful disregard for modesty, tolerance of eccentric behaviour and appalling traffic problems, is one most Brightonians would recognise today.

Detail of fig. 1

Constable scholars had long known the address from letters the artist sent to his friend Archdeacon John Fisher, but its precise location was problematic. He was writing from a town in the throes of an immense building boom. Whole neighbourhoods were springing up almost overnight as brick kilns and scaffolding invaded sheep fields and farmland to the west and the east. Street names could be informally adopted for a few years, then overtaken by the march of what the architect Charles Busby proudly described on his map of his own developments in 1825 (fig. 2) as 'The Magnificent Building Arrangements Now in Rapid Progress'.[4] Sober's Gardens appeared briefly in a few scrappy records and vanished in less than a decade.

During the search for the history of the street (now called Sillwood Road) the inhabitants of other houses began to come vividly to life. The magnificently unorthodox Mrs Sober herself – what a name for a seaside landlady! – was the sister of Thomas Read Kemp, the builder of Kemp Town, the sprawling new development to the east of Brighton. Brother and sister were both at one time members of an evangelistic sect or, as Constable told Fisher with some amusement: 'She is of the *good*, and has built a Chapple in which she preaches herself. I have heard this story – a man was taken before the magistrates quite drunk – when asked what

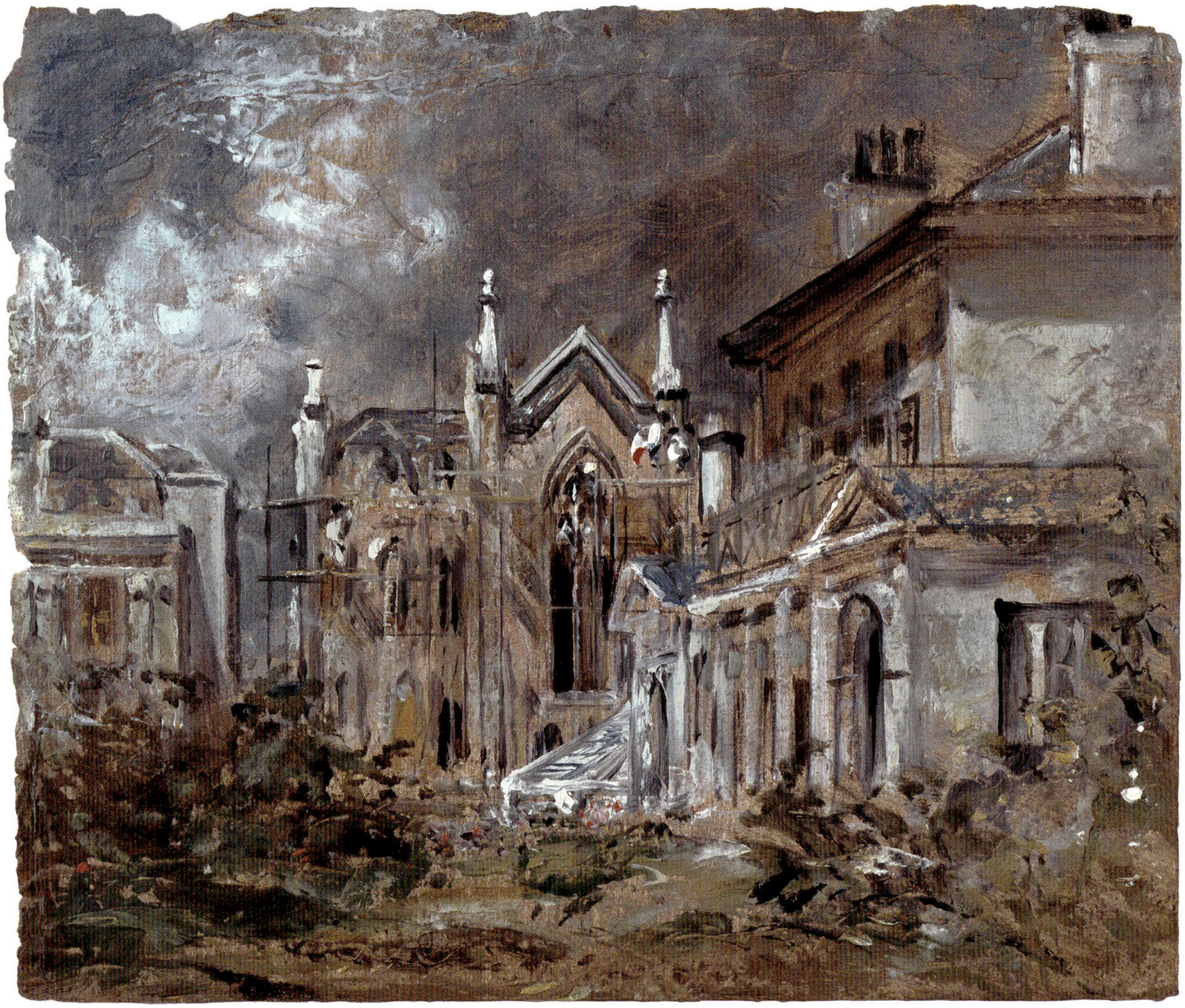

he was he said he was one of Mrs Sober's congregation.'[5]

The residence of Mrs Ann Sober was Western Lodge, a grand villa at the top of Sober's Gardens that was redeveloped in the 1870s and vanished under the shops and homes of what is today Sillwood Terrace. Her brother Thomas Kemp was Lord of the Manor of Brighton,[6] and Mrs Sober was therefore not strictly 'the Lady of the Manor', but the connection lent her considerable status in the town. She built her 'chapple' in an earlier home in Warbleton, east Sussex, in 1816,[7] and became quite famous for her fiery sermons. By the time the Constables encountered her, she and her brother had both returned to the fold and become more orthodox in their religious views, but her reputation as a lady preacher – and the jokes –followed her for the rest of her life.

Another colourful neighbour was a fellow artist, John James Masquerier – irrepressible, effusively sociable, French and a painter of portraits, who lived next door at 8 Sober's Gardens and became another long-standing connection.

One exciting discovery that helped establish the exact location of number 9 – for the street numbering as well as the name changed at least twice between 1822 and 1850 – came from scrutinising *The Gothic House, with Western Lodge, Brighton* (fig. 1), a painting by Constable made from a vantage point a few yards north of Harrap's home of a view that is now blocked by later Victorian villas. The building partially seen, at the top right of the picture, is Western Lodge. The Gothic House still stands at 95–96 Western Road.

Fig. 1
The Gothic House, with Western Lodge, Brighton
2 August 1824
Oil on paper, 25.5 × 30 cm
R.24.15A
Private collection

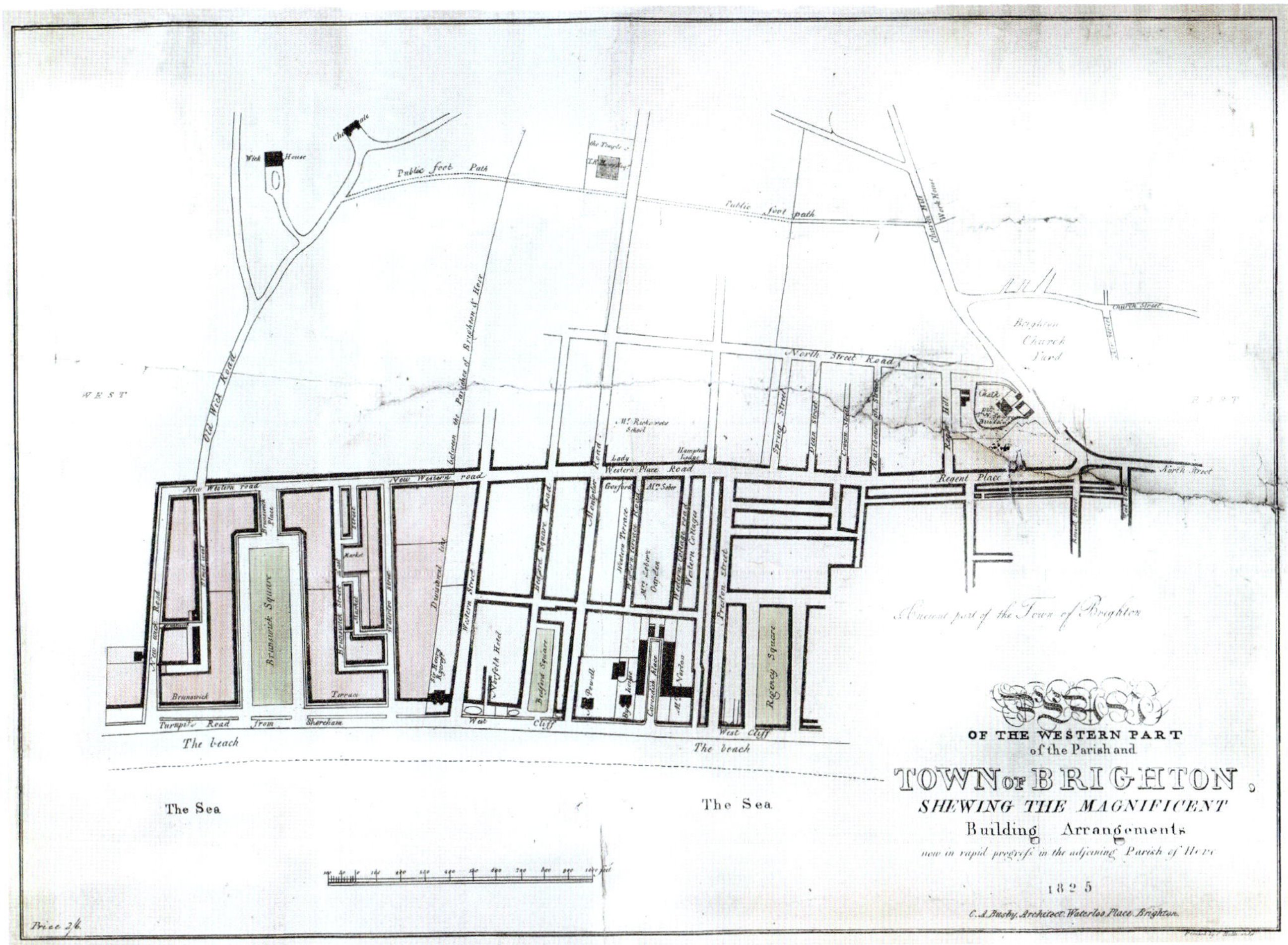

Fig. 2
CHARLES BUSBY
(1786–1834)
Plan of the Western Part of the Parish and Town of Brighton Shewing The Magnificent Building Arrangements Now in Rapid Progress in the Adjoining Parish of Hove
1825
East Sussex Record Office

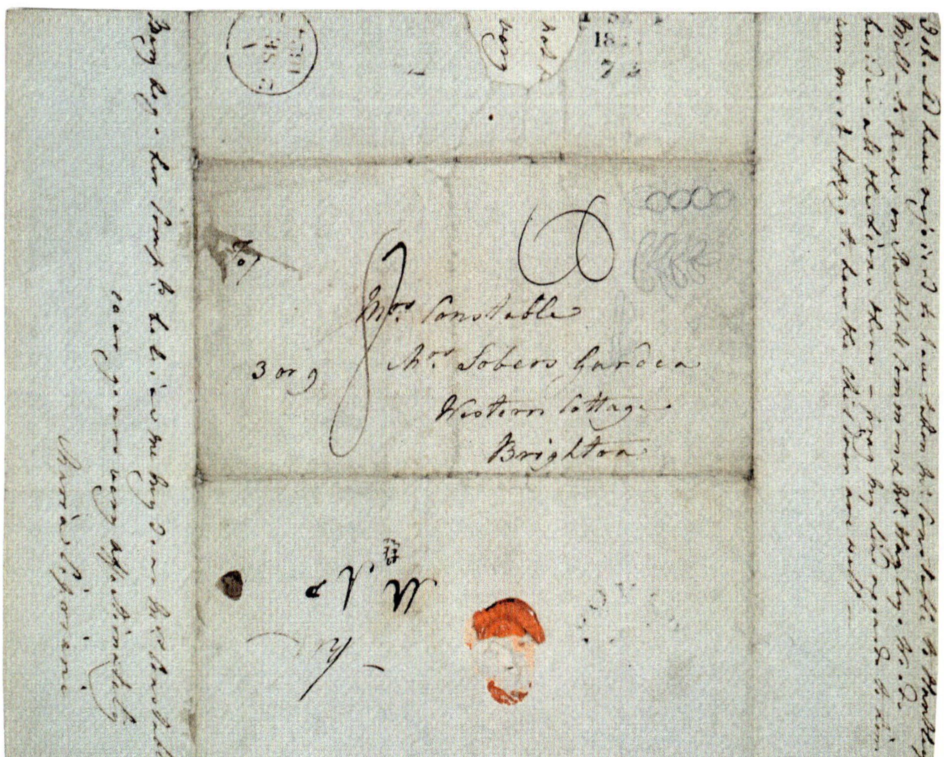

Fig. 3
Letter addressed to 'Maria Constable at 3 or 9 Sober's Garden, Western Cottages, Brighton'
Constable Family Collection

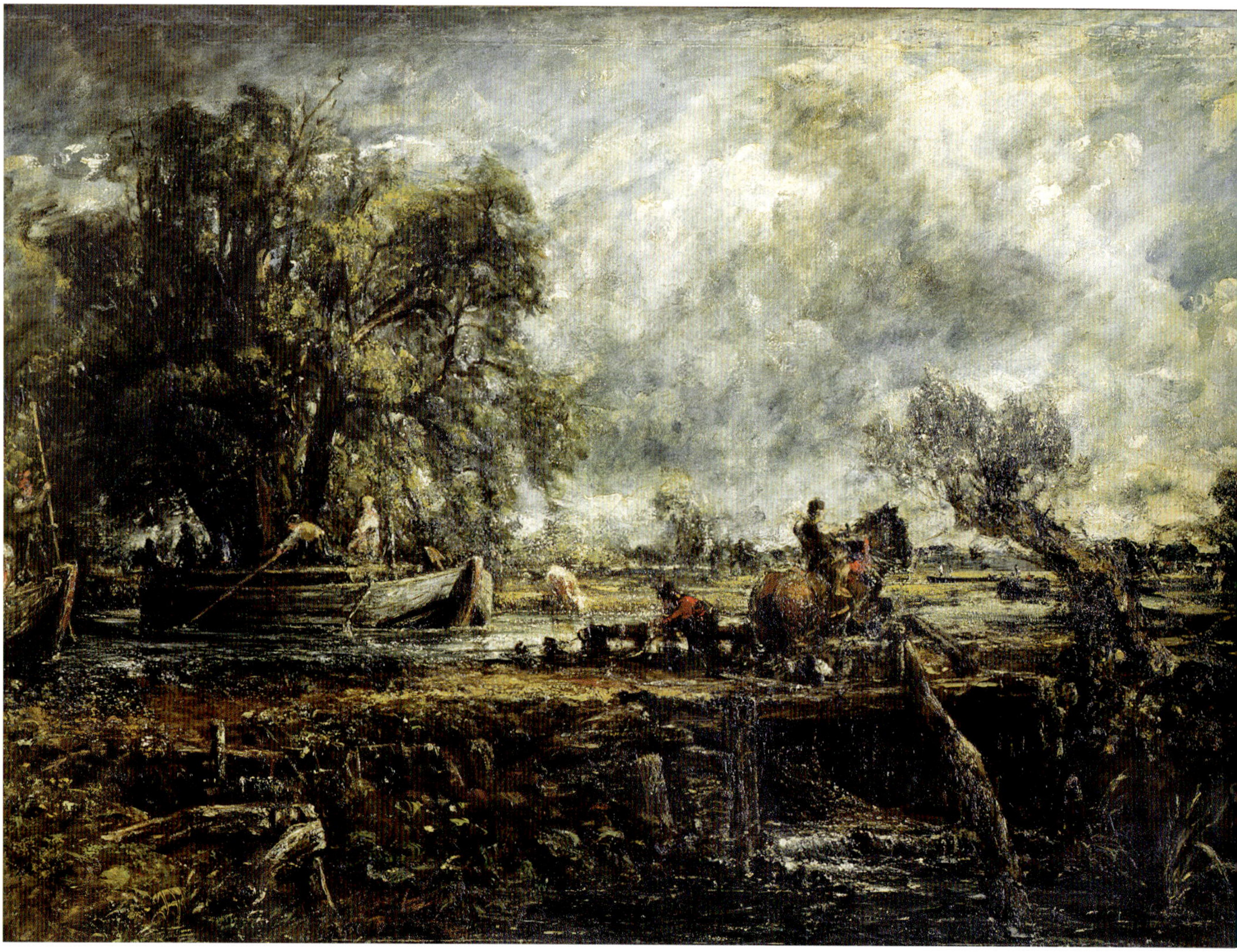

Another even more conclusive find was a letter in the Constable family collection addressed to Maria Constable (fig. 3) at '3 or 9 Sober's Garden, Western Cottages' – Western Cottages being the name formally adopted for the street in the 1830s and the first manuscript link between the addresses.

These and other findings confirmed the house as the one where Constable lived and worked for many weeks in 1824, a visit that was the first of many during a four-year period when Brighton was genuinely important for the artist, both as his best hope of a cure for his dying wife, Maria, who found the sea air offered some relief from her tuberculosis, and as a source of artistic inspiration.

It gave him some much-needed 'repose' which allowed him to complete small commissioned works away from the constant interruptions that plagued him in his busy London studio, where he was also trying to finish his real priority: the last of his great series of Suffolk canal scenes, *The Leaping Horse* (fig. 4). It also afforded him the rare opportunity to step out of his front door with sketchbook and paint box and, within minutes, to be close to nature, where he could make small, exquisite sketches of the 'breakers and the sky'[8] or the tranquil countryside of the Downs, dotted with his beloved windmills.

For Harrap this was more than an historical curiosity. His deep appreciation of Constable

Fig. 4
The Leaping Horse
(full-scale sketch)
c.1825
Oil on canvas,
129.4 × 188 cm
R.25.2
Victoria and Albert
Museum, London

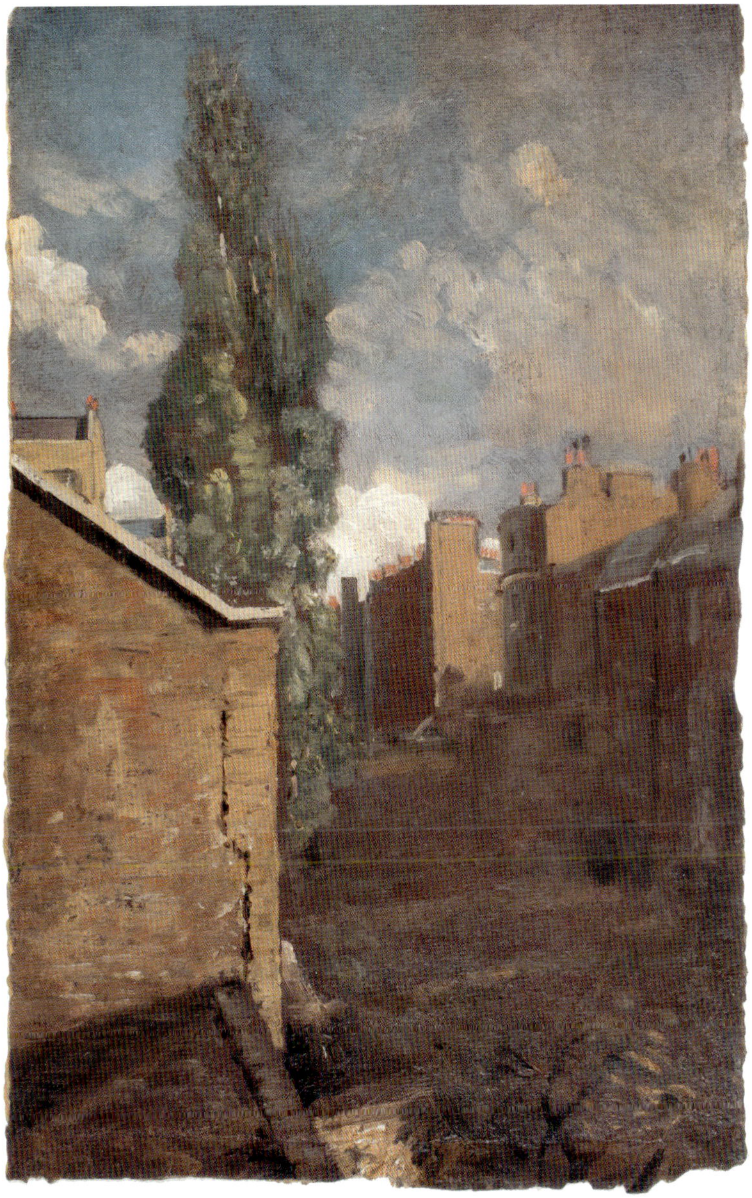

Fig. 5
Houses at Hampstead
Oil on paper,
28 × 18.1 cm
R.22.51
Private collection

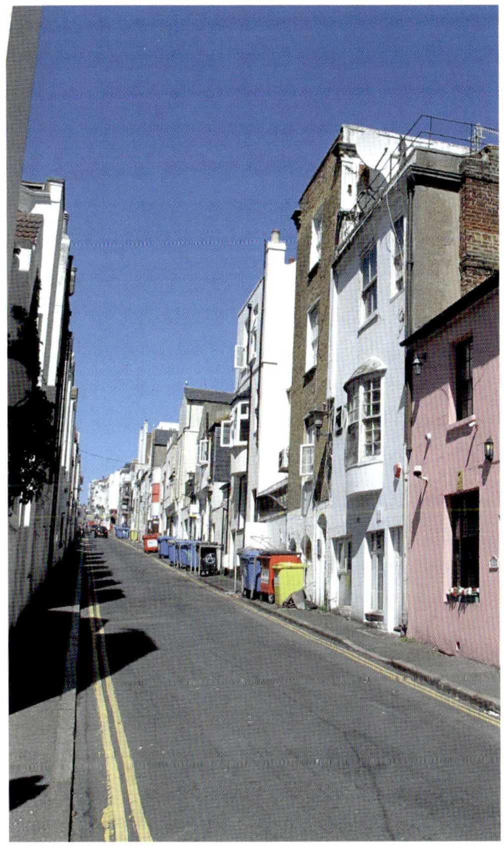

Fig. 6
Little Preston Street,
Brighton (rear of 9 Sober's
Gardens)
2016
Photograph, Shân Lancaster

both as an artist and as an inspiration to thoughtful young painters from the 1820s until the present day led him to plunge into further research. This has directly linked almost 200 works to the Brighton visits and inspired fresh appraisals of works previously attributed to other locations and times. Brighton is being re-evaluated much as Salisbury was when the successful exhibition *Constable and Salisbury* at The Salisbury and South Wiltshire Museum (now the Salisbury Museum) in 2011 expanded and clarified much of what was known about the artist's connections with that city, its characters and its countryside, and led to the location being considered for the first time as a subject complete in itself.

New acceptance by the art world of the importance of 9 Sober's Gardens led to a Blue Plaque, unveiled by Constable's great-great-grandson Richard Constable in 2013 and a new role for Harrap, as curator of the *Constable and Brighton* exhibition at Brighton Museum and Art Gallery.

During preparations for this exhibition two more fascinating discoveries have been made. The first arose from a suggestion by the distinguished art historian and Constable scholar Conal Shields that it could be worth looking very closely at a painting that has intrigued him for years: *Houses at Hampstead* (fig. 5). Shields confided that he had long believed that the

Fig. 7
Sketch at Brighton/ Williamstown Strand, 1824–26
Oil on board, 17.2 × 27.3cm
R.26.11
Private collection

architecture suggests the location is Brighton, not Hampstead. As a meeting of authors of this book discussed this theory, Ian Warrell, a Turner specialist, author of Chapters 3 and 4 of this book and a Brighton resident himself, suddenly exclaimed, 'Have you looked out of your back door recently?'

A scholarly stampede to the rear of the house confirmed that the view over the neighbouring yard and up Little Preston Street (fig. 6), a passage of small early nineteenth-century buildings, did indeed correlate closely with the bow fronts, arched doorways and distinctive orange-red brickwork in the painting. A small north-facing room on the upper floor of Harrap's house had already been identified as the probable location of the improvised painting room used by Constable in 1824. Given the high elevation and north orientation of the painting, it is now possible to speculate that *Houses at Hampstead* records what he saw from his studio window in Brighton. Constable is known to have painted views from the rear of several of his other homes, in East Bergholt (*A View at East Bergholt*, V&A) and from lodgings in Hampstead. Now *Houses at Hampstead* may be the next to be reidentified as a result. Research into the building pattern of the street in the 1820s is already under way with the historian Dr Sue Berry, the author of Chapter 6.

The other unexpected connection may solve the mystery of a puzzling small seaside painting by Constable described as 'famously enigmatic' when it was sold at Christie's in 1988. It is inscribed on the reverse 'Williamstown Strand' (fig. 7), and the sale catalogue explains: 'it does not refer to an identifiable stretch of coastline near Brighton which is the most likely coastal scenery … and while with the inscription ending rather abruptly it has been suggested that it may once have read "Williamstown Stranded" there is no documentation of a ship of that name being wrecked at the time.'

The answer may arise from the fate of Henry Fauntleroy, the last banker to be hanged for fraud in England. Constable, who knew several of the families ruined by the collapse of Fauntleroy's bank, followed the case in the papers and wrote to Fisher describing him as 'villainous'.[9] After the sentence of death had been passed, the usually gentle Constable wrote: 'Of the wretched Fauntleroy – no one seems to sympathise with him – a greater instance of moral depravity they say never existed. [He is] the only man that I ever felt I *could* see hanged.'[10]

No researcher could resist a hanged banker. A quick check in the archives of Constable's favourite paper, the *Morning Post*, revealed that Fauntleroy was not only on Constable's mind but also on his doorstep. He was a very near neighbour in Brighton, his elegant Grecian villa (see fig. 84), with 'a billiard room in the form of Napoleon's travelling tent',[11] occupying the corner site at the top of Sober's Gardens where Hampton Place meets Western Road today.

Less than a mile to the south-east lived Jeremy Botting, the official hangman for Newgate Prison in London, where he eventually executed Fauntleroy on 30 November 1824. His home in a tenement just off West Street was notorious in Brighton as 'Botting's Rookery', and it is strange to think of the two men crossing each other's path in Brighton, as they must certainly have done, and then both meeting in London, one to face the death penalty and the other to carry out the execution.

Constable is likely to have been aware of the added piquancy of hangman and prisoner both living a few minutes' walk from Sober's Gardens.

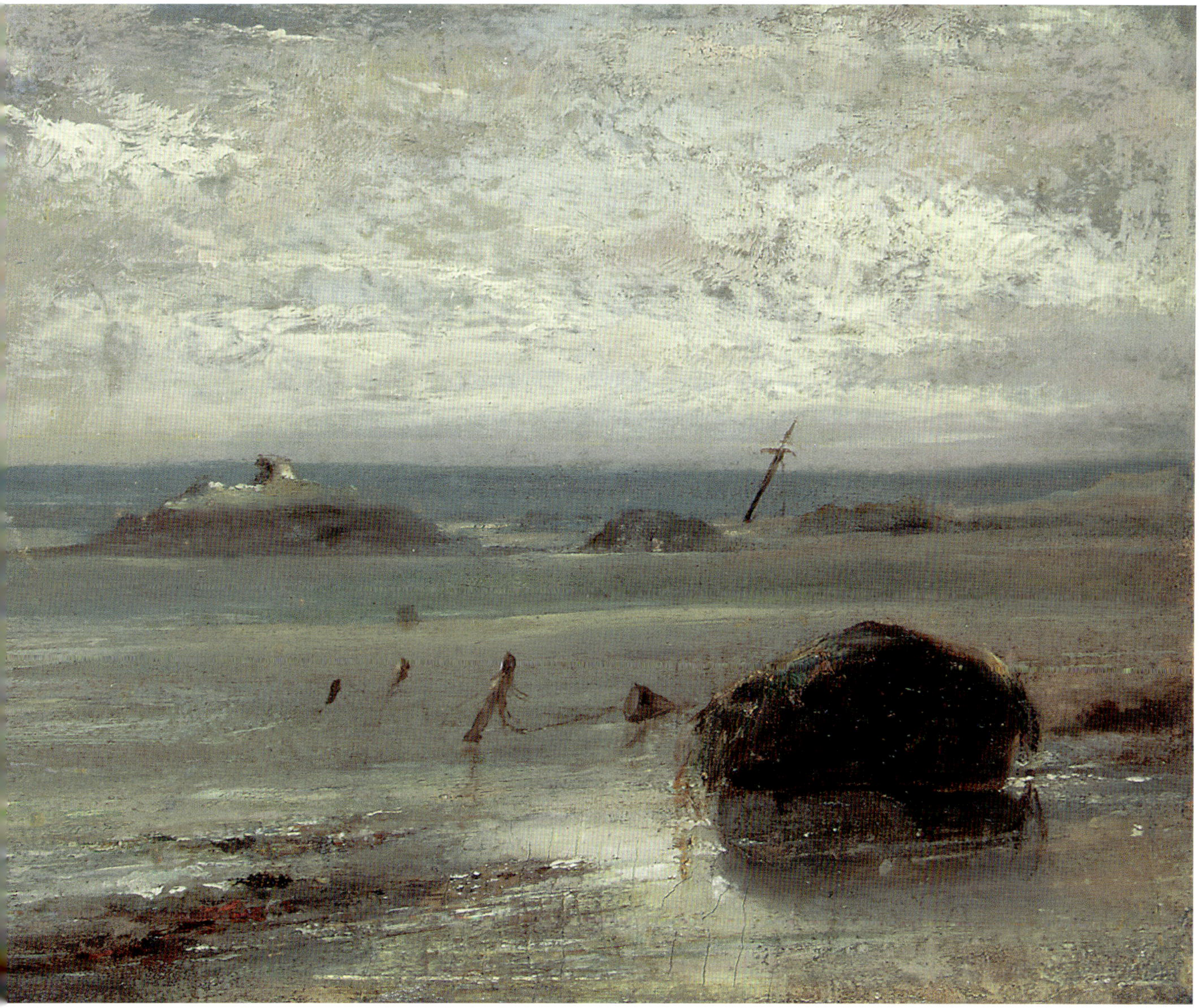

He certainly read the *Morning Post* regularly, and followed the calamitous fortunes of Fauntleroy, so it is interesting to discover that on 16 October 1824, a date when he was still in Brighton, there was, on the same page as a dramatic account of the developments in the trial of Fauntleroy, a report of a shipping disaster off the coast of Dublin. Two ships, the *Mary Frances* of Drogheda and the *Don* from Shetland, were 'stranded at Williamstown'.[12] The description of the stranding is exactly what the painting shows, and, as the sale catalogue noted, the inscription on the painting ends abruptly. Did it originally say 'Williamstown strandings'?

Constable was under pressure to find marine subjects for the Anglo-French dealer Arrowsmith at the time. Perhaps the story of the *Mary Frances* and the *Don* inspired him to dash off this little painting as an *aide-mémoire* with a scribbled reference to the incident for future use.

Connections such as these will fuel yet more findings about Constable in Brighton, linking the artist more and more strongly with the town, about which he had such mixed feelings. For, in spite of his initial shock at the crowds and the vulgar bustle of the popular beaches, he did mellow as he made new friends and acquaintances, explored the coast and the hinterland and enjoyed seeing his family blooming in the fresh air. By 1826, during a visit to his friend Henry Phillips in Bedford Square, he was referring to it affectionately in a letter to Maria: 'I wished much for you when I heard – and saw – and smelt – the dear old sea, which has always done you so much good.'[13]

The end has not yet been written to the story of Constable's Brighton period.

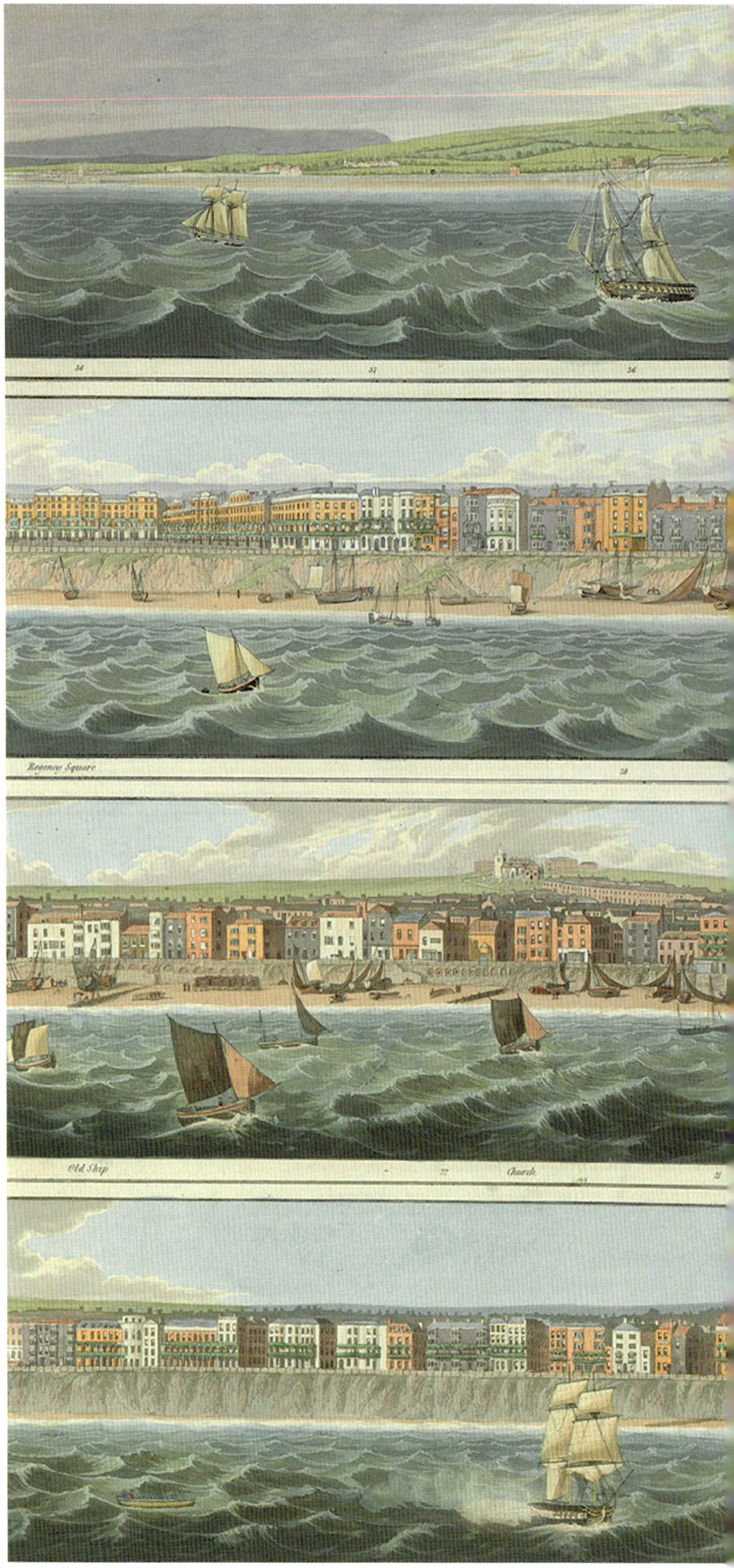

Fig. 8
Robert Havell Jr
(1793 –1878)
A Coasting View of Brighton, the drawing taken from nature
1824
Hand-coloured aquatint on paper, 11 × 320 cm
Paul Mellon Collection, Yale Center For British Art, New Haven, CT

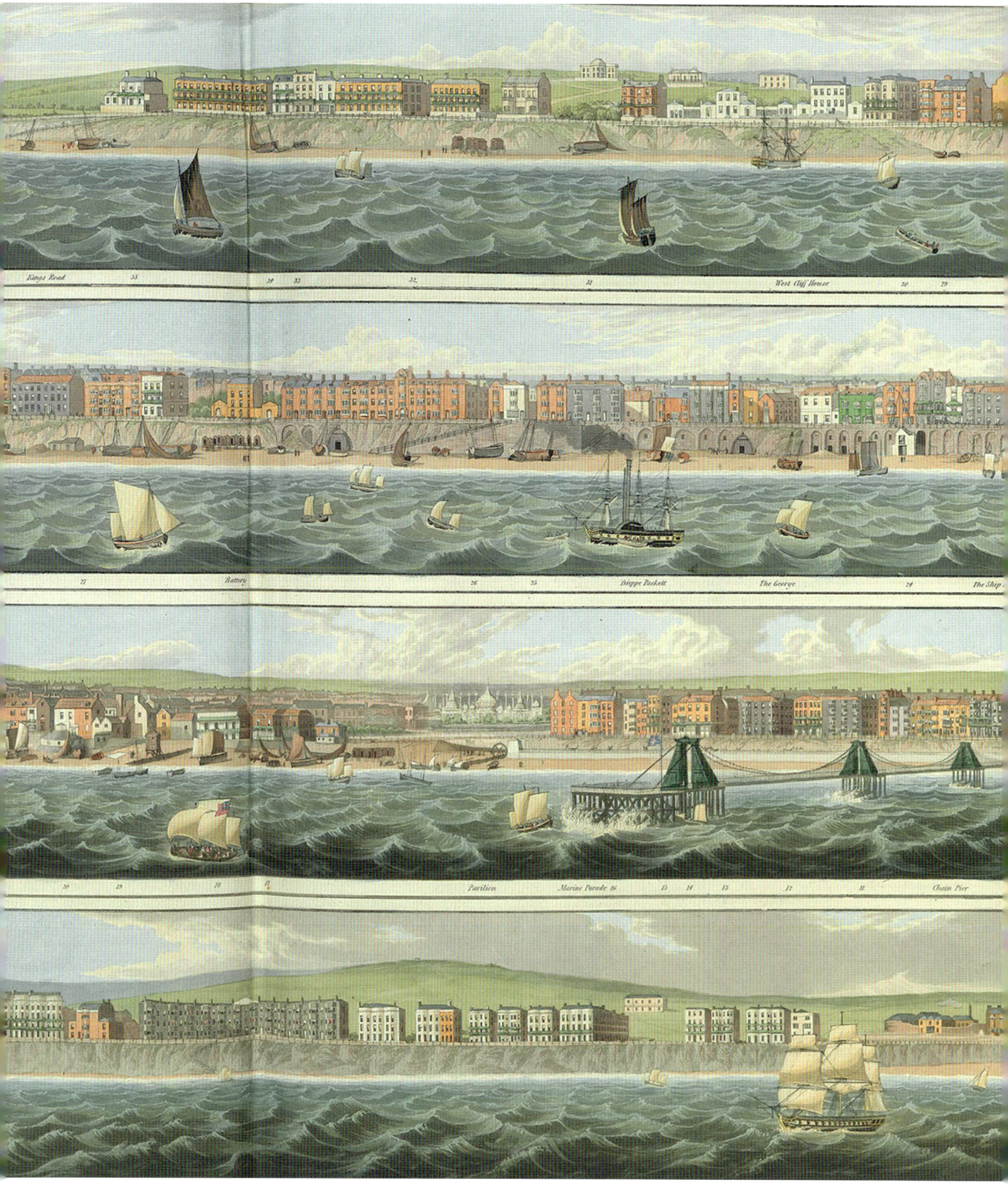
Kings Road
West Cliff House
Battery
Dieppe Packett
The George
The Ship
Pavilion
Marine Parade
Chain Pier

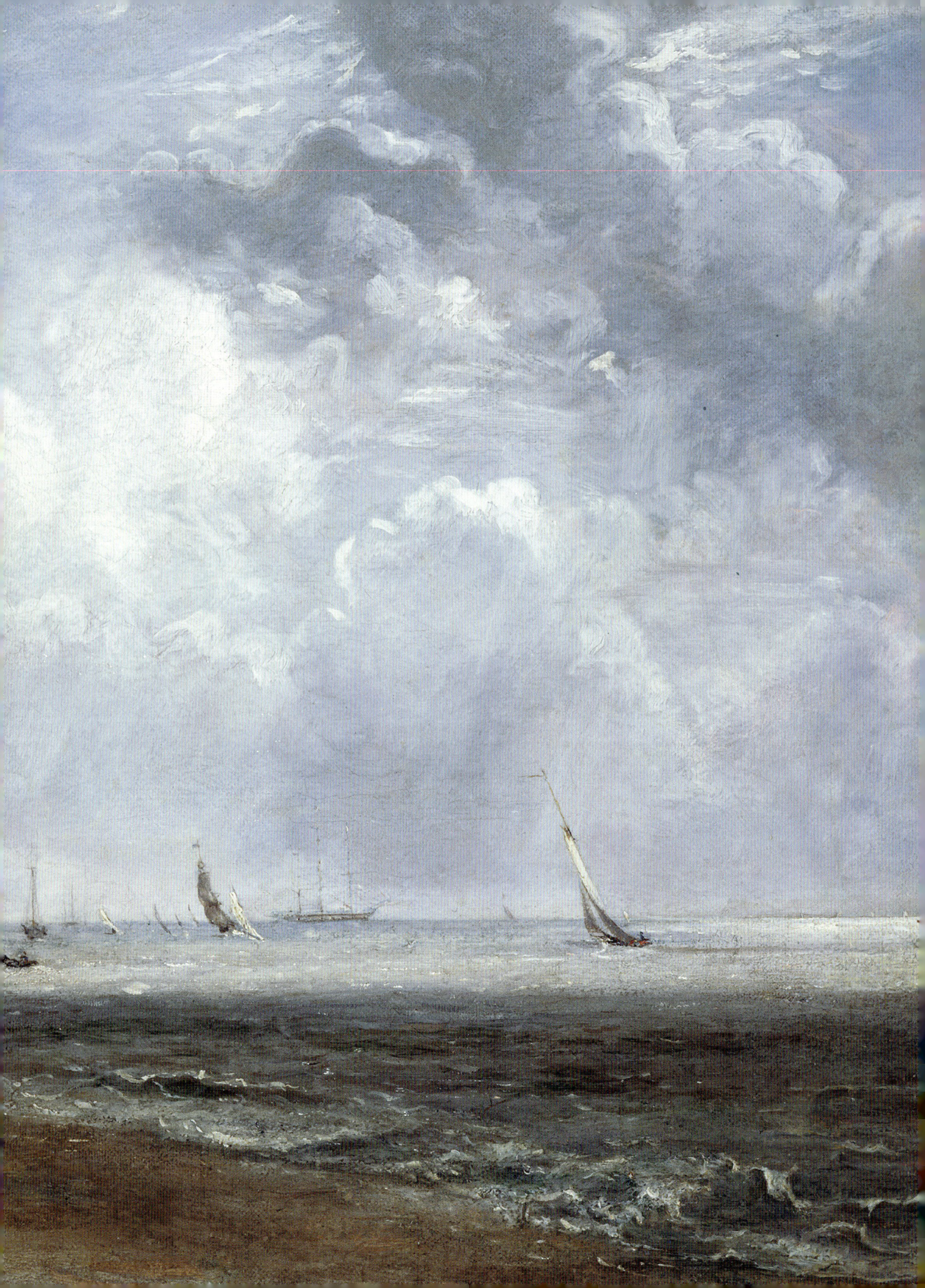

1 Arrival in Brighton and Setting Up a Painting Room

'getting on with my French jobs'

Anne Lyles

On 8 May 1824 Constable wrote to his close friend Archdeacon John Fisher from his central London address in Charlotte Street, situated in the heart of the artists' quarter in Fitzrovia. It was a long and newsworthy letter, in which Constable was able to report on some recent, particularly favourable turns in his professional fortunes, as well as to update him on a new development in his domestic circumstances.[1]

One important piece of news that Constable relayed to Fisher was that he had recently succeeded in selling his key exhibit that year at the Royal Academy, *The Lock* (fig. 9), for the full asking price of 150 guineas. A more remarkable fact was that the painting, for the first (and, as it transpired, only) time in his career, had sold on the opening day of the Academy's annual spring exhibition – to a wealthy merchant, James Morrison. In fact the painting has a more dynamic composition than those of his preceding large landscapes, showing the prominent figure of a lock-keeper straining to open one of the lock gates on the River Stour at Flatford, close to the corn mill that had been operated by Constable's father, Golding, in this pocket of Suffolk close to the border with Essex where the artist had grown up. However, it also seems likely that, being an upright, the picture enjoyed a particularly favourable placing in the Academy's 'Great Room' at Somerset House that year, perhaps hung towards the middle of one of the walls and even 'on the line', a position often enjoyed by portraits of a similar – that is to say upright – format (fig. 10).[2] Both these factors may have helped Constable secure a quick sale on this occasion.

Following his marriage to Maria Bicknell (fig. 11) in 1816, rather than continuing to visit his native East Bergholt in search of new material for his paintings, Constable resided permanently in London and began to set his ambitions on painting larger, more ambitious canvases. Though taking their themes from the scenery of the River Stour or the area around Dedham Vale, these paintings were also imbued with echoes of earlier, Old Master paintings, such as the classical landscapes of the French artist Claude Lorrain or the more homely views of seventeenth-century Dutch landscapists such as Jacob van Ruisdael.

Constable's strategy of producing larger pictures, on a scale of roughly six feet in width, had immediately paid off, as it was on the strength of the first of them, *The White Horse* (fig. 12), exhibited at the Royal Academy in 1819, that he had secured his election as an Associate member of the Academy that same year. It thenceforward became clear to Constable that, if he intended to gain election as a full member

Detail of fig. 14

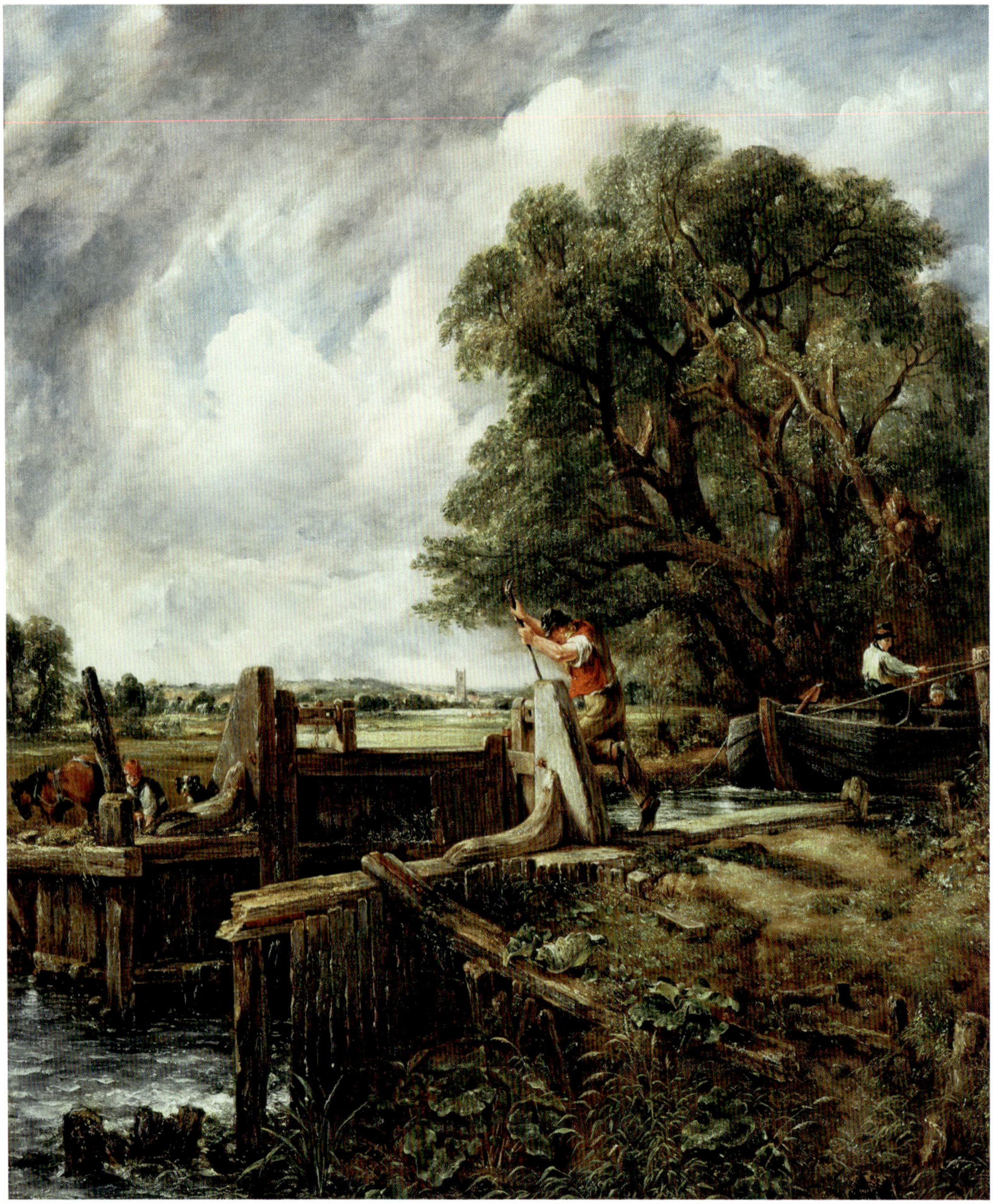

Fig. 9
The Lock
1824
Oil on canvas,
142.2 × 120.7 cm
R.24.1
Private collection

one day, he would need to continue painting in a similar vein, on a large scale, even though as a landscape painter (as opposed to a history painter) it was always more difficult to secure the necessary votes from the Academicians on the jury. In this sort of climate, sales and positive reviews from the critics offered at least some measure of an artist's likely success.

Another piece of good news Constable was able to pass on to Fisher was the successful outcome of his recent negotiations with the Anglo-French dealer and print publisher John Arrowsmith over the purchase of some of his pictures. Fisher already knew, from previous communications with Constable, that Arrowsmith had first approached Constable in 1822 with an offer to purchase *The Hay Wain* (see fig. 25), the third of the artist's six-foot landscapes that he had sent that year to the British Institution – the other key exhibition venue in London – following its showing at the Academy the previous year.[3] Fisher also knew that Constable had on that occasion turned down Arrowsmith's offer of 70 guineas, being under half the asking price of 150 guineas.[4] However much Constable had needed the

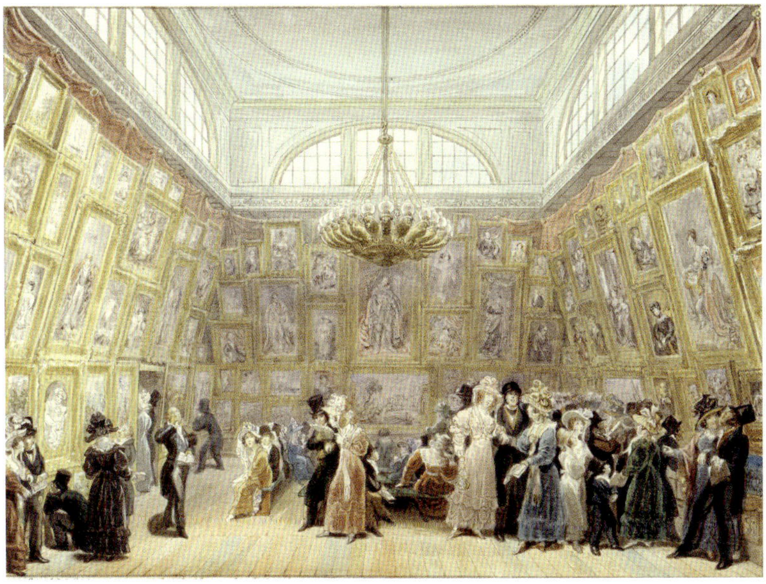

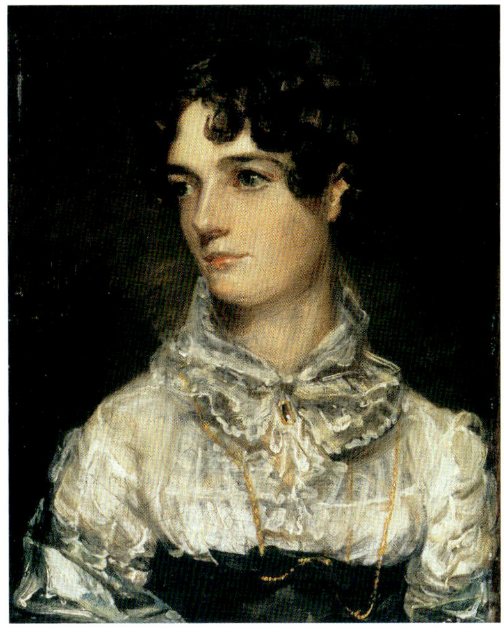

Fig. 10
George Scharf
(1788–1860)
Exhibition at The Royal Academy, London: 1828
1828
Watercolour,
18.9 × 26 cm
Museum of London

Fig. 11
Maria Bicknell, Mrs John Constable
10 July 1816
Oil on canvas,
30.3 × 25.1 cm
R.16.13
Tate, London

money at the time, he had been reluctant to accept an inferior offer, he told Fisher, especially from a 'Frenchman', betraying here – however playfully – something of the 'little Englander' mentality that would characterise his general reaction to his new-found popularity in France around this time.[5]

However, when Arrowsmith returned to London in 1824 to try to persuade Constable to change his mind, explaining that he intended to make a feature of *The Hay Wain* at the Paris Salon later in the year, Constable finally came to terms – albeit only after he had secured Fisher's willing agreement to waive his own interest in acquiring the picture.[6] Now Arrowsmith had committed himself to pay 250 guineas for *The Hay Wain* in a package that included another of his large pictures, the recently painted *View on the Stour near*

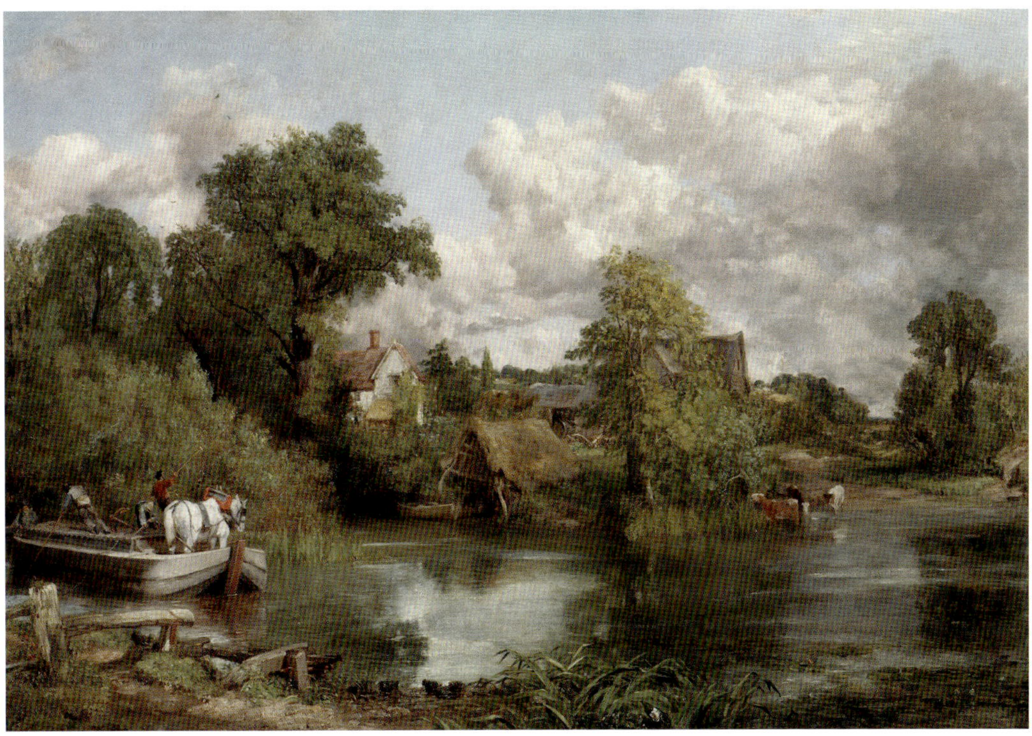

Fig. 12
The White Horse
1819
Oil on canvas,
131.5 × 187.8 cm
R.19.1
The Frick Collection,
New York

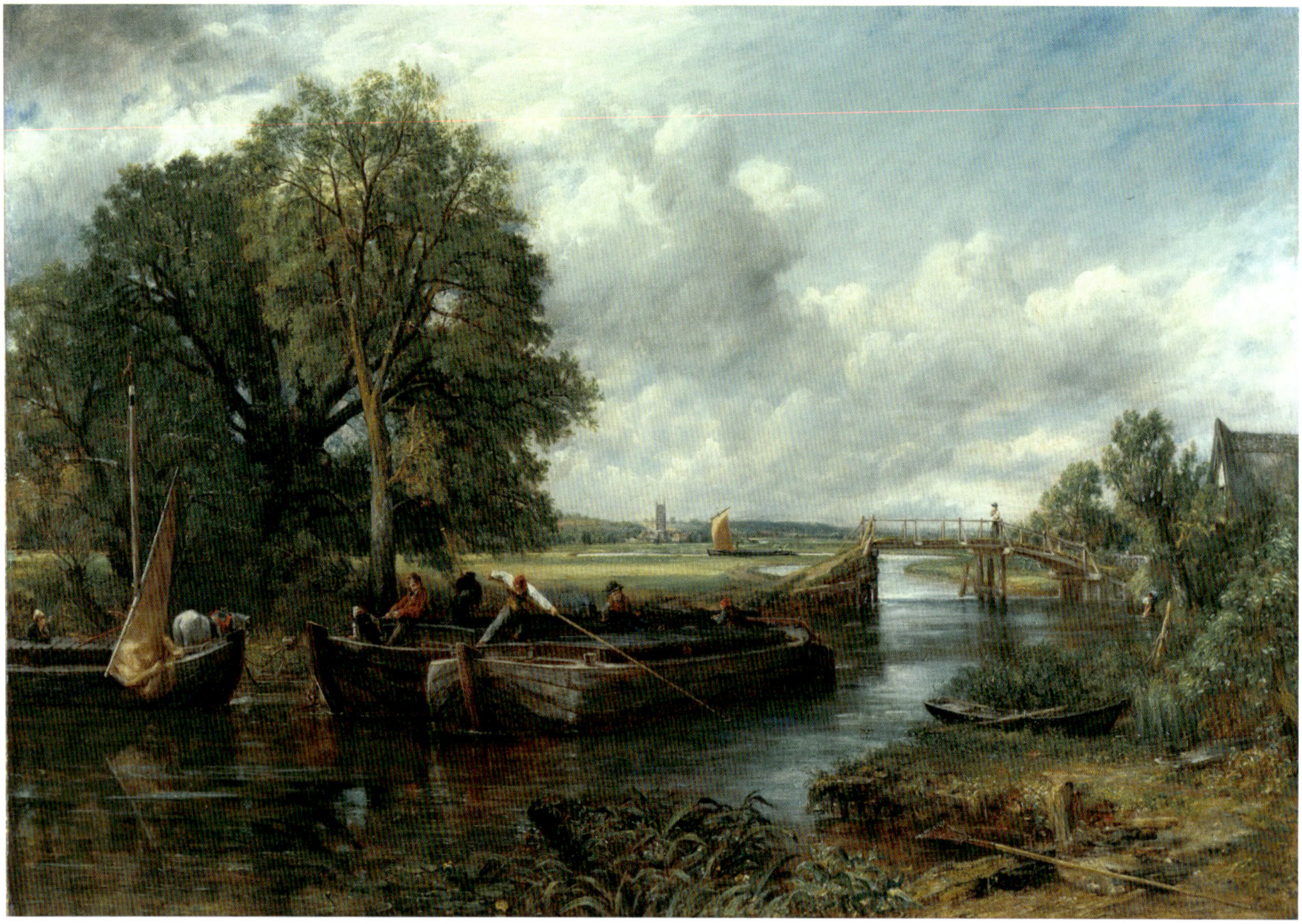

Dedham, of 1822 (fig. 13), and also a small sea piece, *Yarmouth Jetty*, also of 1822 (fig. 14), which the artist had in effect thrown in to help secure the deal.[7] Constable had been reluctant to let the pictures out of his studio until the money from Arrowsmith was in his account, and now – he was happy to tell Fisher – it was.[8] Thus, with the addition of 150 guineas for *The Lock*, Constable told Fisher he now had £400 in the bank. In the spring of 1824, then, Constable's professional fortunes were riding high indeed.

It was just as well that Constable felt financially secure at this juncture. Not only did he already have four children with Maria – in the following few years, before Maria's death towards the end of 1828, there were to be three more. His wife's health was delicate and, as he explained to Fisher in his letter of 8 May, had recently been affected by the warm weather, with the result that they had been told to try the sea. He mentioned to Fisher he would shortly be sending the family to Brighton.[9]

Such a change in circumstances would be sure to bring disruption to Constable's painting routine, as well as further expenditure. As it happened, Constable had already been moving the family between different premises since 1819, when he first took lodgings in Hampstead, a village to the north of London free from the pollution associated with the capital, for the benefit of Maria's health and their (then) two children. He was to rent houses in Hampstead every subsequent year, with the exception of 1824, until he took a lease on a residence in Well Walk late in August 1827, enabling him in effect to secure the advantages of a more or less permanent second home there. Now, in 1824, and on various subsequent occasions until 1828, Constable was to add a third location, Brighton, to those of Hampstead and central London, between all of which he now had to juggle his work and domestic arrangements.

The advantage of Brighton, as Constable was to explain to Fisher the following year, was

Fig. 13
View on the Stour Near Dedham
1822
Oil on canvas,
130 × 188 cm
R.22.1
Huntington Library and Art Gallery, San Marino, CA

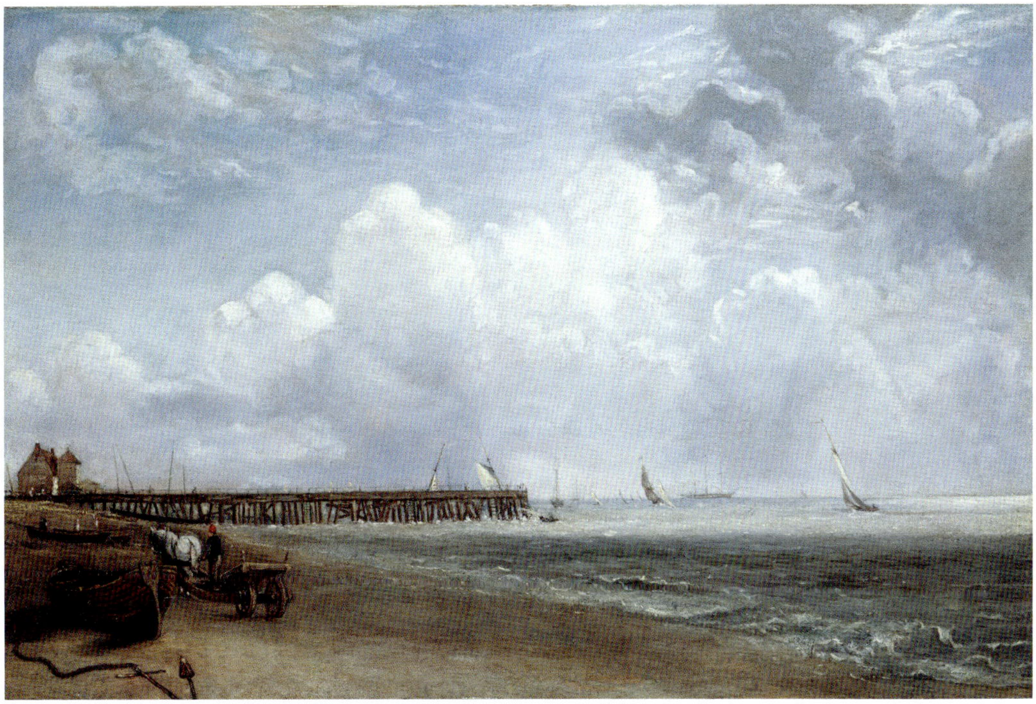

Fig. 14
Yarmouth Jetty
1822
Oil on canvas,
32.2 × 50.5 cm
R.22.38
Tate, London

that it was considerably cheaper than Hampstead while also having a good coach service.[10] Moreover, precisely because Brighton was much further away from central London than Hampstead, Constable's visits to the resort ended up being more productive. One option, then, was to accompany his family there on the coach, settle them into their lodgings and, in between, perhaps fit in a bit of sketching on the beach, or a little inland on the Downs. He would then return to Charlotte Street to work in the purpose-built studio that he had inherited, and then adapted for his own needs on first moving into the house (previously occupied by the Academician and famous diarist Joseph Farington) in 1822.[11] Alternatively, if he could spare the time for a longer visit to Brighton – as in the summer of 1824 and, to a lesser extent, over the Christmas and New Year of 1825–26 – Constable might then settle down to making progress on some of his commissions there.

In fact when, in May 1824, Constable planned to take the family to Brighton for the first time, he had more than enough work on his hands. On 22 May, Arrowsmith had called on him again in Charlotte Street to discuss arrangements for sending to Paris the three pictures he had just paid for (two more were subsequently to be added to the crate).[12] On this same visit Arrowsmith also brought with him another French dealer and print publisher, Claude Schroth, with whom Constable was ultimately to enjoy more cordial professional relations than Arrowsmith. Schroth immediately ordered three pictures from Constable: two Hampstead views (at this stage specified to measure about 21 × 30 inches each) and an unnamed smaller picture (measuring 13 × 10 inches).[13] Arrowsmith returned on the following two days, confirming in writing not only Schroth's order but also his own, new commission – that is, a second transaction – for four more small pictures (two of which were to measure 12 × 20 inches, and two more 10 × 12 inches).[14] Although smaller pictures were not as time-consuming to paint as a six-footer, Constable – ever the perfectionist – intended to apply equal care to their execution.[15]

As if all these French commissions – and there were to be others over the next few months[16] – were not demanding enough, Constable had to juggle them alongside other orders for existing English clients and patrons. For example, in the spring and summer of 1824 alone he was tied up with continuing work for John Pern Tinney, a lawyer from Salisbury for whom Fisher had bought, as a gift, the second of Constable's six-footers, *Stratford Mill*, of 1820

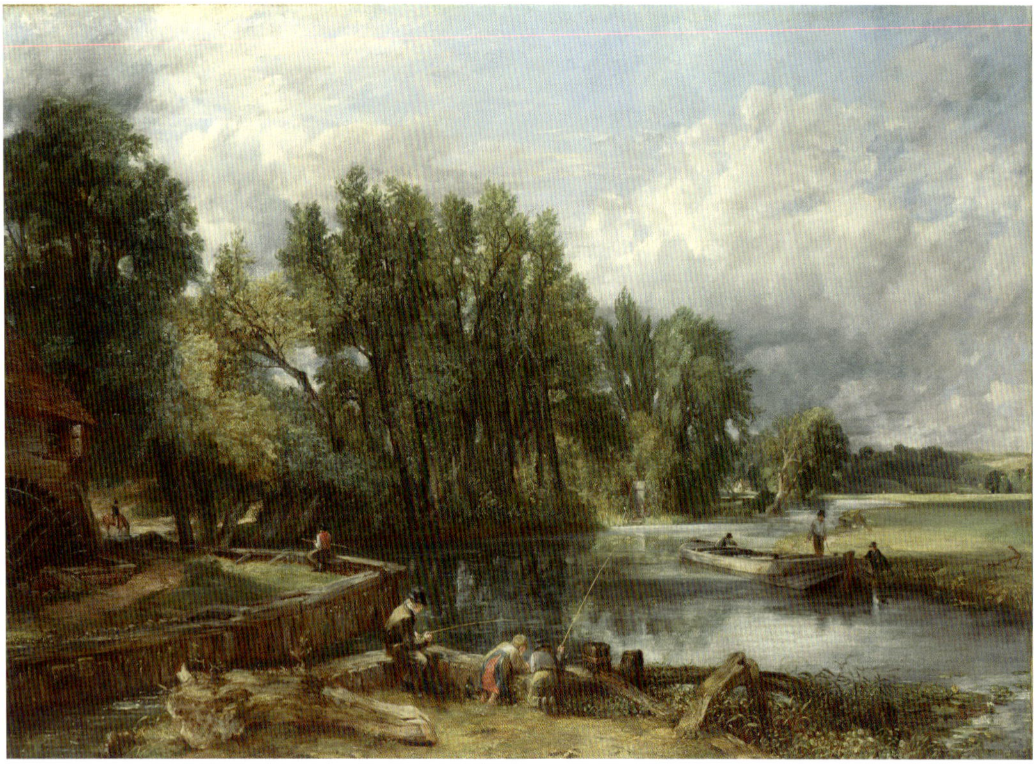

Fig. 15
Stratford Mill
1820
Oil on canvas,
127 × 182.9 cm
R.20.1
National Gallery, London

(fig. 15), and which Constable was either cleaning or retouching at this date, or whose frame he was 'doing up', and a commission for Fisher himself for a small picture of *Parham's Mill, Gillingham*, where the cleric had a living, as well as two versions of a view of *Salisbury Cathedral from the Bishop's Grounds* (fig. 16) – one for Fisher's uncle, the bishop of Salisbury, and another for the latter's recently married daughter, Mrs Mirehouse. There was also a replica of a portrait to finish for Henry Greswolde Lewis and 'a little coast' (a view of *Harwich Lighthouse*) for his old Suffolk friend James Pulham; and he had also recently embarked on a second full-scale version of *The Lock*, perhaps speculatively, with the aid of his studio assistant John ('Johnny') Dunthorne, the son of his old Suffolk friend and amateur artist John Dunthorne the Elder. To make matters worse, Constable would then find himself having to spare the precious services of Johnny to attend to other tasks he might otherwise have had to take on himself: for example, the painting requirements of his patron the amateur artist Sir George Beaumont (which included mending holes in some of his canvases) or fielding similar such demands from another of his long-standing patrons, Lady Dysart.[17]

On top of all these commissions there were, of course, the artist's family obligations. Constable, an attentive father and loving husband, hated to be away from his wife and children for any period of time. In 1825 he told Francis Darby – the son of the famous Midlands industrialist Abraham Darby, who built the first iron bridge at Coalbrookdale – who had just agreed to buy two of Constable's Hampstead views (replicas of a pair he had painted for Schroth in 1824), that he was 'not happy apart from them for a few days, or hours'.[18] However, the artist had little choice in the matter. Maria's health, and that of the children, was paramount, and Constable had to work to support them – especially until the death of his father-in-law, Charles Bicknell, early in 1828, when Maria received a substantial legacy.

On the various occasions when, during the Brighton years, they were apart, Constable would usually keep a journal, which he would send to

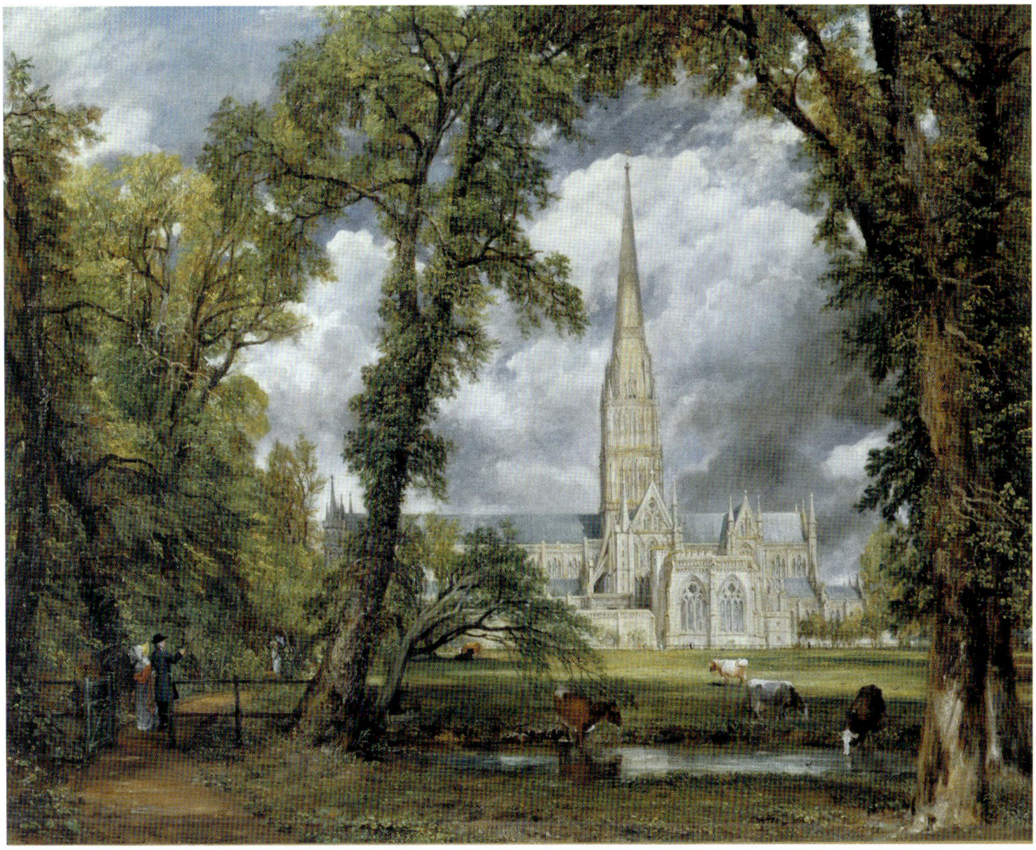

Fig. 16
Salisbury Cathedral from the Bishop's Grounds
1823
Oil on canvas,
87.6 × 111.8 cm
R.23.1
Victoria and Albert Museum, London

Fig. 17
A Mouse with a Piece of Cheese
1824
Oil on paper,
10.1 × 13.3 cm
R.24.82
British Museum, London

Maria in instalments, in lieu of a letter, often via a friend who might be travelling between London and the resort to save on the cost of postage. One of these was a neighbour in Mrs Sober's Gardens, the wealthy, semi-retired portrait and history painter John James Masquerier, whom Constable rather disliked but who, like Constable himself, was frequently travelling between the two locations, so was presumably tolerated by him for his usefulness as a courier.

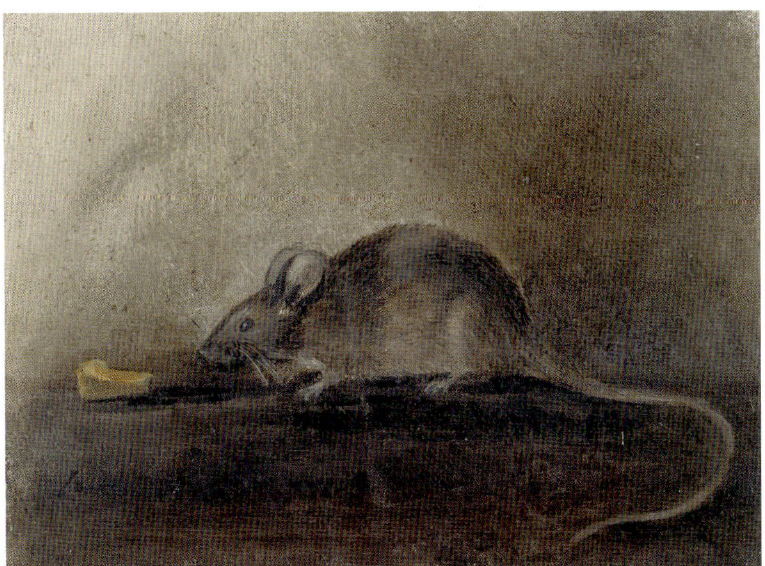

As well as telling Maria in his journal around this time about the pictures he was busy painting, Constable would also mention the people or exhibitions he had recently seen, or the visitors who had called, many of whom – Maria called them his 'flies' – took up his valuable time; indeed on one occasion, when the ever persistent Peter Coxe happened to call, the artist confessed to Maria that Johnny had pretended that Constable was away in Brighton.[19] Constable would also record in his journal some of the domestic, daily goings-on at the house in Charlotte Street, perhaps describing his, or the maid's, physical ailments or the arrival in the back drawing room of a sparrow, some pigeons or a 'pretty goldfinch [which] came to perch on the bars of [the] window', or the cats knocking down the flower pots on the landing, or else Dunthorne's recent sighting of the mouse, now 'getting very fat' as Constable could not resist giving him rinds of cheese (fig. 17).[20]

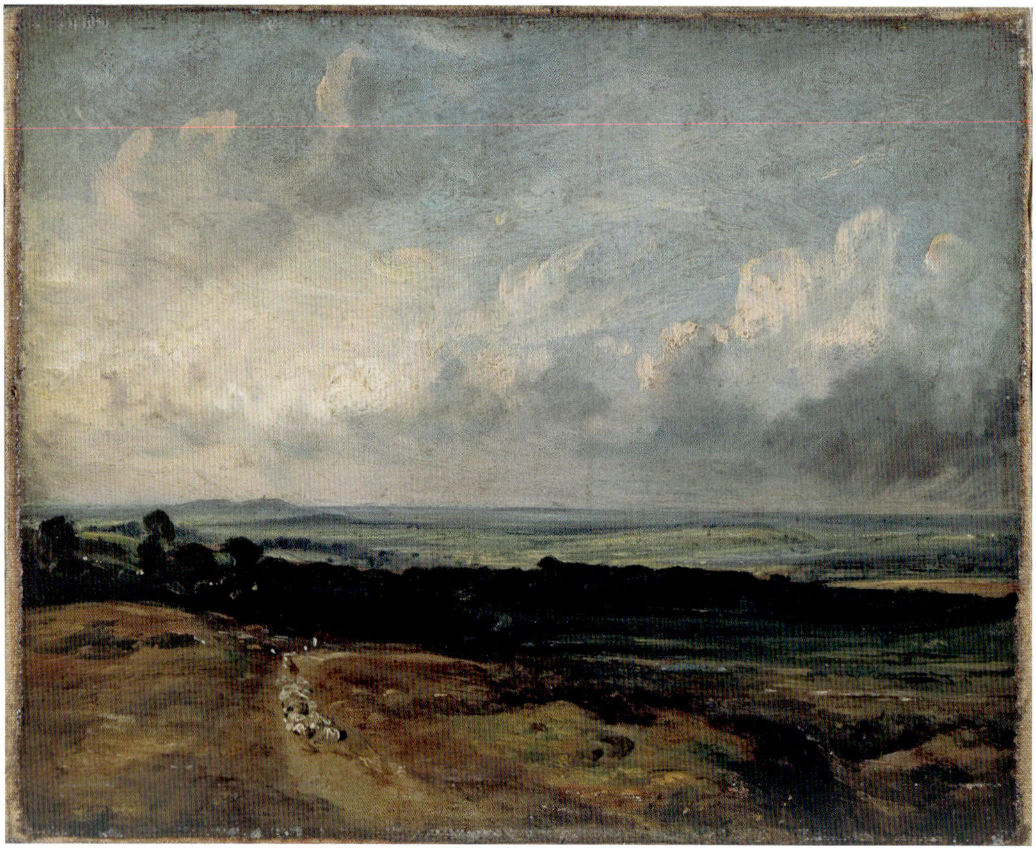

Fig. 18
Child's Hill: Harrow in the Distance
c.1820–30
Oil on canvas, 19.7 × 25.1 cm
R.25.12
Victoria and Albert Museum, London

A key priority for Constable, then, when moving his family to 9 Sober's Gardens in Brighton in 1824, was to ensure that he had a suitable space there for painting so he could work on his commissions – which he would refer to as his 'jobs', his 'French jobs' or his 'dead horses' – and thus attempt to extend his visits there for as long as possible. He presumably started assessing a suitable space as soon as he first arrived at the house, to install the family there, in mid-May, before returning to London only a few days later. In early June he was back in Brighton for another brief stay, this time bringing with him Johnny Dunthorne, who had helped 'to do up [his] painting box' shortly before they set off, and who may also on this occasion have helped him set up his painting room.[21]

It is not entirely certain which room at 9 Sober's Gardens (now 11 Sillwood Road) Constable used as his painting room. As well as himself, Maria and the four children, the house had to accommodate the cook, Mrs Inskip, and her husband and, at various stages, the children's nurse, Mrs Roberts, and often a maid as well. Indeed we know that, owing to constraints of space, Constable had to share the room he used for painting with the cook and her husband (Mrs Inskip offered to sit in the kitchen during the daytime).[22] Assuming the current back extension to 11 Sillwood Road was already in place by 1824, Shân Lancaster and Peter Harrap think it likely that a small room on the upper floor at the back, of a type often allocated as servants' quarters, may well have been the one Constable used for painting. Since this small room faces north – the orientation most favoured by painters for their studio spaces because of the mellow, even quality of the light – this does seem highly plausible.[23]

By 19 June, by which time Constable had already been back in London for a few days, Maria was clearly making ready the allocated painting room for his next visit, although she wrote that she feared he would not like it 'now that it is decorated'.[24] Although ambiguous, this comment seems to imply that the room had recently been decorated in a colour or shade that she knew Constable would not have chosen him-self. Perhaps the room had even been decorated

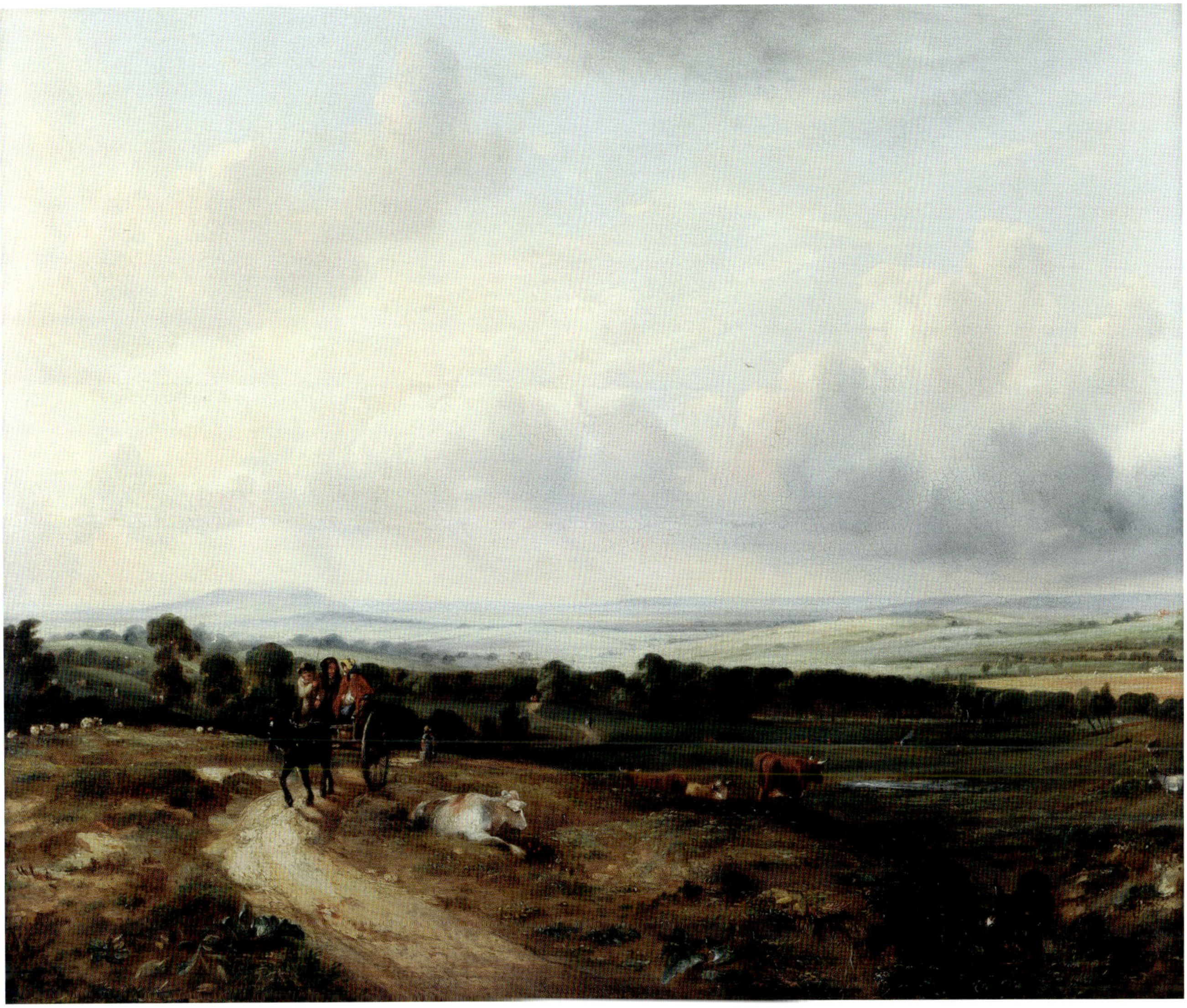

Fig. 19
Child's Hill: Harrow in the Distance
1825
Oil on canvas,
59.6 × 77.4 cm
Not in Reynolds
Dick Institute, Kilmarnock

in white, which he had told her some ten years earlier was 'disagreeable to a painter's eyes, near pictures' – a comment he had made when redecorating his then painting room (at a different address in Charlotte Street) in a colour of his own choosing, 'a sort of purple brown'.[25] As the house at Sober's Gardens was rented (almost certainly from Mrs Sober herself), the choice of colour may have had to be approved by her in advance.[26]

We know that when Constable set off from London for Brighton on 16 July, with the intention of staying there for about a month over the summer – though in the event he was to stay for three – he took with him, packed up with Johnny Dunthorne's help, a number of pictures.[27] R. B. Beckett speculated that these paintings would surely have been his French commissions – canvases to which, with Johnny's help, Constable had perhaps already transferred the designs of the subjects he intended to work up and finish there for his French dealers.[28] For the day after his arrival in Brighton in mid-July, Constable wrote to Fisher mentioning that he had brought with him 'several works to complete', and some six weeks later, on 29 August, without having returned to London in the interim, Constable was still writing, in another letter to Fisher, about his progress on his 'French jobs'.[29] When setting off for Brighton from London in mid-July, Constable also carried with him some canvas, presumably blank, on which he may have intended to start some new pictures.[30] Alternatively, this canvas may have been intended for cutting up into smaller fragments for *plein-air* sketching – some,

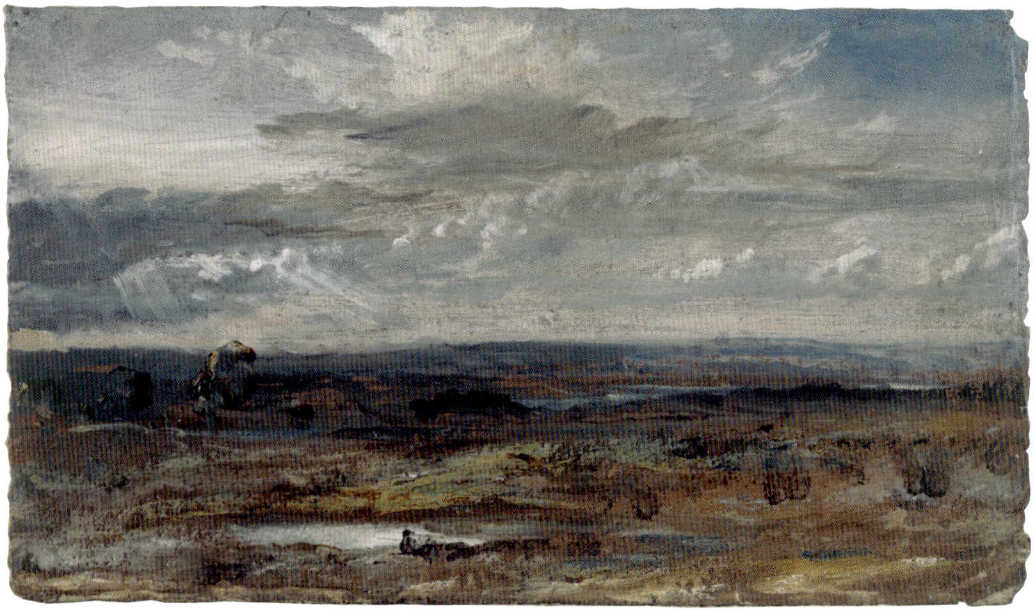

Fig. 20
A View at Hampstead: Evening
31 July 1822
Oil on paper,
16.5 × 29.8 cm
R.22.14
Victoria and Albert Museum, London

no doubt, of a size to fit into the lid of his paint box.[31] He also took an easel.[32]

Whatever the size of the room set aside at Sober's Gardens as his painting area, it seems almost certain that Constable would only have used it in the summer of 1824 – and indeed would only have used comparable painting spaces at his other residences in Brighton in subsequent years – for working on his smaller commissions. Even if the painting room at Sober's Gardens was large enough to have accommodated a fully stretched, six-foot-wide painting – as well as, alongside it, a full-scale preparatory compositional sketch of the sort Constable was accustomed to paint for his large pictures at this date (see figs 4 and 141) – it would have been highly inconvenient to transport the finished painting back to London. Indeed, only three years earlier Constable had even experienced problems in getting large pictures out of his London house in Keppel Street.[33] As it happens, we can be almost certain that the large exhibition pictures he was working on during the Brighton years – *The Leaping Horse, The Cornfield* and *Chain Pier, Brighton* (see figs 4, 66, 48) – were painted in his Charlotte Street studio, given that he mentions in his correspondence working on most of them from that address.[34] It is true that in the spring of 1827 Constable sent *The Chain Pier* to the Academy from his rented house at Downshire Hill in Hampstead.[35] However, it seems more than likely that the latter had been started, and probably substantially painted, in his studio in Charlotte Street and then subsequently finished by him in Hampstead.

Two of the commissions that we know Constable did paint in the summer of 1824 in Brighton are the mid-scale pictures of Hampstead, a pair, executed for Claude Schroth: *Child's Hill: Harrow in the Distance* and *Branch Hill Pond, Hampstead*.[36] The former, *Child's Hill* (see fig. 19), is based on a small oil sketch of this same subject in the Victoria & Albert Museum (fig. 18) which was probably in Constable's studio when Schroth visited him in May 1824 and placed his order for the picture.[37] Although no equivalent small sketch has been

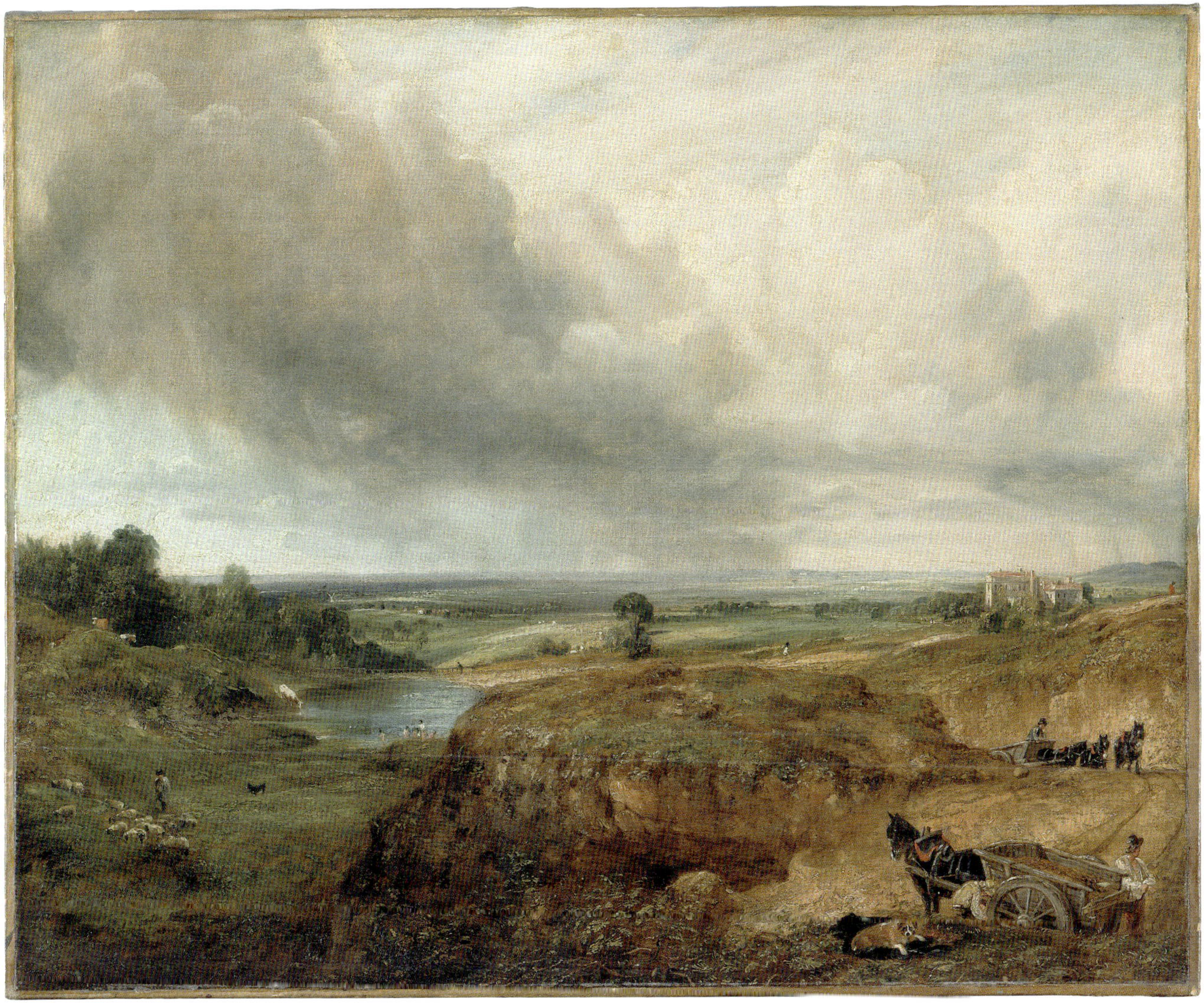

Fig. 21
Branch Hill Pond, Hampstead
1825
Oil on canvas,
59.7 × 76.2 cm
R.25.7
The Oskar Reinhart Collection 'Am Römerholz', Winterthur, Switzerland

identified to date for Schroth's view of *Branch Hill Pond* (fig. 21) it seems possible that the small sketch *A View at Hampstead: Evening*, from 1822, also in the Victoria & Albert Museum (fig. 20) and inscribed 'Schroth' on the verso, may have supplied the original germ of the idea.[38]

Constable painted the finished versions of *Child's Hill: Harrow in the Distance* and *Branch Hill Pond, Hampstead* for Schroth on a slightly larger scale than originally specified, pictures now in a private collection (albeit reproduced here in a different version in the Dick Institute Kilmarnock) and Oskar Reinhart Collection in Winterthur, Switzerland respectively (see figs 19 and 21).[39] By the end of the year Constable had made replicas of them for sending to the exhibition at the Royal Academy in 1825, the versions subsequently purchased by Francis Darby.[40] They were clearly popular with collectors, as a third pair exists in the Dick Institute (see fig. 19), whilst the composition of *Branch Hill Pond* is also known in an additional, somewhat inferior repetition in Bury Art Gallery, perhaps made with the help of John Dunthorne.[41] An intriguing, near same-size, broadly handled version of the *Branch Hill Pond* composition by Constable also exists in the Tate (fig. 22). Although this may, as tradition narrates, be a version left deliberately unfinished at the request of the buyer, it may on the other hand represent an interim same-size composition sketch of the sort that Constable was making at this date for his six-foot landscapes.[42] If it was the latter, it is just possible that Constable took it with him to Brighton as well.

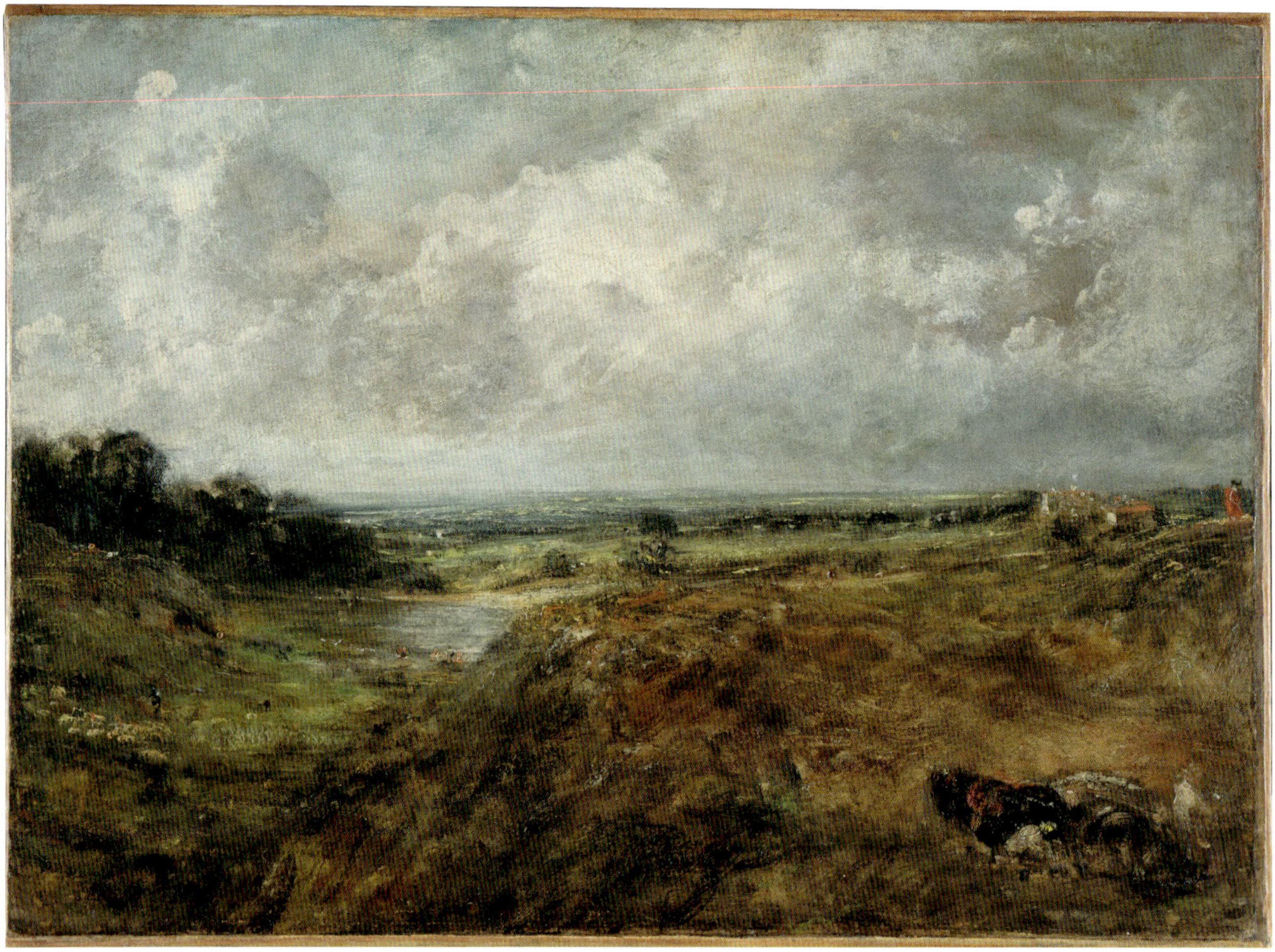

Fig. 22
Branch Hill Pond, Hampstead Heath, with a Cart and Carters
1825
Oil on canvas, 53.6 × 76.8 cm
R.25.9
Tate, London

Schroth had originally hoped that Constable would complete the two Hampstead views – and the third small painting he had commissioned from him – in time for him to submit them for inclusion in the Paris Salon exhibition due to open in August 1824, to which Arrowsmith had already promised Constable he would send *The Hay Wain* and *View on the Stour Near Dedham* (figs 25 and 13).[43] However, when Constable wrote to Schroth from Brighton to say that this would not be possible, Schroth replied urging him not to hurry his work on the pictures.[44] By 29 August, Constable wrote to Fisher to say he was getting on with his French jobs, adding that 'one of the largest is quite complete', clearly referring here to one of the two Hampstead views he had painted for Schroth.[45] On the recommendation of a friend, he showed this Hampstead view to the third Earl of Egremont, who had a town house in Brighton in addition to his main country residence at Petworth. However, Constable told Fisher that the earl had mentioned the picture – and other examples of his work with which he was already familiar – only to point out 'their defects' (this episode is discussed in greater detail by Ian Warrell in Chapter 4).[46]

It seems unlikely that, in addition to painting the two Hampstead views for Schroth in Brighton, Constable would also have embarked on his repetitions of these subjects there.[47] However, among the batch of pictures he took with him to Brighton in July 1824 there may well have been one or two of his earlier commissions for his English clients, bearing in mind he was often juggling these with his French ones. There is also the likelihood that he had taken with him any outstanding works for Arrowsmith, for the latter's second order, even though he had already made good progress on some of these in his London studio the previous June. On 23

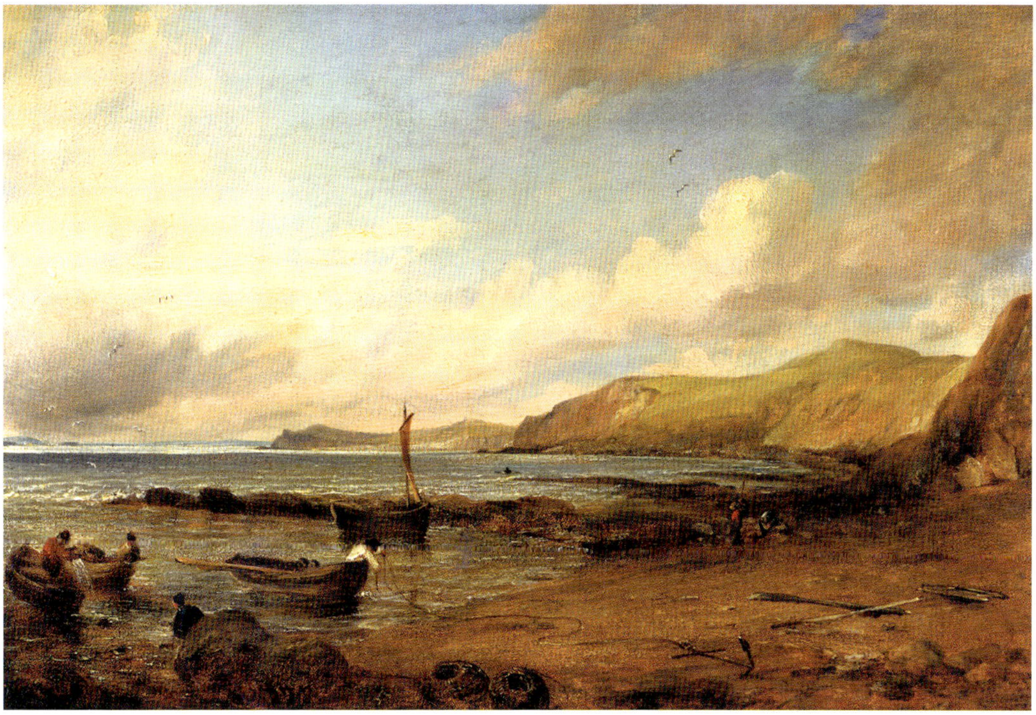

Fig. 23
Osmington Bay
1824
Oil on canvas,
36.8 × 54.6 cm
R.24.5
Dayton Art Institute, Dayton, OH, lent by the Harold and Mary Louise Shaw Foundation.

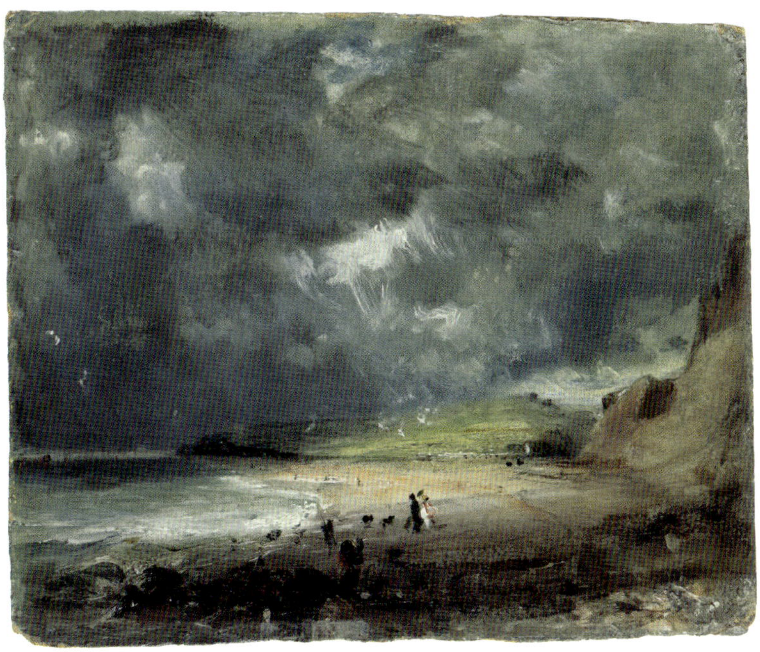

Fig. 24
Weymouth Bay
1816
Oil on millboard,
20.3 × 24.7 cm
R.16.78
Victoria and Albert Museum, London

June, for example, he had written in his journal that 'tomorrow … [I] shall complete 2 out of 3 of Mr Arrowsmith's pictures'.[48] One of these was probably the 'little picture of Cum Paul's' – that is, a view of Hampstead with St Paul's Cathedral in the distance, currently unidentified – that he had mentioned he was working on 'for Mr Arrowsmith' two days before.[49] The other was probably *Osmington Bay* – today identifiable as the version known to have been commissioned by Arrowsmith and currently on loan to the Dayton Art Institute (fig. 23) – that he wrote he was painting on 18 June.[50]

Whether Constable, as anticipated, did actually finish these two pictures before he left London for Brighton in mid-July is not known. He was frequently over-optimistic about how long it would take him to complete a picture, and he could rarely resist doing further work on his paintings even if he had himself once stated them to be 'finished'. If he did take *Osmington Bay* with him to Brighton to complete there over the summer, there would have been an inherent irony in the fact that he would have been painting a coastal scene there – one near Fisher's living at Osmington village, where he and Maria had spent their honeymoon in the autumn of 1816 – which the artist would have remembered for its almost deserted beaches and sense of solitude (fig. 24). Those quiet stretches of Dorset shoreline were a far cry from the bustle of the beach scenes Constable witnessed in Brighton in August 1824, teeming with visitors, and prompting his notorious outburst to Fisher in his letter that month that the resort seemed to him no more than 'Piccadilly … by the sea-side'.[51]

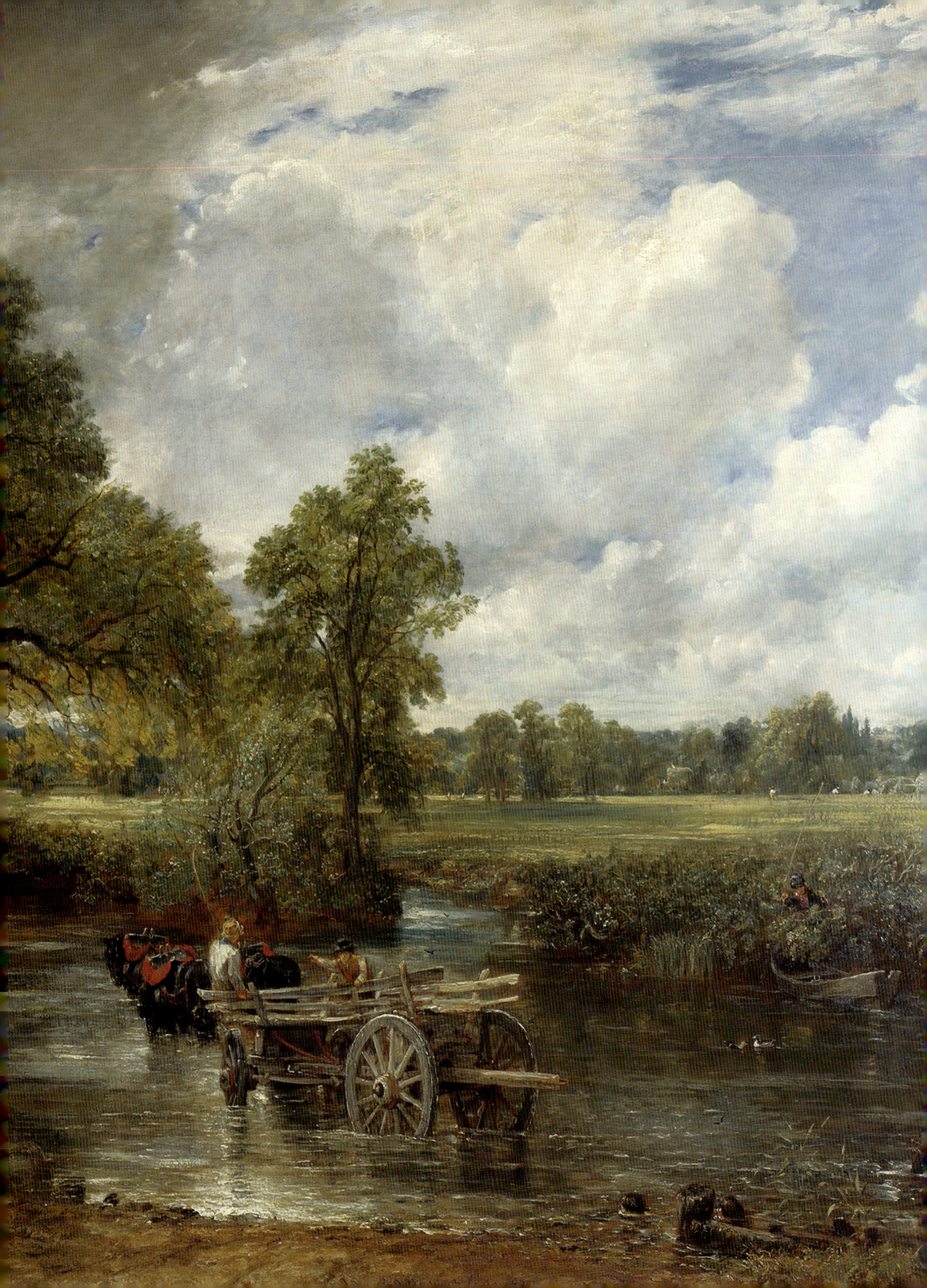

2

The 1824 Paris Salon

'a most complete and deserved success'

ANNE LYLES

Detail of fig. 25

IN THE ENTRY Constable wrote in his journal for 22 June 1824 – the diary he was keeping in London for Maria's benefit in lieu of a letter while she was in Brighton with the children – there was the usual mix of news. He told her of the paintings he had been working on that day and also cited, at length, one of the reviews of the picture he currently had on display at the Royal Academy, *The Lock* (see fig. 9). There was also mention of the visitors he had received that day – one of them was Fisher, with whom he had dined 'on a new peice [*sic*] of roast beef' – and of the table ale that local maltster Kennedy was now brewing for them, and an update on some household expenses. Among all this news there was a short paragraph in which Constable mentioned that he had just received a letter from Mr Arrowsmith in Paris, informing him of the safe arrival of his pictures there – *The Hay Wain*, of course (fig. 25), *The View on the Stour Near Dedham* and the small *Yarmouth Jetty* (see figs 13 and 14) – and telling him 'how much they were admired'. The letter was, Constable added, 'quite flattering'.[1]

Arrowsmith's letter was indeed most flattering. 'I can now Sir assure you', the Anglo-French dealer had written, 'that no objects of art were ever more praised or gave more general satisfaction than your pictures and it is with great impatience that I wait for the Exhibition of the Louvre to insure [*sic*] you a most complete & deserved success.' He had then added that he hoped Constable would come over to Paris to receive 'the congratulations of my country men' in person.[2] As far as this latter invitation was concerned, Constable's riposte – as stated by way of forewarning to Maria in his journal entry – was that 'I hope not to go to Paris as long as I live. I do not see any end it is going to answer.'[3]

Arrowsmith was clearly not exaggerating in his letter to Constable when he spoke of the impact Constable's pictures were having on French artists and critics shortly after their display in Paris in June. In fact, this highly positive reaction was something on which Arrowsmith had no doubt gambled when negotiating his deal to buy the pictures from Constable, having presumably assumed that he might well, as it were, be backing a winning horse.

In the years following the defeat of Napoleon at the Battle of Waterloo in 1815 the Continent had been opened up again to travellers, and by the early 1820s there was a steady flow of visitors moving in both directions. Theodore Géricault, leader of the new Romantic movement in France, had come over to London in 1820 to exhibit his huge painting *The Raft of the Medusa* (1819) at the Egyptian Hall in Piccadilly. He had then remained in London for most of the

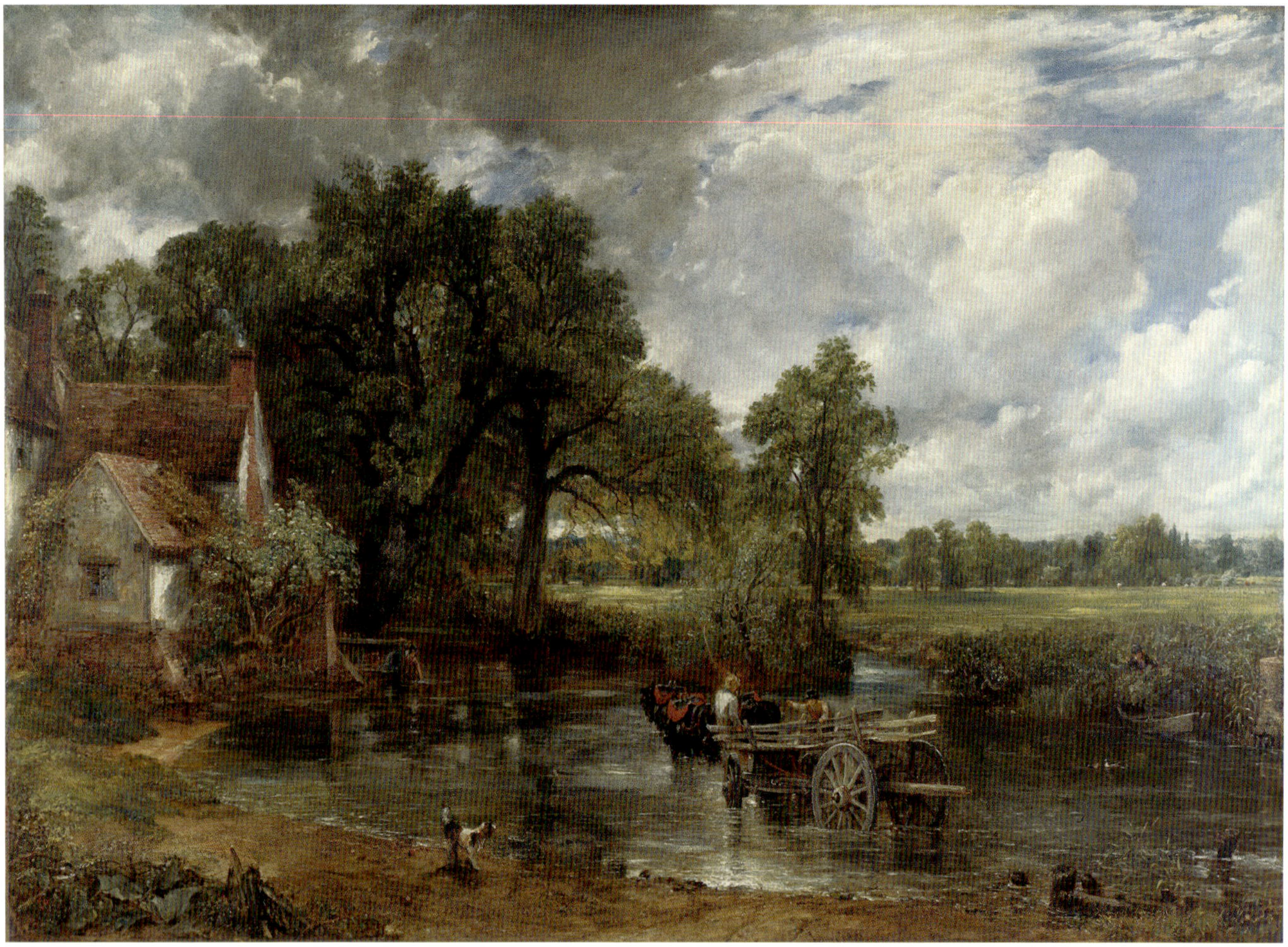

following year, when he saw Constable's *The Hay Wain* on exhibition at the Royal Academy, reporting back to artistic colleagues on his return to France that he had been quite stunned ('tout étourdi') by the painting.[4] Then there was the influential French author Charles Nodier, who, following a trip to England and Scotland in 1821, when he also visited London and admired *The Hay Wain*, had the same year published an account of his travels, *Promenade de Dieppe aux Montagnes d'Écosse*, in which he similarly singled out the painting for favourable attention.[5]

As Linda Whiteley has pointed out, Arrowsmith probably met Nodier at some stage around this time through his brother-in-law Louis-Jacques-Mandé Daguerre, a scene painter and co-inventor (with Charles Bouton) of the Diorama and later, of course, to become famous for his pioneering work in photography.[6] So it was presumably on the strength of hearing (or reading) accounts of *The Hay Wain* from the likes of Géricault and Nodier that Arrowsmith had first arrived at Constable's studio in 1822 with an offer to buy the picture.[7] Meanwhile, the Diorama, a type of moving, illuminated panorama, had been so successful on its launch in Paris in 1822 that Daguerre had decided to open a branch of the spectacle in London, in Regent's Park, entrusting the task of establishing it there to his two brothers-in-law, John and Charles Arrowsmith.[8] John (and no doubt Charles) – whose family, as it happens, was of English origin – would thus have been making frequent visits to London between 1822 and the opening of the London Diorama in September 1823. Constable himself attended the private view for the Diorama's opening at Regent's Park, telling Fisher that, however impressive, it was in his view beyond the realm of true art, as its object was deception.[9]

By early 1824 Arrowsmith clearly felt the time was right to approach Constable with an improved offer for *The Hay Wain*, and this time,

Fig. 25
The Hay Wain
1821
Oil on canvas,
130.5 × 185.5 cm
R.21.1
National Gallery, London

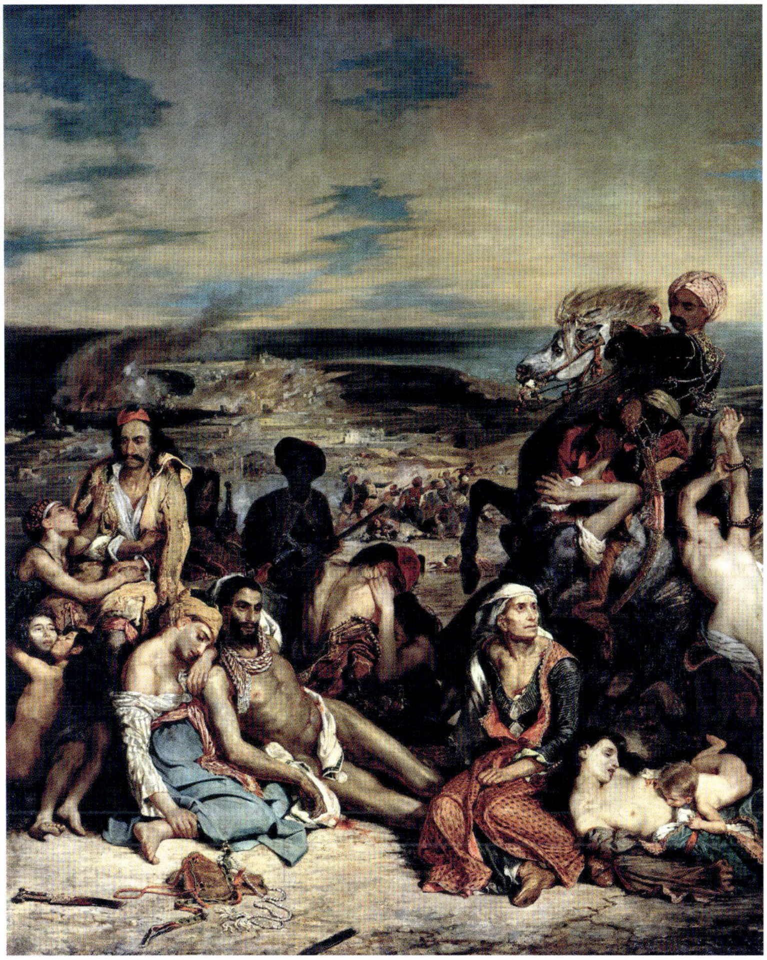

Fig. 26
Eugène Delacroix
(1798–1863)
Massacre at Chios
1824
Oil on canvas
419 × 354 cm
Musée du Louvre, Paris

of course, he was successful, purchasing the picture in a package with two other paintings by the artist.[10] In the interim between his first offer and the spring of 1824, when he concluded his negotiations, the English artist's reputation in Paris had risen, if anything, still further. By the autumn of 1823, for example, the French landscape artist Jacques Auguste Régnier had succeeded in acquiring a small painting by Constable.[11] On seeing it in Paris that year, the young Eugène Delacroix – shortly to take over the mantle from Géricault as the leading figure of the French Romantic movement – described the small picture as quite astonishing ('admirable chose et incroyable').[12]

It is no surprise, then, to hear that Delacroix, who at this time was working on his big Salon painting the *Massacre at Chios* (fig. 26), was among those who flocked to Arrowsmith's premises in Rue Grange-aux-Belles in June to see *The Hay Wain* and Constable's other paintings there. He noted in his journal for the day he visited, 19 June (the same day Arrowsmith had written to Constable to tell him how much his pictures were admired), of the remarkable impression they had had on him on that occasion ('Ce Constable me fait un grand bien[13])'. Indeed, it is presumably a measure of how much interest Constable's paintings were attracting at this time that visitors were prepared to make the journey to Arrowsmith's gallery in what is now the 10th *arrondissement* in Paris, bearing in mind, for example, that Claude Schroth's gallery boasted a much more central, prestigious location, in rue de la Paix, in the heart of what is now the 2nd *arrondissement*.[14]

It is perhaps difficult for a modern audience – bearing in mind not only our deep familiarity with *The Hay Wain* but also all that has happened in painting since Constable's own day – fully to appreciate quite what it was about the picture (and about the artist's work in general) that caused so much excitement among French artists and critics at the time. A younger generation of French painters was now emerging who were reacting against the austere neo-classicism of Jacques-Louis David and his followers – and in fact Constable himself on one occasion referred disparagingly to David's paintings as 'loathsome', on another to the artist's 'stock and heartless petrification of men and women'.[15]

This young French avant-garde particularly admired the qualities in British art they found lacking in their own more rigid – and thoroughly academic – painting tradition. They commended, for example, the way that British artists selected for their subject-matter scenes from everyday life or from contemporary poetry or literature. (Géricault particularly liked David Wilkie's genre scenes, and Régnier started to

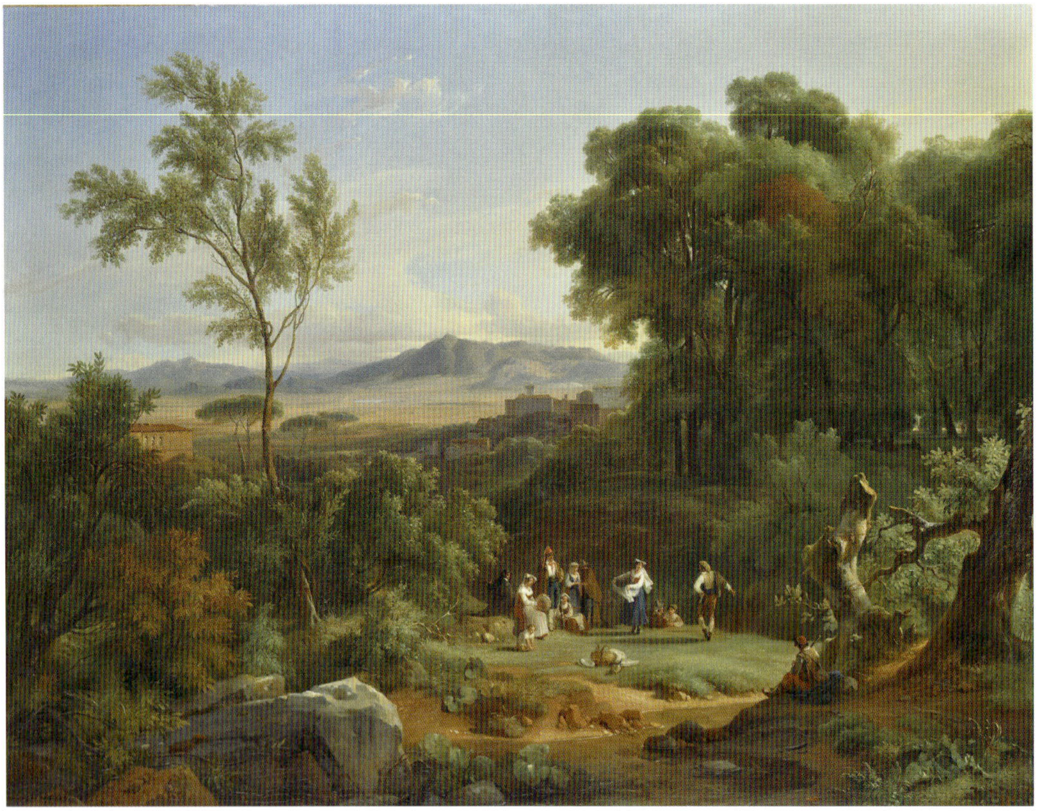

Fig. 27
ACHILLE-ETNA MICHALLON
(1796–1822)
Landscape Inspired by the View of Frascati
1822
Oil on canvas,
127 × 171 cm
Musée du Louvre, Paris

paint scenes drawn from the historical novels of Sir Walter Scott.[16]) In landscape, meanwhile, they warmed to the emphasis in British art on native – that is to say, local – scenery, something Nodier had remarked on in his *Promenade*.[17] Furthermore, one could hardly get more local than Constable's views of the River Stour at Flatford, important to the artist for their personal associations rather than for any widely acknowledged picturesque qualities such as were found in more popular (and more commonly represented) British scenery: for example, the Lake District or north Wales. What they seemed to appreciate in Constable's art is what one writer has referred to as his 'intimacy of spirit'.[18]

Above all, to French eyes, Constable's Suffolk scenes must have represented a refreshing change from the classical landscapes with Italian or Italianate associations still most esteemed in their own country at this date, such as those painted by Prix de Rome winner Achille-Etna Michallon (fig. 27). Michallon's pictures were modelled on those of the earlier, eighteenth-century French landscape painters Pierre-Henri de Valenciennes and Jean-Victor Bertin (under both of whom Michallon trained), and these artists in turn had taken inspiration from a tradition of landscape painting stretching as far back as the seventeenth century, to the venerable Nicolas Poussin.

Indeed, when feedback began to reach Constable in London concerning the opinions of the French critics about his paintings (still at this stage at Arrowsmith's gallery in rue Grange-aux-Belles), it soon became clear to him just how much of their criticism concerned his apparent move away from the art of the past. In the letter Constable wrote to Fisher on 18 July – the day after he arrived in Brighton for what was to become a three-month stay there – he informed him that although the French critics admired the 'look of nature' in his paintings and also his rich colour, they nevertheless bemoaned the extent to which his work departed from '*what has been* done' and were worried, he reported, as to 'what [was] to become of the great Poussin &&'. 'Angry' with the French artists for admiring his pictures, Constable told Fisher, the critics were now anxious that those same artists might seek to imitate the 'seductive' qualities in his paintings.[19]

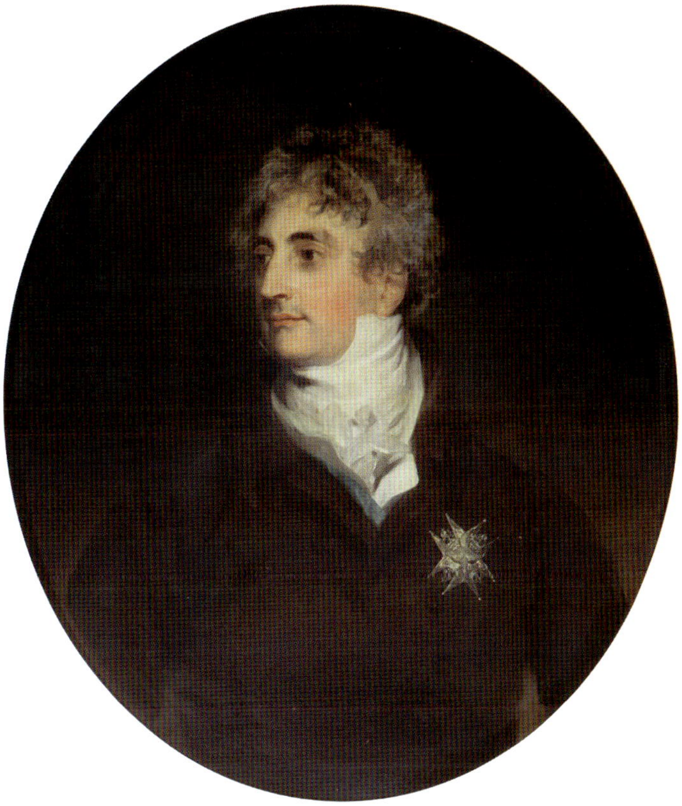

Fig. 28
THOMAS LAWRENCE
(1769–1830)
Duc de Richelieu
1823
Oil on canvas,
89 × 79 cm
Sorbonne, Paris

The 'seductive' qualities to which the critics referred almost certainly concerned his handling. Since the later part of the eighteenth century – the period dominated by David and his followers – it would be true to say that French painting technique had generally been characterised by an attention to smooth, even brushwork. The younger generation of French artists, eager to embrace new trends in art, was highly responsive to the rather looser, more expressive painting style adopted by certain English artists at this date – not just Constable but also, for example, Thomas Lawrence, President of the Royal Academy (fig. 28), and (the admittedly Anglo-French) Richard Parkes Bonington.

Of course, Constable's exhibited paintings at this date did not share the highly spontaneous, virtuoso brushwork that one sees in his small *plein-air* oil sketches, such as *Weymouth Bay* (see fig. 24) or those he painted in Brighton between 1824 and 1828 on the beach or the Downs – nor, indeed, was there ever any intention that they should do so, in a period dominated by the idea of appropriate levels of 'finish' in an exhibition picture. Nevertheless, in comparison with French art of the period (and indeed with much British art of this time), Constable's exhibition pictures of the 1820s would have appeared unusual in displaying his tendency to use broken brushstrokes and to introduce lightly impastoed highlights and coloured accents.[20] Delacroix came to admire the way in which Constable would juxtapose small dabs of varying shades of the same colour very close to each other so as to render those colours more intense although – as John Gage pointed out – the idea already had a substantial history in French eighteenth-century aesthetics.[21]

In any case, it is clear that there was already a substantial flurry of interest in Constable's paintings even before Arrowsmith sent them from his gallery in Paris to the Salon in late August – the 'Exhibition of the Louvre' that he had mentioned to Constable in his letter the previous June and which he was anticipating 'with great impatience'.[22] By contrast with the Royal Academy, whose exhibitions took place annually in the spring, exhibitions at the Paris Salon, held in the Palais du Louvre, were biennial – at least in principle, for though there was an exhibition at the Salon in 1824, for example, the next one did not take place until 1827.[23]

The 1824 Salon was later to be dubbed the 'Salon des Anglais' ('English Salon'), although this was something of a misnomer. Certainly it contained a fair amount of work by English artists, not only those pictures by Constable which Arrowsmith had sent in – *The Hay Wain*, the *View on the Stour Near Dedham* and an unidentified view of Hampstead that he had substituted for *Yarmouth Jetty* – but also paintings by, among others, Lawrence and Bonington, including the former's *Duc de Richelieu* (see fig. 28) and the latter's *French Coast with Fishermen* (fig.

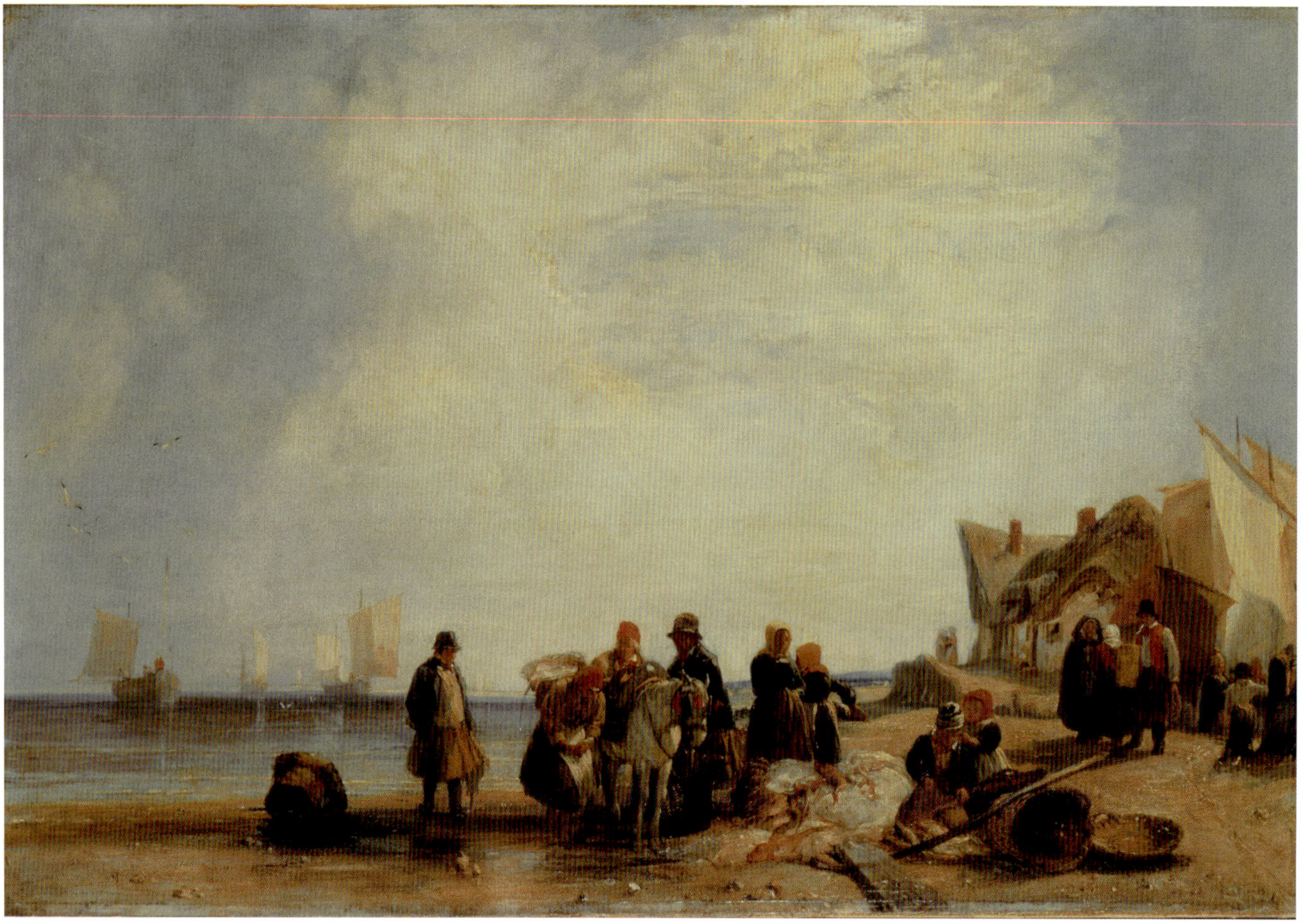

29).[24] In addition there was a good representation at the 1824 Salon of work by English watercolour painters – watercolour being a medium in which, it was widely recognised at this date, the English particularly excelled – by the likes of, for example, Anthony Vandyke Copley Fielding, his brother Thales Fielding, James Duffield Harding, Samuel Prout, Henry Gastineau and John Varley.[25]

In reality, however, the 1824 Salon was still dominated by the work of French artists, and in that particular year it seemed as though battle lines were drawn among the critics between those who favoured the older 'neo-classical' school and those who preferred the new 'Romantic' art, a contest between traditionalists and modernists, especially now that the latter were further encroaching on the former's artistic ground.[26] It was in this climate, as Linda Whiteley notes, that much of what was new in French painting came to be associated by the critics with the influence of English art – to the extent indeed that the critic Étienne-Jean Delécluze began to talk about a division between these two different schools of art as 'homérique' and 'shakespearienne'.[27]

As might have been predicted, of those British artists represented in the 1824 Salon it was Constable whose work drew most attention from the critics. They continued to be divided between those aspects of his work they admired (for example his 'truthfulness', 'vivacity' and 'freshness') and features they disliked (especially the loose brushwork, which they persisted in fearing might set a bad example to imitators).[28] However, as far as the latter was concerned, it was in a sense already too late, for Delacroix was apparently so struck by the power of Constable's novel handling that he is known to have retouched part of his masterpiece *Massacre at Chios* (see fig. 26), although art historians continue to debate exactly which parts of the picture Delacroix repainted and precisely when – that is, before the Salon opening or during the course of the exhibition itself.[29] Furthermore, as

Fig. 29
Richard Parkes Bonington (1802–1828)
French Coast with Fishermen
c.1825
Oil on canvas,
64.3 × 96.7 cm
Tate, London

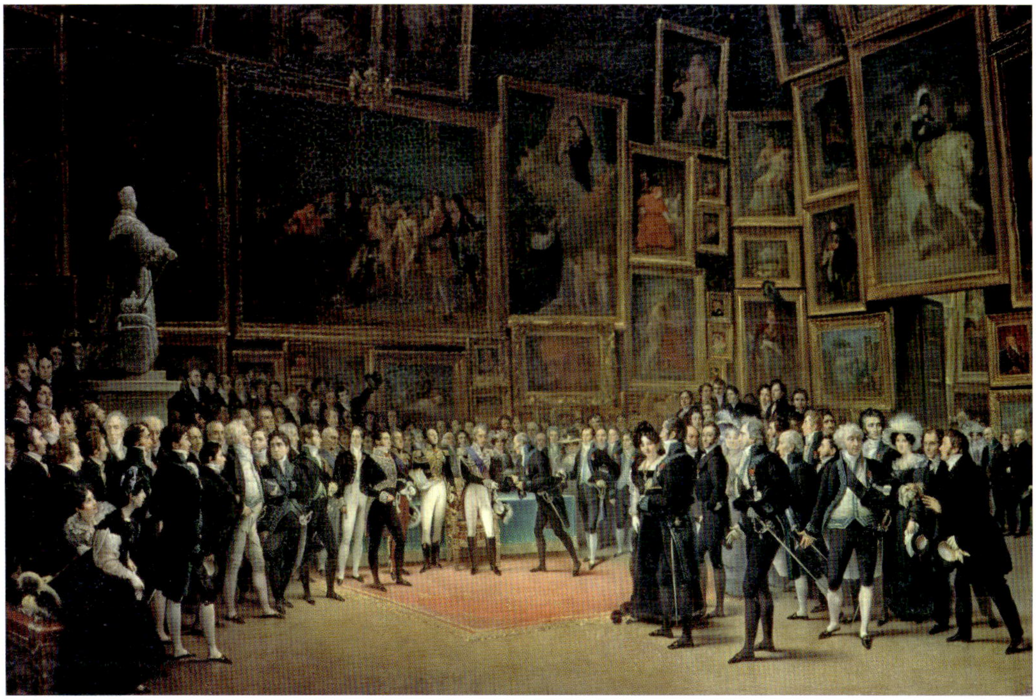

Fig. 30
F. J. HEIM (1787–1865)
Charles X Distributing Awards to Artists at the Close of the 1824 Salon
1827
Oil on canvas,
1.73 × 2.56 m
Musée du Louvre, Paris

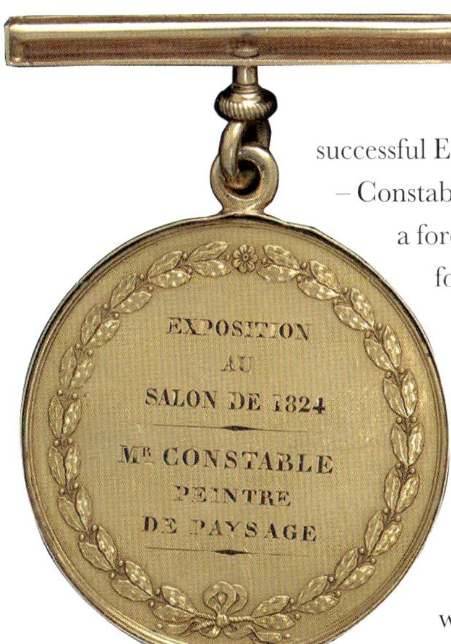

Fig. 31
Gold medal awarded by Charles X of France to John Constable
1825
Diam. 4.3 cm
National Gallery, London

if to reinforce the impact that Constable's work had had at the Salon that year, early in 1825 – as the Salon closed – Constable heard from Arrowsmith that he had been awarded a gold medal by the king of France, Charles X (fig. 31).[30]

This was indeed an honour, albeit one that Constable shared with Copley Fielding and Bonington, while Lawrence was granted the more distinguished Légion d'Honneur. Although the successful English recipients of these awards – Constable included – were not necessarily a foregone conclusion, one should not forget that all these painters, with the exception of Bonington, seem to have been represented at the Salon by invitation, whether directly or indirectly.[31] Moreover, the Comte de Forbin, Director of the Louvre, an artist in his own right and clearly an admirer of Constable's work, had sat on the Salon jury in 1824 and apparently gone out of his way to secure good positions for the latter's paintings in the hang. Forbin was later to have Constable's pictures moved, during the course of the exhibition, to a lower – and more prestigious – position, almost certainly in the Salon Carré (the equivalent to the Great Room at the Academy), so that the richness of handling they displayed could be more readily appreciated.[32]

It was in the Salon Carré that Charles X presented the medals to the lucky recipients, as shown in a picture by F. J. Heim painted three years later (fig. 30). Constable's pictures are not visible in Heim's record of the occasion – they may be out of sight. However, more pertinently, Constable himself is not included in the painting either. True to the prediction he had made to Maria in June 1824, he never did cross the Channel either to see the exhibition during its four-month run or to receive his medal in person. This is despite the fact that Arrowsmith continued to press invitations (and kept ready a room for him in his Paris house) and even though it would have been an easy crossing for Constable from Brighton to Dieppe by packet boat (see fig. 83) and thence a straightforward journey to the French capital.[33]

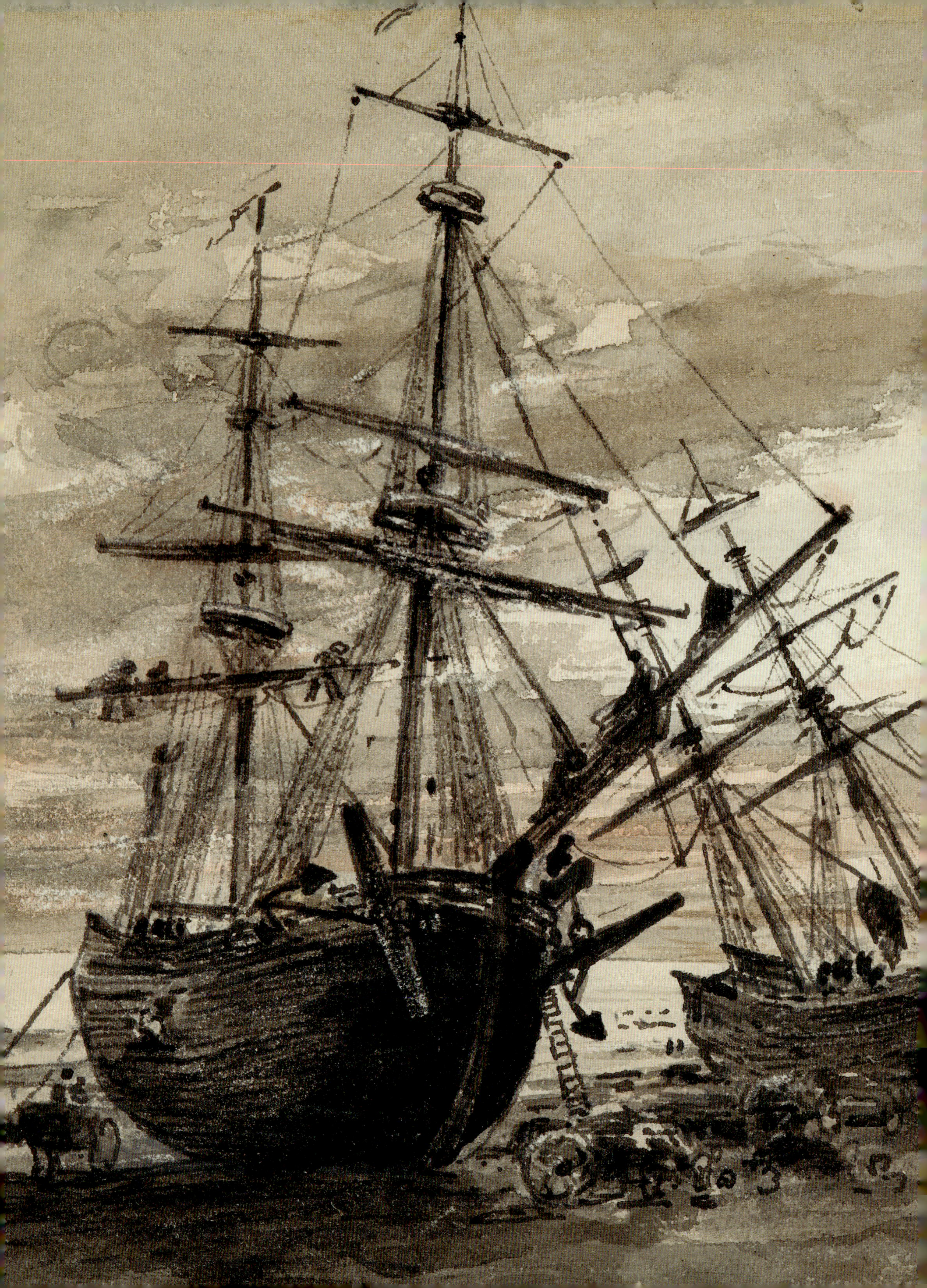

3 In Pursuit of Originality in Brighton

'these subjects are so hackneyed in the Exhibition'[1]

Ian Warrell

Despite being near-contemporaries, with a shared dedication to landscape painting, there are surprisingly few occasions in the careers of Constable and J. M. W. Turner where common subject-matter provides an opportunity for close and meaningful comparisons of their creative responses and their respective objectives. Even at Salisbury, where both men found patronage and friendship, the works they painted emerged from very different circumstances, and are separated by several decades.[2] It is therefore all the more fascinating to examine the period of roughly four years in the mid-1820s when both were suddenly drawn to Brighton. As we will see, Brighton was abuzz with novelty in 1824. So it is not altogether remarkable that it provided the setting where the very independent paths of these artists crossed.

At forty-nine, Turner was a year older than his rival. Unlike Constable, he was not encumbered with familial responsibilities, despite apparently having fathered two illegitimate daughters. (Evelina, aged around twenty-three, was by then married to the diplomat Joseph Dupuis, and Georgiana, only twelve or thirteen, was living with her mother, Sarah Danby.) Unlike Constable, Turner had quickly gained recognition and success, and thereafter maintained his pre-eminence, both in the distinguished circles of the Royal Academy, to which he had been elected in 1802, and in the commercial realm of popular topographical prints.

It was, in fact, his work on three different, but overlapping topographical publications that determined his presence in Brighton in 1824, at the end of a journey that had already encompassed Portsmouth, Chichester, Arundel and Shoreham. Typically, Turner diligently recorded his travel expenses in a sketchbook, but the precise dates of his spell in Brighton have not been identified. Nevertheless, it seems likely to have been early in the summer, perhaps at the very start of June.[3]

He had not exhibited anything at the Academy this year because all his energies during the first half of the year had gone into the notable but troublesome commission from George IV for a vast canvas depicting the Battle of Trafalgar, which was installed in the newly refurbished state rooms at St James's Palace as the pendant to an earlier sea-battle painted by Philippe-Jacques de Loutherbourg (both now at the National Maritime Museum, Greenwich).[4] Turner would undoubtedly have worked right up to the last minute, making final adjustments, and so must have remained in London until at least 20 May, when the king held his first 'Drawing Room' of the season.[5]

Detail of fig. 45

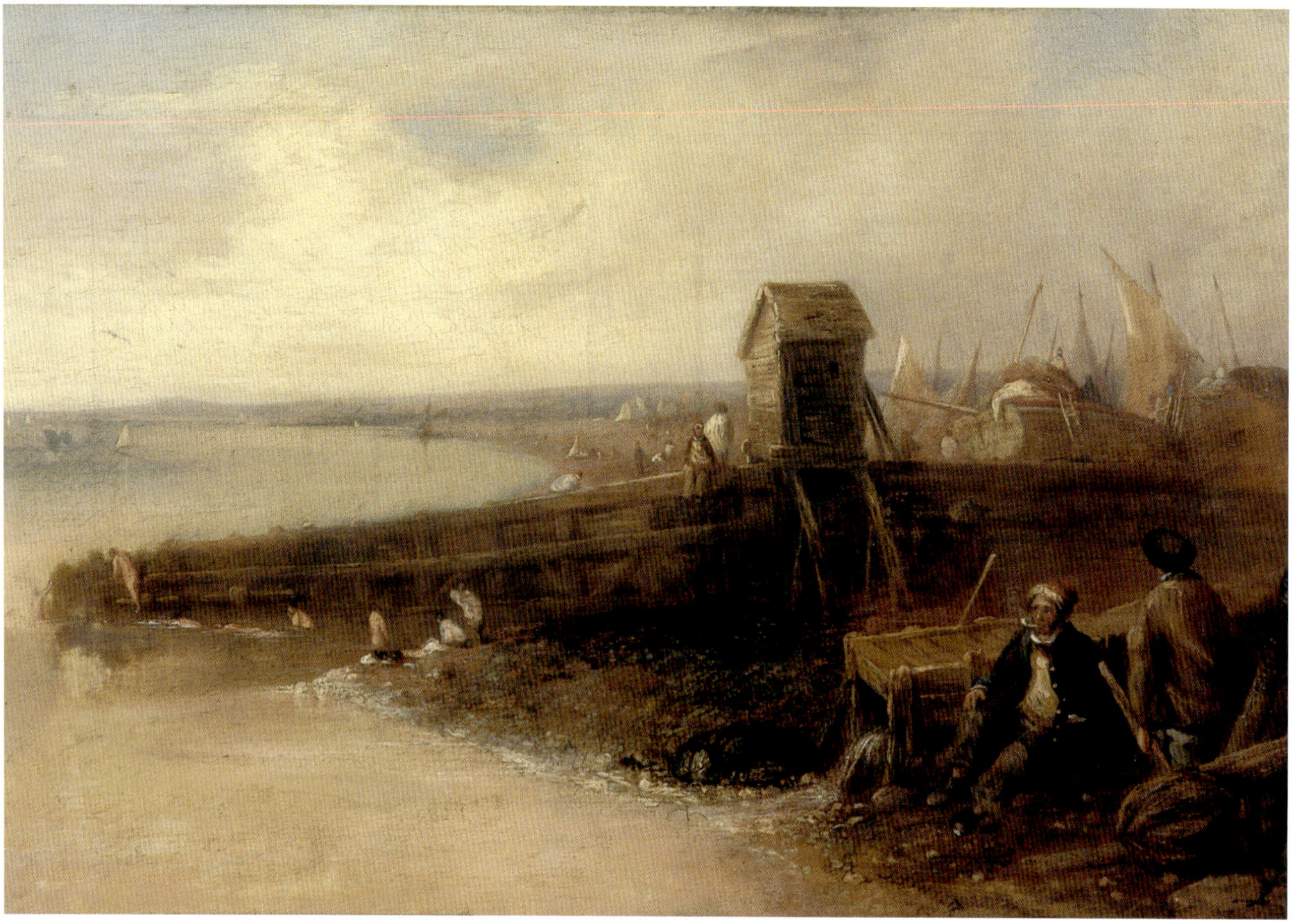

Fig. 32
JAMES BENNETT
(1808–1888)
The Pump House, Brighton
1825
Oil on canvas,
39.4 × 59.5 cm
Royal Pavilion & Museums, Brighton

This was a week after Constable had installed Maria and the rest of his domestic household at Sober's Gardens, and he was not back in Brighton again until 10 June, which makes it probable that Turner's visit fell between those of Constable. Not that they would have sought out each other's company away from London. Constable may well have been pleasantly surprised to discover Turner's 'wonderfull range of mind' during a dinner back in 1813, but in the intervening years they seem to have remained resolutely respectful of their differences, socially at least.

At Brighton, Turner's chief mission was to devise an image that offered a more up-to-date impression of the resort for the *Picturesque Views on the Southern Coast of England* (1814–26). Initiated and issued by William Bernard Cooke and his brother George, this serial publication had become a vehicle for Turner's evocative scenes of the shores of Britain in the years when the threat of invasion from Napoleon's France was finally quashed. Other artists also contributed images, but there was no doubt that Turner was the engine propelling the critical success of the venture. Views of Brighton by Samuel Owen and Henry Edridge had been engraved in 1814, in the earliest stages of the series, depicting St Nicholas's Church and the Pump House.[6] The latter structure, on the beach, drew water up to the fashionable baths adjacent to the Fish Market (fig.33). But by 1824 both of these picturesque features were undoubtedly considered quaint alongside the latest landmarks, the chief of which was the Suspension Chain Pier, inaugurated in October 1823.[7]

The pier was far from being the only new attraction or facility in Brighthelmston, or Brighton (as it was by now usually known). Since 1811 the town's population had more than doubled, to almost 30,000. Evidence of the ongoing expansion of its housing stock, as well as its places of entertainment, illuminated by lighting supplied by a new gasworks, was

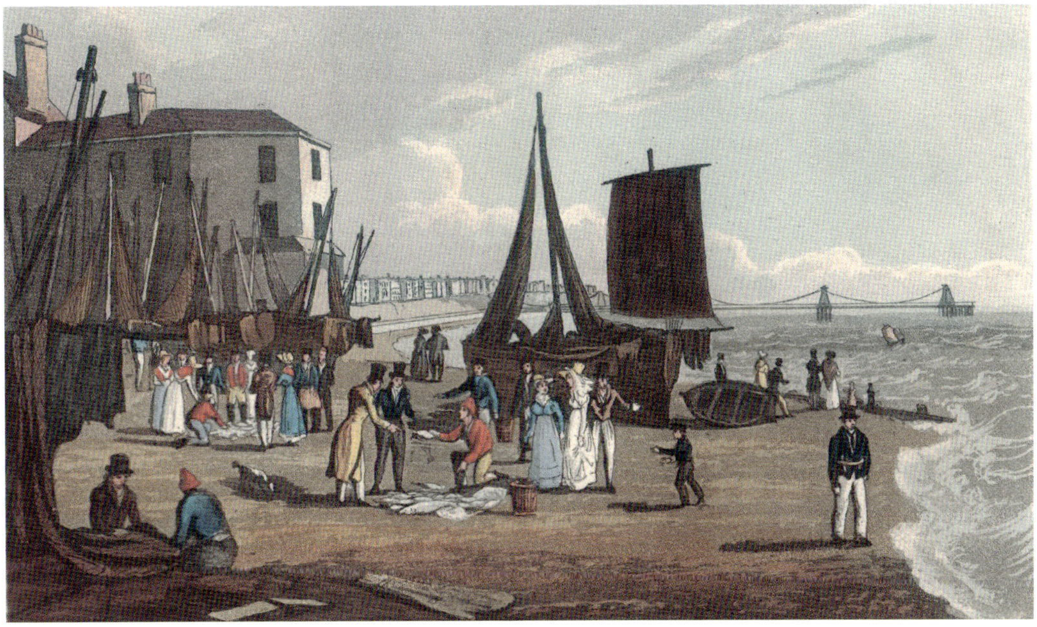

Fig. 33
Robert Havell Jr
(1793–1878)
The Fish Market on the Beach (Plate VI from E. W. Brayley's *Topographical Sketches of Brighthelmston and Its Neighbourhood, 1825)*
1824
Hand-coloured aquatint
8.5 × 14.5cm
Private collection

inescapable to the huge number of visitors, whose presence during the summer months often pushed the number of those resident to well over 50,000.[8] In that era the recent completion of the Royal Pavilion seemed to confer a royal allure on the town, though such affectations were somewhat punctured by the notoriously unregulated attitude to sea-bathing. Whereas other resorts offered discrete areas for male and female bathers, they were not distinct at Brighton; and swimming was even permitted close to the Fish Market, another key location for tourists (fig.32). It was thought shocking that the bathing machines denied women the protective awnings, available elsewhere, to shield them from the impertinent scrutiny of those on the promenade equipped with telescopes.[9]

Downplaying such concerns, guidebooks such as Brayley's *Topographical Sketches of Brighthelmston and Its Neighbourhood* (1825) were quick to reassure their readers of the social distinction of fellow visitors, claiming they came from 'the first Families for rank, splendour, and fashion in the kingdom'.[10] But, in fact, by the 1820s the intermingling of a broader social mix had become an established phenomenon that Constable was not alone in finding troubling. In his well-known, ill-humoured word-picture of Brighton sent to his friend Fisher in late August 1824, he famously lambasted the 'endless & indecent confusion' of what he termed 'Piccadilly … by the sea-side' (see pp. 8–9). Just a few years earlier, in 1819, the Prince Regent's mistress, Mrs Fitzherbert, had remarked disdainfully, 'When I tell you that fifty-two public coaches go from hence to London every day and bring people down for six shillings, you will not be surprised at the sort of company we have.'[11] Haughty comments of this kind may well have encompassed the social types that Constable termed abusively the 'off-scouring of London', but they also make palpable the greater access to travel and leisure, not only for the middle classes, in the years after Waterloo. Other texts, notably those by metropolitan incomers, reveal a similar condescending tone towards Brighton's *nouveau* status. Mary Shelley, for example, penned a sneering account of her time in Brighton in 1826, dismissing it ultimately as a 'seat of barrenness'.[12]

Constable was more even-handed, viewing all he saw dismissively, including the social pretensions of the fashionable set intent on gaining admittance to the peripheries of the royal court at the Royal Pavilion (fig. 34). It is notable, for example, that he made no sketches whatsoever on the Steine; nor did he record the great royal bauble that dominates it, the artificiality of which cannot have appealed to his preference for natural forms. There was, in any case, no need for him to sketch it because the

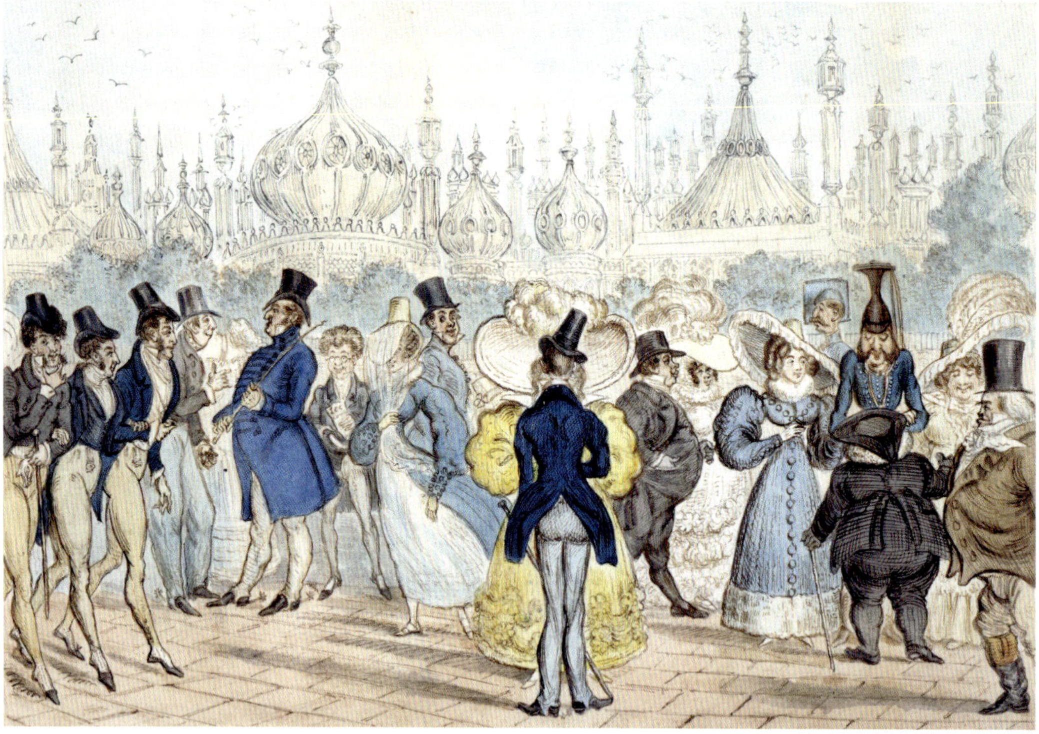

Fig. 34
Alfred Henry Forrester (pseud. Alfred Crowquill) (1804–1872)
Beauties of Brighton
1825
Pen, ink and watercolour, 22.3 × 32.7 cm
Victoria and Albert Museum, London

building's steady transformation from Holland's classical Marine Pavilion to John Nash's oriental fantasy had been thoroughly documented by countless other artists, and so its image was already pervasive – even outside Brighton.[13]

Despite the expressly topographical concerns of his visit to Brighton, Turner similarly paid little heed to the Pavilion, making just two quick sketches from the north, in which its domes and minarets are dramatically silhouetted by an afternoon sun. These are among the thirty sheets of a pocket-sized sketchbook he covered in little more than a day.[14] Seemingly perfunctory on first inspection, the sketches reveal his consummately professional approach to the accumulation of visual information. Each quick schematic outline was part of a cumulative experience, which retained the potential to be reunited with others to create a recognisable whole. They are therefore mostly components, rather than compositions. Constable's tendency, by contrast, was to absorb visual reality as a series of resolved images that grew out of a slower, more reflective assimilation of place, based on a longer inhabitation of the settings. Of course, his sketches remained open to the same kinds of editing and manipulation that Turner pursued away from the motif. But the fragmentary quality of the older artist's method seems closer to the way neuroscientists now believe the eye and brain work together in the fundamental process of seeing and understanding the world.[15]

Take, for example, a sketch he made of the seafront houses and hotels along the rapidly expanding seafront (fig. 35). For once, Turner helped to fix the location by adding an inscription – 'Bedford H[ouse]' – which pinpoints the buildings depicted as those formerly on the

Fig. 35
J. M. W. Turner (1775–1851)
Marine Parade, Looking West from Bedford Street
(from the Brighton and Arundel sketchbook; TB CCX f.29); (D18357)
1824
Pencil, 7.5 × 11.8 cm
Tate, London

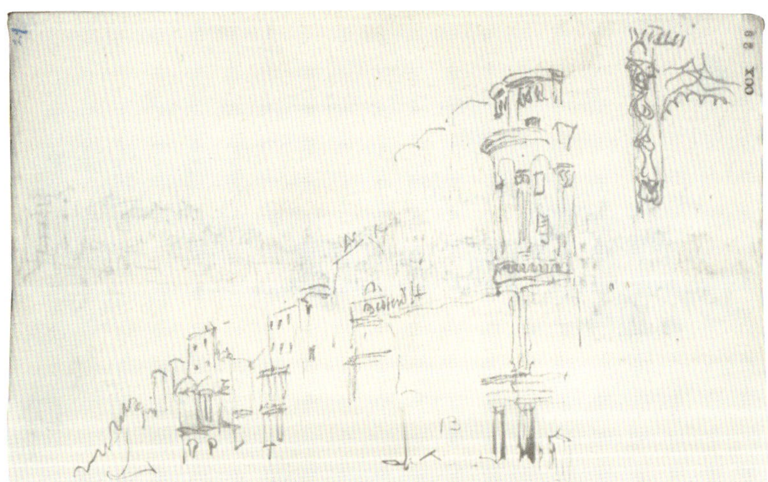

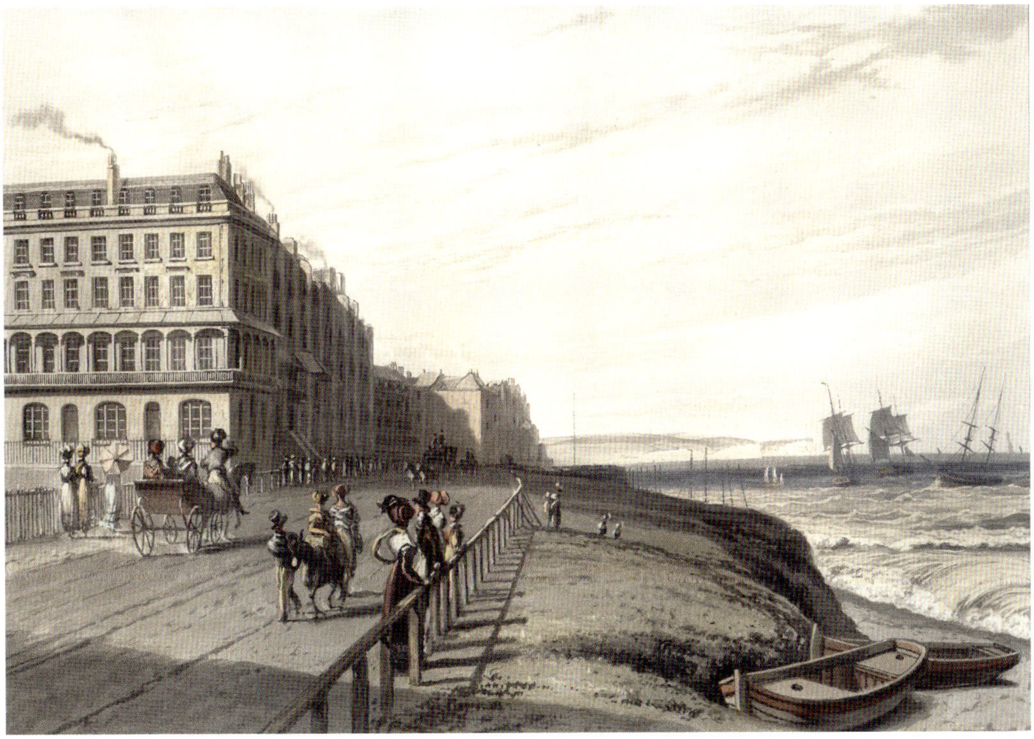

Fig. 36
William Daniell
(1769–1837)
Near Regent's Square
(from *A Voyage round Great Britain*)
1823
Hand-coloured aquatint,
22.7 × 30.1 cm
Private collection

corner of Marine Parade and its junction with Bedford Street. His eye was evidently attracted by the accumulation of architectural features that the writer of a local guidebook highlighted the following year: 'viranda galleries in front, supported by Doric columns fluted; the upper stories are ornamented with pilasters, a bold cornice, and a balustrade parapet'.[16] But rather than repeating this visual information for all four lodgings, only the nearest is delineated; the others are defined merely as blank outlines.

This kind of visual shorthand permitted Turner to encompass far more in a short space of time, with the result that his sketches span Brighton's most ambitious housing developments in the early stages of construction at what were then the two furthest reaches of the seafront. Out to the east he found the façades of Kemp Town, notably Arundel Terrace and Lewes Crescent, while at the other end of town, where Brighton's expansion was beginning to encroach on Hove, work was progressing on the terraces of Brunswick Town, well to the west of Constable's lodgings in the vicinity of Regency Square (fig. 36).[17] Turner's terse outlines perhaps mislead the viewer, suggesting in both cases that building work was more advanced than was actually the case. By completing only the façades of their schemes, the developers were able to fill in the houses behind in a piecemeal fashion, according to demand. But the confidence that pervaded the booming Brighton of 1824 was shortly afterwards punctured by the far-reaching consequences of the financial crisis of 1825–26, which for some time threatened the viability of these schemes, leaving the sites largely vacant. One visitor in 1826 described the speculative development in eastern Brighton as like a ghost town, and, in fact, by 1828 only 11 of the 105 planned houses of Kemp Town had been occupied.[18]

Turner's research for an image that would define modern Brighton was shaped by his knowledge of William Daniell's series of views for the rival publication *A Voyage round Great Britain*, which had begun after his own set of *Picturesque Views on the Southern Coast*, but which had in the meantime come close to a complete circumnavigation of the whole nation. Daniell had issued three aquatints of Brighton in August 1823, showcasing the appeal of the town's fashionable new settings (fig. 36).[19] But his visit had preceded the completion of the Chain Pier, which had quickly become the town's principal landmark. Already during 1824 a deluge of new

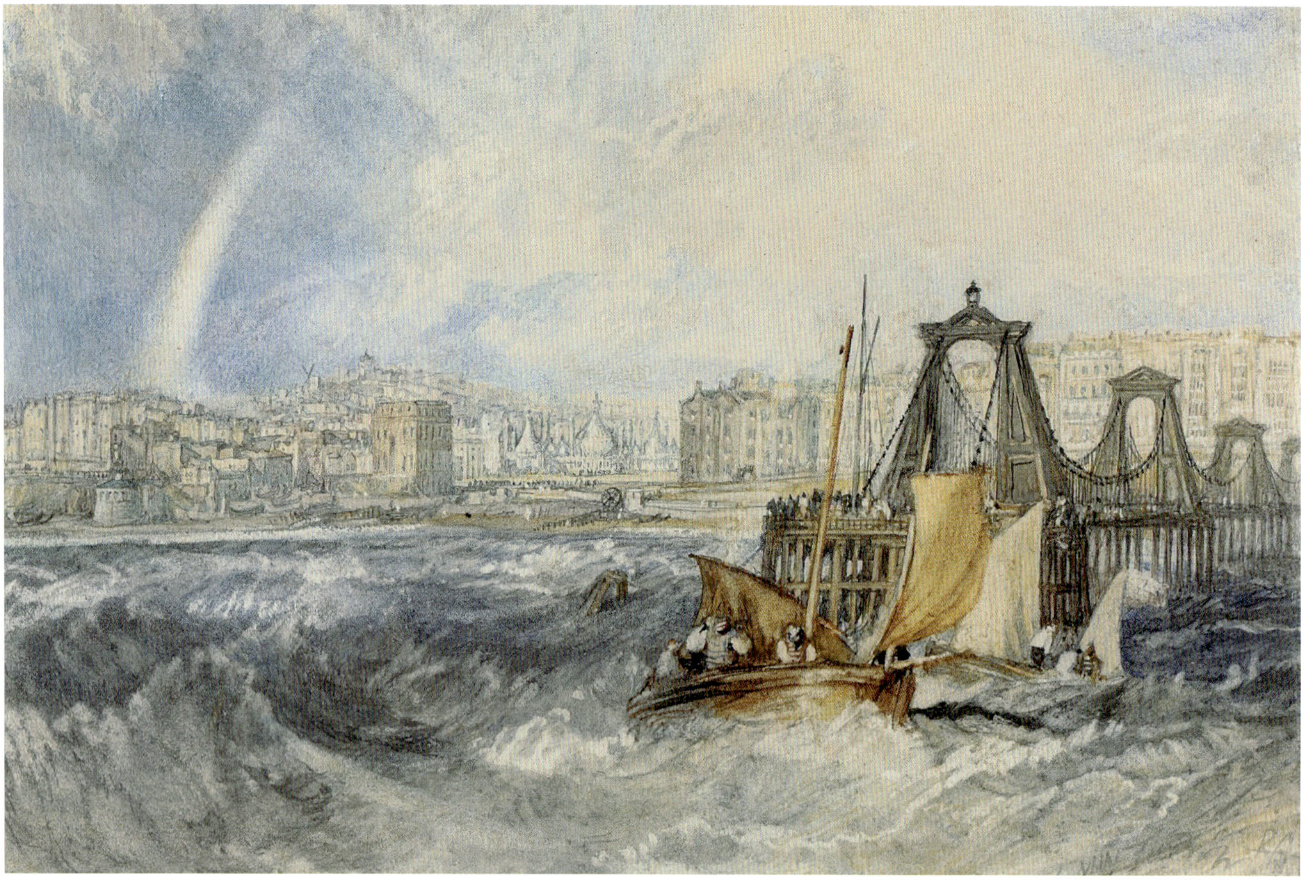

prints was available, published in formats to meet all tastes and pockets.[20] Almost without exception, these earliest images depicted the new structure from the west side, either from the foot of the Steine or from the Fish Market (see figs 33 and 125).

Turner's sketchbook demonstrates his pursuit of novel prospects that combine the pier with the expanded seafront, or juxtapose it with traditionally picturesque subjects such as St Nicholas's Church or the Pump House.[21] But one of the most detailed sequences of sketches suggests that he had determined on a view from the pier itself, looking back to shore.[22] His plan was to combine key manifestations of Brighton's modernity in his composition – Lamprell's Baths (1823), the new Albion Hotel (already constructed but not open for business until 1826), the Royal Pavilion and the pier – the only problem being that the terrace of houses on the seafront actually obscured the palace. Such practical shortcomings were easily overcome with a little sleight-of-hand in the resulting watercolour by imaginatively shifting the viewpoint some way out to sea, beyond the pier's final platform, as the town might be seen from one of the steam-packets arriving from France (fig. 37). The dramatic effect this created was a solution adopted by other artists once the watercolour was published in September 1825, after which it remained in circulation well into the later nineteenth century, retaining its vitality even

BELOW: **Fig. 38**
ROBERT HAVELL JR (1793–1878)
Brighton from the Sea 1824
(Plate II from E. W. Brayley's *Topographical Sketches of Brighthelmston and its Neighbourhood*, 1825)
Hand-coloured aquatint, 8.5 × 14.5 cm
Royal Pavilion & Museums, Brighton

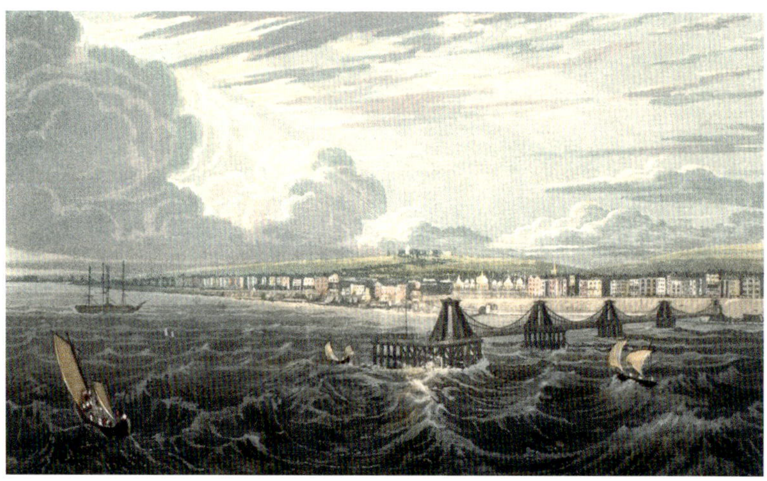

OPPOSITE: **Fig. 37**
J. M. W. TURNER (1775–1851)
Brighthelmston, Sussex (from *Picturesque Views on the Southern Coast of England*), 1824–25
Watercolour, 14.6 × 22.2 cm
Royal Pavilion & Museums, Brighton

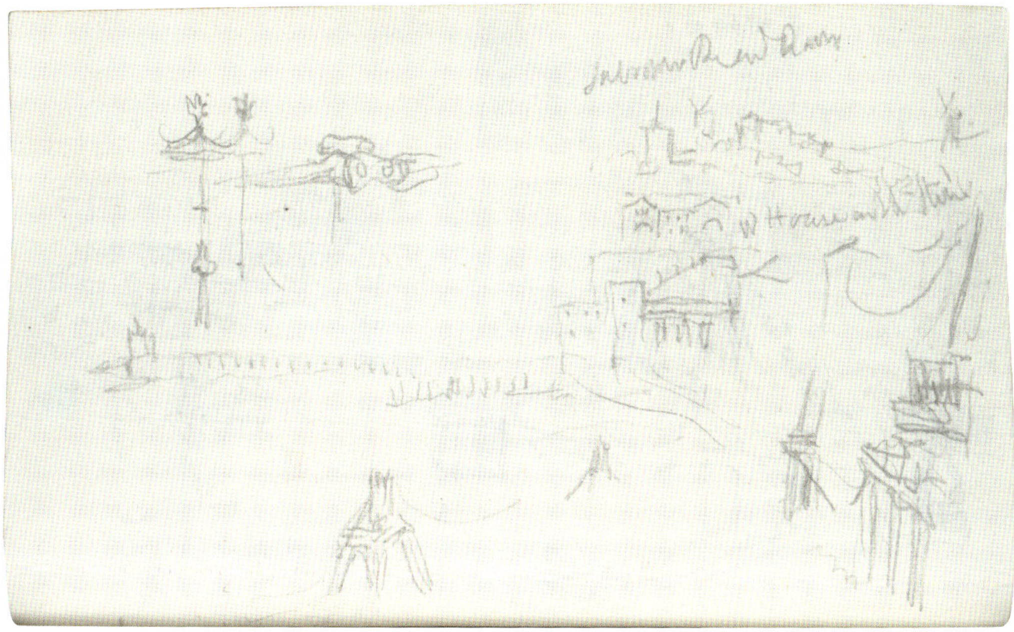

RIGHT: **Fig. 39**
J. M. W. TURNER (1775–1851)
Details of the Chain Pier, Brighton; with Church Hill and Its Windmills
(From the Brighton and Arundel sketchbook; TB CCX f.31a); (D18362)
1824
Pencil, 7.5 × 11.8 cm
Tate, London

after the pier itself was finally destroyed in 1896.[23] Of those who anticipated Turner's way of visualising the town, Robert Havell Jr produced a variant of the viewpoint (fig. 38) that came out too late in 1824 for it to have influenced Turner's sketching process, but his earlier panorama of the full seafront may have provided a useful stimulus (see fig. 8).[24] On other pages of his sketchbook Turner's composite notes furnished him with supplementary observations, including studies of one of the links in the suspended chains, and of the buoys positioned to protect the end of the pier, which were lost in the storm at the end of 1824 (fig. 39).

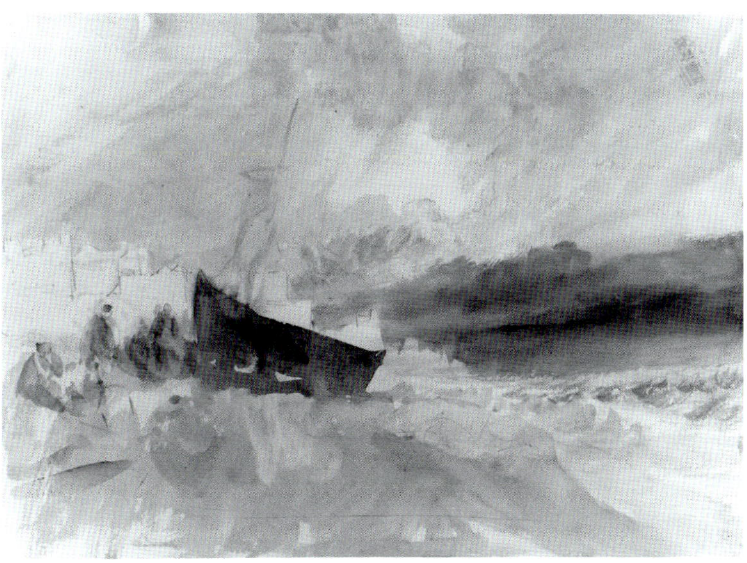

BELOW: **Fig. 40**
J. M. W. TURNER (1775–1851)
Fishing Boats Hauled Up on Brighton Beach
(From the Farnley-Munro sketchbook)
c.1824
Pencil and watercolour, 19.3 × 26.7 cm
Private collection

The leaves of another of Turner's sketchbooks contain a few images that seem to be connected with his time in Brighton (fig. 40).[25] One, in particular, overlaps with Constable's drawings of 1824 in its adoption of monochrome washes and its focus on fishing boats hauled up on the shingle beach. By the time they arrived in Brighton that year, both artists had seen the group of sepia-toned pen-and-ink drawings by Claude Lorrain that had been acquired by the collector Richard Payne Knight, and which had been passed to the British Museum by July (fig. 41).[26] Turner needed no encouragement to think of his own work alongside the seventeenth-century master's. So an article in the *Somerset House Gazette* that made approving comparisons between Claude's studies and the 'sketches of certain masters of our own school' would have been of less significance to him than to Constable, who was also specifically named among the 'ingenious compeers … who sketch with no less spirit and truth' than Claude.[27]

This flattering endorsement may have been a contributory factor in Constable's subsequent decision to undertake his series of monochrome sketches while at Brighton (see figs 42–47, 117–119, 123, 124).[28] He moved on to these at the start of September, when the weather remained fine for the harvest.[29] So the switch from pencil and oil to pencil and wash (added

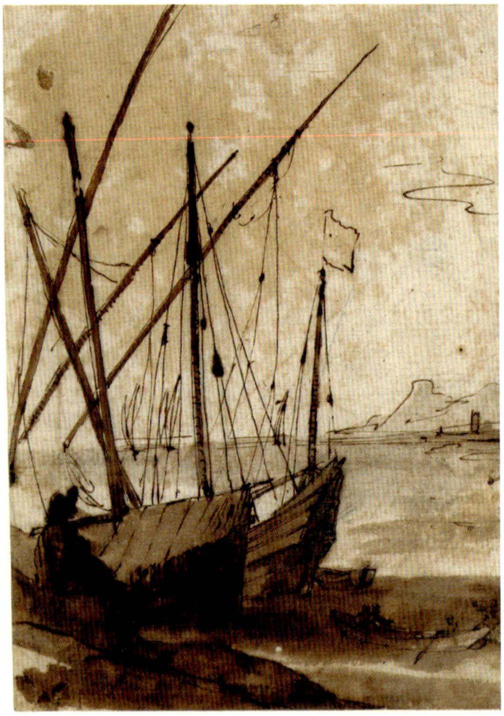

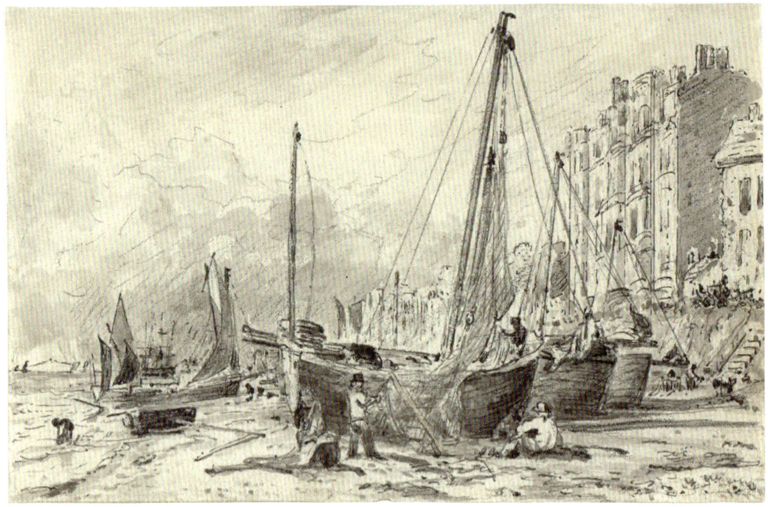

Fig. 41
Claude Gellée, le Lorrain (*c.*1604/5–1682)
Coast with Sailing Boats
*c.*1638–40
Pen and ink, with wash, 23.5 × 17.5 cm
The British Museum, London; bequeathed by Richard Payne Knight, 1824

Fig. 42
Beached Fishing Boats, Mending Nets, Brighton, Looking West
c. 1824
Pencil, pen and ink, with grey and ochre wash on Whatman paper, 11.4 × 18.1 cm
Not in Reynolds
Private collection (Christie's 2016)

either on the spot or later) for these works was not prompted by the practical consideration of a need to change media when sketching in cooler or wetter weather, although conversely the continued and exceptional warmth in the first fortnight of September, which brought yet more visitors to Brighton, would possibly have limited and deterred Constable from working in oils *en plein air*. In any case, the sketchbook in which he made the drawings had already been in use earlier in the summer: a pencil outline on a sheet now in the Horne Foundation in Florence sets out the composition of the oil sketch he painted of the Gothic House on 2 August (see fig. 1).[30] On the same page, but below the outline for that work, is another sketch of a cluster of fishing boats partly obscured by a low cliff. The conjunction suggests that this was also a composition he intended to develop in oils, as does a further sketch of Brighton boats under a cloudy sky at the top of the sheet, worked much more emphatically.[31]

Of course, several of the oil sketches painted in June and July already testify to Constable's fascination with the distinctive qualities of Brighton's fishing boats (see figs 87–89). He would no doubt have viewed the fishermen more sympathetically than the town's other occupants, perhaps succumbing to the widespread perception that Brighton's fishing community had been displaced by the transformation of the town since the arrival of the Prince Regent.[32] So his decision to focus on their boats during his time in Brighton effectively pitted tradition against modernity. Even so, in his dyspeptic critique of the resort on 29 August, Constable hardly conveyed great enthusiasm for them, or gave the impression that he was about to embark on a sustained survey of the fleet of perhaps 90 boats. His appreciation was actually strictly qualified, conceding he could make do with the boats in the absence of more interesting subjects. Moreover, he noted, 'The fishing boats are picturesque, but not so much so as the Hastings boats.'[33] He supported this assertion by making a sketch (which interrupted the text of his now lost letter) differentiating between the luggers of Hastings and the broad-beamed, spritsail 'hoggies', or hog boats, of Brighton, despite apparently not having been to Hastings. He was probably able to make the comparison at Brighton. But the characteristic boats had featured repeatedly, for well over a decade, in depictions of Hastings by Joshua Cristall, David Cox, John James Chalon and, inevitably, Turner, as well as many others.[34] So pervasive were images of boats beside the sea

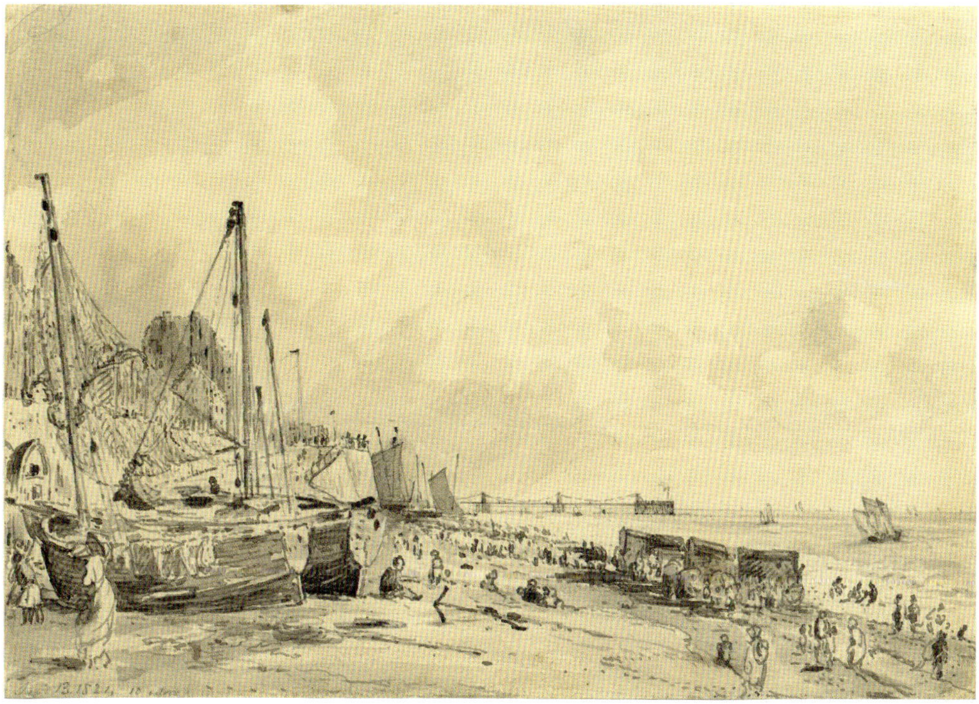

Fig. 43
Brighton Beach Looking East
13 September 1824
Wash over pencil on paper, 17.7 × 26.1 cm
R.24.30
Sterling and Francine Clark Art Institute, Williamstown, MA

that Constable considered such subjects 'hackneyed in the Exhibition' and of a 'class of art much easier than Landscape'.

It is not difficult to detect here a note of peevishness, ironically at a moment when repetitions of his own shore scene of Great Yarmouth were in demand (see p. 24 and fig. 14). That success may have emboldened him to conceive other ways to challenge the dominance of Turner – whom Constable would describe in January 1825, just a few months later, as 'him who would be Lord over all'.[35] So something of this sentiment may have driven him to embark on the series of drawings, with a view (at this stage) to them serving as the basis for paintings. Another possibility, first suggested by Ian Fleming-Williams in his sensitive study of the Brighton drawings, is that Constable's new Brighton associate, the horticulturalist Henry Phillips (*c.*1779–1840), encouraged him to think of creating a set of publishable designs.[36] At this date there still seemed to be a buoyant market for topographical prints. It was an appetite that Turner fed assiduously, simultaneously producing designs not only for the *Southern Coast*, but also *The Rivers of England*, *Views in London* and *The Ports of England*, with his *Picturesque Views in England and Wales* following on from 1825.

The problem in considering the nature and purpose of Constable's drawings of the fishing boats is that we know that some, perhaps most, of them were reworked towards the end of the year, with the result that we cannot be sure what they looked like at the point when Constable went back to London in October. A reasonable assumption is that they were primarily sketches in pencil, sometimes with additional wash, and that the greater degree of finish came only later. At least a handful of sheets were left as simple pencil sketches, but one of these is a much more definitive statement that relates to the 1827 oil painting, so the shading may have been subsequently strengthened.[37] For the most part, however, the later additions were in fine lines of pen and ink, with monochrome wash (see fig. 117); in only a few instances was diluted colour applied to add warmth (see figs 45, 119 and 123).[38] Despite such revisions, the images still retain the informality of sketches, and have more in common with the simple drawings that Daniell prepared for his published series than the brilliant colours and technical flourishes of Turner's topographical watercolours.

On 17 December, Constable explained to Fisher that he had again delayed sending him the sketchbook containing the images of boats

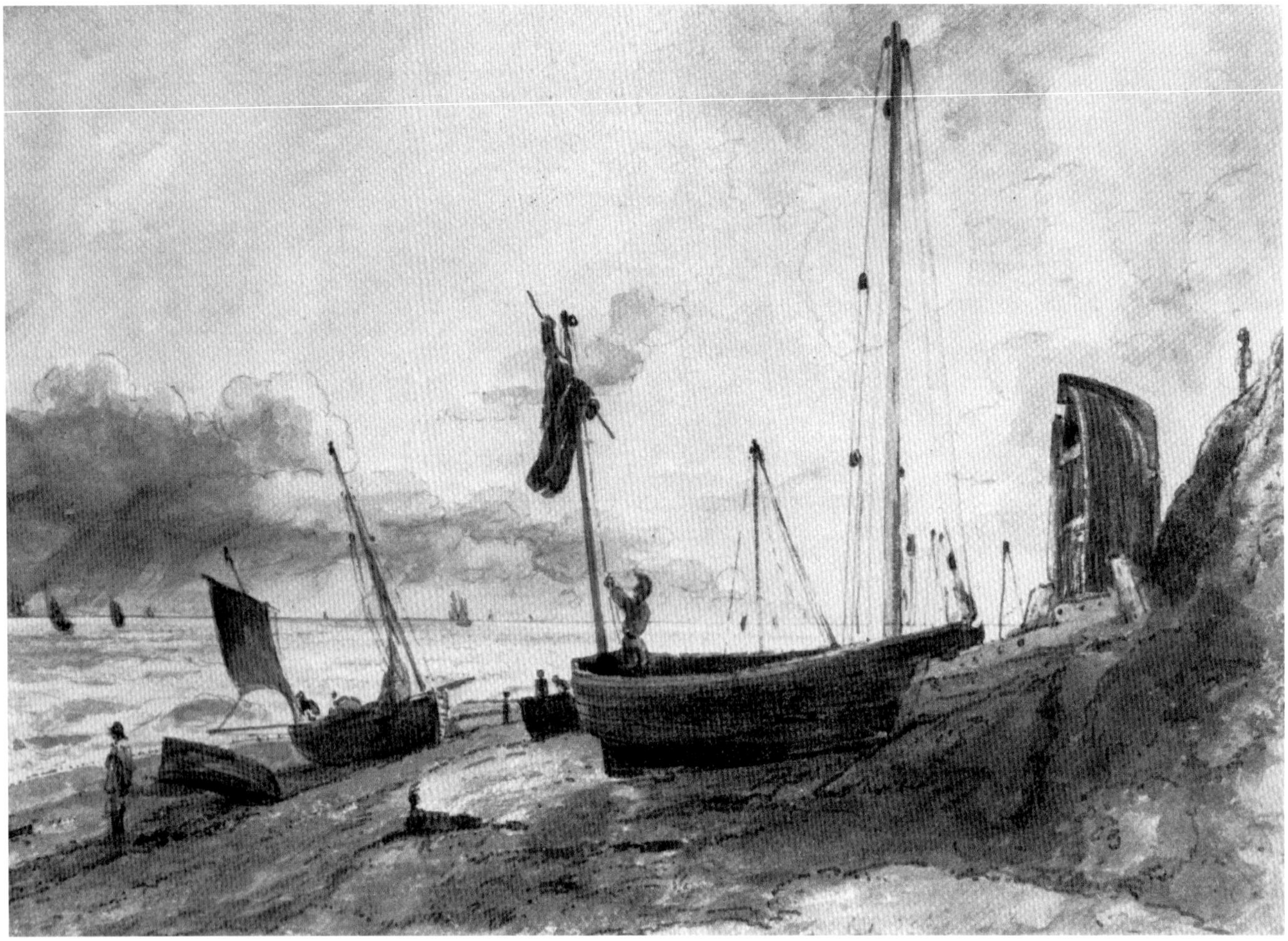

Fig. 44
Beach Scene, with a Fisherman Unfurling a Sail, and Beached Boats
1824
Pencil, pen and grey ink, with grey-brown wash on Whatman paper, c.17.6 × 25.5 cm
Not in Reynolds
Whereabouts unknown (sold at Christie's, 4 March 1975, lot 20)

(which he had first promised in early November) because he had been negotiating with the Anglo-French dealer Arrowsmith: 'We were settling about work and he has engaged me to make twelve drawings (to be engraved here [perhaps by S. W. Reynolds], and published in Paris), all from this book, size of the plates the same as the drawings, about 10 or 12 inches. I work at these in the Evening.'[39] Frustratingly, it is not possible to conclude definitively from this whether the discussions are entirely new or whether they may have first arisen in the summer, when Arrowsmith commissioned various paintings from Constable. The fact that the artist had mentioned those works previously, but not this project, might suggest it is most likely to be a recent idea. Nevertheless, there is a passing reference to the sketchbook in a letter to Fisher on 17 November. There he said he was 'busy' with it, describing its contents again: 'they are all boats – and coast[al] scenes – *subjects* of this kind seem to me more fit for *execution* than sentiment'.[40] The implication is that he saw the original designs as having only descriptive rather than imaginative potential, and it is possible to conclude from this that he was already devising the reproductive project.

Further details can be gleaned from the December letter, where he told Fisher more about the process of transforming his preliminary material: 'The book is larger than my others – and does not contain odds, and ends (I wish it did), but all complete compositions – all of boats, or beach scenes – and there may be about 30 of them.'[41] Constable declined a further request by Fisher for the sketchbook at the start of 1825, sending instead a dozen of his oil sketches (see Ch. 6); and this presumably indicates that he was then still at work on the project. There appear to be no further references to it during that year. But his hopes of creating a set of images that would appeal both to his compatriots and to his new

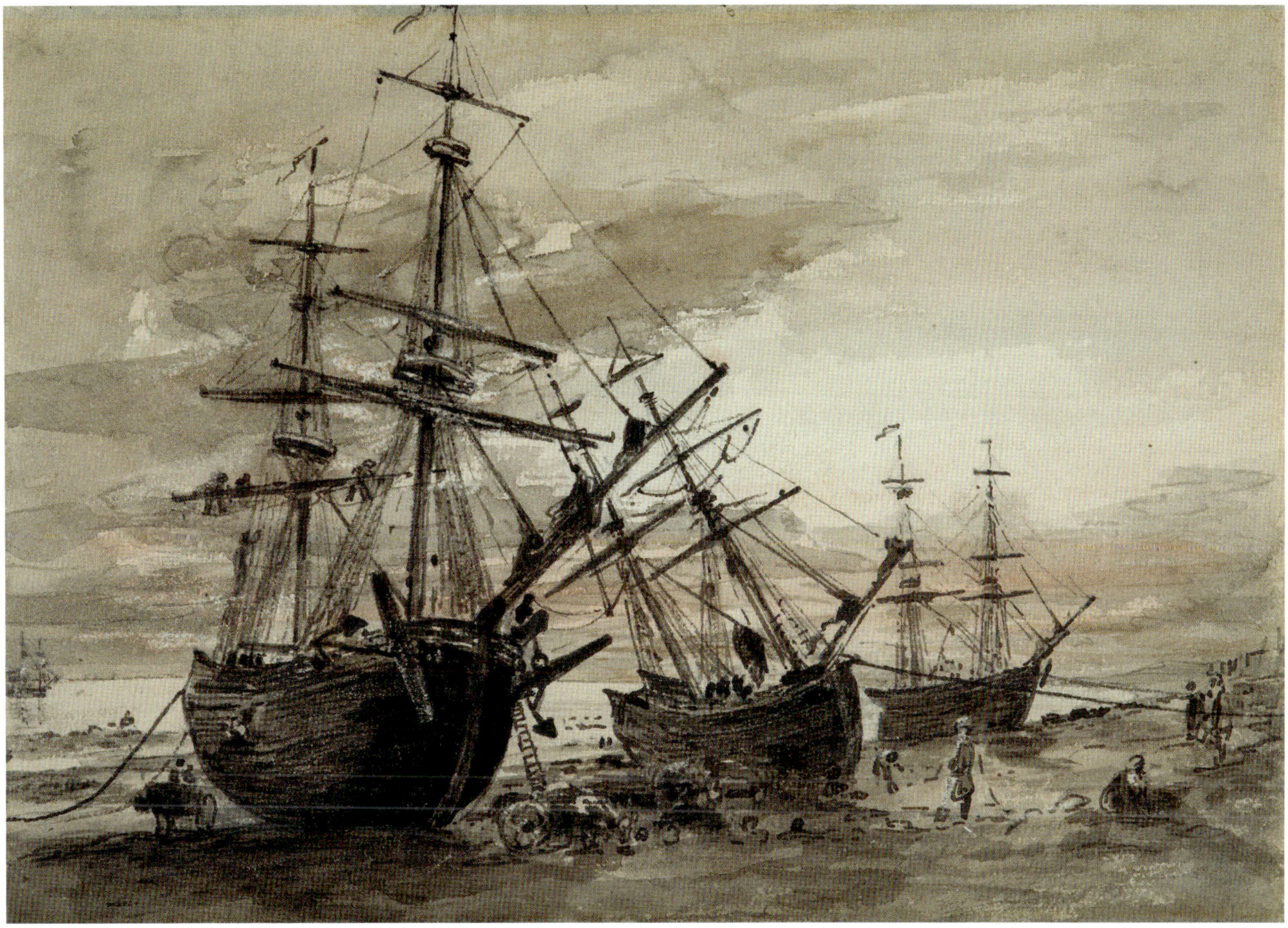

Fig. 45
Coal Brigs on Brighton Beach
1824
Pencil, pen and wash, 17.8 × 26 cm
R.24.47
The Higgins, Bedford

French admirers, evoking more the essence than the bare topography of the place, must have been a casualty of the rupture of his business dealings with Arrowsmith, in November 1825; at this time the dealer's financial position was already precarious, and the ensuing bank crisis toppled him and many others the following month.[42]

Of those drawings that can now be documented, there are at least 24 (and perhaps as many as 29) that seem originally to have been part of the large sketchbook, made up of 1821 Whatman paper measuring 18 × 26 cm. There are also two or three smaller sketches, measuring around 11 × 18 cm, that may have been half-sheets from the book, or possibly pages from a smaller sketchbook, of the kind he is known to have used at Brighton the following year (fig. 42).[43] The smaller dimensions are also the same for the two principal constituents of the panoramic study of the Chain Pier that later served as the basis for Constable's 1827 painting (see fig. 127).

It is much harder to determine conclusively any of the 12 designs that Constable was planning to resolve for publication. Three designs extend onto part of a second sheet, and there are clearly revisions in each to bring it to a greater degree of resolution.[44] There are also two drawings made solely in pen-and-ink outline, with none of the tonal wash or pencil shading that gives the best works in the series the rich chiaroscuro that Constable generally aimed for.[45] Both can be related to other images in the sequence, so may have been tracings of works that no longer exist, exercises in developing potential designs for reproduction from those compositions, or copies by family members or associates.[46]

In addition to the sketchbook pages, there are two much larger sheets and a few intermediate-size sketches that have been linked with Brighton and the south coast.[47] Most depict beached vessels and tapering cliffs, but only one of them depicts a recognisable topographical

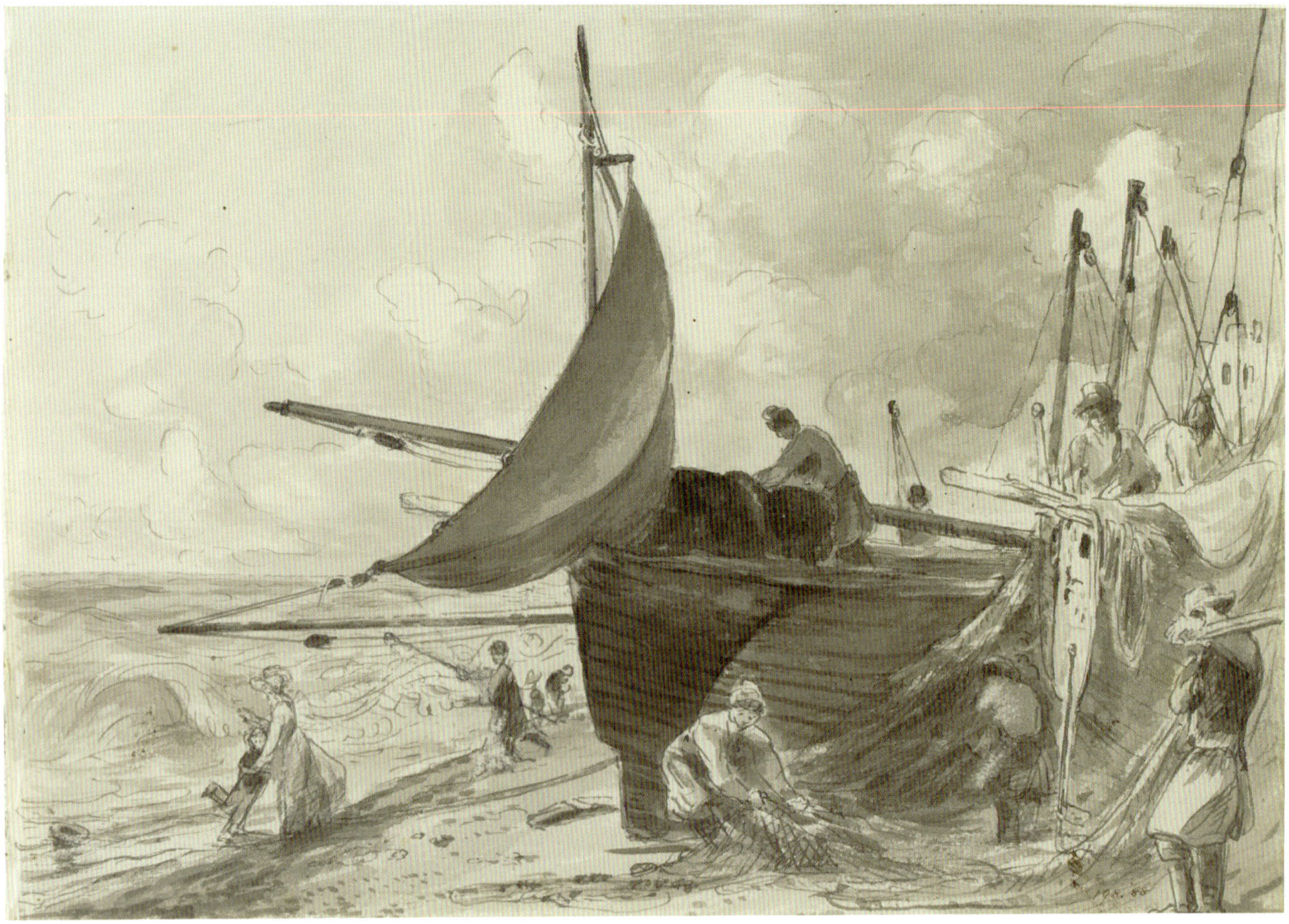

Fig. 46
A Fishing Boat on Brighton Beach, Windy Day
c.1824
Pencil with pen and wash, 18.1 × 26.4 cm
R.24.38
Victoria and Albert Museum, London

feature, the Pump House, bordering the Fish Market, which was also later featured in Constable's 1827 painting of Brighton (see fig. 48). More generally, however, it has to be said that the main group is tightly focused on the boats, the sea and the shore, and is otherwise lacking in the usual kind of local specifics that proved appealing among contemporary topographers. Constable seems much more alert to the nuts and bolts of the fishing trade (see fig. 124), and these sketches do much to challenge Turner's later teasing jibe, reflecting what he considered Constable's shortcomings: 'What does he know about ships?'[48]

Although the Chain Pier appears as a topographical marker in several drawings, Constable frequently avoided delineating, or blurred the specifics of the settings in which his boats are placed. From what he did include, it is possible to locate the majority of the sketches to the beach between the West Cliff and the Battery, then positioned to the east of Cannon Place (more or less in front of the Grand Hotel). The appeal of this location was presumably to some extent determined by its convenience, just a short distance from his lodgings. In a sketch dated 1 September, a plume of smoke rises from the six cannons stationed at the Battery, perhaps to signal the end of afternoon.[49] As well as improvised shelters made from fragments of old boats (fig. 44), many of the fishermen used the capstans located there (see also the Havell panorama, fig. 8).[50] At low tide the exposed sand below the Battery was where brigs, transporting coal from the north-east to fuel the demands of the ever-expanding resort, were beached and their cargo unloaded, a continuing practice that highlighted the limited utility of the 'dandy chain pier' for the town's economy (see fig. 45).[51] This part of the seafront was slightly less 'touristy' than the traditional Fish Market, which Constable seems to have largely avoided.[52] As well as the fishermen, there are occasionally other figures, probably visitors. However, some may well be members of Constable's family. There is, for example, a charming vignette of a mother shield-

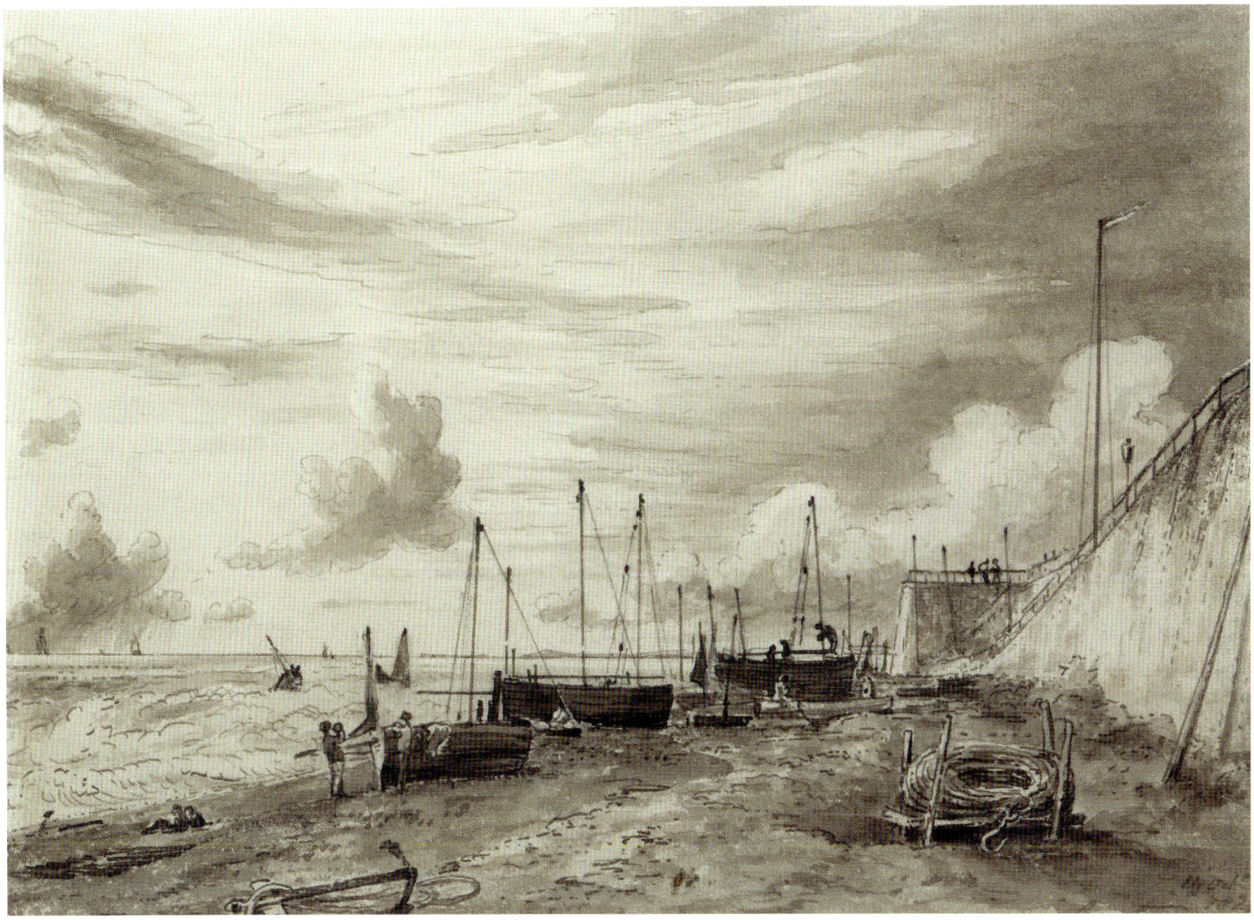

Fig. 47
Brighton Beach
14 October 1824
Pencil, pen and wash,
17.8 × 25.4 cm
R.24.32
Private collection

ing her young son, who has run from an incoming breaker and in doing so has lost his hat (fig. 46); this may well be Maria and the eldest of the children, John Charles (b. 1817).[53] Another drawing, showing an artist in a top hat sketching in front of fishing boats, may feasibly be a self-portrait.[54]

Another strikingly resolved composition depicts a group of beached boats and the signal station at Worthing, set against a panoramic sky, with a long bank of clouds rolling up the Channel.[55] Constable's otherwise exceptional presence in Worthing on 22 September (the date he added to the sheet) is explained by an auction there that day of a 'very choice and valuable collection of paintings' and prints belonging to the local surgeon Michael Morriah; however, it is not known if he acquired anything at the sale (notes about Old Master images, which were presumably included, can be found on the back of another sheet (fig. 46).[56]

Constable's helpful practice of often dating his sketches (unlike Turner) created a sequence of nine fixed points once he started his studies of the fishing boats, spanning Wednesday 1 September to Monday 18 October (see figs 43 and 47). By the end of this time the weather in Brighton had become 'damp and variable – much beyond what has been usual with us at such a season' (as noted in the local newspaper).[57] The arrival of autumnal weather is apparent in some sketches, characterised by more substantial clouds and rolling breakers (see figs 46 and 47).[58] Soon afterwards Constable was back in London, reviewing how to use his sketches. But instead of immediately tapping these new impressions for a work in oils, he plunged into another large Stour subject (see fig. 4), stubbornly rejecting Fisher's encouragement to vary his subject-matter. Consequently, because the Arrowsmith commission came to nothing, it was not until the spring of 1827 that he found a means of channelling his Brighton experiences into a bold public statement, his monumental canvas, *Chain Pier, Brighton* (fig. 48).

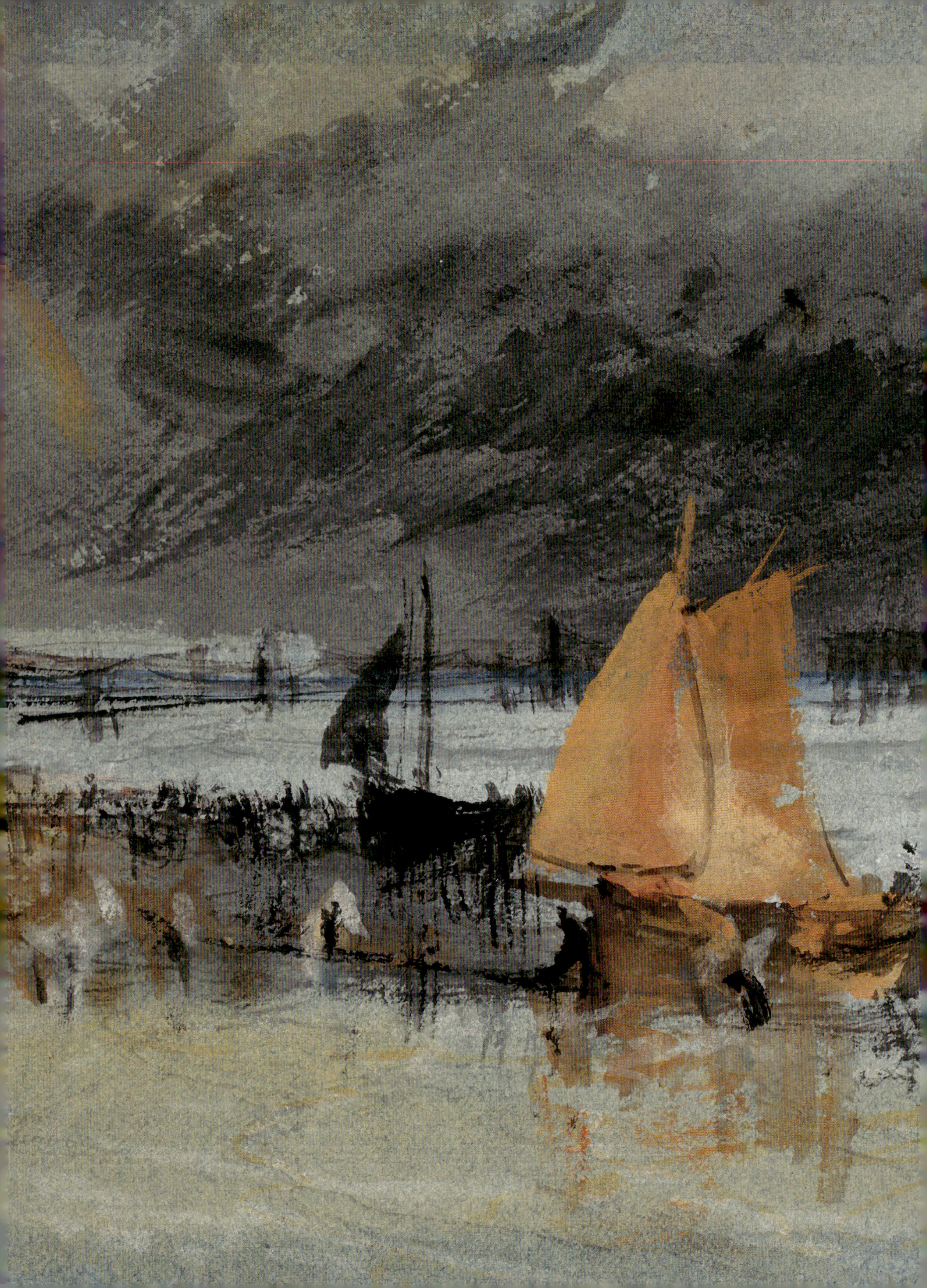

4 Taking on the Chain Pier – and Turner

'I will do his Lordship & myself justice'[1]

IAN WARRELL

THE ORIGINS of Constable's well-known picture of the *Chain Pier, Brighton* (fig. 48) stem from a detailed sketch (see fig. 127). This is now dated to 1824 because Constable's painstaking attention to the structure records the same outlying buoys noted by Turner (see fig. 39), which were destroyed before the end of the year.[2] A clue as to who Constable hoped might eventually acquire the painting can also be found in his garrulous letter of August that year. There he mentions Lord Egremont, one of the most significant figures, after the royal family, on the local scene, whose comings and goings from his residence, East Lodge (sometimes known as 'Neville Lodge') on Upper Rock Gardens, regularly appeared in the newspapers under headings such as 'The Mirror of Fashion'. From these useful but fragmentary details it is clear that, between the end of May and late October 1824, Egremont was only in Brighton for two relatively brief spells: first, around the start of July, when it was thought he was about to set out to Ireland for three months; and then for a second period of a few days around 15 August.[3] On 22 July, in between the two visits, the earl, then in his 73rd year, had a serious fall at Petworth (his main home, in West Sussex) involving 'severe contusions' and requiring a 'phlebotomy' (the drawing of blood).[4] The accident obviously put paid to the planned sojourn in Ireland, but the resulting short restorative Brighton visit in August fortuitously provided the chance for one of Constable's unnamed local friends (probably his pompous neighbour James Masquerier, who was then engaged for a portrait of the earl) to arrange for Egremont to see the more finished of the Hampstead scenes nearing completion for Schroth (see figs 19 and 21). Given its potential significance, Constable presents this course of events in a curiously summary way. Egremont was among the foremost supporters of current British painting and sculpture, so the artist must have been hopeful that this occasion could provide new opportunities for him. Indeed, back in May he had respectfully described Egremont as an 'excellent nobleman', because of the aristocrat's ongoing patronage of C. R. Leslie.[5]

As things turned out, it is apparent that Egremont's inspection of the Hampstead painting did not go well. Constable glosses over much in his account, failing to make clear where the viewing took place, or whether he was actually present himself. Instead he offered a neat construction of Egremont's opinion of his work: 'He recollected all my pictures of any note, but he recollected them only for their defects … The truth is that landscape affords him no interest whatever.'[6] Though pithy, the final allegation is perhaps self-justifying and not a fair reflection of the longer

Detail of fig. 51

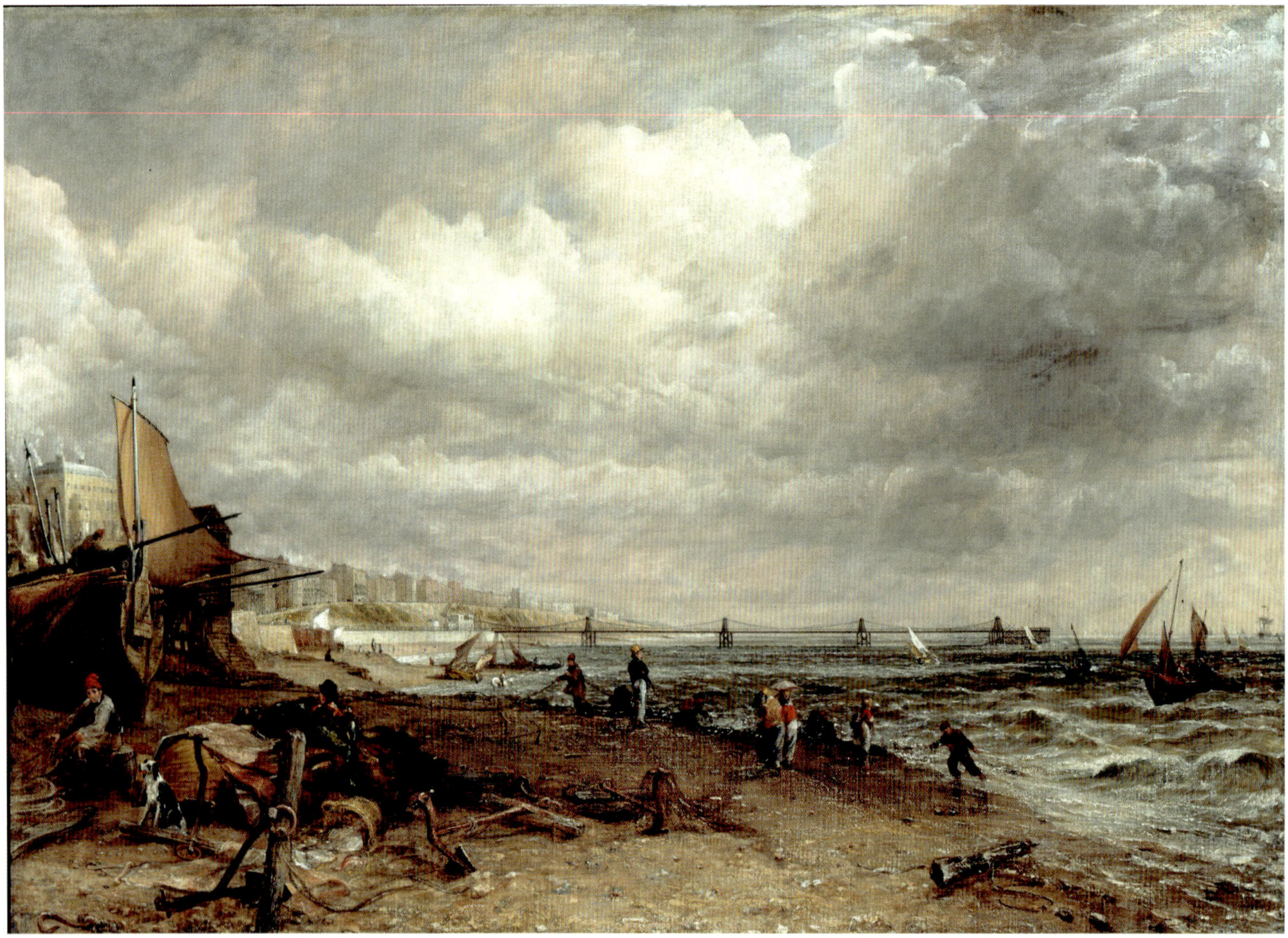

history of Egremont's acquisitions, which had included landscapes by Richard Wilson, Thomas Gainsborough and de Loutherbourg, and which would go on to encompass scenes by popular contemporaries such as A. W. Callcott, T. C. Hofland, Henry Howard and William Linton.[7] More significantly, of course, Egremont had bought 14 oil paintings by Turner in the period up to 1814 (the largest group anywhere). But artist and patron had thereafter fallen out over Turner's appropriation of an image by Claude in the Petworth collection when making a political point at a time of bitter divisions in the art world.[8] Landing on opposing sides, Turner found himself no longer welcome; and so Constable was in one sense correct about the earl's apparent disdain for contemporary landscape – or at least its chief representative – in 1824.

Crucially, the quotation from Constable's letter to Fisher – as given above – omits the very telling phrase 'But I will do his Lordship & myself justice'. This generally overlooked statement of intent clearly reveals an ambition to produce something of direct appeal to Egremont that would also address his criticisms. There was, of course, one obvious Brighton subject that would meet these criteria: the Chain Pier. Despite Egremont's many acts of charitable munificence, in 1824 his 'deservedly esteemed' status (to quote the *Morning Post*) was enhanced by the lead he had taken in supporting the construction of the pier.[9] After Captain Samuel Brown (the instigator of the scheme), Egremont was first on the list of investors, securing a batch of three shares (numbers 4 to 6) at £100 each towards the total cost of £30,000.[10] The prominent nature of this support meant that he was invariably associated with its success.

Constable's decision to make the meticulous sketch of the Chain Pier this year consequently marks his first step in identifying a subject that would reflect Egremont's public-spirited

Fig. 48
Chain Pier, Brighton
1826–27
Oil on canvas,
127 × 182.9 cm
R.27.1
Tate, London; Purchased 1950 (N05957)

OVERLEAF:
Detail of **Fig. 48**

generosity while perhaps winning future support for himself. In recognising this as the inherent purpose of the sketch, its significance is all the more notable in having been undertaken at exactly the moment when everything else Constable had to say about Brighton indicates how much it was not to his taste. However, while the urban subject-matter perhaps appears to constitute a decisive break from Constable's usual material, shortly before moving to Brighton he had embarked on a new version of his depiction of the opening of Waterloo Bridge.[11] The most intriguing thing about his plan for a Brighton picture, in the light of his stated resolve, is why he did not complete it until nearly three years later. One pressing reason may have been the greater receptiveness of his French patrons just then, which could naturally have induced him to stick to subjects with a ready market. But the resulting picture undoubtedly benefited from his greater familiarity with Brighton during the intervening years, which must have continued to impress on him the popularity of the pier.

As noted in the previous chapter, the majority of the earliest representations of the pier showed it from the west, much as it would be seen by a visitor approaching from the town centre, with its full span stretching across the horizon. These contemporary engravings tend to include either bathing machines or fishermen, depending on whether artists adopted a viewpoint adjacent to the Steine (see figs 80, 82 and 125) or the beach near the Fish Market (see fig. 33). Constable combined both types of staffage in his finished picture to provide a more comprehensive survey of those frequenting the shore (inherently evoking the list of objectionable Brighton types classified in his letter). Typically, he chose to follow the less fashionable option of the two standard formats, rooting his scene in the activities of the fishing community. These were already presented as one of the distinctive tourist sights of Brighton in the guidebooks available to Constable, which also listed the range of fish types caught at different seasons. They also noted the greatly diminished size of the fleet, as well as the ways in which its practices had been circumscribed, most infamously by the recently introduced restrictions to the open ground bordering the beach known as the Steine, where the fishermen had traditionally dried and mended their nets.[12] In Constable's painting the fishing boats are menaced by dark clouds, in contrast to the brilliant sunshine illuminating the distant promenade and the Chain Pier. He had similarly used clouds previously to underscore the concerns about moves away from tradition that led him to paint one of his views of Salisbury Cathedral.[13] So once again he seems here to be enlisting the weather to dramatise a key moment of transition from what Andrew Hemingway has described as 'an older and more natural social order contrasted with the rapidly growing …

Fig. 49
Unknown Artist
(Monogram 'A')
British School
Brighton Beach with Chain Pier
c. late 1820s
Oil on canvas, 46 × 75 cm
Felbrigg Hall (The National Trust)

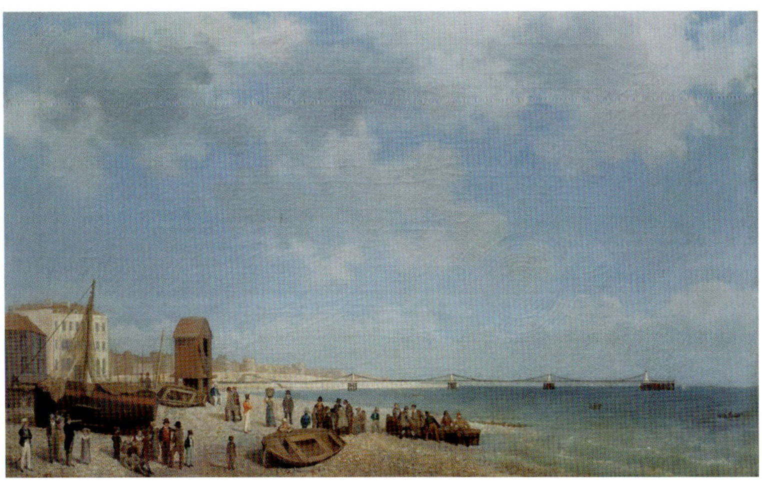

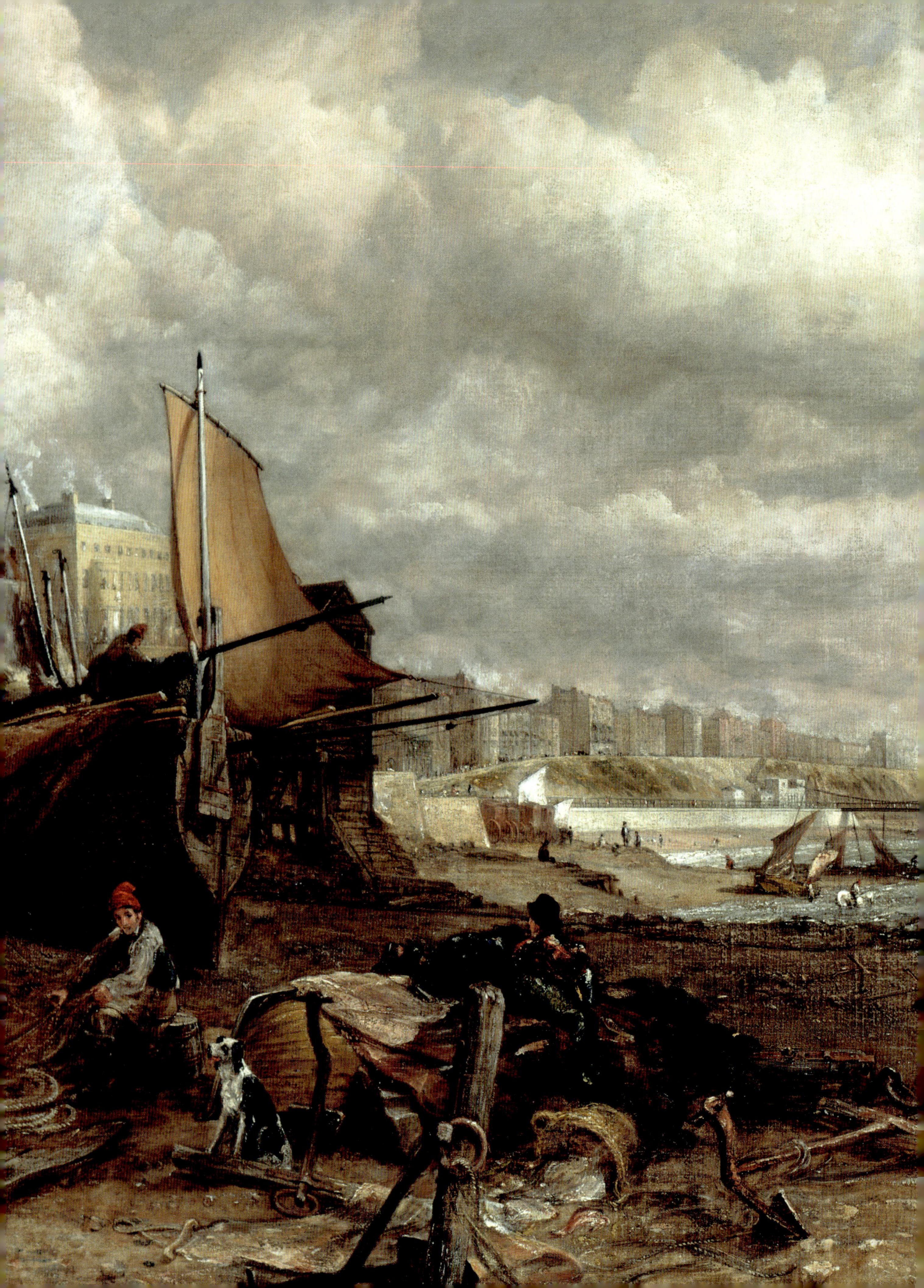

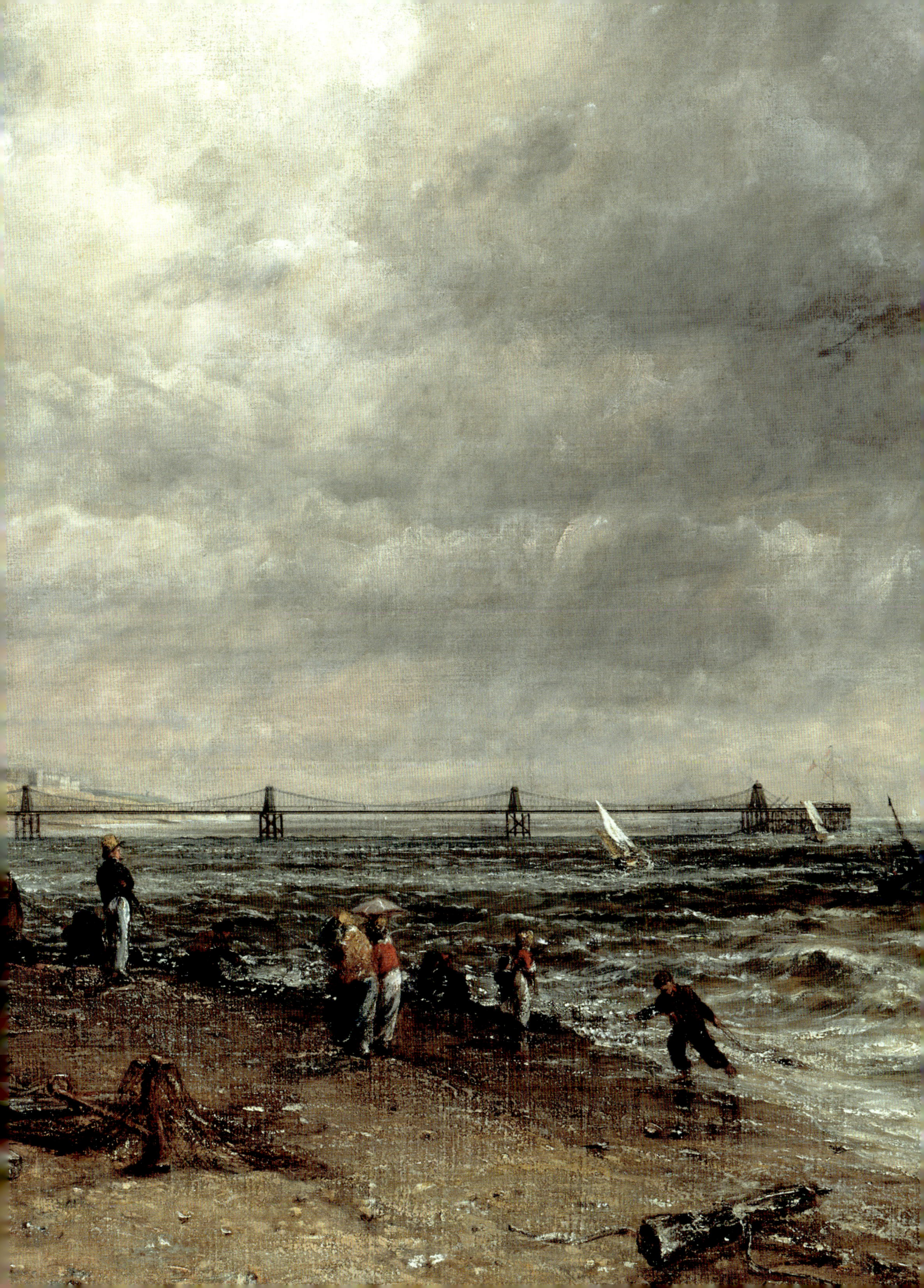

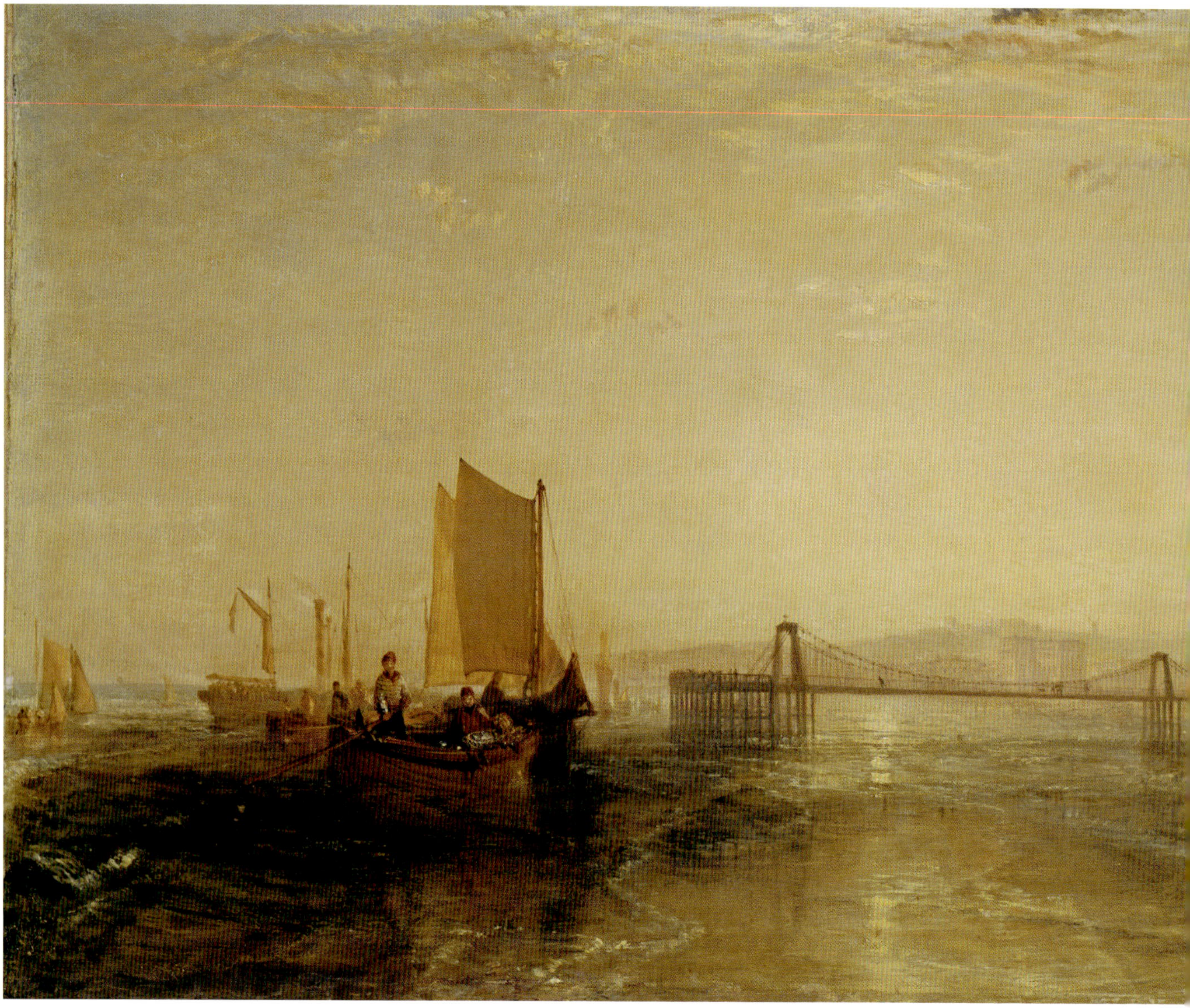

distasteful, new social order, which is signified by the physical evidences of modernization'.[14] An indication of how forcefully the image conveys its urgent sense of flux can be apprehended by comparing it with another painting from the period by an unknown artist (fig. 49). Adopting almost exactly the same standpoint, this painter offers a charming representation of the scene, with a similar emphasis on a vast expanse of sky. It even features a man thought to be a customs official (or perhaps a 'preventive service' man) in straw hat, blue jacket and white trousers who can also be seen in Constable's images (see figs 48, 87 and 88). But ultimately the picture lacks the sense in Constable's representation of a deeper meaning beyond the topographical facts.

Constable's painting was shown at the Royal Academy in 1827, and received a lukewarm critical response. *The Sun* felt it had 'a characteristic humidity about it that almost imparts a wish for an umbrella', but was disappointed that the town was not given more prominence.[15] However, a note in *The Times* described it as 'one of his best works', and expressed surprise that Constable's pictures did not sell.[16] Far from remedying this pattern, the comment anticipated the fate of *Chain Pier, Brighton*. Whether Constable continued to hope it would find a home at Petworth remains uncertain. Later in the year he mentioned to Fisher that 'a man of rank' had enquired about the price, but no sale had resulted, and once again he seems rather guarded about sharing

Fig. 50
J. M. W. Turner (1775–1851)
Brighton from the Sea
c.1828–30
Oil on canvas, 63.5 × 132 cm
Accepted by HM Government in lieu of tax and allocated to the Tate Gallery, 1984. In situ at Petworth House (T03886)

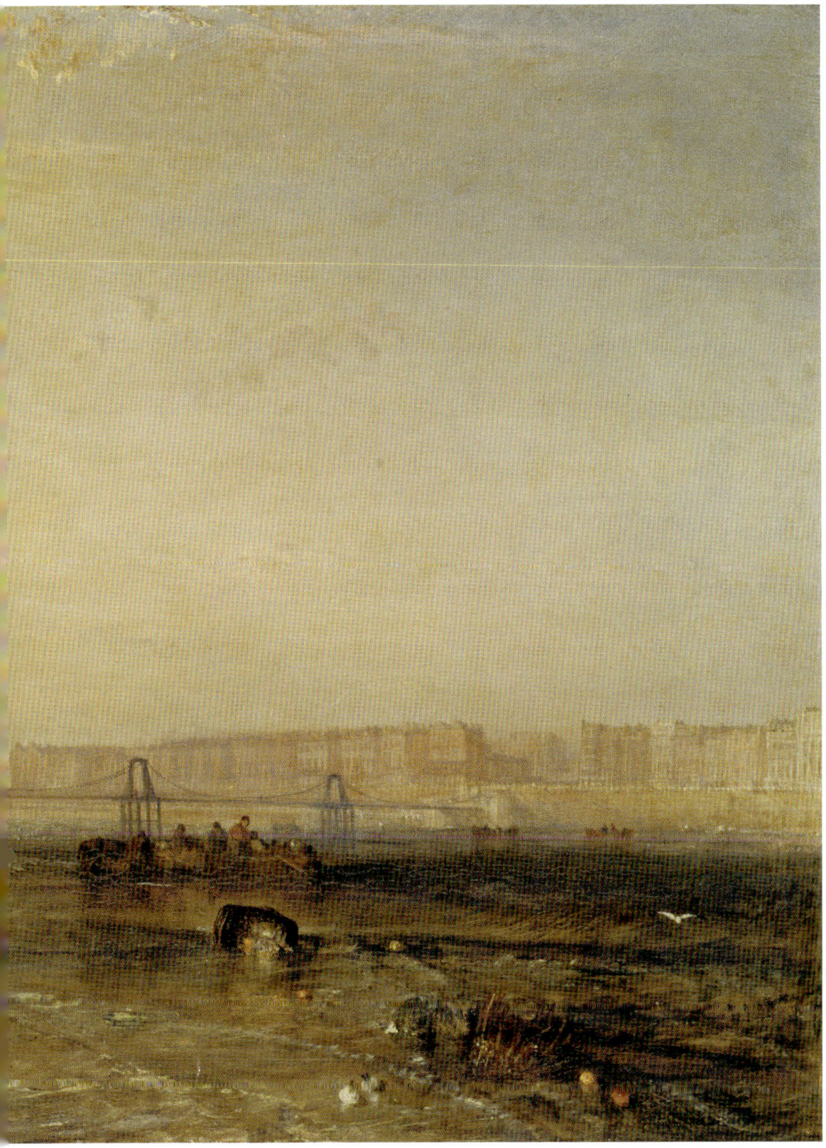

the full details, perhaps to protect his pride.[17] Lord Egremont certainly saw the exhibition, and acquired from it Callcott's *Heavy Weather Coming On, with Vessels Running to Port,* which hung in the Great Room very close to Constable's canvas.[18] Also on display in that great forum were three of Turner's paintings, two of which were marine or coastal subjects.[19]

Since his visit to Brighton in 1824 Turner had continued to thrive. His works were beginning to attract greater hostility for their extreme colours, but in 1826 Constable confessed that Turner's exhibits had never before given him 'so much pleasure – and so much pain'.[20] A year later Turner was on the point of a rapprochement with Egremont. He had passed through Petworth for some reason around 1825, but it was in early July 1827 that the two men were truly reconciled, at the sale of Sir John Leicester's celebrated collection of contemporary British art. In order to protect his market position Turner bought back at least two of his own works at a loss, and was grateful to Egremont for buying one of four other pictures by him in the sale. Evidently an invitation to stay once again at Petworth also ensued, for Turner was at the house by late October, and it was on that visit he painted the well-known series of brightly coloured, informal 'snapshots' on blue paper that evoke the life of the country house so vividly.

Exactly how long he stayed remains unknown, but during this productive visit he probably also began work on the series of landscape paintings that remain in the Carved Room (fig. 50).[21] In the first instance he tried something unusual by setting out the proposed images as fairly advanced, full-scale compositions, which allowed Egremont to see how they would work in situ and to choose a sequence of four designs from six alternatives. To the modern eye these preliminary ideas (all at Tate Britain) are seductive in their economy, resembling Turner's contemporaneous unfinished watercolour 'beginnings'. It is tantalising to ponder whether Turner could somehow have gleaned information about Constable's laborious method of creating oil sketches of exactly the same format as the major works they anticipate.[22] Although Turner's Petworth prototype images lack his colleague's rigour and subtle modifications, he perhaps developed this otherwise unparalleled way of working as a kind of experimental response.

One of the four images he went on to finish for the Carved Room was a view of the Chain Pier at

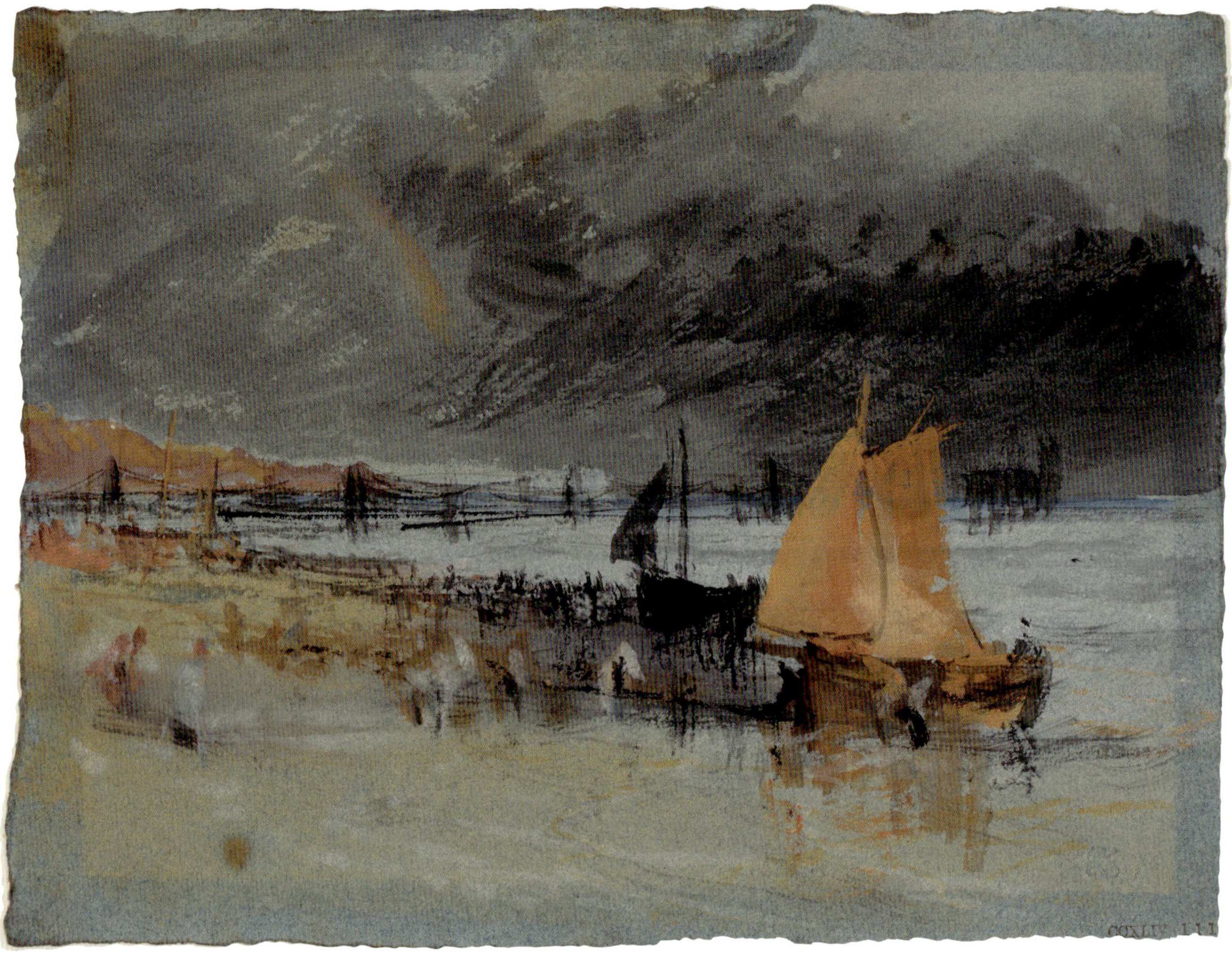

Brighton (see fig. 50); his motives for selecting the subject for inclusion there undoubtedly coincided with Constable's back in 1824, since all the images in the group celebrate Egremont's estate, or his interests. Turner's canvas was not completed until after he got back from Italy in 1829, but the related study (in the Tate collection) is known to have been on the walls at Petworth by early August 1828.[23] In preparing the composition he was obviously able to go back to the sketches for his *Southern Coast* watercolour (see fig. 37). However, a group of five colour studies of the pier, made on the same blue paper as the Petworth series, provides evidence that he also made a quick excursion to Brighton from Petworth at the end of 1827 (figs 51–53).[24] In a couple of them Turner seems to explore the foreshore as depicted in Constable's recent exhibit, demonstrating that (as Fisher had warned) he recognised its subject as a deliberate incursion onto his territory.[25]

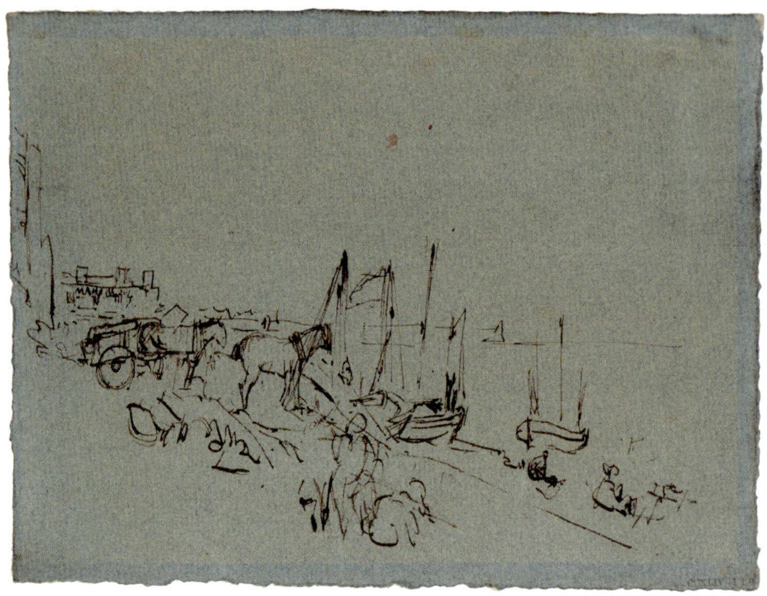

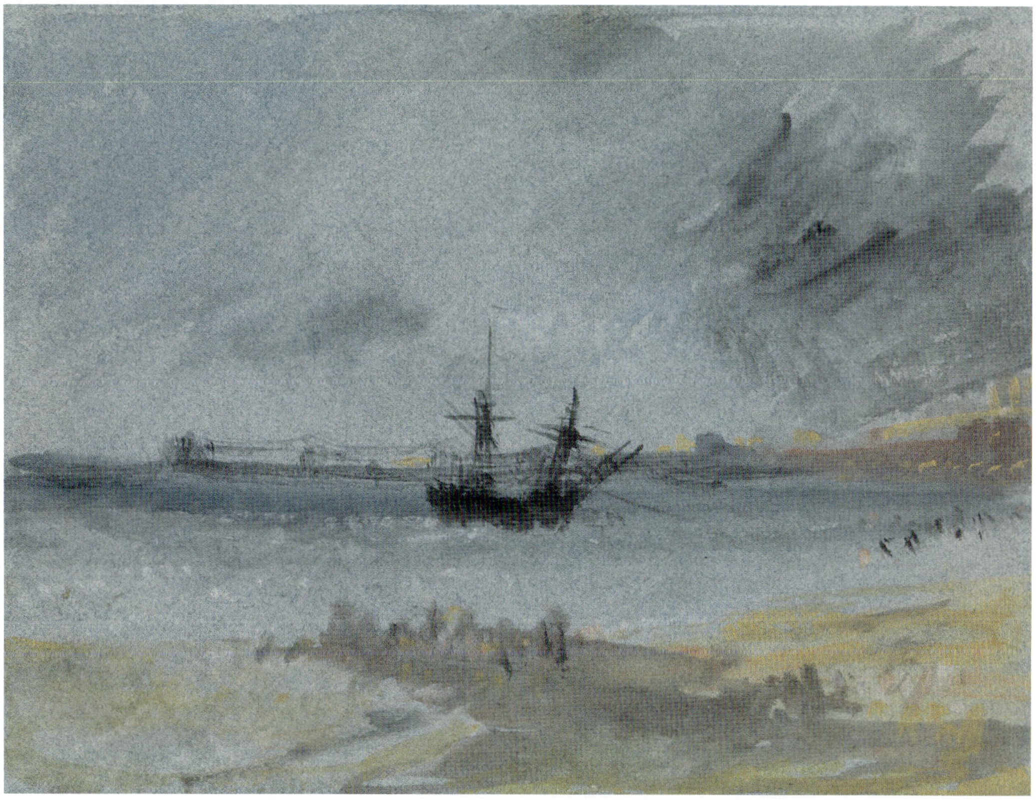

Fig. 53
J. M. W. Turner (1775–1851)
A Collier on the Beach at Brighton with the Chain Pier (sometimes known as *'Ship Aground, Brighton'*)
c.1827
Watercolour and bodycolour on blue paper,
14.2 × 19.5 cm
Yale Center for British Art, New Haven, CT

OPPOSITE ABOVE:
Fig. 51
J. M. W. Turner (1775–1851)
The Old Chain Pier from the West
c.1827
Bodycolour and watercolour on blue paper (faded),
14.2 × 19.3 cm
Tate, London

OPPOSITE BELOW:
Fig. 52
J. M. W. Turner (1775–1851)
On the Coast at Brighton, with Mahomed's Baths in the Distance
c.1827
Pen and ink on blue paper (faded),
13.9 × 19.3 cm
Tate, London

An unfinished canvas, begun in the late 1820s, is a more direct attempt to assimilate Constable's composition in his own manner (fig. 54); Turner's image coincidentally preserves the full sweep of his rival's canvas before the left side was trimmed, as does the engraving issued in 1829 (fig. 55).

Closer in spirit to the viewpoint that Turner went on to develop are the other three colour sketches, which show the pier from the east, not far from Egremont's Brighton home (see fig. 53). Turner's sooty brushwork proves the perfect emanation of the collier beached further along the shore. Appealing though these vessels were to Constable and himself, Turner chose not to include one in his painting for Egremont. Rather, since the Chain Pier was specifically constructed to overcome the absence of a natural harbour, he diplomatically highlighted its principal function by featuring the arrival of one of the steam-packets – possibly the *Rapid* or the *Union* – that guaranteed a link between Brighton and Dieppe.[26] Its inclusion makes it all the more noticeable that Constable deliberately eschewed these symbols of modernity in all his Brighton works, despite the fact that the cross-Channel service had been inaugurated and was a regular feature throughout his extended visit in 1824. Meanwhile the painters of topographical prints were less squeamish about the dirty chimneys of these boats, and readily assimilated them into their images (fig. 56).

Nevertheless, the contrast between Constable and Turner on this point is not as simple as it at first appears. For there is a certain ambiguity in the way Turner presents the steamboat, its form partly obscured by the group of fishing boats, whose occupants stare directly at the viewer.[27] As in his later images of *The Fighting Temeraire* (1839) or *Rain, Steam and Speed* (1844),

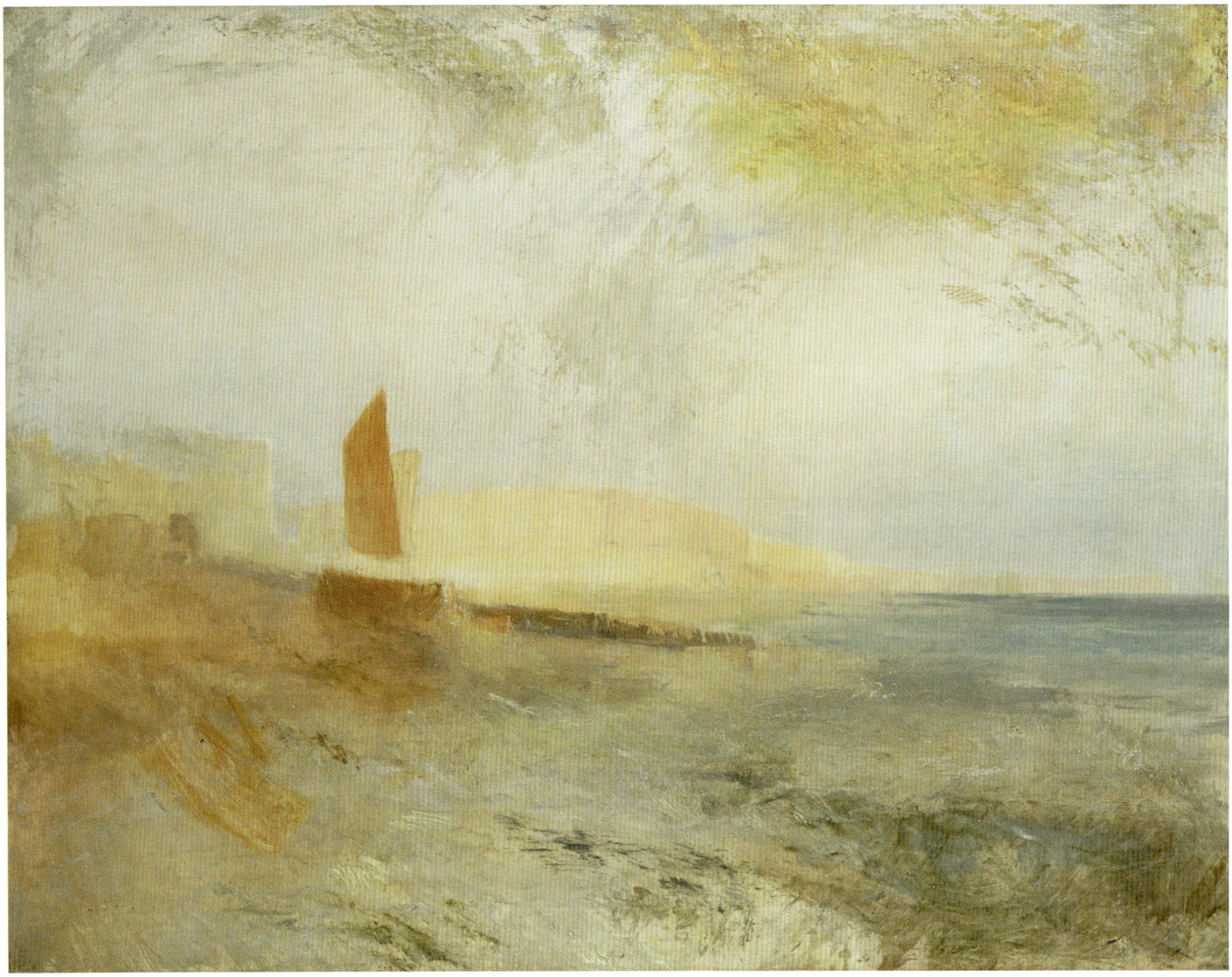

Fig. 54
J. M.W. TURNER (1775–1851)
Brighton Beach, with the Chain Pier in the Distance, from the West
late 1820s, reworked after 1843
Oil on canvas,
91.3 × 121.9 cm
Tate, London

Turner clearly fully accepted, welcomed even, the inevitability of technological progress. But such advances are invariably represented in a way that tugs the emotions for what is passing away, or in danger of being superseded. In this picture Turner demonstrates he had recognised the reservations lurking within Constable's earlier view of the town. Surprisingly, given the context for which the painting was created, he is much more explicit about the consequences of Brighton's rapid expansion. As well as depicting the wide expanse of new squares and promenades, he suggests the palpable impact that the ever-increasing population was having on its environment. This is present in the form of a discarded basket of vegetables spilling out across the foreground waters. While, on a formal level, this provides variety of colour, more essentially it recognises the casual pollution that accompanies urban expansion. It is an extraordinary and unavoidable detail, which would have been at eye-level for diners in the Carved Room. So it was inevitable that it provoked comment. However, rather than disagreeing head-on about the desirability of their presence, the tactful Egremont chose to challenge the likelihood that the vegetables would float, (something that was then tested, using real vegetables in a bath tub).[28]

By the time Turner was resolving the canvas in 1829, Constable had begun a series of bold and highly expressive mezzotints, in collaboration with David Lucas.[29] These were issued collectively as *Various Subjects of Landscape, Characteristic of English Scenery, from Pictures Painted by John Constable, R.A.*, but the title is generally abbreviated to *English Landscape*. In addition to paintings that had been exhibited, the published plates reproduced much more informal works.

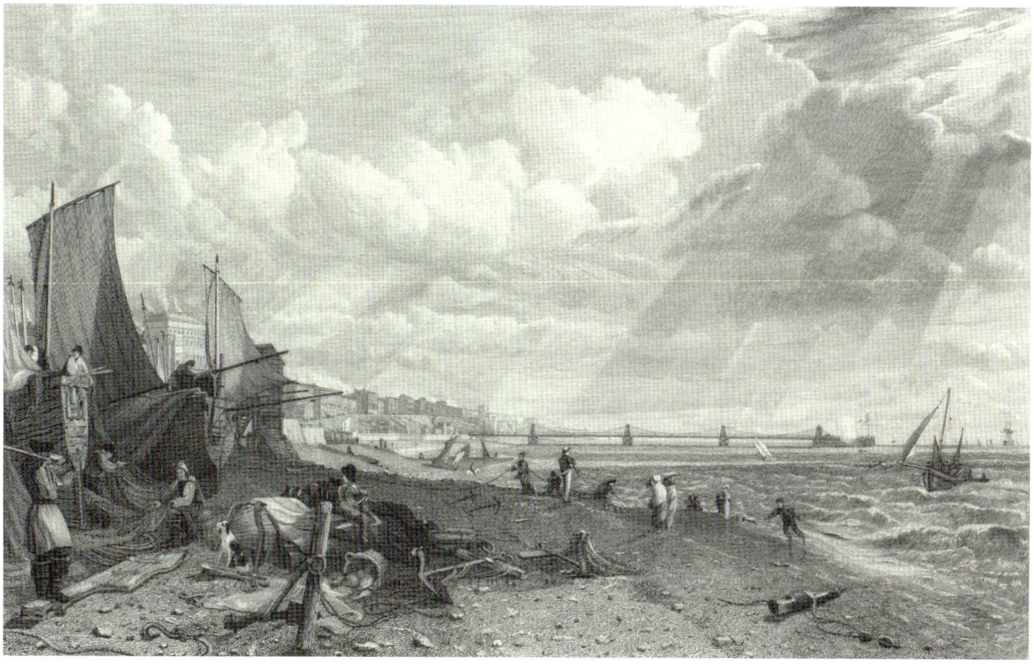

Fig. 55
Frederick Smith (1805–1879), after Constable
View of Brighton with the Chain Pier
12 August 1829
Line engraving, 27.8 × 37.8 cm
Royal Pavilion & Museums, Brighton

A handful of the sketches painted in Brighton were among the subjects selected for the project, but in the end only the *Sea Beach* (see fig. 62) was resolved in mezzotint before the series came to a halt after only 22 images had been distributed. The subject is curious as the sole representation of Brighton, but it neatly summarises Constable's pictorial concerns during his stay in 1824, effectively condensing his numerous studies of boats with his fascination for the churning foam of the sea. His focus on the fishing boats surely grew out of his frustrations over the failure of the Arrowsmith commission (see p. 53), but may also have been coloured by the publication of E. W. Cooke's etchings of Brighton boats in his series of *Shipping and Craft*, afterwards reissued as *Twelve Plates of Coast Sketches, Brighton* (1830; fig. 58), which share something of Constable's aesthetic and spirit of enquiry (see fig. 87). There may also be a more personal element in the image, which has its origins in the tender monochrome sketch showing the mother and child (see fig. 46). If the

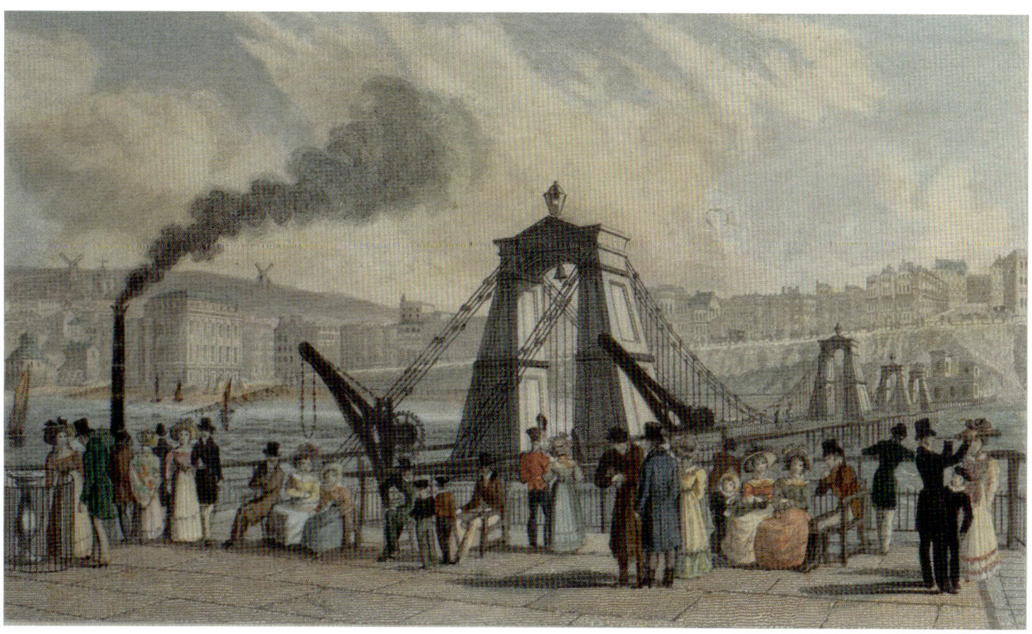

Fig. 56
William John Cooke (1796–1865), after Nathaniel Whittock (1791–1860)
Brighton, from the Chain Pier, 1829
(from *Allen's History of the Counties of Surrey and Sussex*, 1829)
Line engraving, 9 × 15.5 cm
Royal Pavilion & Museums, Brighton

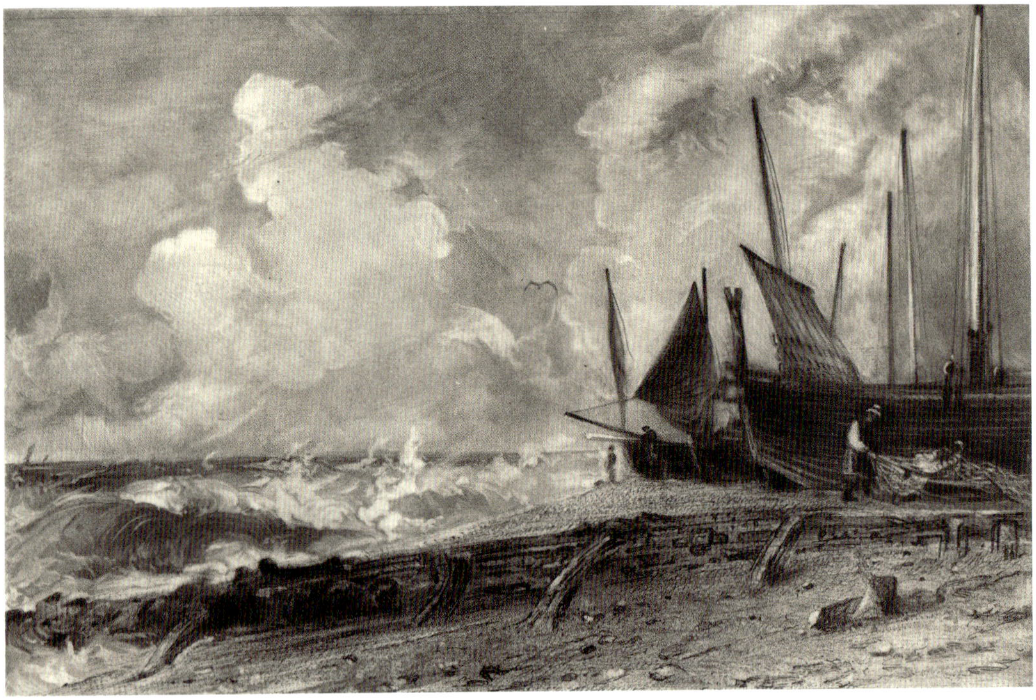

Fig. 57
David Lucas (1802–1881), after Constable
A Sea Beach, Brighton, Heavy Surf – Windy Noon (Plate 10 of *English Landscape*)
1830
Mezzotint and drypoint on cream laid paper, 30.5 × 44.5 cm
Yale Center for British Art, New Haven, CT

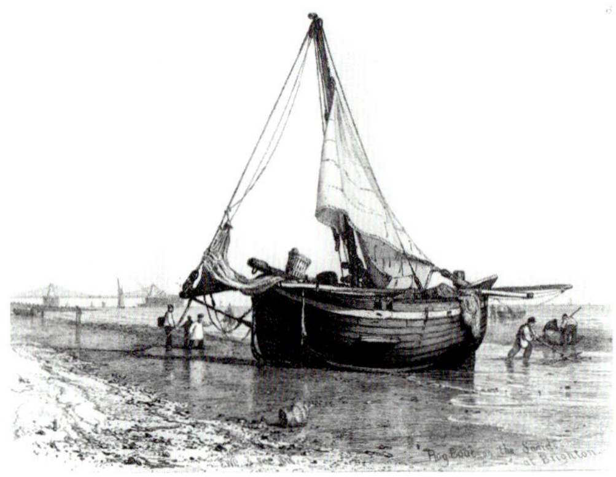

Fig. 58
Edward William Cooke (1811–1880)
Hog Boat on the Sands at Brighton
1830
Etching, 20 × 27 cm
Private collection

identification of the woman is credible as Maria, who had by then died, her absence in the wide expanse of beach, coupled with the timeless crash of the breakers, lends the scene a particular poignancy.

The image was accompanied by a letterpress text that may have been compiled either by Constable himself or by Henry Phillips, using a quotation from the Suffolk poet George Crabbe. It also shares, or possibly borrows, details of the commentary used for Turner's earlier *Southern Coast* image, helping to shed a more positive light on Brighton than Constable's own correspondence. By the time the image was in circulation, at the end of 1830, he had already abandoned work on the upright windmill subject (figs 59 and 60), and although he pressed on with his other Brighton view, of the cornfields on Church Hill, which in 1824 had been right on the outskirts of town (see fig. 61), it was not engraved until after his death, probably around 1843.

This was also the year in which C. R. Leslie published the first edition of his *Memoirs of the Life of John Constable*, based chiefly on the artist's correspondence, including the diatribe about Brighton that opens this book. Turner is not known to have owned a copy, but he would have been surprised and flattered to find his intellectual abilities described so appreciatively in 1813 (though Leslie had prudently cut Constable's comment that the 'wonderful range of mind' was all the more remarkable because it resided in someone essentially 'uncouth'). In the years after Brighton had first brought them into direct competition they had repeatedly sparred at the Academy, culminating in 1832 in the incident where Turner seemed deliberately to undermine the long-delayed exhibition of Constable's depiction of the *Opening of Waterloo Bridge* by his addition of a flash of red in one of his own sea pieces. Constable was surely right to see this as an act of provocation, but it may have been more an act of collegiate playfulness than has often been assumed. The two men certainly

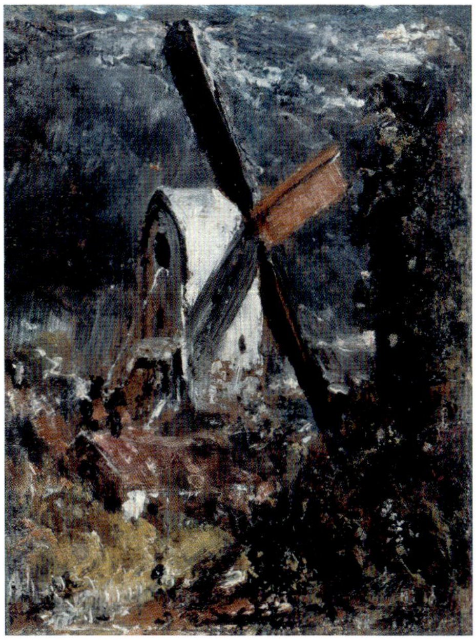

Fig. 59
A Windmill near Brighton
1829
Oil on paper, later lined on canvas, 14.6 × 11.4 cm
R.29.60
Victoria and Albert Museum, London

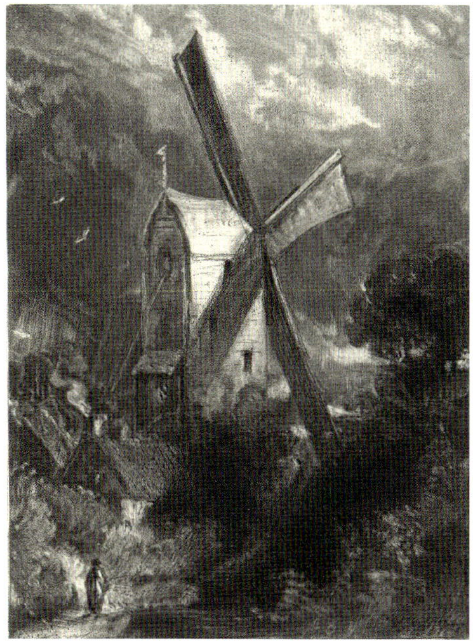

Fig. 60
David Lucas (1802–1881), after Constable
A Mill near Brighton
1829
Mezzotint and drypoint on cream wove paper
43.2 × 28.9 cm
Yale Center for British Art, New Haven, CT

monitored each other's work sufficiently closely to know the other's strengths and failings, and to play on them. Research into Turner's pigments has highlighted that the one-upmanship that peppered their relationship in the early 1830s continued for Turner even after Constable's death. Dr Joyce Townsend has demonstrated that the unfinished canvas dating from the late 1820s, which Turner put aside after merely sketching out a version of Constable's great view of Brighton of 1827, was reworked across the sky with a yellow that was not available until at least 1843 (see fig. 54).[30] Perhaps Turner was prompted to go back to it following the publication of Leslie's *Memoirs*. But far from resolving the picture, the new layers of paint add a discordant note, seemingly causing Turner to abandon it once more, as if he recognised that, when it came to Brighton, he had to concede to Constable a draw, if not quite a win.

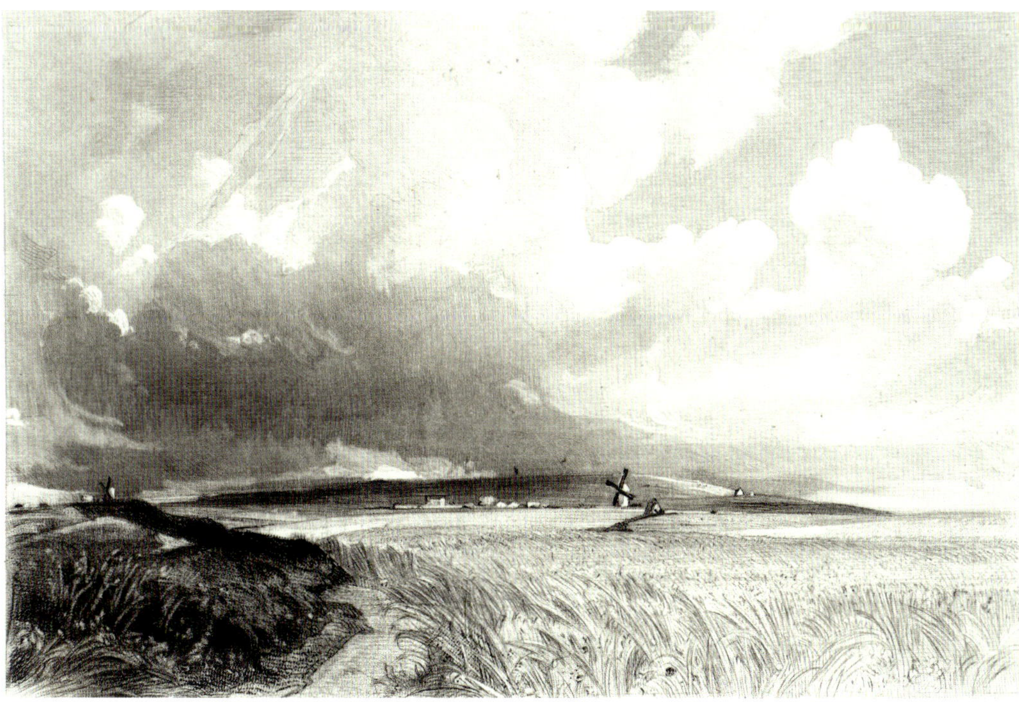

Fig. 61
David Lucas (1802–1881), after Constable
Cornfields near Brighton, after John Constable
1855
Mezzotint on paper, 13 × 19.8 cm
Tate, London

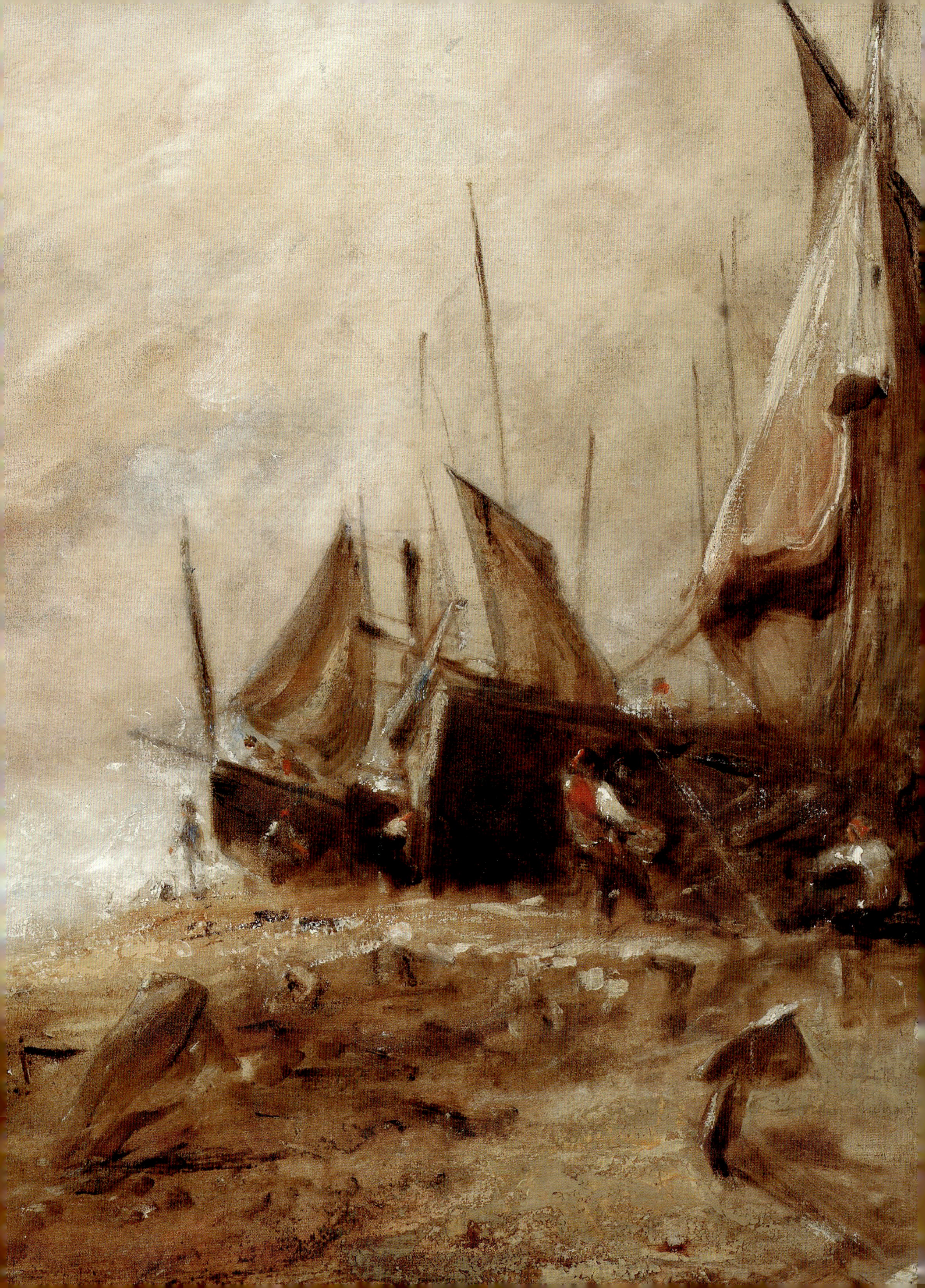

5

Later Brighton Visits and Posthumous Acclaim in France

'making the family name a mark of distinction'

ANNE LYLES

THE YEAR 1825 started well for Constable with news of his gold medal from the French king Charles X, following the successful reception of his work at the 1824 Paris Salon (see Ch. 2). He wrote to his friend Fisher in late January to tell him about the award, content that he had 'added to the respectability of my family by making the family name a mark of distinction'. He added, however, that the award of a gold medal was as nothing compared with the value of their friendship, Fisher having loyally supported him during the years of his 'obscurity'. Furthermore, it would make little difference to his painting habits. He knew 'the difficulty of gaining reputation in the first instance', he told Fisher, and was 'dayly [*sic*] made sensible of the still greater difficulty of maintaining it'.[1]

Aware that he could not afford to rest on his laurels, Constable knew he would need to continue painting large pictures for the Academy for the sake of his professional reputation. Furthermore, as the six-footers were speculative ventures – and it was unpredictable as to when or whether they might sell – he needed to complement them with his smaller commissions to ensure a regular income. Nor was there to be any respite from what was now becoming an established pattern of moving the family between houses in London, Hampstead or Brighton.

Not long after his return from Brighton towards the end of 1824, Constable had told Fisher that he was working in his studio on his next large picture, adding that he was not inclined to vary his favoured subject-matter of River Stour scenery simply to feed the expectations of a public who craved variety.[2] From a large preliminary compositional sketch, he produced his next six-footer, *The Leaping Horse*, (see fig. 4) which went to the Academy in the spring. Although the picture did not sell, at this stage Constable might reasonably have hoped that it might do so at some other point during his lifetime – although, as it happens, it did not. (And indeed it was perhaps just as well that he could not have known then either that, with only one exception in the 1830s, every large picture he would paint for the Academy in future would fail to find a buyer.[3])

In 1825, meanwhile, a larger number of Constable's large pictures (four of them) happened to be on display in London, at the same time, than at any other, subsequent stage during his lifetime. For as well as *The Leaping Horse* at the Academy, three more of his large canvases – *The White Horse*, *Stratford Mill* and *The Lock* (see figs 12, 15 and 9) – were lent by their owners to an exhibition of the work of *Living British Artists* that the British Institution mounted that summer instead of its more usual display of Old Masters.

Detail of fig. 62

With the exception of a negative review by *The London Magazine* in connection with the pictures by Constable included in the 1825 British Institution exhibition, nearly all the reviews were favourable towards Constable's work around this time.[4] Indeed 1825 was something of a high point in terms of positive criticism of his work. The true turning point, it could be argued, came with his exhibition at the British Institution in 1828 of *Chain Pier, Brighton* (see fig. 48), the handling of which one reviewer found so rough that he likened it to someone leaving the scaffolding up on a house after the building work was finished.[5]

Aided no doubt by the extra boost to his reputation following the success of the 1824 Salon – and indeed English artists who visited Paris in 1825 continued to report back to him how widely he was still talked about there[6] – luckily Constable still had plenty of orders from French dealers that year. When, in late January, Schroth called to collect his two Hampstead views from Constable (see figs 19 and 21), he put in a request for three more small pictures.[7] On 8 April these were outstanding, as were two small works for Arrowsmith.[8] That same April, Constable mentioned he also had a further three paintings on order from another French admirer of his work, the great Paris publisher Firmin Didot, whom he had first met at his London studio the previous March, courtesy of an introduction from Arrowsmith.[9]

In mid-May, meanwhile, Schroth wrote to Constable to tell him that he would be returning to London in August and that he hoped that his pictures might be ready for him to collect by then. In the same letter he tactfully asked Constable to attempt to paint the foregrounds of the commissioned paintings in as highly finished a manner ('très rendues') as possible, to suit the taste of his Parisian clients.[10] Schroth entrusted the letter to Delacroix to deliver to Constable by hand in late May, having added a few words of recommendation about the young French artist in the hope, no doubt, that Constable would receive him at Charlotte Street and show him the paintings in his studio on which he was then engaged. Although we know that Delacroix did indeed deliver the letter, we do not know whether Constable was at Charlotte Street when he called, and thus whether the two great artists ever met – the current art-historical consensus is that they probably did not.[11] It seems that Delacroix later came to own a sketchbook that Constable may at one stage have used in Brighton, but the status of this little book is fraught with issues relating to attribution, especially given that more than one hand appears to have been at work on the drawings it contains.[12]

Nor is it possible today to identify the subjects of the paintings in Schroth's second order, nor those requested by Didot, although at various stages during the year Constable refers to painting pictures for the two men.[13] A little more is known, however, about the paintings he may have been working on for Arrowsmith in 1825. In late December of the previous year – around the time Arrowsmith was also discussing with Constable a project to engrave some of the artist's drawings of Brighton fishing boats (see Ch. 3, p. 52) – he asked the painter to 'think of my companion to Hampstead Heath – & the Brighton sea piece'.[14] The former subject may perhaps have been intended as a pair to the small Hampstead picture ('Cum Paul's') that Constable had painted for him the previous year (see Ch. 1, p. 33). However, the 'Brighton Sea piece', which Arrowsmith reminded Constable about again in March,[15] is more difficult to pin

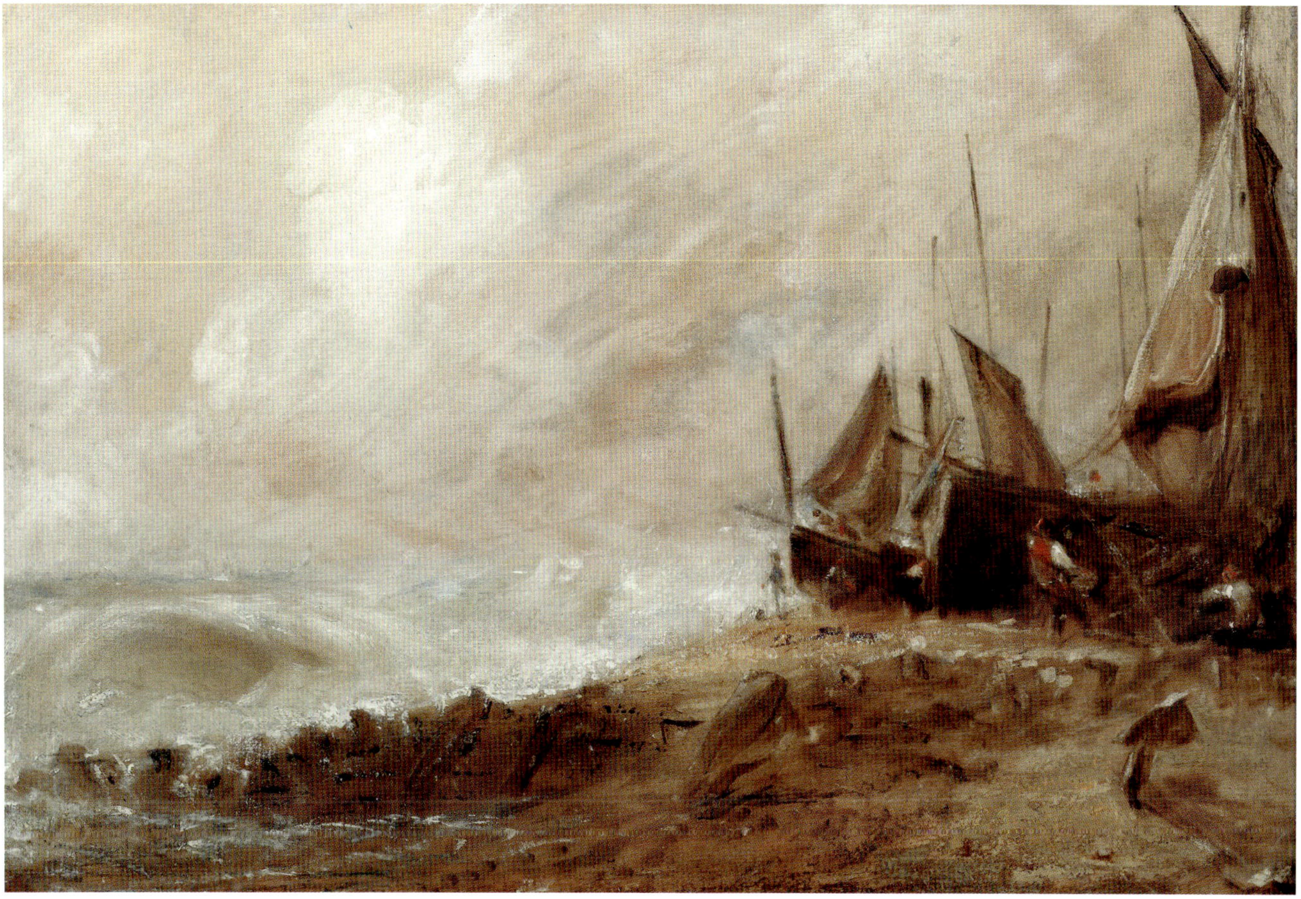

Fig. 62
A Sea Beach, Brighton
c.1825–27
Oil on canvas,
65.6 × 100.5 cm
Private collection,
Detroit, MI

down; we cannot even be sure, of course, that it was ever painted.

One possibility, however, is that the large composition sketch by Constable of *A Sea Beach, Brighton*, formerly at the Boston Museum (fig. 62), may be connected with Arrowsmith's commission.[16] When this painting was cleaned recently, in connection with an episode of the BBC television programme *Fake or Fortune*, it was revealed by Sarah Cove that it has the same type of pink stippled priming that we know Constable was using, perhaps exclusively, in the 1820s.[17] Although larger than most of the paintings Arrowsmith ordered from Constable following his original purchase in 1824 of the two six-foot landscapes for the Salon, there is still the possibility that the Frenchman had commissioned something larger in this instance – after all, beach scenes of this sort were very popular at this date on both sides of the Channel (hence, no doubt, Arrowsmith's involvement in the proposed engraving project with Constable on a similar theme). Like that project, the *Sea Beach* may then have become a casualty of the rift (see p. 53) between Constable and Arrowsmith later in the year.

If not connected with the Arrowsmith commission, the other possibility is that *A Sea Beach, Brighton* was started by Constable as an idea for a large Brighton exhibition picture that was later abandoned, but which may originally have been planned as an alternative to *The Chain Pier* (fig. 48) – even, perhaps, as a complementary view, given that the two pictures show views in opposite directions. In the end, the subject of *A Sea Beach* was engraved instead, for Constable's publishing project *English Landscape* in the 1830s (see Ch. 4, p. 68), although the specific prototype for the mezzotint was a small, related oil sketch in Detroit.[18]

Just when, in the summer of 1825, things seemed to be going so well for Constable professionally, illness struck again in the family, this time affecting the artist's eldest son, John

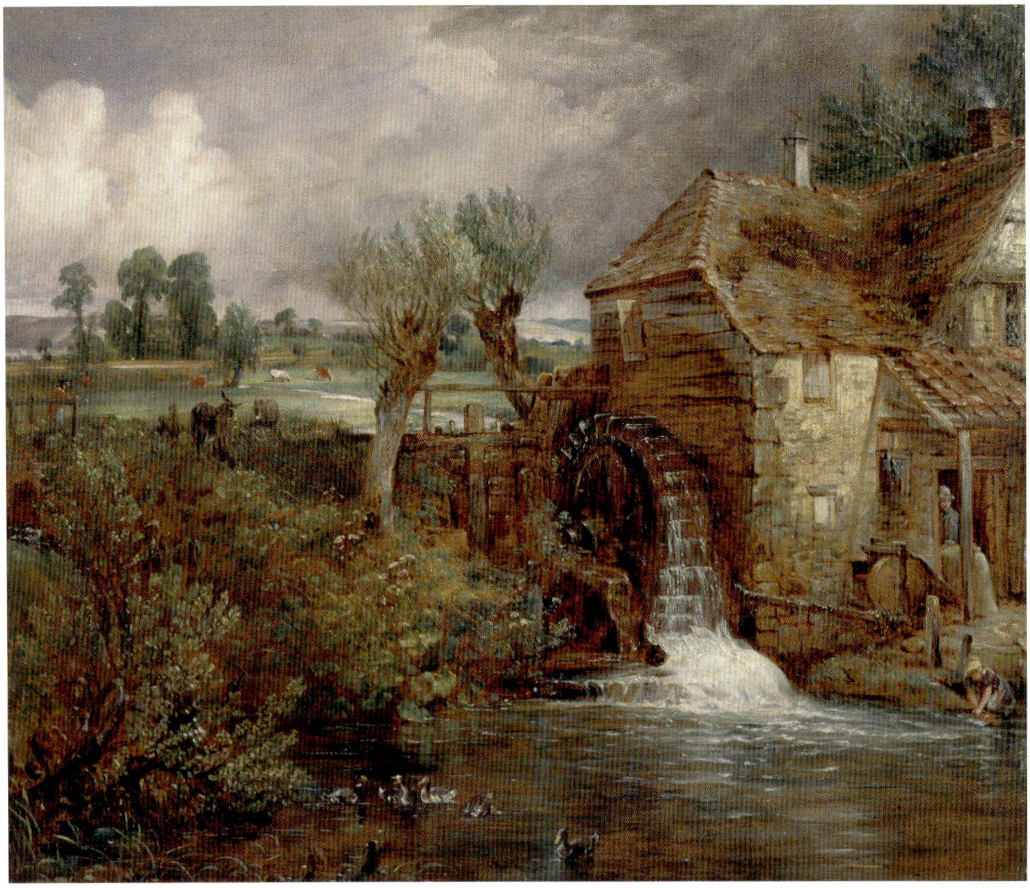

Fig. 63
Gillingham Mill, Dorset
c.1826
Oil on canvas,
50.2 × 60.3cm
R.26.4
Paul Mellon Collection,
Yale Center for British Art,
New Haven, CT

Charles. Brighton was once again decided upon, both for its sea air and also so that John Charles might try the curative properties of sea bathing.[19] Perhaps because the family was looking for accommodation at shorter notice than the previous year and also somewhat higher in the season – they were to travel down to Brighton on 31 August – in 1825 they initially took what transpired to be unsatisfactory lodgings in Russell Place. Constable meanwhile resumed a routine similar to that which he had adopted the previous year, travelling down with the family to settle them in, returning to London to work and then making snatched visits to Brighton as and when he could. One of the latter was a trip there at the beginning of December to move the family to a more suitable residence in Cannon Street.

It seems unlikely that Constable would have been able to paint any of his outstanding commissions in Brighton towards the end of 1825, given how infrequently he was there. However, we do know of one commission, a view of *Gillingham Mill* (fig. 63), that he painted in Brighton when staying at Cannon Street for two weeks over Christmas and New Year of 1825–26 (and, on New Year's Day itself, he painted the remarkable *plein-air* beach study in the Tate; see fig. 121).[20] *Gillingham Mill* was painted for a London acquaintance called Mrs Hand, on a slightly larger scale than the version he made for Fisher the previous year (ironically, the mill itself, near one of Fisher's livings at Gillingham in Dorset, had burned down in the interim).[21] Constable told Fisher that, while he was painting the picture, Maria read to him from a recently published book of Nicolas Poussin's letters, observing there were very few differences between 'painters now and painters then', their point in common being the frequent apologies they made to patrons or 'friends for not doing their pictures sooner'.[22]

It is surely telling that the one commission we know Constable did work on in Brighton in this period, *Gillingham Mill*, was for an English client rather than, as was the case during his stay in the resort the previous year, for one of his

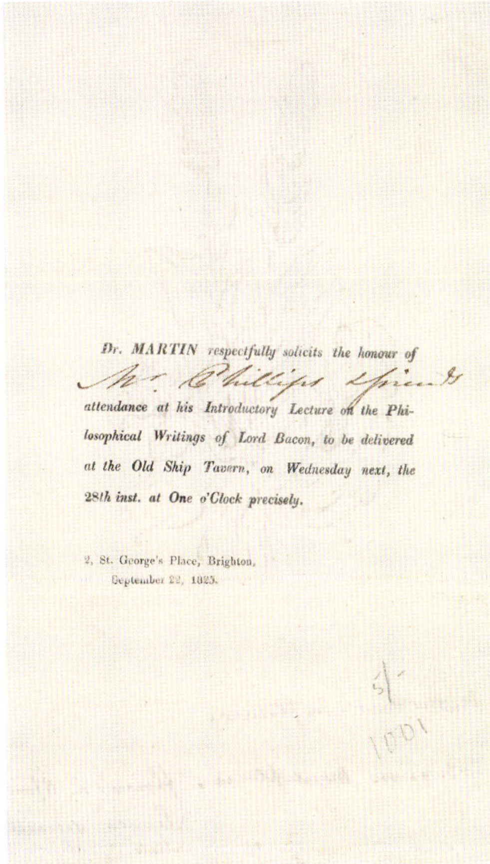

Dr. MARTIN respectfully solicits the honour of Mr. Phillips friend's attendance at his Introductory Lecture on the Philosophical Writings of Lord Bacon, to be delivered at the Old Ship Tavern, on Wednesday next, the 28th inst. at One o'Clock precisely.

2, St. George's Place, Brighton,
September 22, 1825.

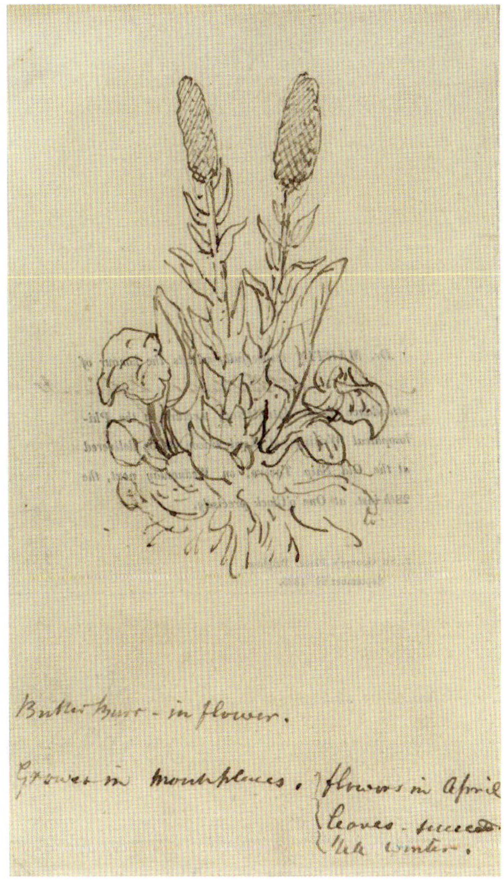

Fig. 64
Invitation to a philosophy lecture
(verso of *The Butter Burr in Flower*)
22 September 1825
Printed on paper,
19.3 × 11.8 cm
Courtauld Gallery, London

Fig. 65
The Butter Burr in Flower
(recto of Invitation to a philosophy lecture)
c.1825
Pen and brown ink on paper,
19.3 × 11.8 cm
R.26.7
Courtauld Gallery, London

French patrons. It seems that the artist painted no further pictures for Arrowsmith after a quarrel the previous November, although around this time Arrowsmith was in any case beginning to default on his payments and in due course, beset with financial difficulties, had to liquidate his stock.[23] He had been badly hit by the so-called 'Panic of 1825', a London banking crisis that soon afterwards spread to other European markets. Schroth was to find himself in a similarly difficult trading position by the following July, when he wrote to Constable to apologise that he would no longer be able to commission any more pictures from him. He did, however, tell him that he intended to retain for his own personal collection the pictures by Constable he already owned, bearing in mind the poor prices fetched by Arrowsmith's paintings when recently offloaded on to the market.[24]

It seems likely that, when trying to find accommodation in Brighton in 1825, the Constables had been offered help from Mr and Mrs Phillips, a couple they had first met – and got to know well – on their first visit to Brighton the previous year. Henry Phillips was a botanist, whom Constable took to immediately on first meeting him when walking on the Downs, as he mentions in the letter of 29 August (see pp. 8–9).[25] Phillips had many an ambitious plan around this time to design public gardens in Brighton and erect conservatories for tropical plants, such as the Athenaeum and Oriental Gardens (discussed in greater detail by Sue Berry in Chapter 6), most of which eventually foundered – indeed one glasshouse actually collapsed during the course of construction.[26] However, Constable described him as 'the most amiable of men & the cleverest … of all I have ever known'.[27]

In late September 1825 Phillips passed on to Constable an invitation (which he himself presumably could not use) to a lecture at the Old Ship Tavern in Brighton concerning 'The Philosophical Writings of Lord Bacon' (fig. 64). Although it is not known whether Constable attended the lecture, we do know that he used the other side of the invitation card to draw a *Butter*

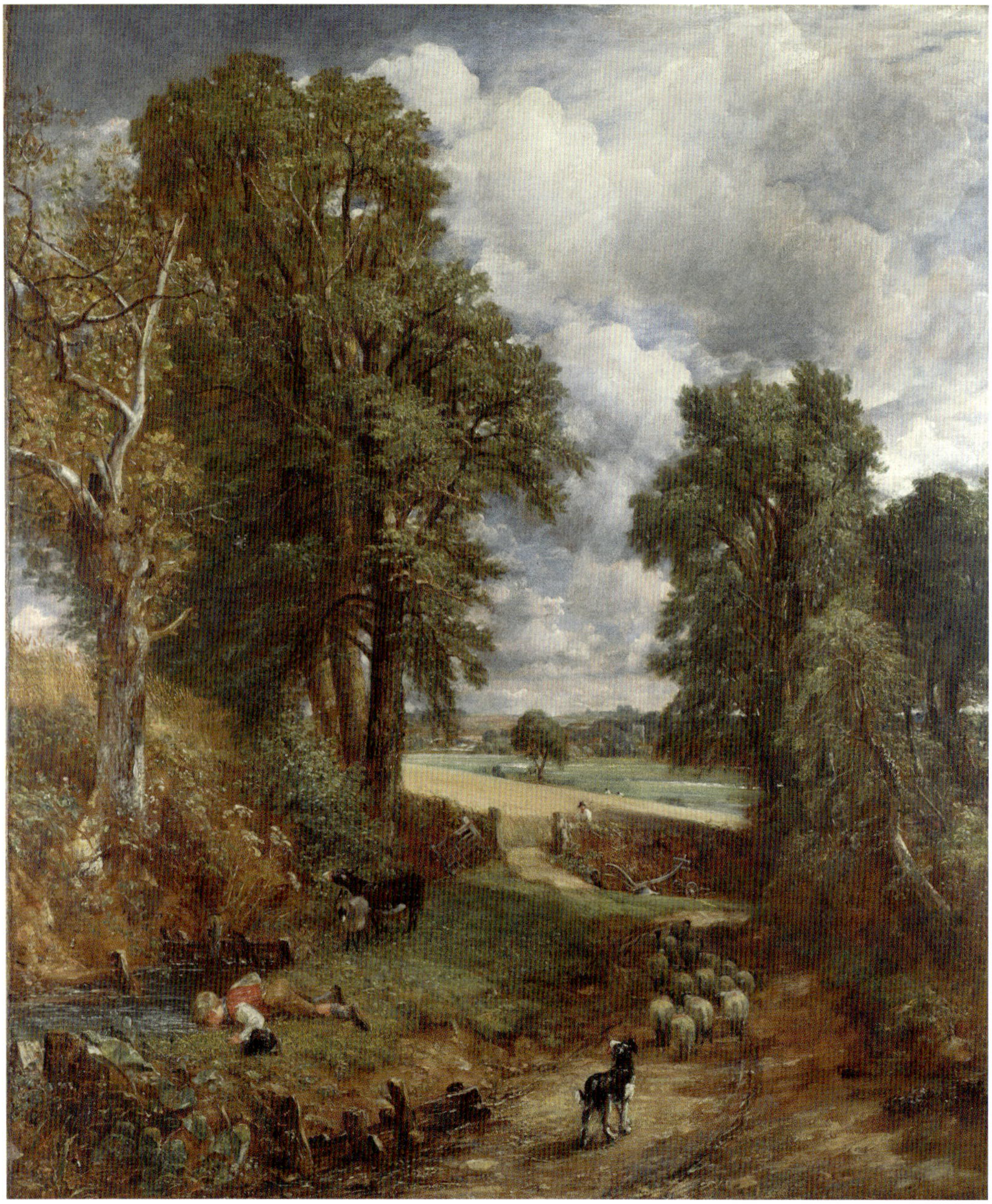

Fig. 66
The Cornfield
1826
Oil on canvas, 143 × 122 cm
R.26.1
National Gallery, London

Burr in Flower (fig. 65). It has been suggested that he may have made this on the next flowering of the plant, around April 1826.[28] However, it seems just as plausible that he drew it at Cannon Street in Brighton a few months earlier, in January, perhaps copying it from a botanical illustration, and conceivably when in company with Phillips.[29]

While Constable was a great admirer of Phillips's publications on botany, the latter took a great interest in the artist's paintings and would often visit Constable in his Charlotte Street studio when on one of his trips to London for meetings at the Horticultural Society or other learned bodies. Early in 1826 he found Constable at work on his next large picture for the Academy, *The Cornfield* (fig. 66), and subsequently wrote to him from Brighton to advise him on the various flowers, plants and grasses such as wild carrot, hemlock, cow parsley and water plantain that would be in season in July, and which Constable wished to introduce into the foreground.[30]

It was also around this time that Constable's eldest child, John Charles, was sent back to Brighton to be placed under the care of Mr and

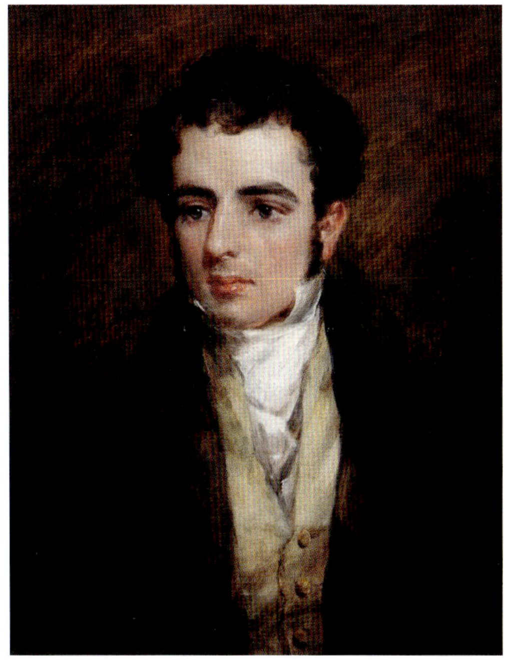

Fig. 67
Dr Herbert Evans
*c.*1829
Oil on canvas, 30.2 × 25 cm
R.29.53
Evans Family Collection

Mrs Phillips for his education – Mrs Phillips ran an academy there – as well as for his health.[31] Except for short visits made in connection with visiting his son, Constable was not to return to Brighton again for any length of time until May 1828. There seemed no pressing need to make another family visit to the resort in 1827 once Constable had taken a lease on a dwelling in Well Walk in Hampstead, in late August, and the family had settled into what he described as 'our comfortable little house'.[32] Thus, as it happens, the only picture of Brighton that Constable painted with a view to its being exhibited in public – *Chain Pier, Brighton* (see fig. 48) – was sent to the Academy in the very year, 1827, that he spent so little time at the resort.

It was in the autumn of 1827, in Hampstead, that Constable first met Herbert Evans (fig. 67), who was to become the family's doctor and – in due course – a close friend, as well as an admirer of the artist's work.[33] Presumably Evans would have been consulted about the advisability of another trip to Brighton in May 1828, when Maria's health was failing fast – her pulmonary tuberculosis had probably by now reached the 'galloping' phase. In any case, the family decided on what was to be their final visit together to Brighton that year, and this time it seems possible they returned to 9 Sober's Gardens. Constable again took an easel with him and now, bearing in mind that Maria was so ill, seems to have spent a much larger portion of his time there (rather than in London), during a stay that lasted two months, until late July.[34] It must have been hard for him, in Brighton in 1828, to be able to concentrate on advancing any of his commissions.

What Constable did manage to do, however, during his Brighton visits in 1828 was to go down to the beach when the opportunity arose. Shortly after the family's arrival in late May, for example, he was particularly intrigued to find on the shore a stranded collier (a coal-bearing sea vessel) called the *Malta*; he recorded it in a number of drawings, one of which shows various figures 'filling in' under the hull of the boat to prevent it heeling over any further (fig. 68). A second vessel, to the right of the *Malta*, another collier, still has the sea washing around its keel, but a cart and team of horses are moving towards this boat to unload its coal.[35]

Constable occasionally sketched in oils on this visit as well. There is a big difference in mood, however, between the tranquil sunset scene he made on 22 May (see fig. 107) and the vigorous oil sketch *Stormy Sea, Brighton* (see fig. 128), which he painted on the beach two months later, shortly before he left the resort, the latter painting's substantial palette-knife work helping evoke a turbulent-looking sea and sky and no doubt also reflecting his anxious state of mind.[36] He commented that they experienced 'most untoward weather' that summer in Brighton.[37] It may perhaps have been owing to this – or else because Maria was so unwell – that a few days later, instead of attempting to continue painting outdoors, Constable brought nature inside in the form of some dock leaves and grasses, and

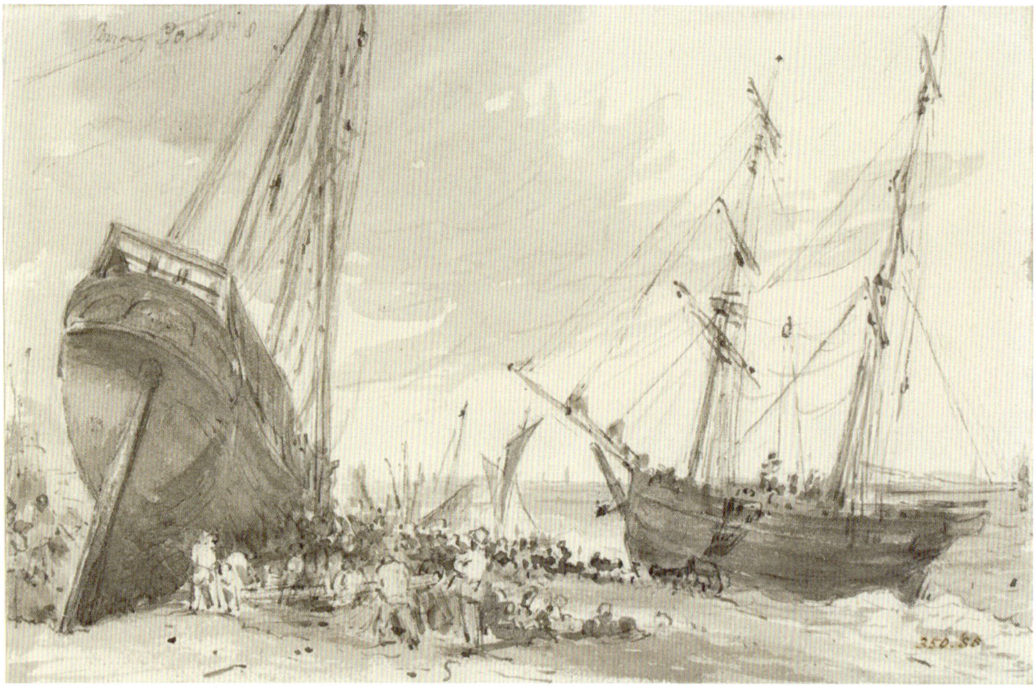

Fig. 68
A Coast Scene with Colliers on the Beach
30 May 1828
Pencil and grey wash,
11.4 × 18.1 cm
R.28.8
Victoria and Albert Museum, London

proceeded to make sketches of them in the house (figs 69–71).[38]

Maria was to die in Hampstead, at their house in Well Walk, towards the end of the year, and for many months afterwards Constable was inconsolable. Painting was to prove a welcome distraction for him, although he found it particularly upsetting that, when he was finally elected a full Academician in February 1829, he was unable to share the news – as he had so long anticipated doing – with Maria.[39] It seems that Constable's election as a full Academician had been delayed so long because of the long-established prejudice against pure landscape painting (as opposed to the sort of historical landscape with which Turner had made his name). He was subjected to a galling comment from Thomas Lawrence, the Academy's President, of course, who told him how lucky he was, as a landscape painter, to have been elected when there were so many talented history painters on the shortlist.[40] However, one Academician, the portrait painter Thomas Phillips, seems to have thought that Constable, by seeking fame abroad (as Phillips saw it), had shown disrespect for the Academy, and this may conceivably have delayed his election still further.[41]

Nevertheless, Constable was to prove a devoted Academician, dedicating himself wholeheartedly to the various duties he took on in connection with his new position. A pencil drawing by the Irish artist Daniel Maclise shows him at work in 1831 while serving as 'Visitor' in the Academy's Life School, where his role was to set the models' poses and supervise the work of the students (fig. 72).

Constable also continued to send in large pictures to the Academy's annual exhibitions – although not necessarily every year, now that ill health often intervened; when that happened, he might send in highly finished watercolours instead. With the exception of a view of *The Opening of Waterloo Bridge* (1832; Tate Britain, London) these later subjects tended to draw either on his Salisbury material (see fig. 130) or his earlier Suffolk subjects. An interesting exception is his last exhibition oil of *Arundel Mill and Castle* (1836–37; Toledo Museum of Art, OH), which was shown posthumously at the Academy's spring display in 1837, at its new premises in Trafalgar Square (Constable had died just a month or so before).

This painting is an interesting tribute to the friendship that Constable made late in life with his namesake (but no relation), the Arundel brewer George Constable, with whom he often stayed in the 1830s; together they would visit

Fig. 69
Study of Docks and Grasses
24 July 1828
Oil on paper laid on canvas,
15.2 × 24.1 cm
R.28.14
British Museum, London

Fig. 70
Study of Dock Leaves
25 July 1828
Oil on paper,
11.4 × 14.9 cm
R.28.15
British Museum, London

Fig. 71
Study of Foliage
c.1828
Oil on paper,
15.2 × 24.2 cm
R.28.24
Victoria and Albert Museum, London

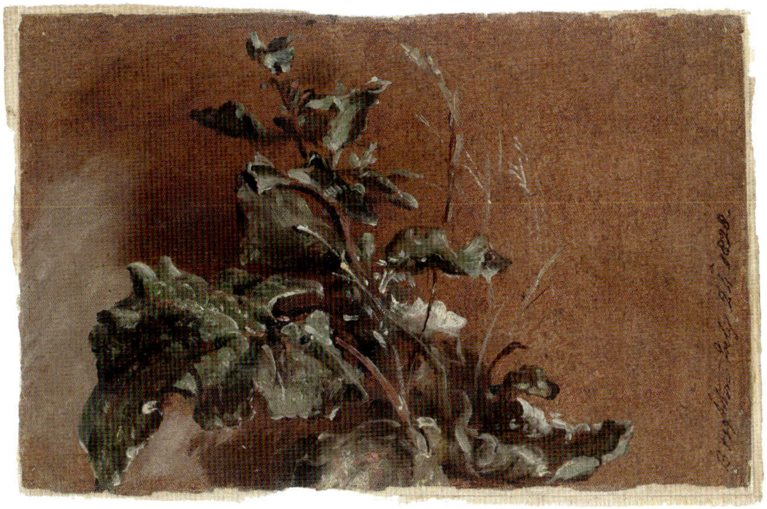

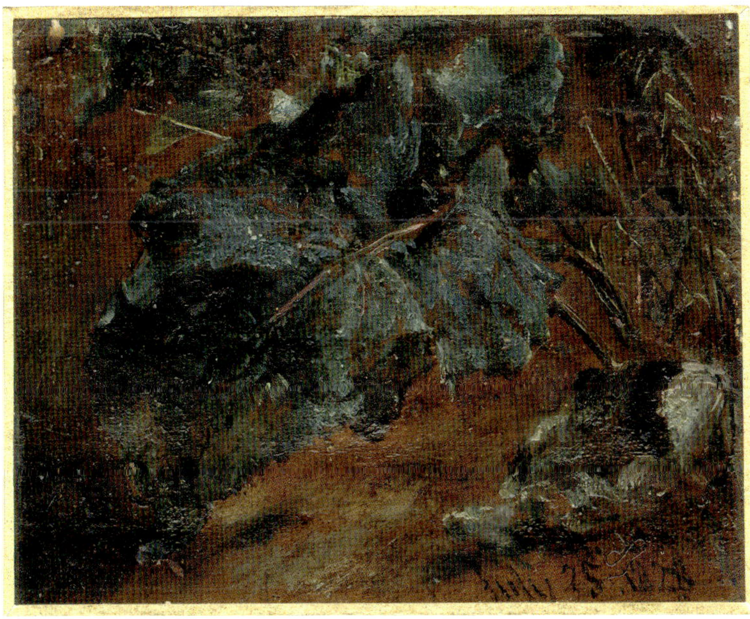

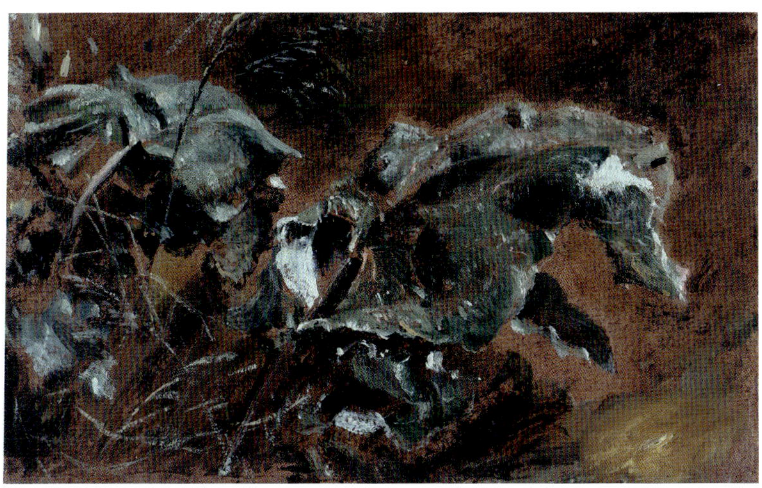

Fig. 72
Daniel Maclise
(1806–1870)
John Constable
c.1831
Pencil,
14.9 × 11.4 cm
National Portrait Gallery, London

many local Sussex sites, including some on the coast, such as Littlehampton.[42] Constable also visited Folkestone in the 1830s, as John Charles and Charles Golding, the artist's second son, spent some time there at school. He even occasionally visited Brighton again after Maria's death – for example in 1830, when John Charles was once more staying at the resort owing to poor health – although such visits must have brought back painful memories of his late wife's decline.[43]

Nevertheless – and despite his famous outburst about the resort in August 1824 (see p. 11) – the four years spanning the time when Constable visited and stayed in Brighton had been highly creative and productive ones for him. As evidence of this, we have the rich range of material he sketched on the beach and on the Downs behind the resort, a substantial and striking corpus of work in its own right. There is also the remarkable large painting

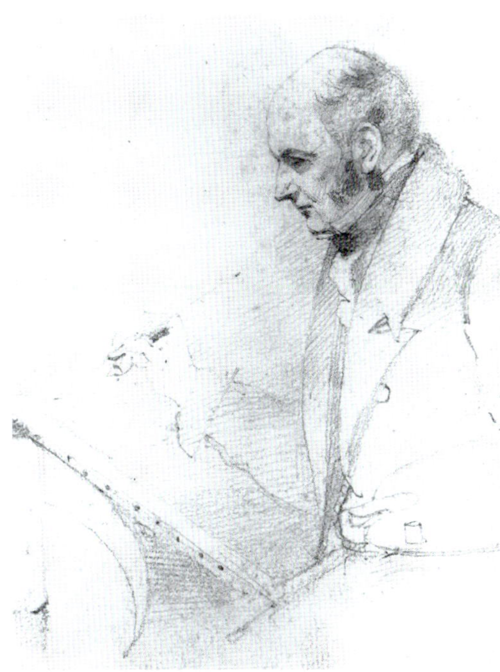

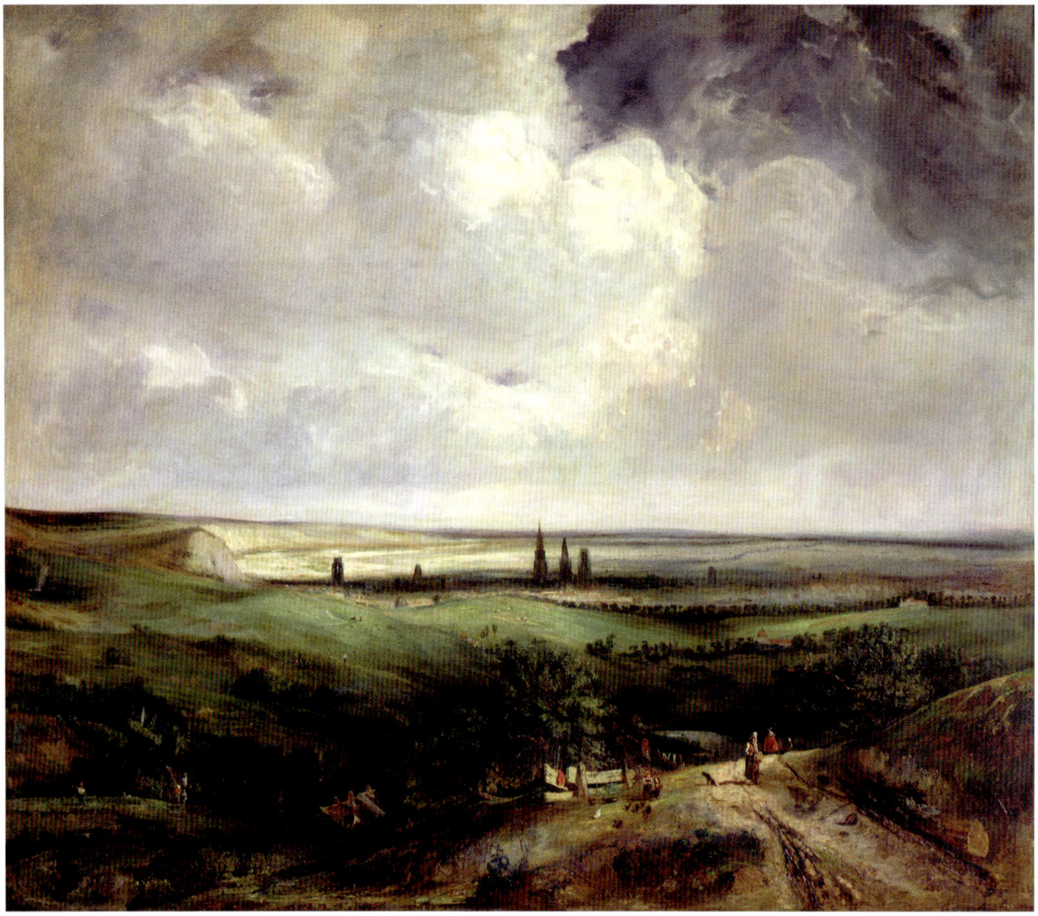

Fig. 73
Paul Huet (1803–1869)
View of Rouen from Mont Aux Malades
1831
Oil on canvas, 1.95 × 2.25 m
Musée des Beaux Arts, Rouen

Chain Pier, Brighton (1827), in which he created a memorable portrait of a coastal town at a key moment of historical transition (see Ch. 4, pp. 58–62), as well as the pictures of non-Brighton subjects (especially the commissioned views of Hampstead) that he is known to have painted at his seaside lodgings. Of no less importance, of course, was the impact that many of his canvases, albeit some of these painted a little before his visits to Brighton, had in France between 1824 and 1828, during the period when he was moving between residences at the resort, in central London and in Hampstead (see Ch. 2).

Yet it was in France that, after his death, an enthusiasm for Constable's art was not just to linger on in the memory but also powerfully to influence – much more so than in Britain – the next generation of landscape painters. Not only had Constable won a gold medal in 1825 following his success at the 1824 Paris Salon, but he also went on to win another French medal in 1826 after being invited to send in work to an exhibition at Lille the year before, of which the highlight was *The White Horse* (see fig. 12).[44] In 1827 he decided to send *The Cornfield* (see fig. 66) to the Paris Salon, this time using the London print-sellers and publisher Colnaghi's to help with the practical arrangements.[45] Although the painting drew less comment from the French critics than his work had done three years earlier, the 1827 Salon itself was said to be teeming with his imitators, just as those same critics had foreseen.[46]

Nor did the admiration of French artists end there. As long as Constable continued to be talked about – and as late as 1835 he was still being informed that no Englishman was as famous in France as he was[47] – and as long as some of his pictures were still circulating among painters, it is clear that his influence was likely to persist. Schroth's two views of Hampstead by Constable, *Branch Hill Pond* and *Child's Hill*

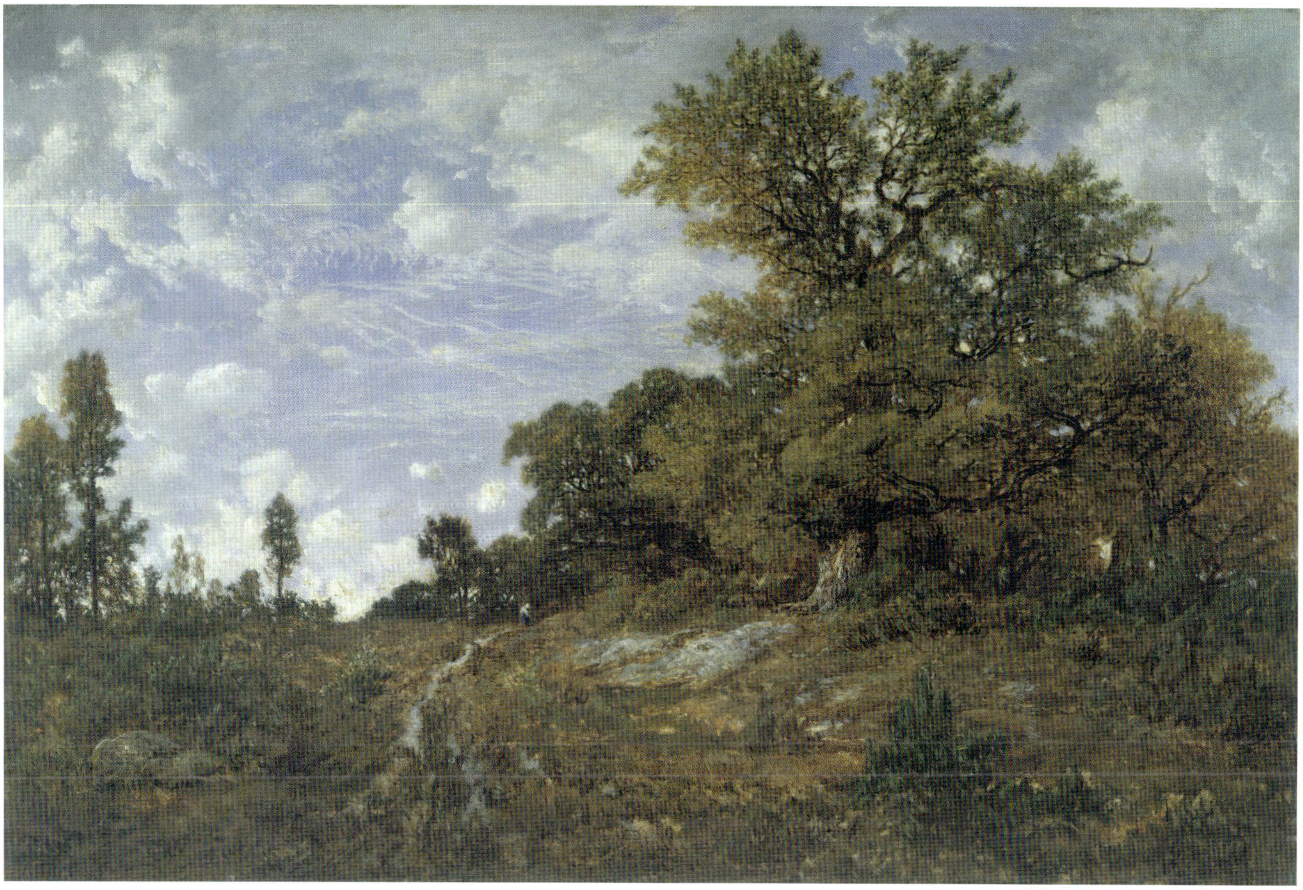

Fig. 74
THÉODORE ROUSSEAU (1812–1867)
The Edge of the Woods at Monts-Girard, Fontainebleau Forest
1852–54
Oil on wood, 80 × 121.9 cm
The Metropolitan Museum of Art, New York

(see figs 19 and 21), which had been widely praised on their arrival in France in 1825,[48] must have continued to be available for viewing in subsequent years, given that the former picture dealer, now trading in prints and retaining his long-standing links with artists, had been true to his promise to Constable and kept them for his personal collection. Paul Huet, for example, must surely have known the two Hampstead paintings, given the extent to which his picture of Rouen (1831; fig. 73) is clearly indebted to them both.[49]

Huet, twenty-one at the time of the 1824 Paris Salon, later recalled the excitement generated by Constable's work that year.[50] Not only did Huet himself later become a great admirer of Constable's work, absorbing its influence more generally (as in his *View of Rouen from Mont Aux Malades*), but he also made a number of direct copies after the Englishman's paintings.[51] In this way he became the critical link – in terms of transmitting ideas about, and examples of, Constable's work – between Delacroix and those in his circle and the next generation of artists, such as Théodore Rousseau, Constant Troyon and Jules Dupré, who, with others, were to form the Barbizon school. Huet was later to acknowledge the importance of Constable's work in pointing the way forward towards a new type of landscape painting in France.[52]

Rousseau must also have heard about Constable from Arrowsmith, who, like Schroth, remained active in artistic circles after his bankruptcy and, indeed, was to become a friend of Rousseau and an active promoter of the latter's paintings.[53] It is, in fact, Rousseau (fig. 74) who, of all the artists of the Barbizon school, most closely approximates Constable in spirit, even if his painterly style is very much his own. Clearly it was not just Delacroix, then, who could claim that 'Ce Constable me fait un grand bien'.

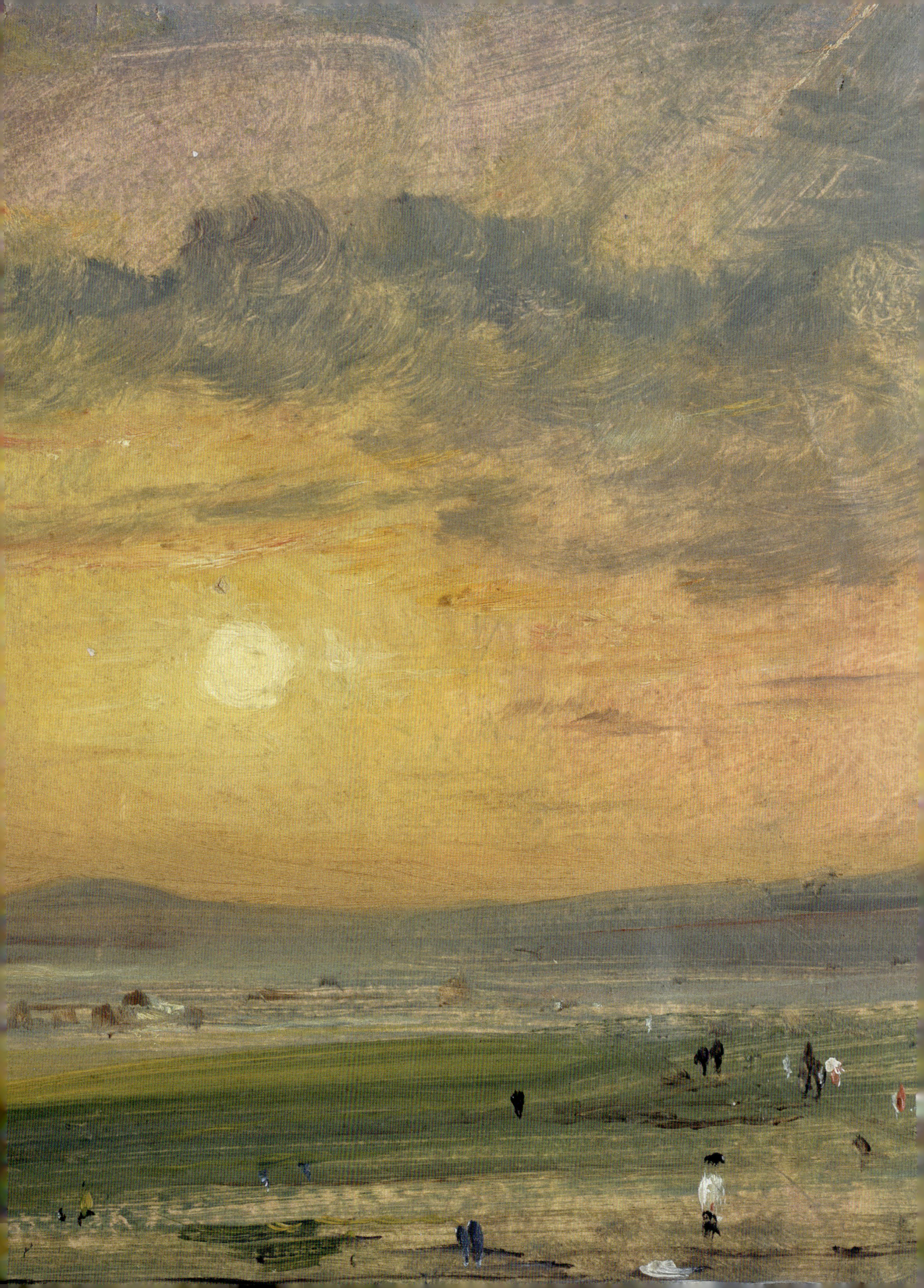

6 Walking with Constable

'my Brighton oil sketches .. (done in the lid of my box on my knees'[1]

SUE BERRY

THIS IS AN INTRODUCTION to Brighton as it was when John Constable and his family visited, followed by three short studies in the form of walks in the localities where Constable sketched and painted. Peter Harrap, curator of the *Constable and Brighton* exhibition, arranged this sequence of images, based on his analysis of the subjects and dates of Constable's works.

For artists, Brighton and its surroundings offered a variety of views, which altered as the resort grew and spread. The need to protect ever-increasing lengths of coastline from erosion changed the look of the seafront. This meant that artists such as Turner, who first came in the 1790s, were able to return to provide new interpretations of the changing prospect. From the 1760s, as the town became fashionable and a possible market for prints, paintings and drawings, the numbers produced proliferated. In 1981 John and Jill Ford made a sterling attempt to itemize the proliferation of prints showing the town before the end of the nineteenth century, listing over twelve hundred subjects; nevertheless, more have surfaced since.[2] So when Constable made his first visit to Brighton in 1824, there were already many images of the resort's most fashionable areas in circulation.

He immediately began exploring his new environment with sketchbook and paint box, as he always did when given the opportunity to observe nature at first hand, dashing off a series of exquisite small paintings capturing the beaches and the rolling hills behind the town, leading up to the Sussex Downs, all of which were an easy walk from the family lodgings in the western end of the town. Surprisingly, given his many reservations about Brighton as a subject, Constable produced a substantial group of works here, so perhaps in his original observations he overstated his view. Most of these works are personal responses: small sketches in a pocketbook; monochrome studies refined in pen and ink; as well as the more familiar evocations in oil of the shoreline and the light falling on the sea – all small enough to fit inside the lid of the box in which he carried his painting materials. As in other settings, it is in these more informal works that we can detect his sheer pleasure in nature and in light, and it appears to have been the process of making the sketches that overcame some of his apparent distaste for Brighton – the 'indecent' resort. No matter what his view was of the character of Brighton, Constable had to consider how he might use it to provide ideas for pictures because he had to make a living. So some aspects of his sketching probably had a commercial end in mind. For example, he told his friend Archbishop Fisher in 1823 that his paintings of marine views were so popular he

Detail of fig. 107

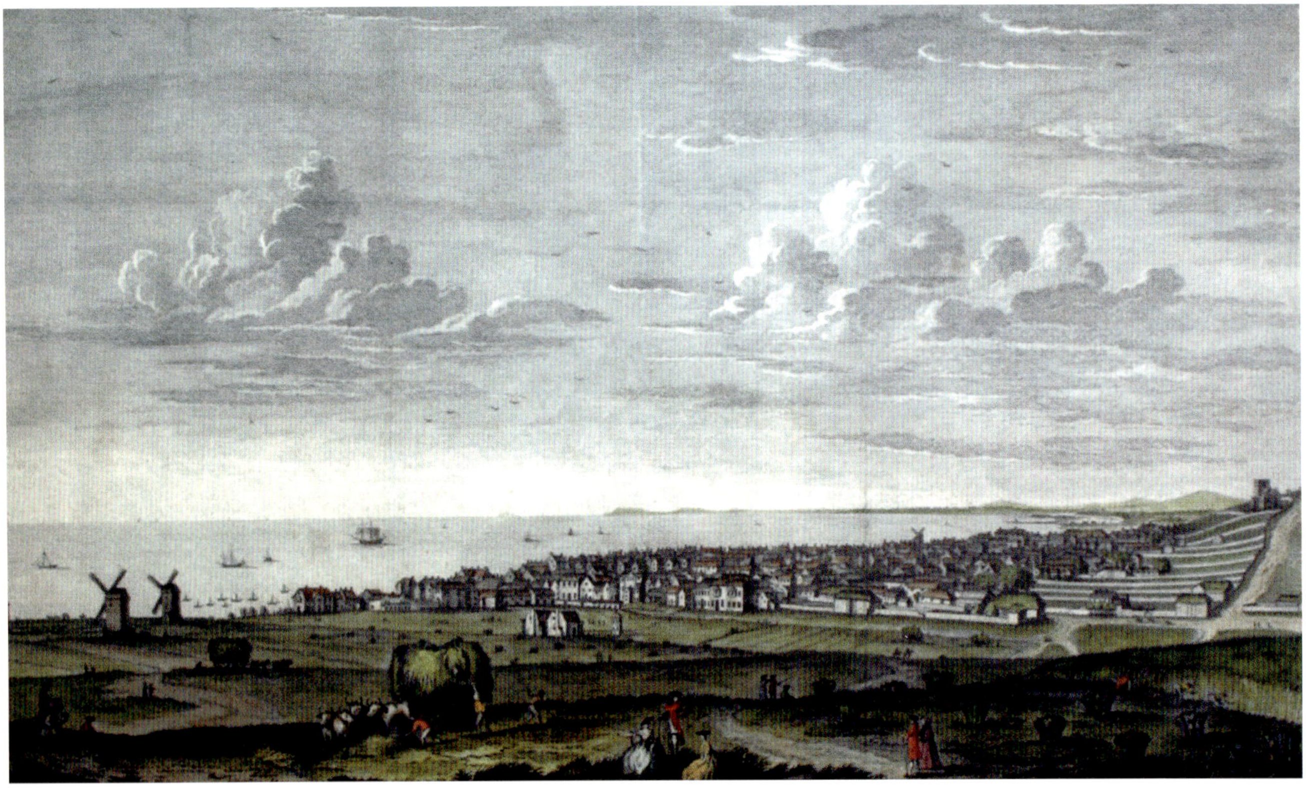

Fig. 75
JAMES LAMBERT
A Perspective View of Brighthelmstone and of the Sea Coast as Far as the Isle of Wight
1765
Engraving
Private collection

had none left to sell,[3] and in 1824 he received a commission from the Anglo-French picture dealer Arrowsmith for shore scenes which were to be engraved and issued as a group (see Ch 3). It is also possible that as early as 1824 Constable developed the germ of his idea for a large canvas, or 'six-footer' featuring the Chain Pier (see Ch. 4). Like the majority of artists, he sought an impression of a place, and so his work cannot be depended on by those seeking accurate topographical evidence.

One of the earliest images of Brighton, or Brighthelmston/Brighthelmstone (a name for the town which was rapidly going out of fashion by 1810), was by James Lambert (fig. 75). It shows features that were subsequently recorded by Constable some sixty years later: the windmills at the edges of the developed resort, the South Downs wrapping around its perimeter, a hint of the low-lying area stretching from Hove, just to the west of Brighton, to Shoreham, and the bay curving westwards towards the new little resort of Worthing.

While the landscape provided a natural setting for a resort, its successful development owed much of its character to the networks of family and friendship that helped to sustain it. The resort was well established when George, Prince of Wales (later the Prince Regent, then George IV), first visited in the mid-1780s. Some historians have over-estimated the impact of the well-publicised periodic presence of the prince at the Royal Pavilion (fig. 76).

The Constables' attachment to Brighton illustrates the importance of contacts. Maria Constable's father, Charles Bicknell, a solicitor to the Prince Regent who drafted some of the contracts for the land the prince acquired around his ever-growing Marine Pavilion, regularly stayed in the resort, and this family connection meant that she already knew – and liked – the town, enabling her to overcome her husband's misgivings.[4]

Until the later 1820s visitor numbers continued to rise, and the majority, despite Constable's remark about 'the offscouring of London', remained predominantly wealthy, although more came from professional and business backgrounds, reflecting the national development of the service and industrial sectors. How and when visitors used the resort changed, which affected the provision of accommodation and services. By 1818 the season was shifting to

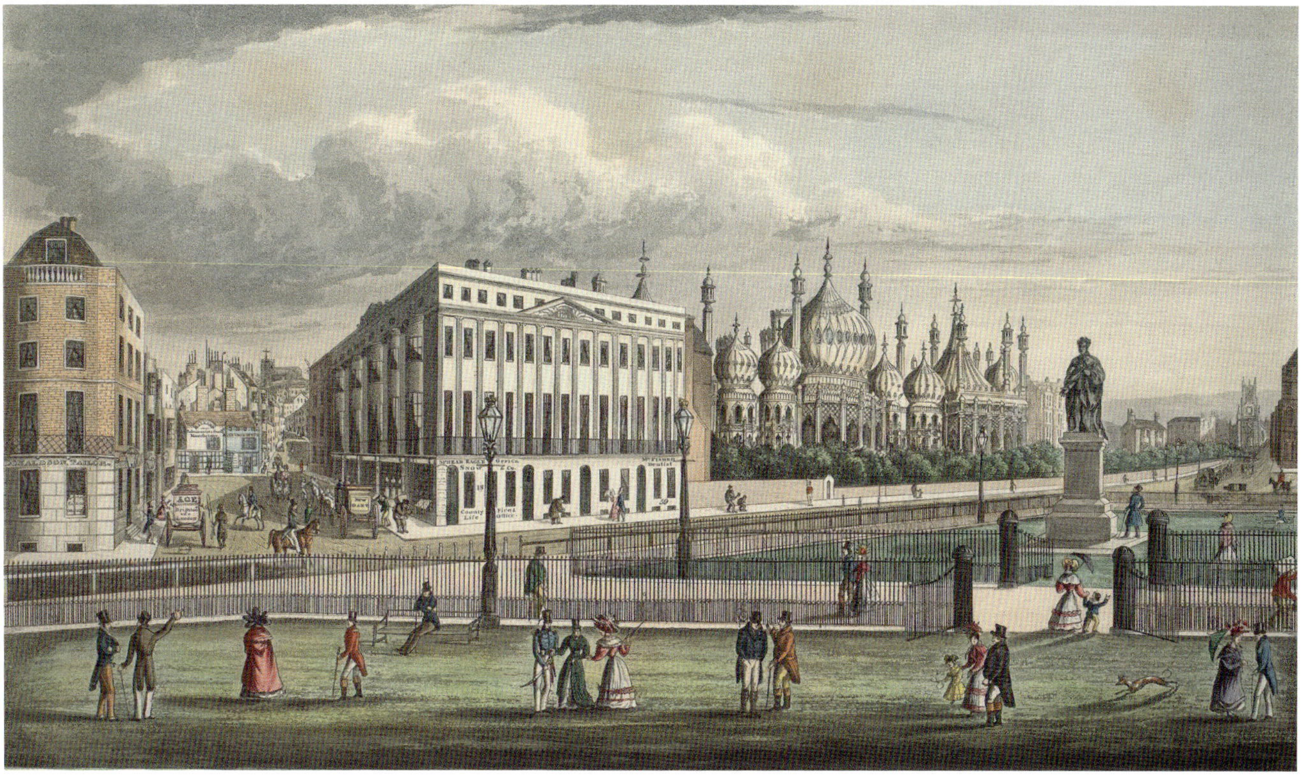

Fig. 76
J. Bruce (active 1820s)
The Carriage Road from *Castle Square to St James Street, and other Important Improvements on the Old Steine*
1830
Private collection

the later autumn, away from the June-to-early-October peak, and lasting longer, a trend that continued into the 1850s. If an account of the number of visitors in the season from 1822–23 is roughly accurate, then around 10–14,000 visitors were accommodated in the later autumn peak period. Most arrived using the forty-nine coaches that conveyed 2,000 passengers a week from London to Brighton, a typical trip taking six hours.[5] By coming in June and July for at least two of their visits, the Constables (short of cash as a rule) were visiting during the slightly cheaper periods; the chief exception being the last three months of 1825, when their son John Charles suddenly fell ill and needed sea air.

When the Constable family first visited, in May 1824, Brighton was still a bustling and rapidly changing resort. But by the end of the 1820s its long phase of prosperity was ending because a national recession was hitting it hard. Holidays, even for the wealthy, were less frequent and shorter. One of the attractions of Brighton was, of course, sea-bathing. During the early 19th century this would have necessarily have involved the bathing machine. These substantial wooden vehicles were common to all seaside resorts and usually, as in Brighton, without a big, unwieldy hood at the front, as Margate for example used to hide bathers from public view while dipping. Bathers changed in them before the machines were trundled into the surf by a horse. They then walked down the steps to be immersed (or 'dipped', as it was then described) in the sea by one or two bathing men or women, who stood in the sea (fig. 77). These machines can be seen in the background of some of Constable's images, including both the large exhibited canvas of 1827 and its related study (see pp. 124–125).

Between 1810 and 1836 the area of Brighton more than doubled, but the demand for easy access to the sea by visitors and wealthy residents reinforced the triangular shape typical of resorts in bays. The front lengthened on either side of the old town, which became the business and leisure area, with light industry and other essential services mainly clustered on its north side. More modest but still quite expensive middle-class accommodation in smaller developments such as Russell Square and Sober's Gardens, where the Constables stayed, were near the sea but not facing it (see fig. 79).[6] Yet although Brighton had replaced Bath as the favoured resort of wealthy and influential people by the mid-1810s, it was less than half the size, and the total population of Brighton and Hove did not overtake Bath until 1851.[7]

The demand for bigger houses pushed up rental prices, to which developers quickly responded. Between 1816 and 1818 over 500 houses were completed, and in 1818 alone about 330 were being built. Older schemes such as Blucher Place and Russell Square, begun before 1815 just west of the old town centre, speeded up. The former was completed by 1820, and Russell Square in 1824. The houses in both developments were smaller than those which then followed,[8] as the building boom continued well into the 1820s. In 1826 the architect C. A. Busby compiled a list of 489 houses and a shop under construction, pointing out that the number was small compared with an estimated 8,000 buildings in the resort. Development was funded with capital from London or local people and banks, by traders supplying building materials giving generous credit times and by the builders from their own funds.[9]

By 1815 the preference among wealthy visitors for entertaining privately was quickly replacing the older one of attending public entertainments co-ordinated by a master of ceremonies. This demand persuaded Thomas Read Kemp (of Kemp Town) to go to the expense of co-operating with co-owners to enclose pastoral land surrounding the resort for development, and Thomas Scutt (of Brunswick Town) to sell an old brickfield on the coast and also valuable freehold farmland for the building of Brunswick Town. The two 'Towns' needed the large areas that these owners made available (see fig. 79).[10]

By this time the town's businesses were already responding to other changes in the use of accommodation. More visitors rented apartments in hotels for short stays or while finding a house or lodgings to rent for several weeks. New hotels such as the York (1819), Royal Albion (Amon and Henry Wilds, 1824), Norfolk and Bedford (Thomas Cooper, 1825 and 1828–29) were built. The Royal Hotel in New Steine on the East Cliff, which began as linked houses, was rebuilt in 1820, and the Pavilion Hotel in Castle Square, also created from amalgamating houses, re-faced in 1824. The investment in improvements to older hotels and bigger, purpose-built hotels reflected the more sophisticated expectations of visitors, who in the past might have accepted a single room or a suite of only two rooms.[11]

Expansion tailed off about 1828, when the dramatic slow-down recorded in the census between 1831 and 1841 began (Table 1). Many bankruptcies among builders and other businesses from the late 1820s marked the stagnation of the building industry related to the decline in the number of visitors resulting from the recession.[12]

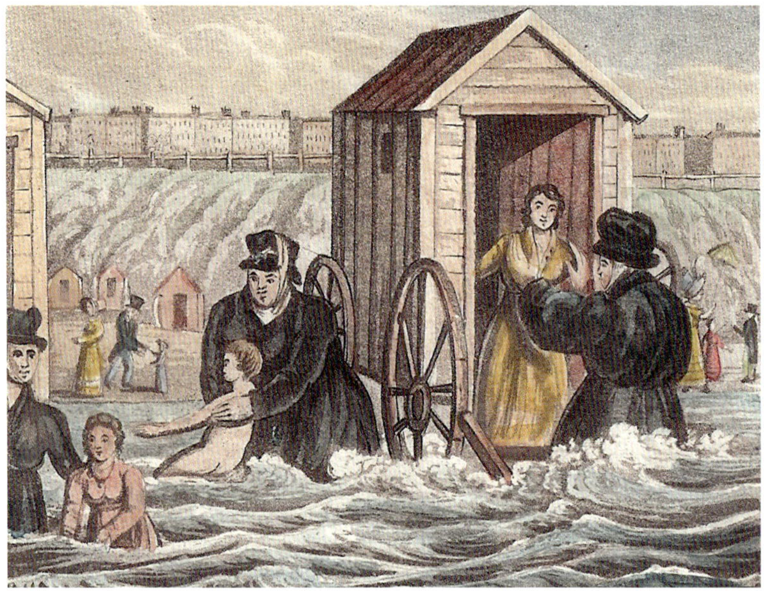

Fig. 77
Bathing Machines (from *Harry and Lucy's Trip to Brighton*, published by J. Whittemore)
c.1829
Private collection

Table 1

POPULATION OF BRIGHTON AND HOVE 1794–1841			
YEAR	BRIGHTON	HOVE	TOTAL
1794	5669		
1801	7339	101	7440
1811	12012	193	12205
1821	22429	312	22741
1831	40634	1360	41994
1841	46661	2509	49170

Between 1815 and 1828 the resort developers learned that, in order to attract affluent visitors, it had to improve urban management by taking on essential responsibilities for which many were unwilling to pay. The Town Commissioners took on street cleaning, drainage and a seafront road, improved the gardens in the Steine and largely mastered the erosion that threated houses from Regency Square in the west to Kemp Town in the east.

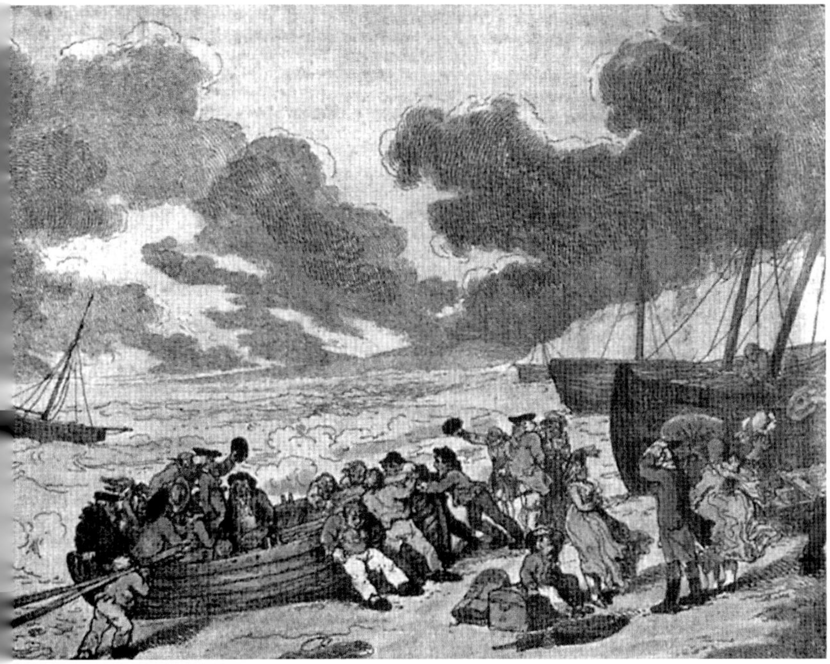

Fig. 78
THOMAS ROWLANDSON (1756–1827)
'Embarking for the Ferry' (from Henry Wigstead and Thomas Rowlandson, *Excursion to Brighthelmstone*)
1790
Private collection

Visitors and local people who depended on tourism were by 1815 very critical of the state of the valley north of the Royal Pavilion (then called North Steine) and called for improvements. Between 1816 and 1820 gardens were formed by clearing the land of flints and rubbish and adding low walls topped with railings, and with four gates as the boundary. Once the landscaping had settled in, the gardens became a popular subject for prints. The Level, to the north of St Peter's Church, was given to the town in 1822, having been simply landscaped by the addition of trees by local people supervised by a gardener, and adopted by the Commissioners.

In 1824–25 a zealous mapmaker, John Pigott- Smith, tried to get into every nook and cranny of the town to map it as accurately as he could, exploring it far more thoroughly than most, including Constable. The map (fig. 79) shows every project that Constable could or would have seen – most of which, to judge from his work and letters, he ignored. Yet for Maria, his wife, like most visitors, these were probably attractions that made the town of interest.

Brighton flourished because of the ease of access to London, but the resort's role as a link in the quickest route to Paris also contributed to its success. The route to Paris via Dieppe had been in use since the 1760s, and the desire to keep it going was one reason for the construction of the Chain Pier. Until it was built, travellers were conveyed to and from the ferry, waiting offshore, by rowing boat (fig. 78). This was uncomfortable and sometimes dangerous. The resort was finally pushed into finding an alternative means of loading and unloading passengers and goods with the advent of steam ferries, which had to wait further out owing to their draught. This resulted between 1822 and 1823 in the con-

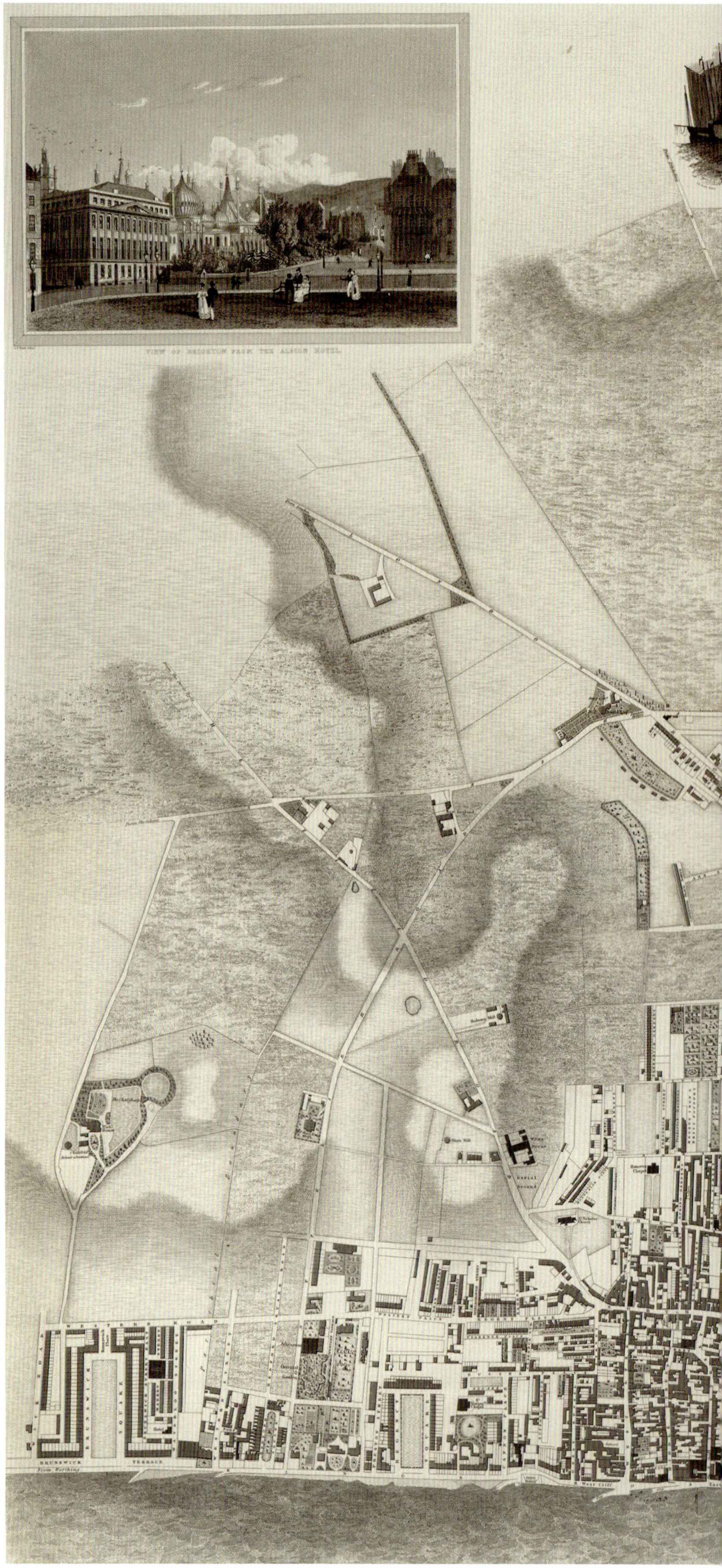

Fig. 79
J. Piggott-Smith
Map of Brighton
1824–25
Private collection

struction of the Chain Pier, one of the first of such seaside structures in the country, financed entirely by subscription (fig. 80). The Earl of Egremont, owner of a villa in Brighton as well as of Petworth House in Sussex, was a keen supporter of this project and a major investor, as well as being a patron of Turner. Constable was keen to enjoy such patronage as well (see Ch. 4 pp. 58–59), which may help to explain why both Constable and Turner decided to paint the pier.

Another new development scheme that Constable encountered in Brighton was the Athenaeum and Oriental Gardens which was proposed for land west of and adjoining Sober's Gardens. This was the joint project of Henry Phillips, a botanist and garden designer and Constable's greatest friend in Brighton, and Henry Wilds, a local developer and architect. Constable visited the site (now Sillwood Place) in August 1826, probably to please his friend, but there are no known sketches of it by him.

A prospectus for the Athenaeum and Oriental Gardens was advertised in July and August 1825. A committee of local worthies, such as Thomas Read Kemp, of Kemp Town, the wealthy and influential vicar of Brighton, the Rev. Henry Wagner, and local businessmen such as the brewer Richard Tamplin, was formed to supervise the project. To publicise the venture, Henry Wilds produced both an aquatint of the scheme, which Hunt engraved, and a model (which has not survived). The cost of the total design, which included a library, was projected as £20,000, to be raised by shares of £100 apiece. Wilds and Phillips claimed that the design, based on the 'celebrated Cave of Elephants' on the Indian island of Salsette, would take two years to build. In September 1825 there were sufficient funds to buy land for

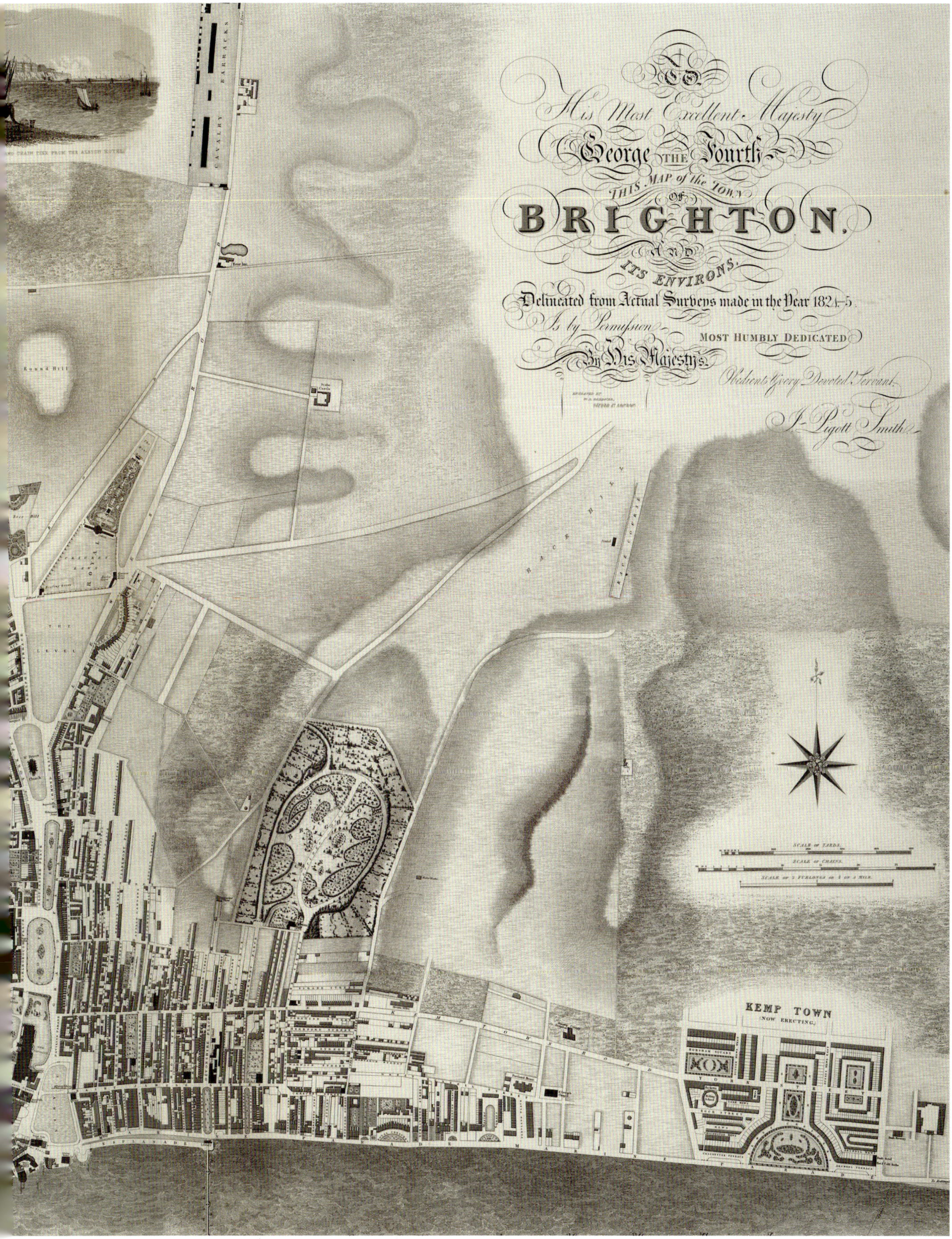
To
His Most Excellent Majesty
George the Fourth
This Map of the Town of
BRIGHTON.
and
Its Environs,
Delineated from Actual Surveys made in the Year 1824–5.
Is by Permission
MOST HUMBLY DEDICATED
By His Majesty's
Obedient & very Devoted Servant.
J. Pigott Smith
CAVALRY BARRACKS
Round Hill
THE LEVEL
RACE HILL
KEMP TOWN
(NOW ERECTING)

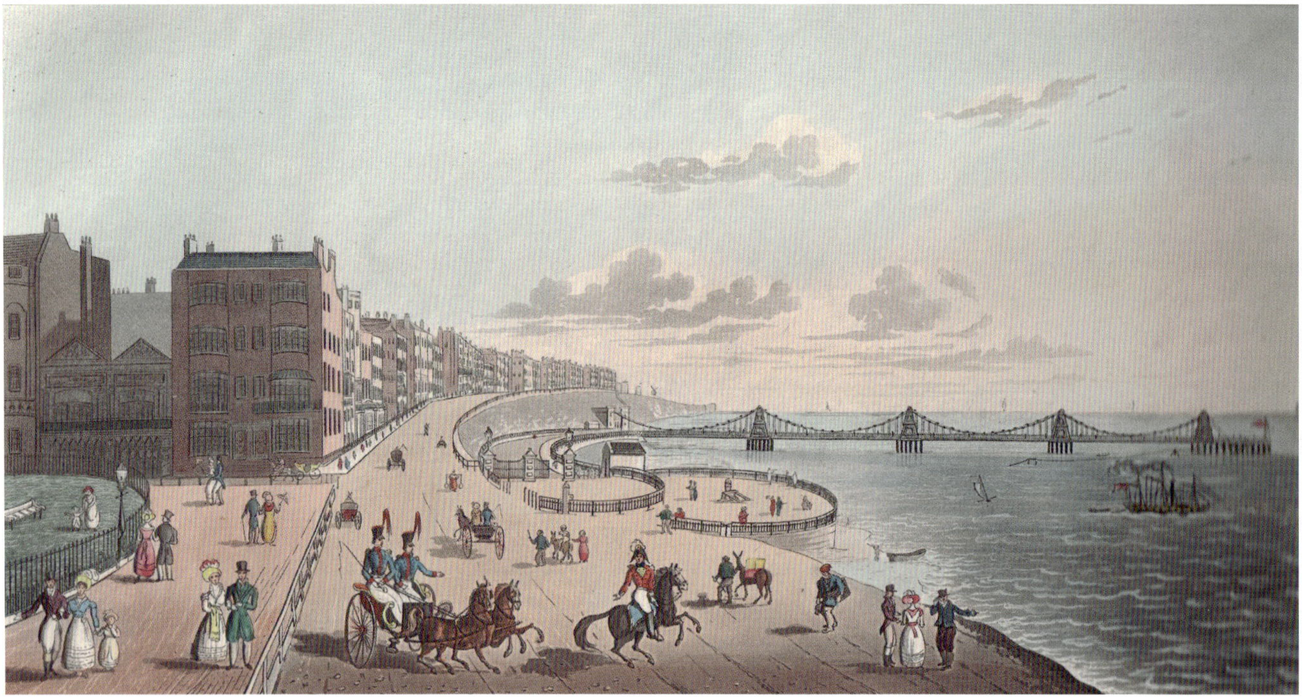

the project, and it is shown in detail on a large map of the town (see fig. 79).

By March 1826 some of the grounds were laid out, and a forcing house was in use, in which a rare plant was reported to have flowered. The Western Pavilion (still standing just off Western Road, in Western Terrace) was probably complete, serving as the north entrance to the grounds. Its 'Indian' style picks up the Mughal references in the windows of the building erected for the library and museum, which became Sillwood House. By April 1826 insufficient money had been raised to build the Athenaeum, and although the committee met again to consider its erection, nothing happened. Henry Phillips did not give up the 'Hindoo' theme, returning to it in the 1830s when he laid out the Surrey Zoological Gardens, with the largest conservatory of its kind in England.

The housing boom ensured that the Constable family had a choice of accommodation.

Fig. 80
J. BRUCE (active 1820s)
The Chain Pier from the South End of the Steine (from his *Select Views of Brighton*)
c.1824
Aquatint
Private collection

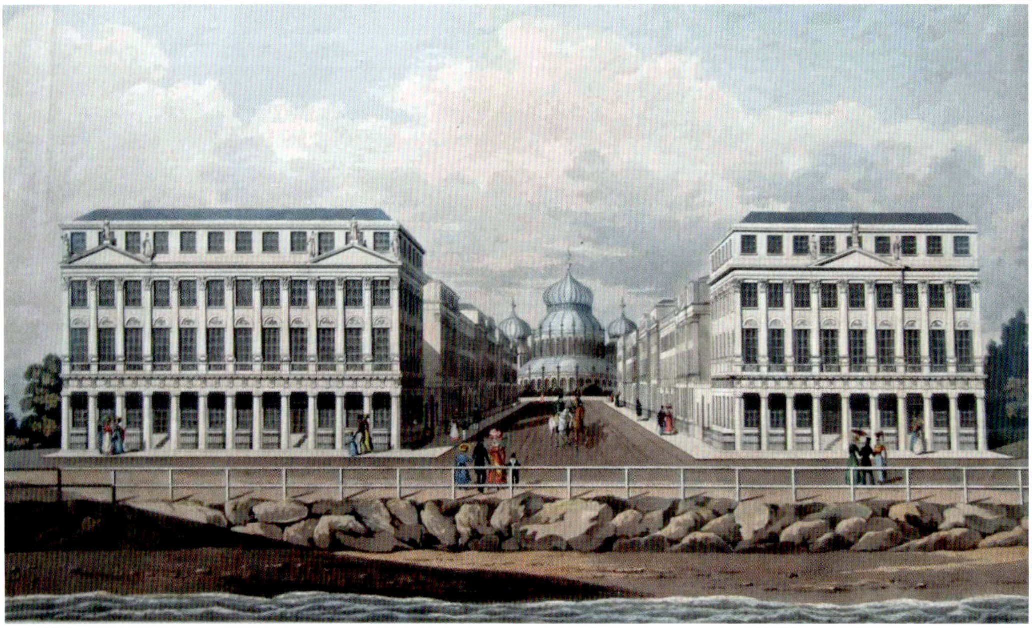

Fig. 81
A. H. WILDS (?1790–1857)
Oriental Place
c.1825
Engraving
Private collection

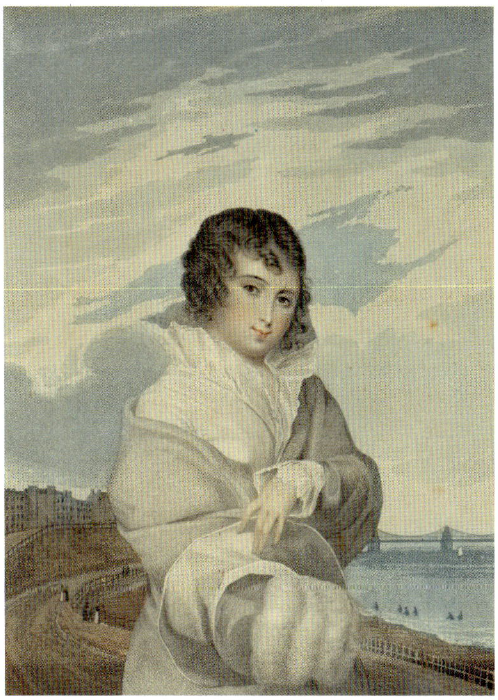

Fig. 82
Thomas Harper (d. 1843) and engraved by A. M. Huffman
Beauty of Brighton: The Chain Pier
c.1829
Mezzotint
Private collection

They rented lodgings on the western side of the flourishing seaside resort, presumably because the edge of town was cheaper, and the easy access to neighbouring fields would have made walking easier for the ailing Maria. However, this more open landscape would also have appealed to Constable. From the house, even weighed down with artist's equipment, it was easy to get down to the seashore from the low-lying cliff. By contrast, the houses on the east side of the resort were built on the sharply rising cliff-top, which made access to the beach harder. Royal Crescent, on the East Cliff, for example, had a series of steps down to the beach.[13]

The family rented 9 Sober's Gardens from 13 May to 3 November 1824. On 31 August 1825 the family occupied a house in Russell Place on the north side of Russell Square, shown clearly on the map by Pigott-Smith (see detail of fig. 79 on p.92). Constable joined them there on 17 September for an unspecified period.[14] On 23 October 1825 he wrote to Maria from London to say that he wanted her to leave Russell Place, which was damp and where she suffered from a bad cold: 'Pray get another house when and where you can ... warmer.'[15]

In November 1825 Constable helped to move the family from the damp lodgings in Russell Street to greater comfort in Cannon Street. They all spent Christmas there together, and he returned to London on 12 January 1826. The family stayed on towards the end of the month, although the exact date of their departure is not known.[16]

Later in 1826 Constable took his sons, John and Charles, to Brighton to place them at the school run by Mrs Phillips (the wife of Henry), and stayed in the Phillips family's house at 3 Bedford Square.[17] But it was clear by August

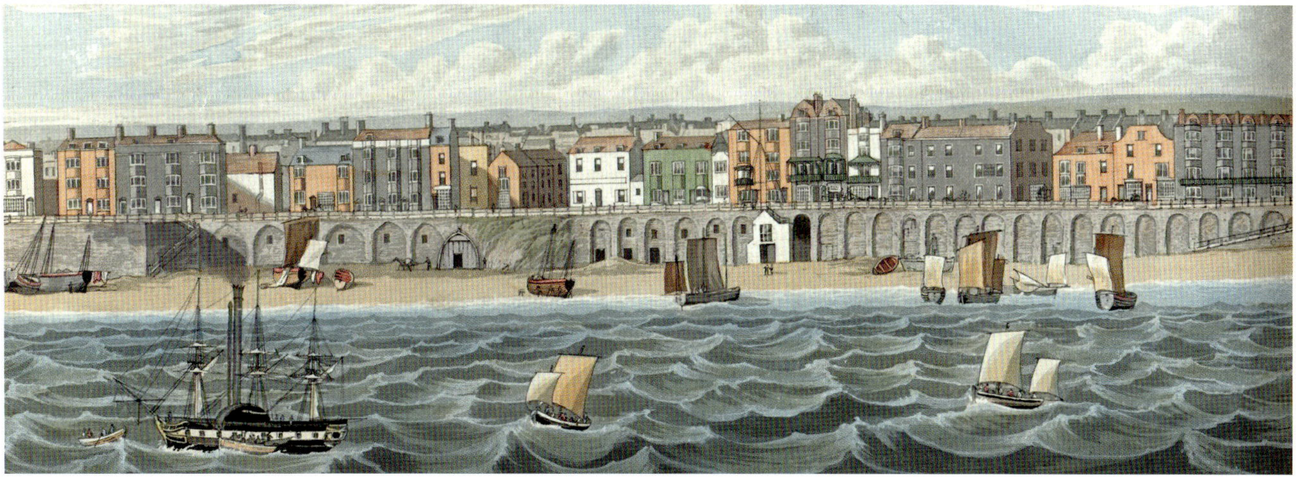

Fig. 83
Robert Havell Jr (1793–1878)
The seafront to the west of the Old Ship with the Dieppe Packet, from *A Coasting View of Brighton, the drawing taken from nature*
1824
Hand-coloured aquatint on paper, 11 × 320 cm
Private collection

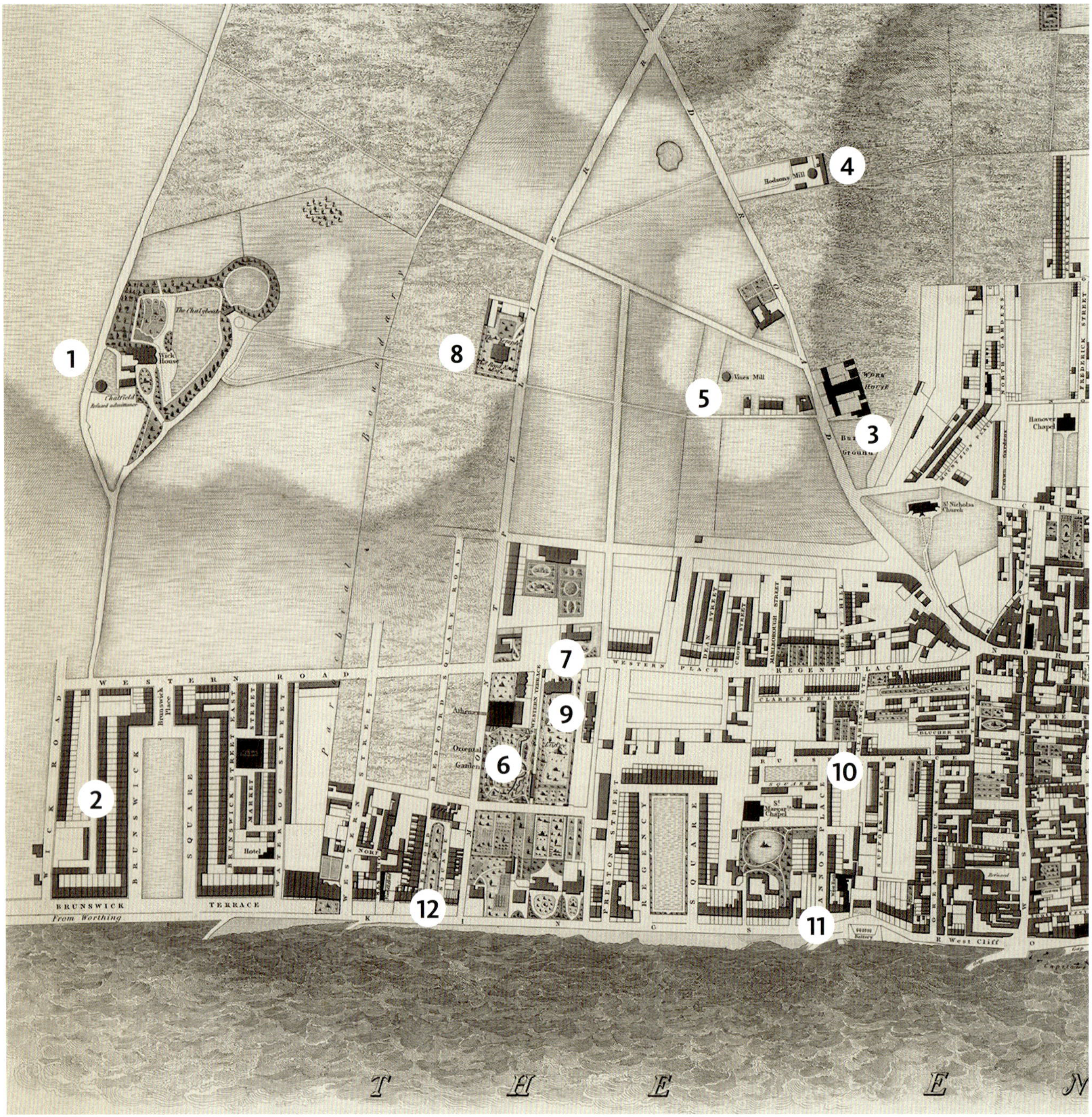

Detail of fig 79 showing Constable's lodgings and other West Brighton and Hove features.

that the family as a whole would not return to the coast that year. In 1827, the year in which *Chain Pier, Brighton* was exhibited, the family did not have a Brighton holiday, and we have no evidence of visits to the resort by the artist.

Between May and late July 1828 the family were in back in lodgings in Brighton, but no address has been found on correspondence from that period. Because the Constables made a point of sending new address details when they moved, the presumption is that they stayed at lodgings they had rented before. Maria was now very ill, with a new-born baby to care for as well, and Sober's Gardens may have been chosen because it had previously proved satisfactory, and its familiarity would have been comforting for her.[18]

As far as we know, Constable painted only two of the houses in the resort and did so from 9 Sober's Gardens, where he could see them on the west side of the house. There he produced

1. Chalybeate
2. Brunswick Town
3. Workhouse
4. Hodsons Mill
5. Vines Mill
6. Oriental Gardens
7. Mrs Sober's Villa
8. Kemp's Villa
9. Sober's Gardens
10. Russell Place
11. Cannon Street
12. Bedford Square

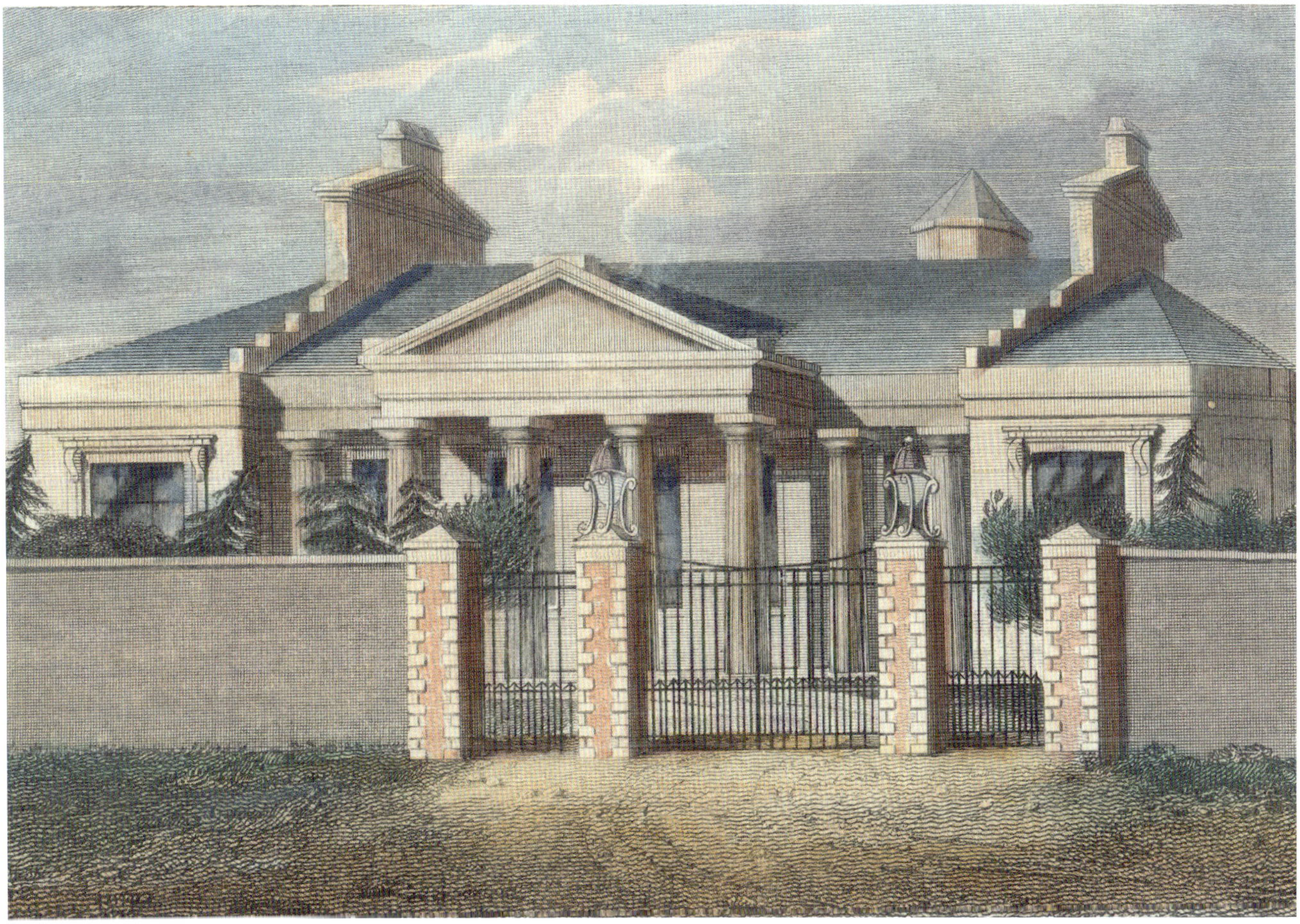

Fig. 84
UNKNOWN ARTIST and ENGRAVER
Hampton Villa (home of Laud Fauntleroy)
c.1825
Engraving
Private collection

a small oil painting of the south side of Mrs Sober's villa (now demolished), with the Gothic villa just to the west of it in the background (see fig. 1). That building still stands, on the junction of Western Terrace and Western Road. He was not swayed by the notoriety of the occupiers of some of the houses. For example, to the north of Sober's Gardens stood Hampton Villa, which became the subject of prints and a lot of press coverage owing to the fraudulent activities of the owner, Henry Fauntleroy (fig. 84 and see pp. 16 and 17).[19]

According to Peter Harrap, who researched the pictures and their dates and locations, Constable explored the resort through a series of walks, each of which he followed three times on foot. These provide the structure for the rest of this chapter. With each successive stay in Brighton, Constable returned to the spot in each excursion where he had left off on his previous visit, painting onwards in the chosen direction of the walk.

His main interest was the coastline, not the urban area. During his first short break in Brighton in 1824, between 8 and 14 June, he wandered from the Battery along to Regency Square. He returned to Brighton in mid-July (for a three-month stay, his longest spell in Brighton) and began exploring the area around the Chalybeate Wells at Wick (now St Ann's Well Gardens) as well as going back to the seafront around West Cliff, making studies of boats on the shore, and continued along Hove and Southwick beach until he could just see Shoreham harbour. He produced a distinctive cluster of pictures of the view west, using the changing weather as his theme.

Constable subsequently explored Hove and the west side of Brighton extensively between

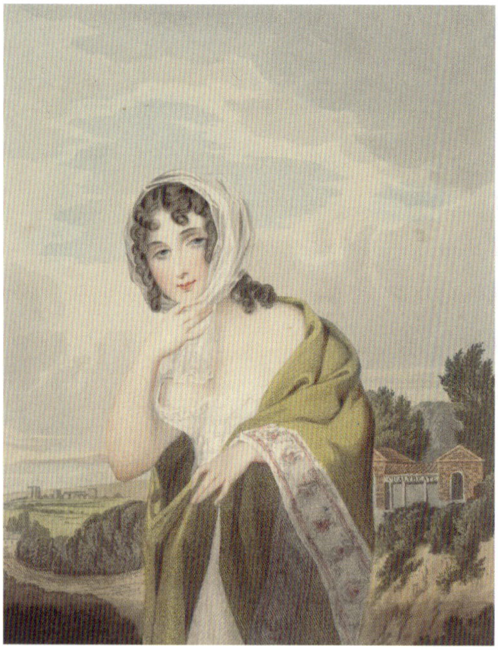

Fig. 85
Thomas Harper (d. 1843) and engraved by A. M. Huffman
Beauty of Brighton: Hove Chalybeate
c.1829
Mezzotint
Private collection

1824 and 1828, working first on a rectangular format for three paintings and then a panoramic series for the next three. It is most likely that he drew Old Shoreham Church and Shoreham Bay on 22 May 1828, just before ending the final family visit to Brighton (see fig. 107).[20]

The Downland north of Brighton became another subject for repeated exploration and interpretation. On 3 August 1824, for example, he was up at Hodson's Windmill (see fig. 113), one of a series of windmills that studded the slopes of the Downs. Their presence was a reminder of the importance of grain locally as a key cash crop and as a major source of food, especially bread, for the many working people who kept the resort functioning. As the son of a miller and grain merchant, he was on familiar ground here.

Constable's third series of walks was east along the seafront towards the Chain Pier. The contrast between his work looking east at Brighton with that looking west to Hove shows in this selection of paintings and sketches. And in many of them the tourist appears, possibly in response to that commission for charming studies of seaside scenes from Arrowsmith (see Ch. 3).

Notes on the back of his paintings suggest that a quick oil sketch might take him two hours, and in general the distance between the sketches was often small – a change of view or a rotation round a capstan, boat or windmill was sufficient to generate a new painting. Constable stated at the time that his overall intention was to create 'freshness and sparkle – with repose'.[21]

Peter Harrap notes that Constable set up his painting box on his knees, pinning prepared surfaces to the lid, using rough paper, canvas or millboard and thus 'painting from the lid of his box'. This portable painting box contained bladders of pigment and brushes, rags and a palette knife, along with a variety of strengthened laminated papers which were prepared with a range of coloured backgrounds which ranged from blue to brown and warm ochres. These were selected as appropriate to the subject he was observing, without any correlation to the time of day. The background colours contributed to the effect in the sky where they were allowed to grin though, suffusing the whole painting. Once the paintings were 'touch dry', he would stack them away in the painting box and head back home.

Fig. 86
J. Rouse (active c.1810–1830)
Hove, Chalybeate Spa
c.1823
Print
Private collection

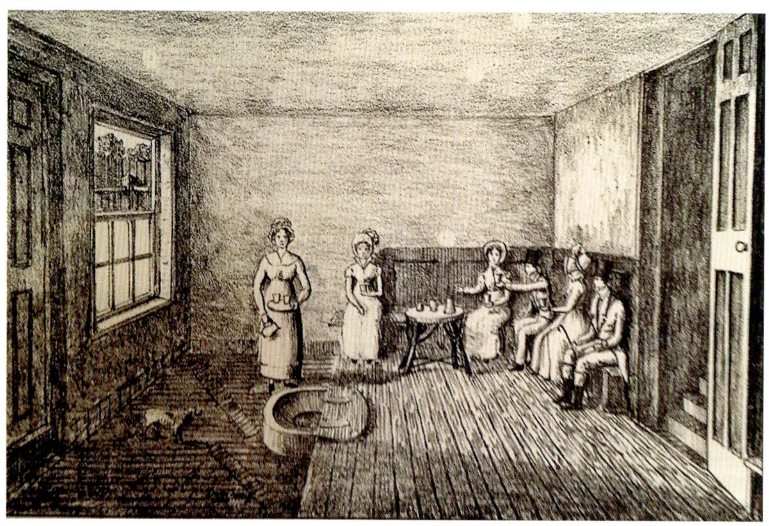

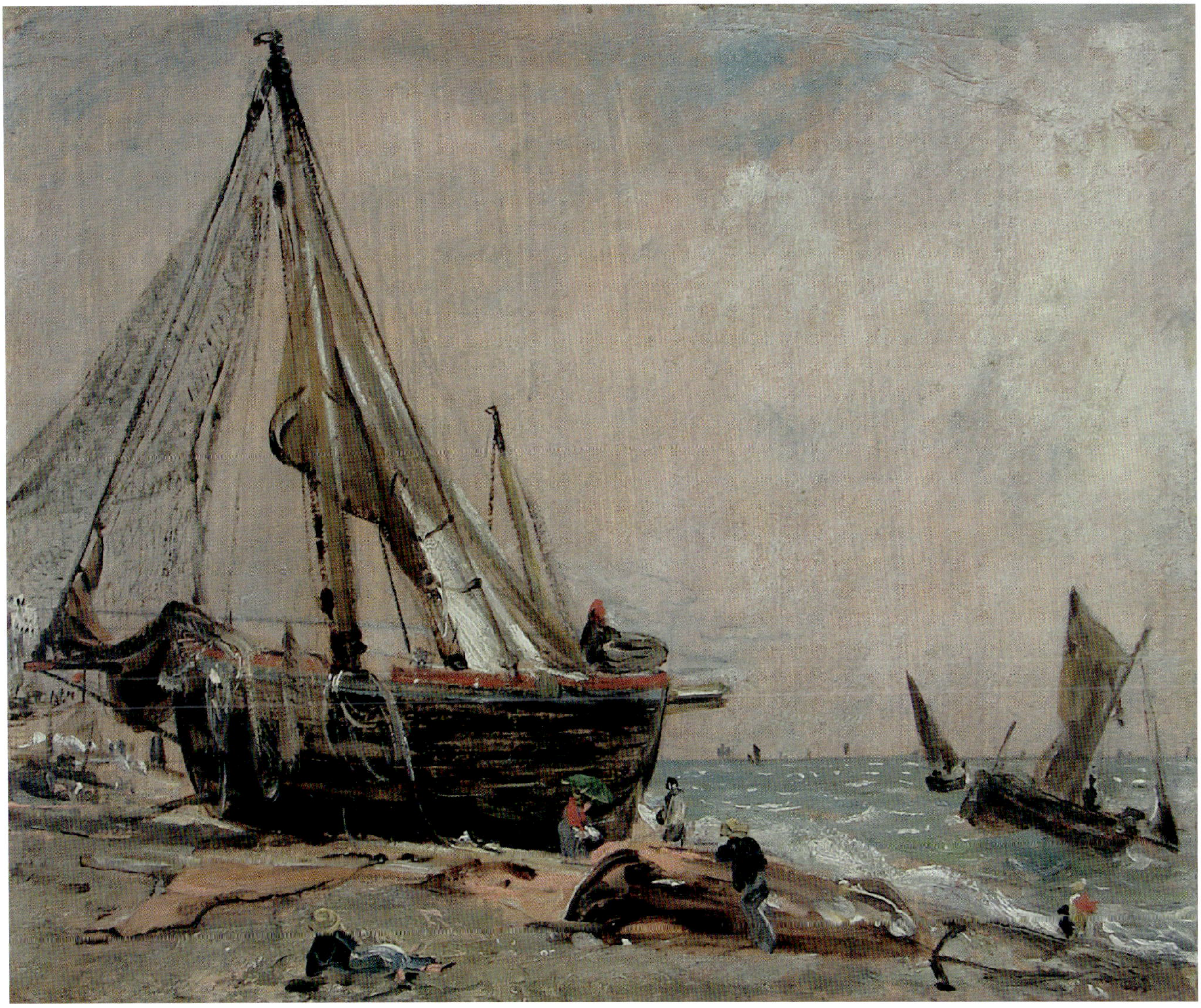

1. Hove and Brighton West End

'nothing here for a painter but the breakers – & the sky' [22]

Fig. 87
Brighton Beach
c.1824–26
Oil on paper laid on canvas,
23.8 × 29.3 cm
R.24.63
Dunedin Public Art Gallery

From his first foray along the coast of western Brighton and on into Hove, Constable started to paint fishing craft, despite complaining in his famous letter of August 1824 (see pp. 8–9) that they were not very interesting. In his first painting (fig. 87) he just hints at the western end of the buildings of Brighton on the left of the picture, and sketchily shows one of the ramps up the shallow cliff. Two ladies with parasols – one green one just in front of the hog boat and another on the beach – and someone sitting on the beach in the foreground remind us of the visitors. But the emphasis is very much on the local fishing boats – how they sat on the beach and looked as they sailed out.

In another sketch (fig. 88), as the crew beach one of these small inshore fishing vessels, furling the sails and pulling on the ropes attached to the prow, they are watched by a well-dressed observer, wearing a hat, a blue jacket and light-

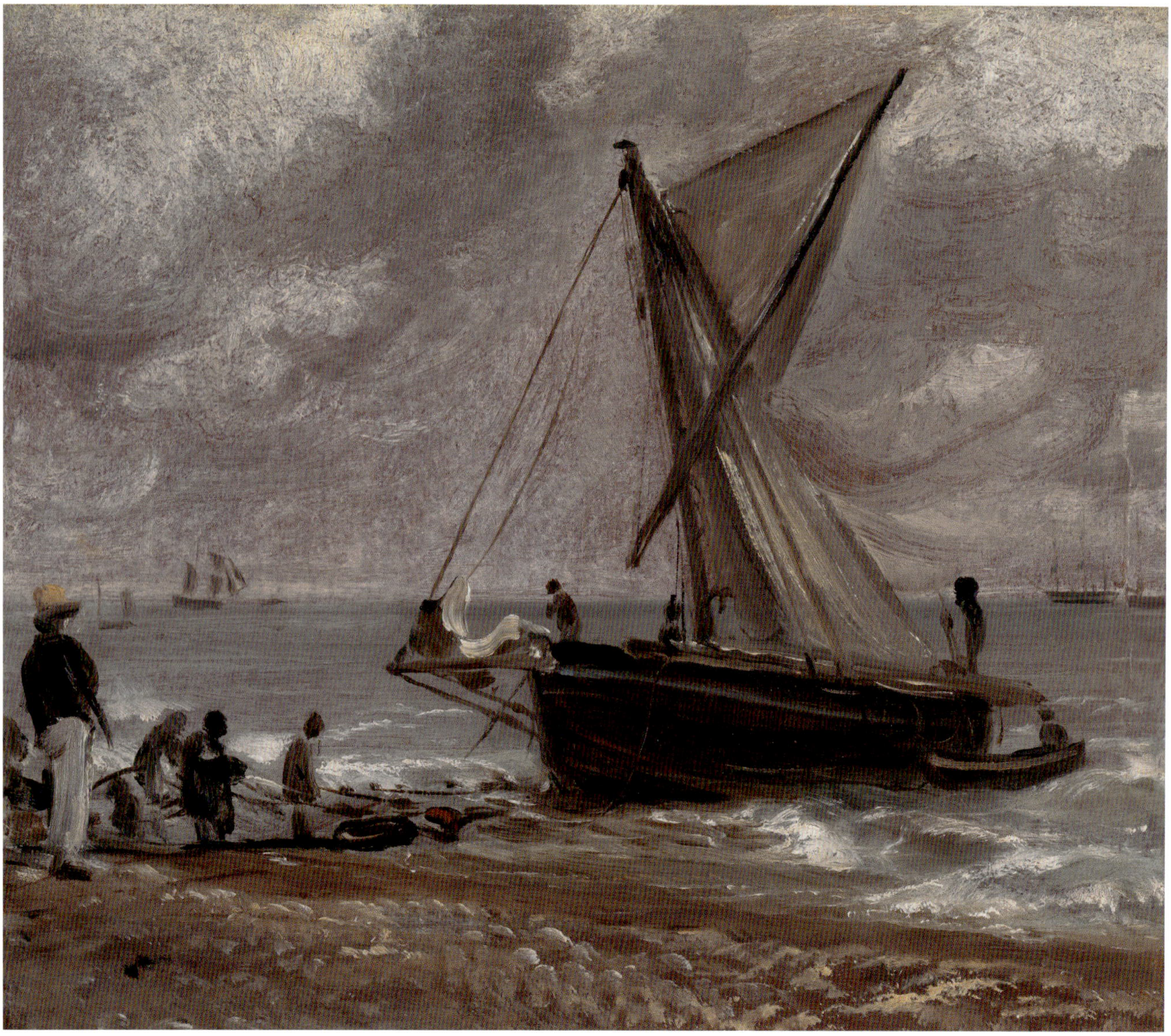

coloured trousers. This figure has sometimes been identified as one of the customs officials who regularly patrolled the beach. Selecting almost the same position, but facing west, Constable sketched a vessel on the beach, its crew occupied with the sails (fig. 89). Is it the same vessel from the other side, but without the observer perhaps?

Peter Harrap comments on fig. 89 that a new development in the Brighton period is the use of some underdrawing in pencil to firm up the forms before committing paint to the surface. It does not seem unreasonable to suggest a fine pen nib dipped into the liquid paint or shellac was utilised in the straighter lines of the rigging.

Fig. 88
Beaching a Boat
1824
Oil on paper laid on canvas, 25 × 30 cm
R.24.64
Private collection

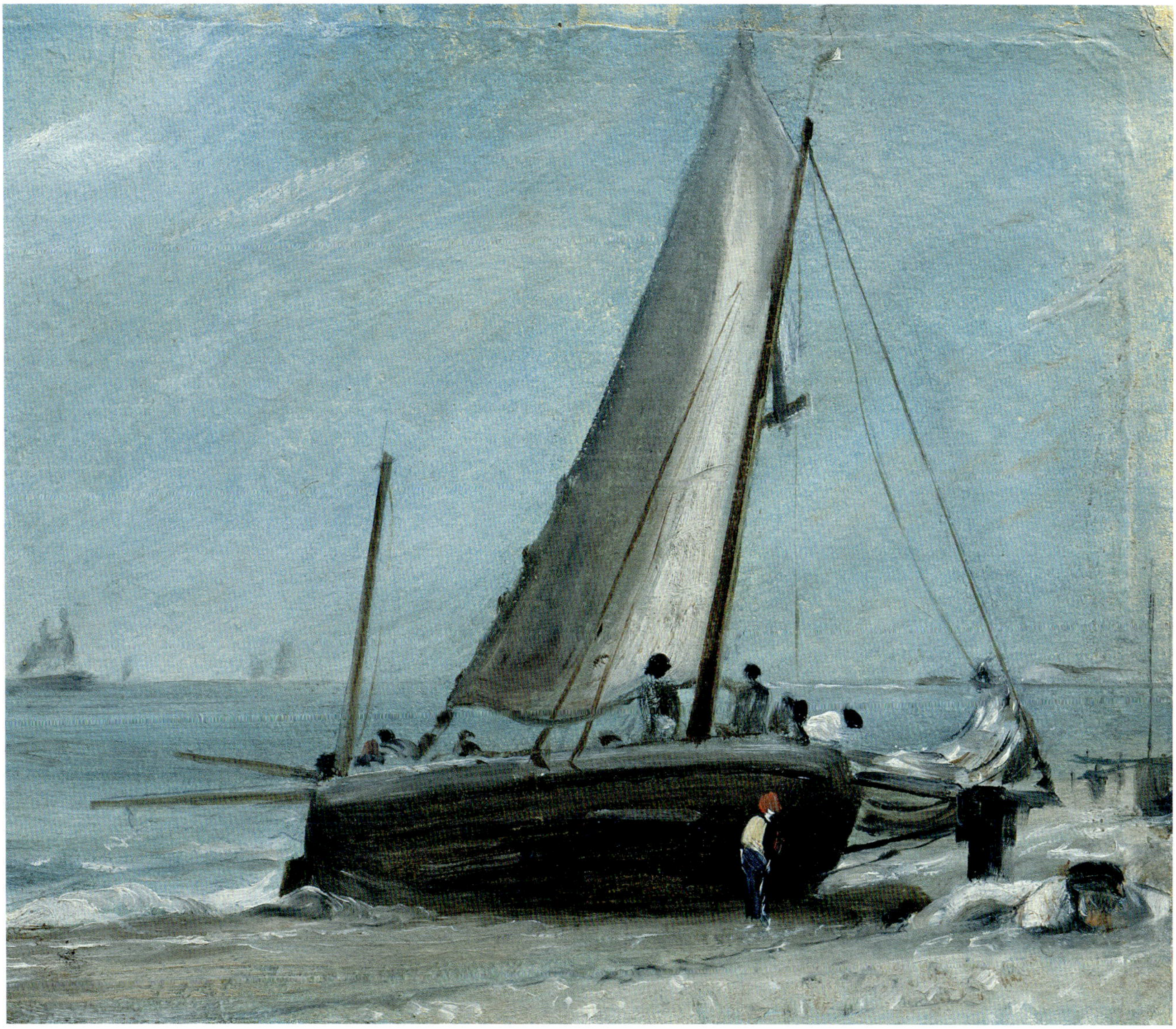

Fig. 89
Brighton Beach with a Fishing Boat and Crew
10 June 1824
Oil on paper,
24.4 × 29.8 cm
R.24.8
Victoria and Albert Museum, London

Constable was more adventurous with adding visitors in *Brighton Beach with Shipping and a Gig* (fig. 90), in which the gig is very lightly painted. He and Turner both thought this use of horses on the difficult terrain of a shingle beach like Brighton's interesting (see also fig. 52), and here again is a possible visual note for a subject to be worked up later or inserted into a more developed scene. Two ladies walking on the beach enliven another oil, again called *Brighton Beach* (fig. 91), which evokes the shallow-shelving shore of the beach at Hove, as does a further view looking westwards at noon (fig. 92), while Constable rotates to paint the view east in the evening (see fig. 93).

Fig. 90
Brighton Beach with Shipping and a Gig
June 1824
Oil on paper laid on board, 12.4 × 28.6 cm
R.24.79A
Private collection

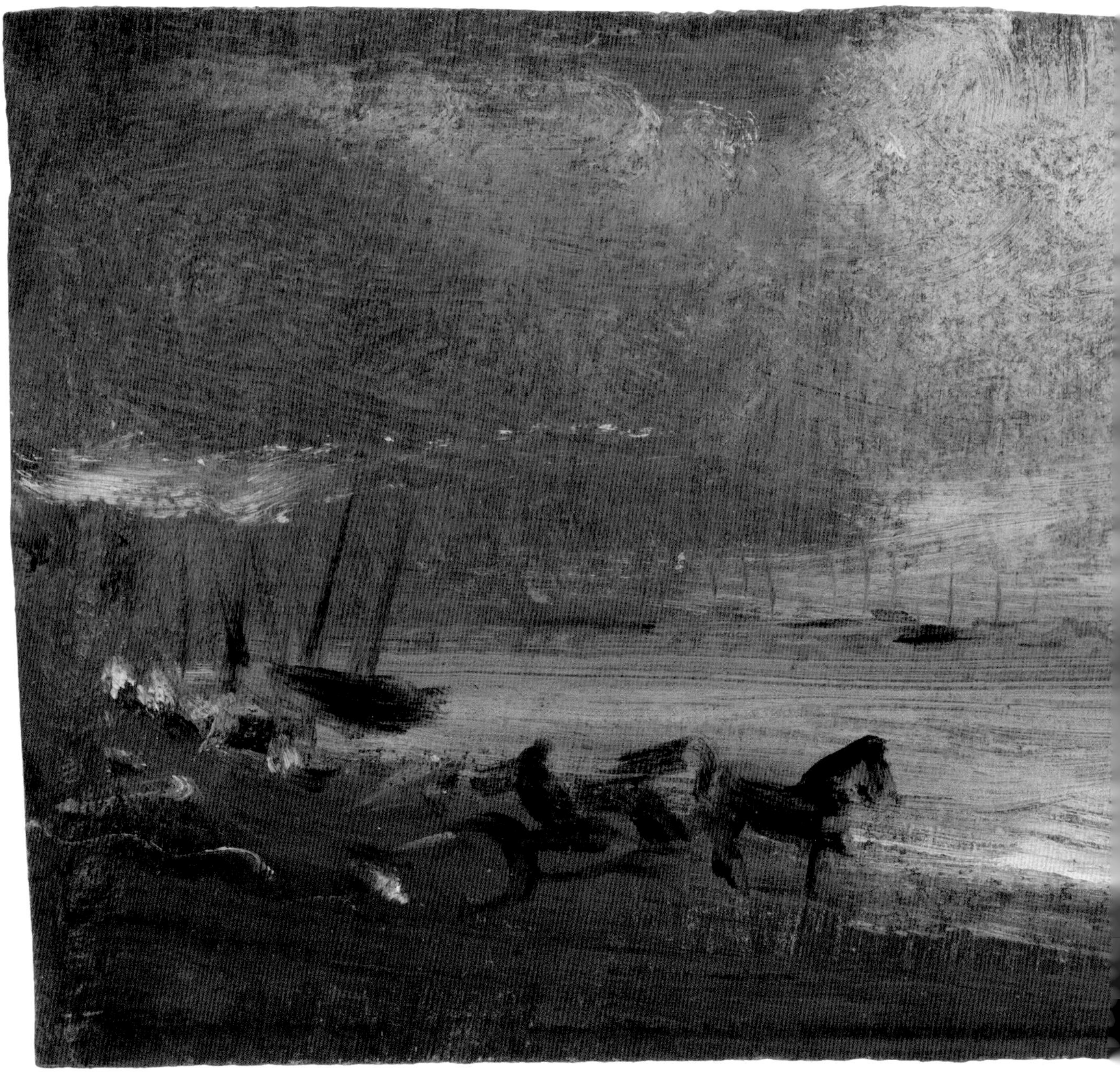

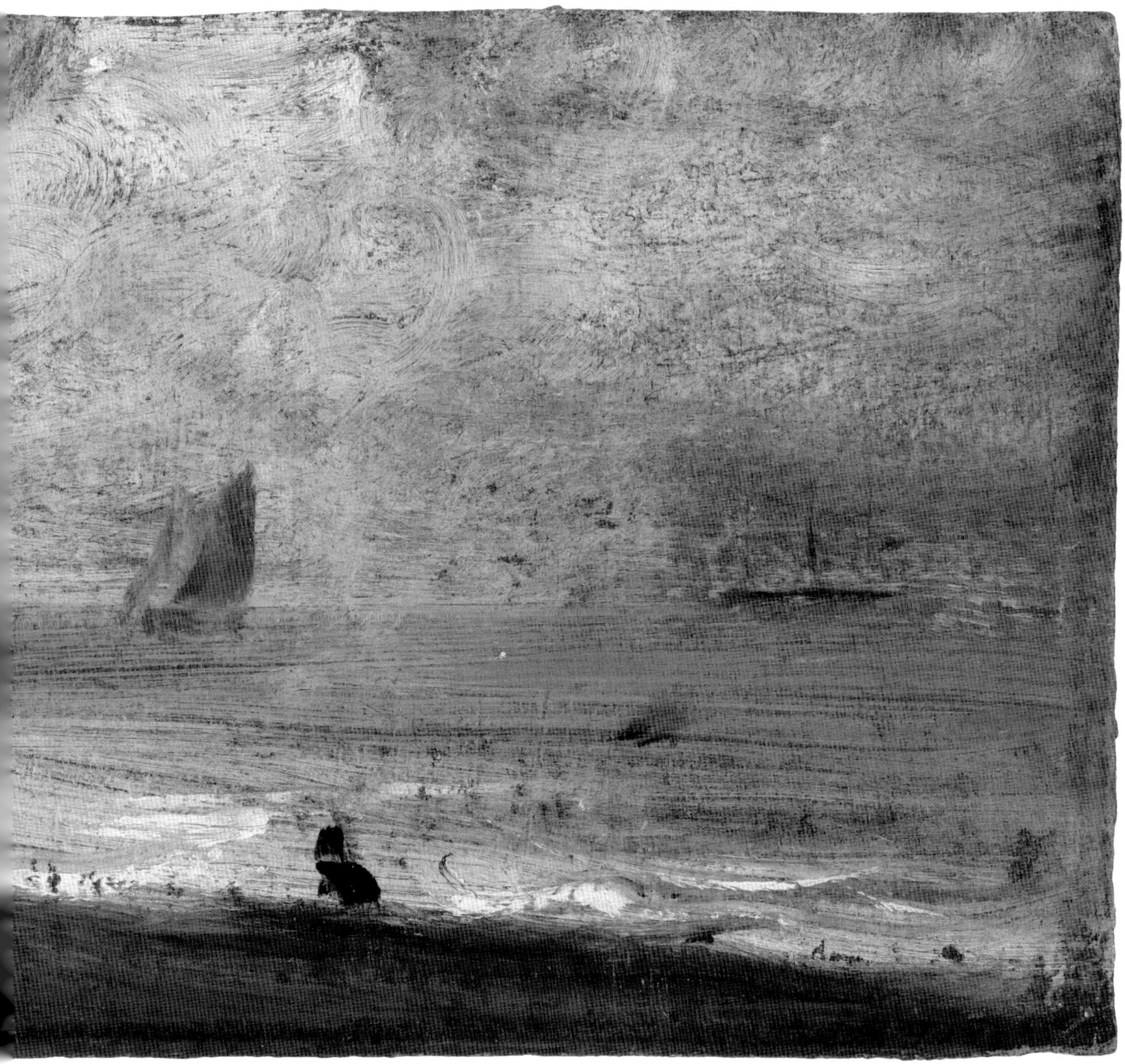

Fig. 91
Brighton Beach
12 June 1824
Oil on paper, 12 × 29.7 cm
R.24.9
Victoria and Albert Museum, London

Fig. 92
Brighton Beach
19 July 1824
Oil on paper, 13.6 × 30.2 cm
R.24.10
Victoria and Albert Museum, London

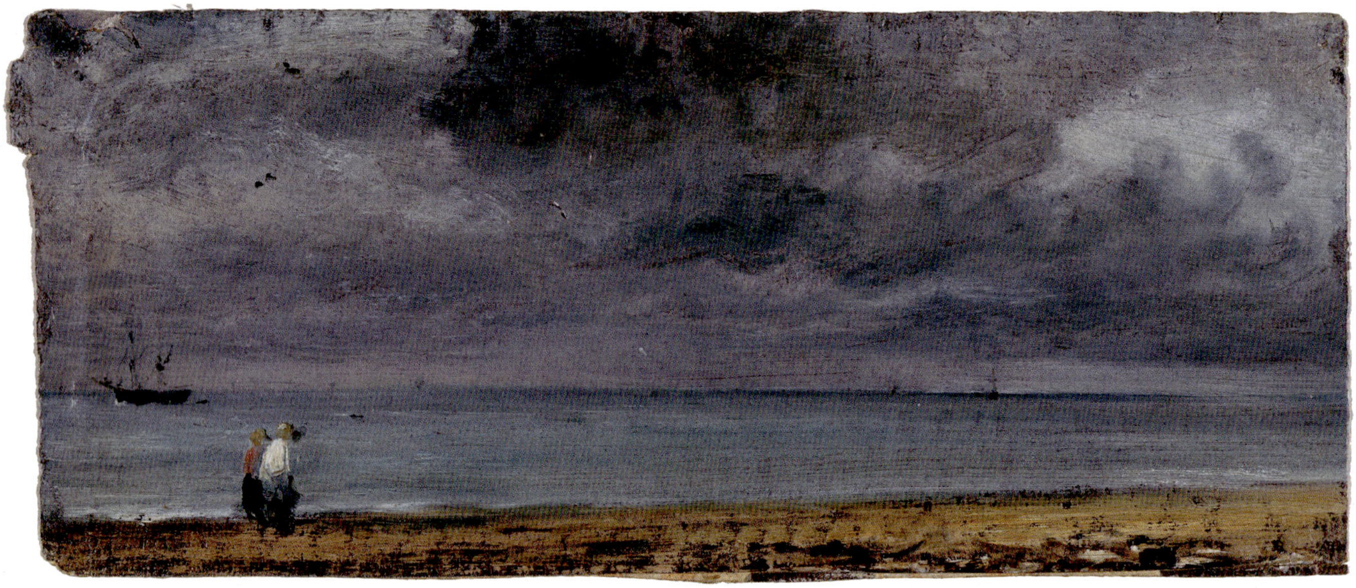

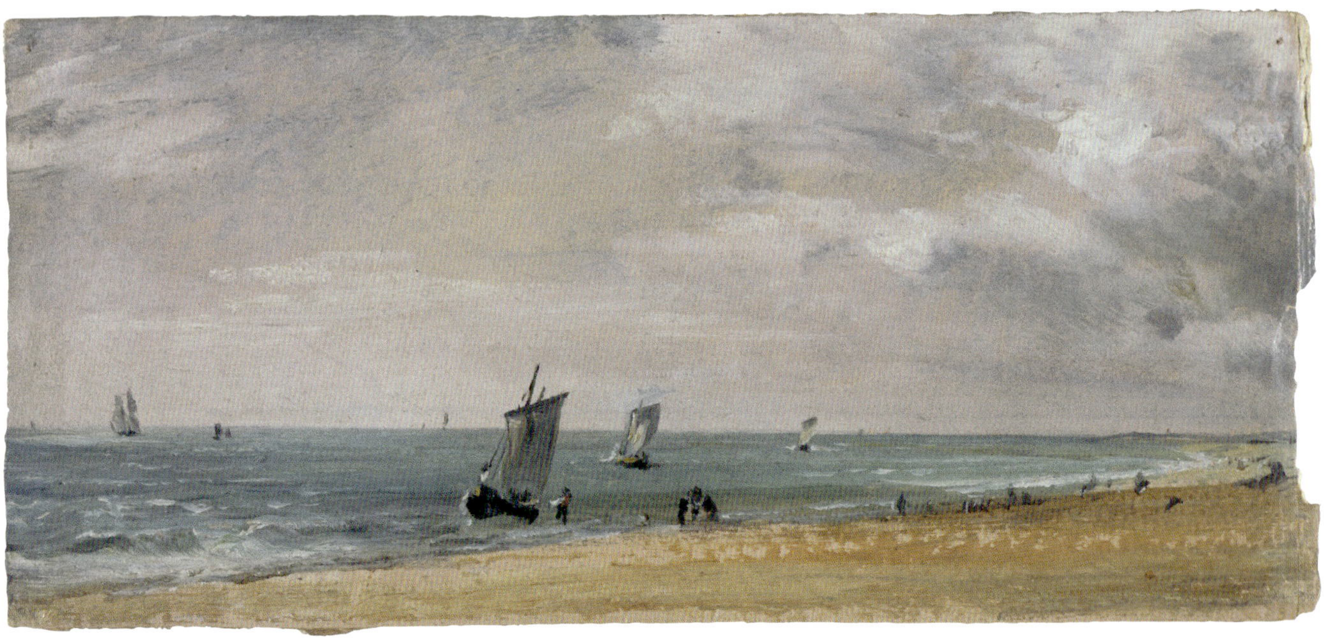

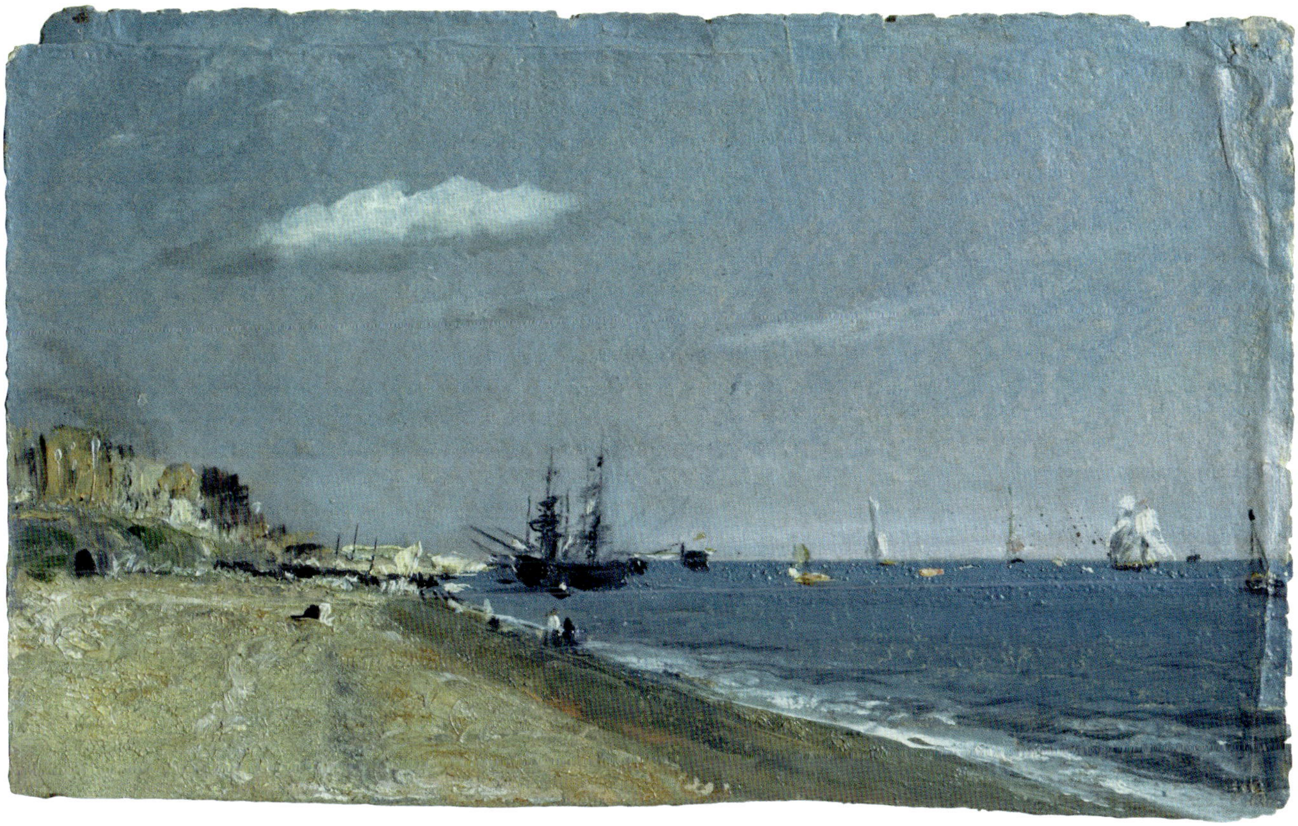

Fig. 93
Brighton Beach, with Colliers
19 July 1824
Oil on paper,
14.9 × 24.8 cm
R.24.11
Victoria and Albert Museum, London

Constable's views gave the impression that the coastline stretched without seafront buildings from Hove to Shoreham. In some of the series the horizon is defined by the promontory and hills of Worthing, which mark the west end of the bay (fig. 96). Sketching the low-lying land of the coastal fringes of Hove, Aldrington and Shoreham also enabled him to concentrate on the sea and sky, experimenting at the same time with colour effects (figs 94, 95, 97, 100, 102 and 104), and the exposed location gave him good views of storms coming up the Channel. At this date the crumbly coast lacked wooden groynes (sea defences) to reduce erosion, and this added to the sense of an undeveloped area. However, Constable did include the brick kilns used to manufacture honey-coloured and red bricks from the local earth (figs 96, 97). These sketches contrast with Constable's views from the west side of Brighton, such as Shoreham Bay on 22 May 1828 (fig. 107).

Peter Harrap notes that here Constable, like Gainsborough, changed his ground colour largely to suit the qualities of his subject. It was during the walk to Shoreham that this highly innovative approach of choosing a coloured ground to correspond to the subject was developed to its full potential; it was abandoned as a working method after 1829.

On 20 July 1824 Constable painted close to Chalybeate, in Hove, where his wife, Maria, had been advised to try the spring water in the hope that its natural properties might help to restore her fragile health. With its open views westwards over the fields and meadows, the Chalybeate was considered by the *Brighton*

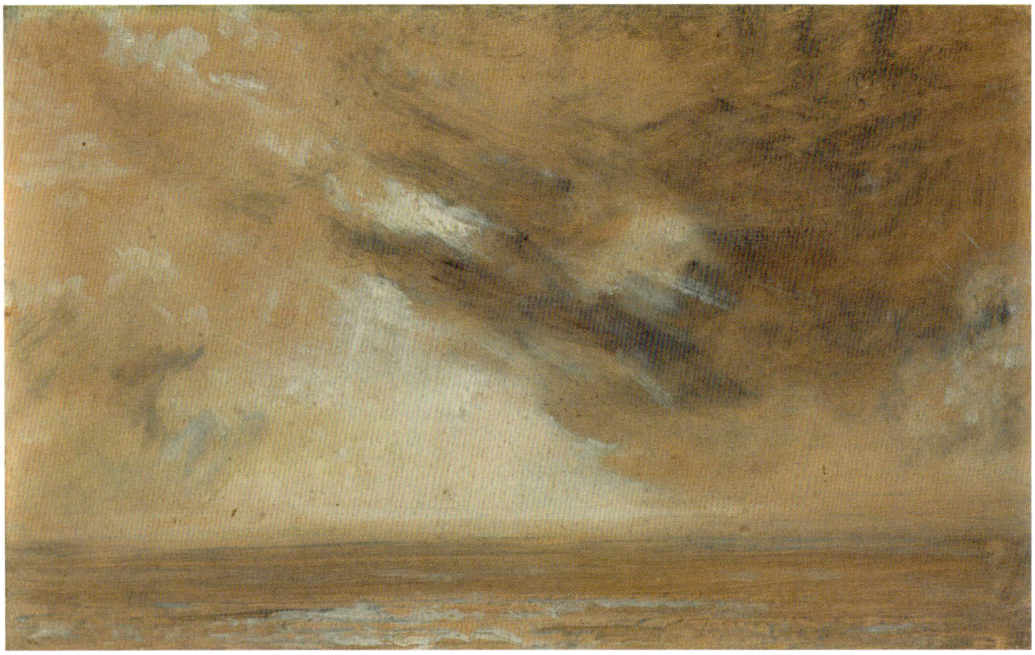

LEFT
Fig. 94
Storm Clouds over the Sea at Brighton
20 July 1824
Oil on paper,
22.2 × 38.1 cm
R.24.13
Dublin City Gallery
The Hugh Lane

BELOW
Fig. 95
Rainstorm over the Sea
c.1824–28
Oil on paper laid on canvas,
23.5 × 32.6 cm
R.24.67
Royal Academy of Arts,
London

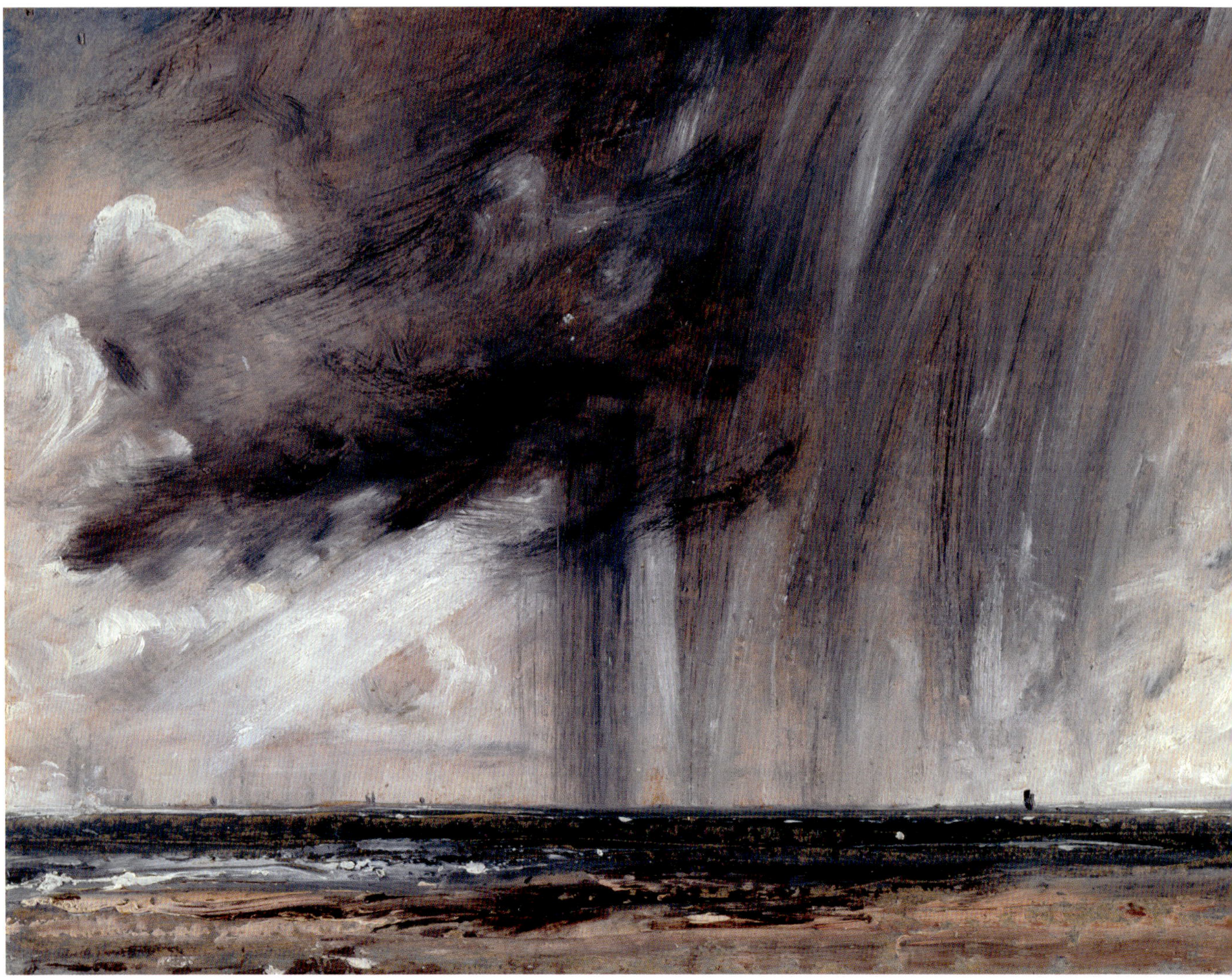

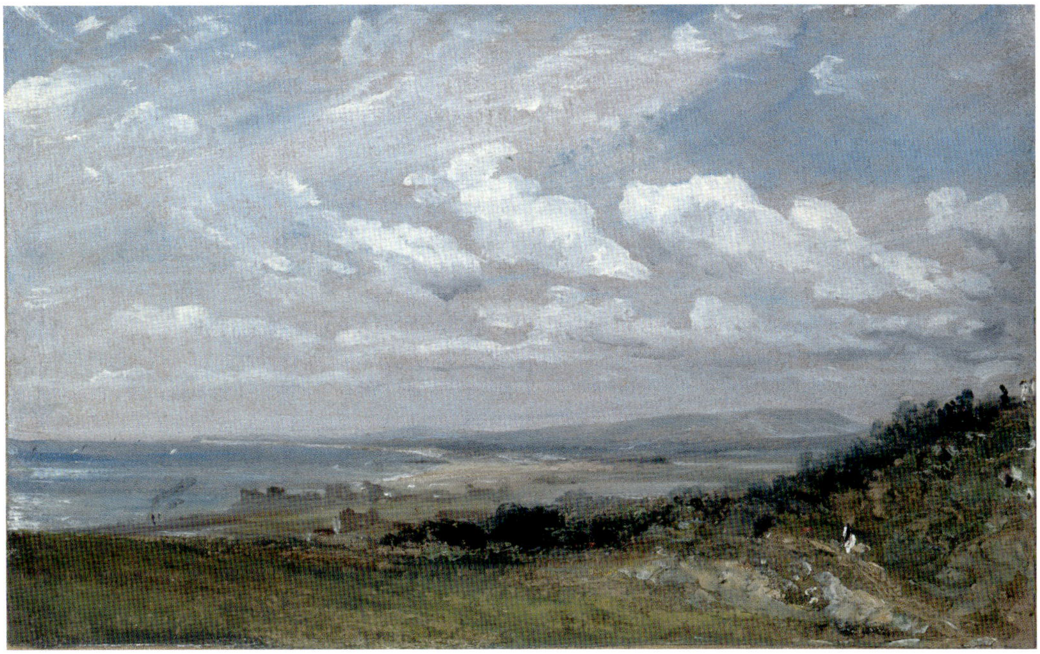

Fig. 96
Shoreham Bay: The Walk to the Chalybeate Wells
Tuesday 20 July 1824
Oil on paper laid on canvas, 14.9 × 24.9 cm
R.24.12
Fitzwilliam Museum, Cambridge

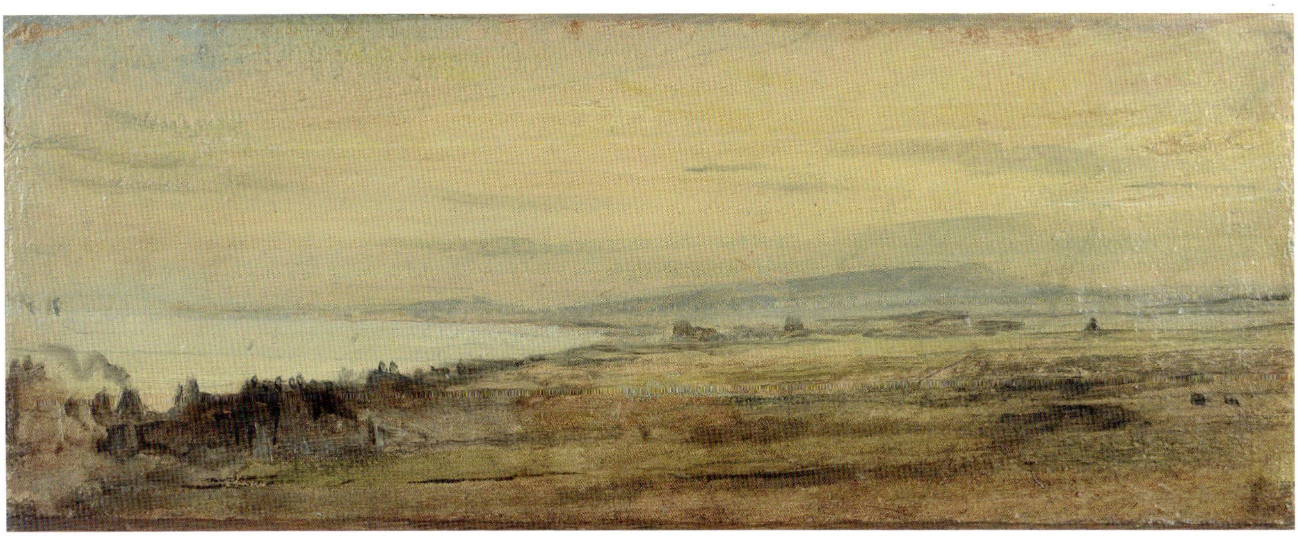

Fig. 97
Brighton (Looking towards Shoreham)
n.d.
Oil on paper laid on canvas, 11 × 29.8 cm
R.24.16
Norwich Castle Museum & Art Gallery

Gazette in June 1824 'one of the most pleasant and rural situations in the vicinity of Brighton'. Situated on the rising ground north of Brunswick Town, it lay within what is now St Ann's Well Gardens, where its spring flows through a capping of a type of ironstone, and surfaces even today as ferruginous waters, staining the little stream flowing from it a rusty colour (fig. 85). In *Shoreham Bay: The Walk to the Chalybeate Wells* (fig. 96) he does include the gorse (locally called furze) along the south side of the hill; now appropriately called Furze Hill. The Chalybeate spa building stood just to the north of this view (fig. 86). Again Constable records the brick kilns on the coast and the tiny village of Hove in the distance, close to the coast, hinting to the right at the presence of the mouth of the River Adur, where Shoreham harbour was being revived to serve Brighton as its port, a development which would remove the coal vessels from the beach.

Peter Harrap observes that, with the stormy weather fronts coming from the south-west and only very occasionally from the south-east, fig. 96 is probably part of a sequence, (figs 94–97), of a storm cloud moving over the sea front from Shoreham towards Brighton on 20 July. These

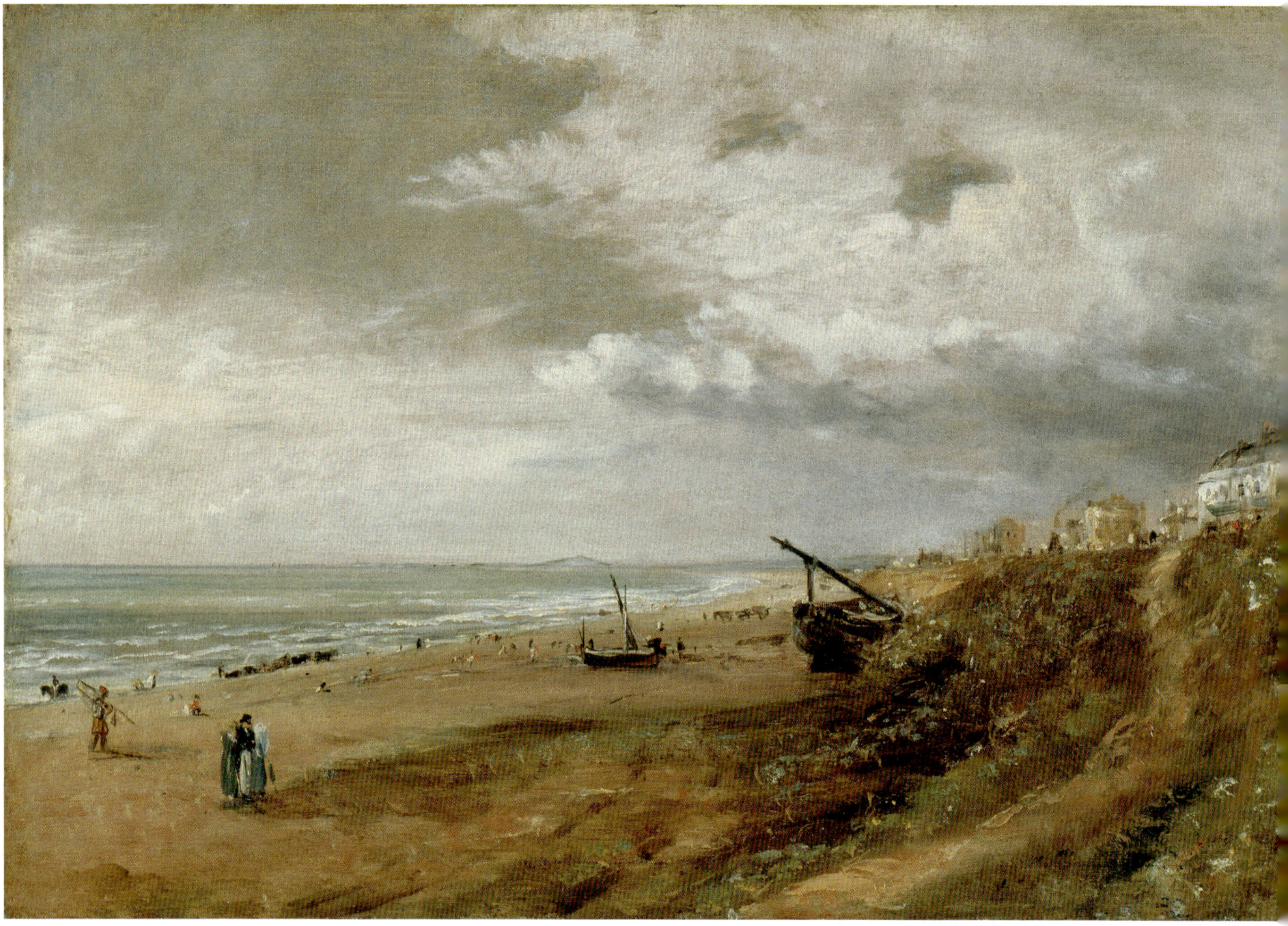

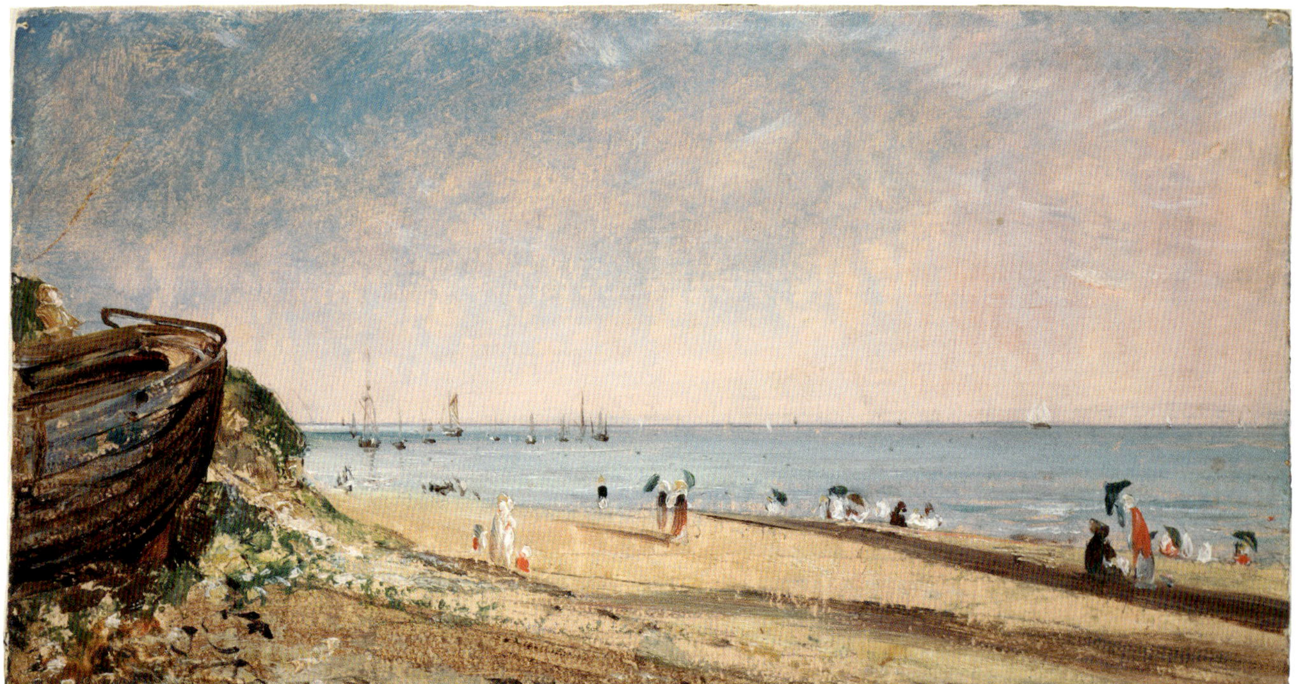

Fig. 98
Hove Beach
*c.*1824–28
Oil on canvas laid on panel, 33 × 50.8 cm
R.24.71
Fitzwilliam Museum, Cambridge

Fig. 99
Brighton Beach
22 July 1824
Oil on paper, 16.5 × 30.4 cm
R.24.14
Victoria and Albert Museum, London

Fig. 100
Coast Scene with Boat and Stormy Sky
*c.*1824–28
Oil on paper laid on board, 15.2 × 18.5 cm
R.24.66
Royal Academy of Arts, London

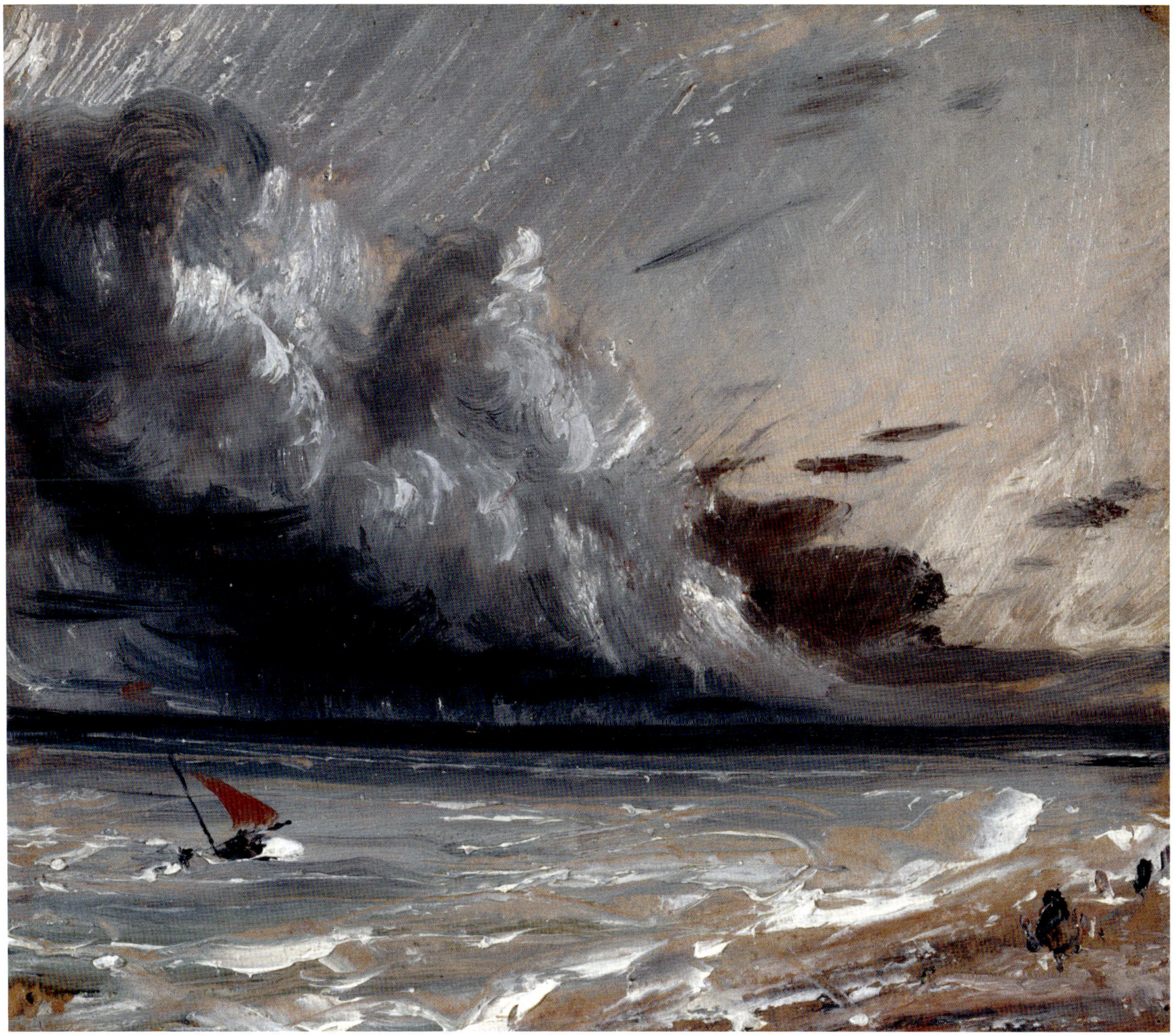

are brief, sporadic, heavy downpours that come and disappear just as quickly as the weather front moves from west to east.

During this period the parish church of Hove, though in disrepair, was still in use. Constable drew it twice in 1825 and again from the same spot in 1828 (fig. 106). Its ruinous state attracted artists and printmakers until the parish rebuilt it to the design of George Basevi in 1833–35. It is now referred to as 'Old St Andrew's', to differentiate it from the innovative and privately funded Italianate 'preaching chapel' designed by Charles Barry and built in Waterloo Street in 1828, which was given the same name, probably because the owner did not expect the old church to survive.

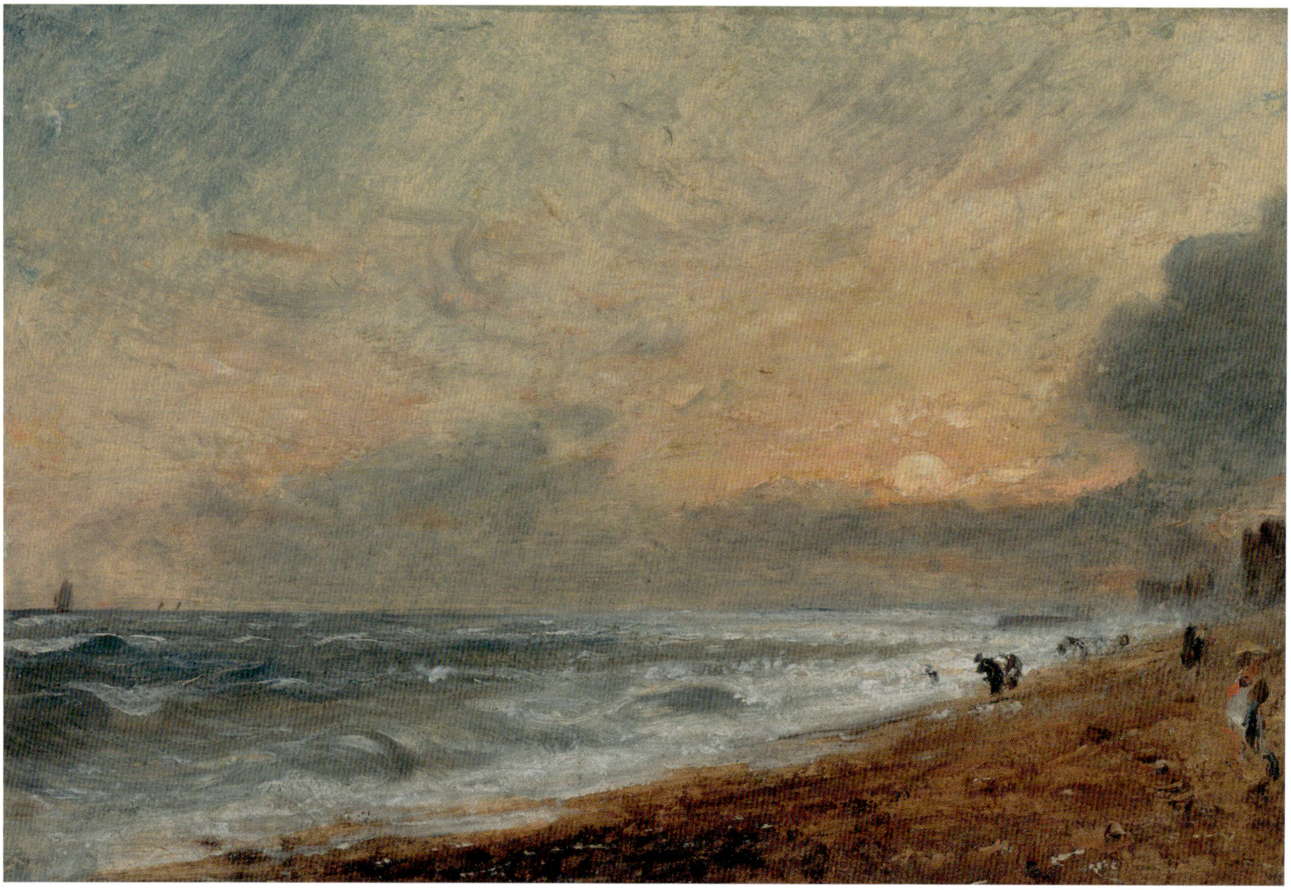

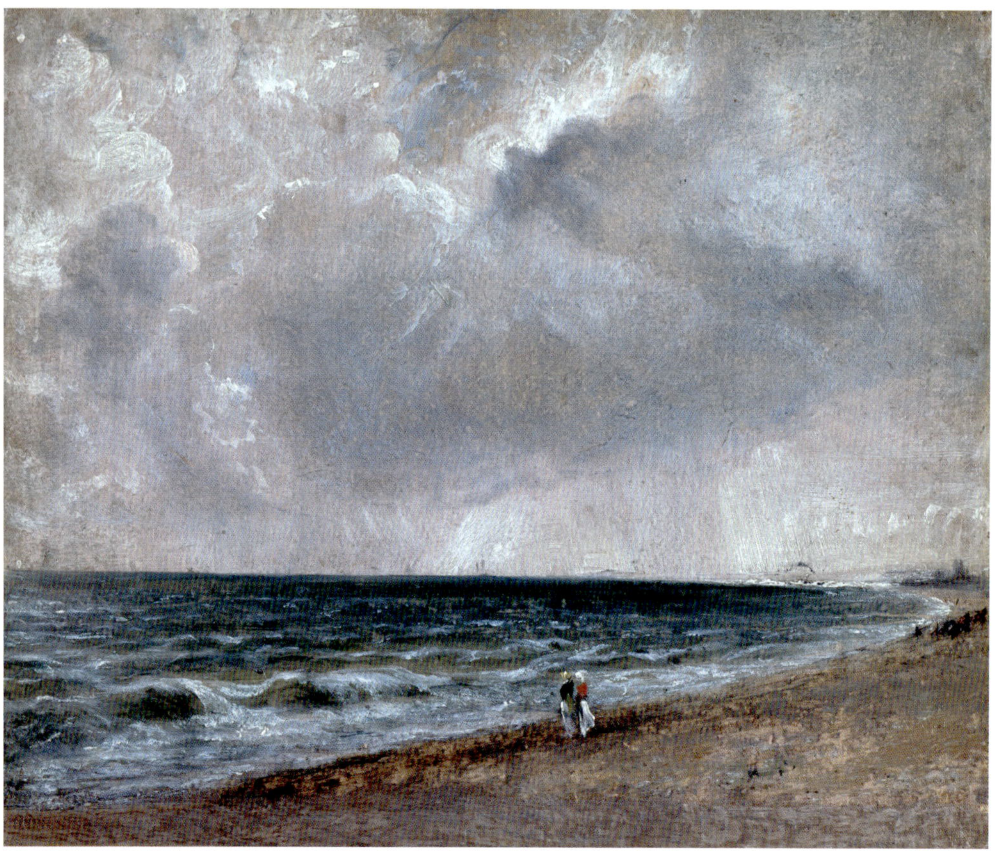

Fig. 101
Hove Beach
*c.*1824–28
Oil on paper laid on board,
23.2 × 35.9 cm
R.24.61
Yale Center for British Art,
New Haven, CT

Fig. 102
Seascape Study: Brighton Beach Looking West
*c.*1824–28
Oil on paper laid on canvas,
19.7 × 24.1 cm
R.24.65
Royal Academy of Arts,
London

Fig. 103
Hove Beach
c.1824–28
Oil on paper laid on canvas, 31.7 × 49.5 cm
R.24.60
Victoria and Albert Museum, London

Fig. 104
Hove Beach with Fishing Boats
c.1824
Oil on paper laid on canvas, 29.8 × 49.2 cm
R.24.59
Victoria and Albert Museum, London

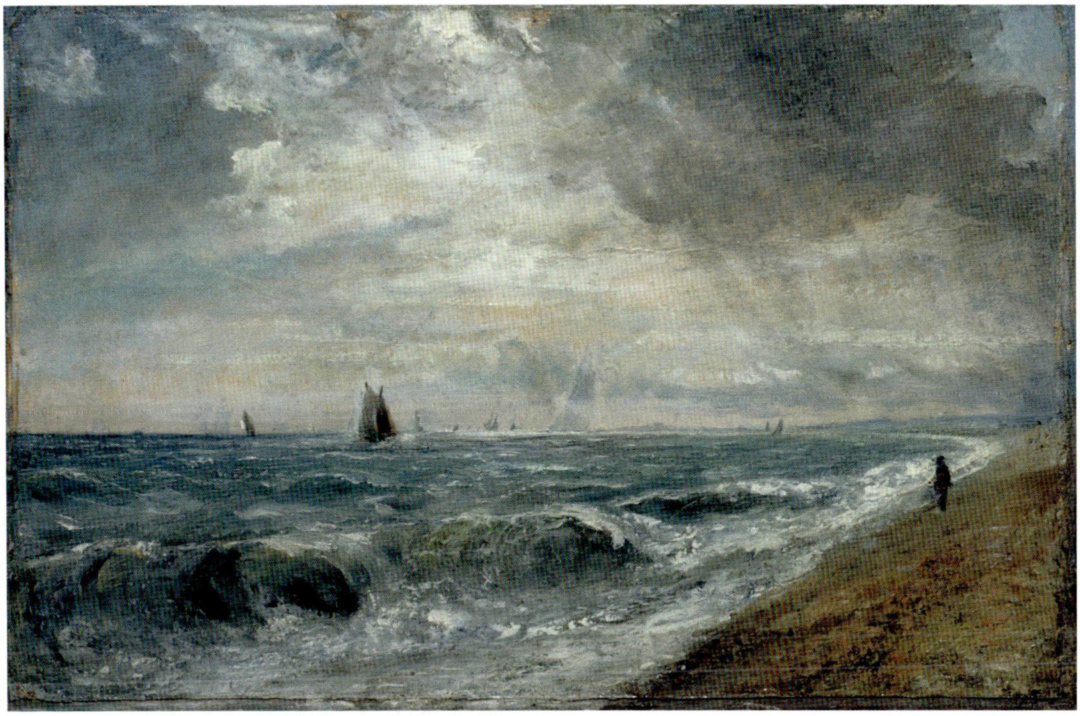

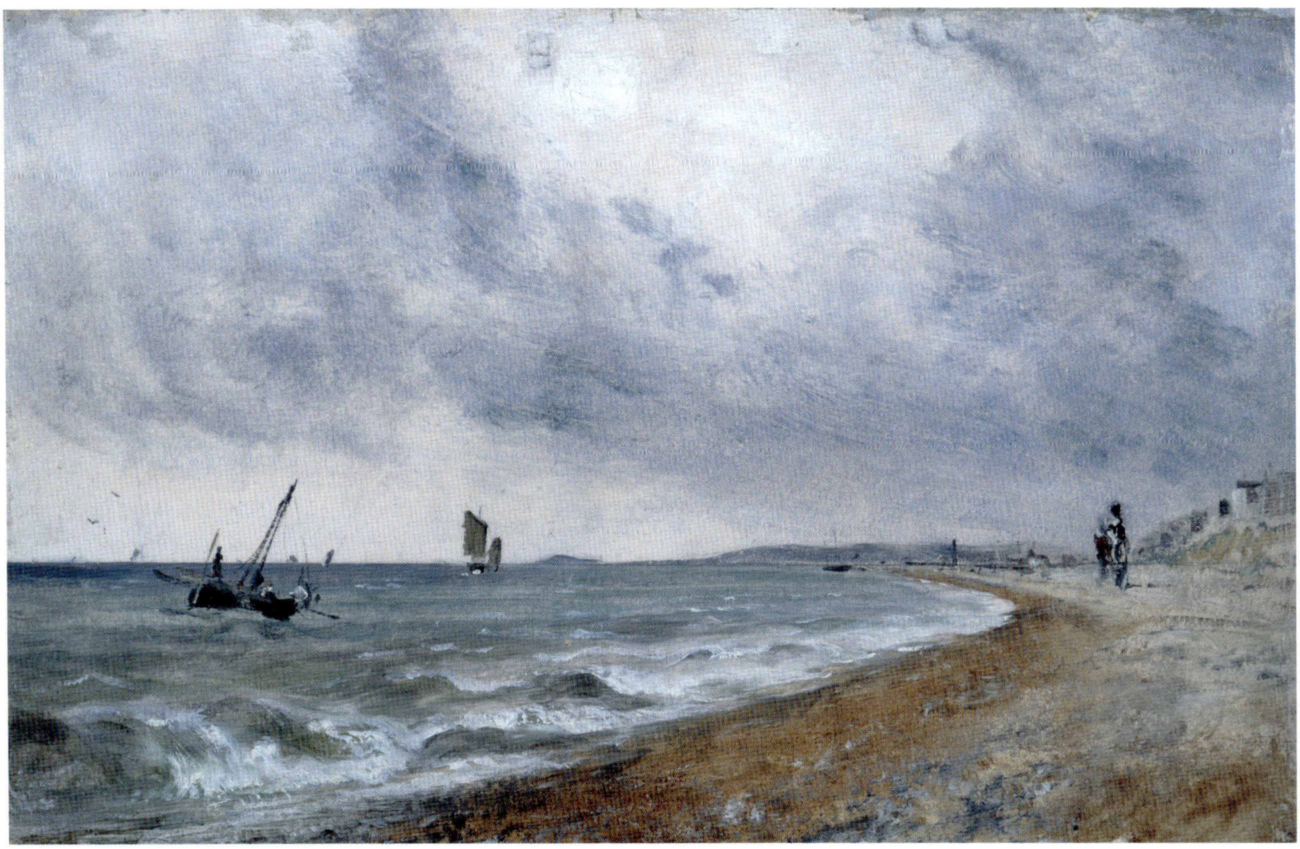

Fig. 105
Blatchington Mill, near Brighton
5 November 1825
Pen and ink on watercolour, 11.3 × 18 cm
R.25.24
Private collection

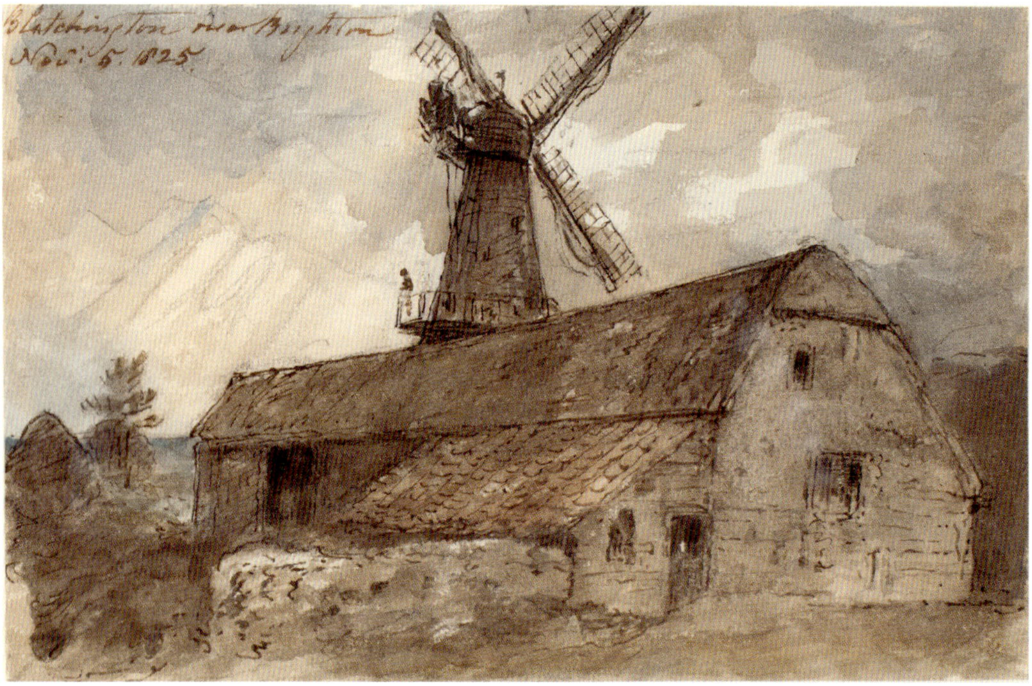

Fig. 106
The Old Parish Church, Hove
16 May 1828
Pencil, 11.5 × 18.6 cm
R.28.5
Victoria and Albert Museum, London

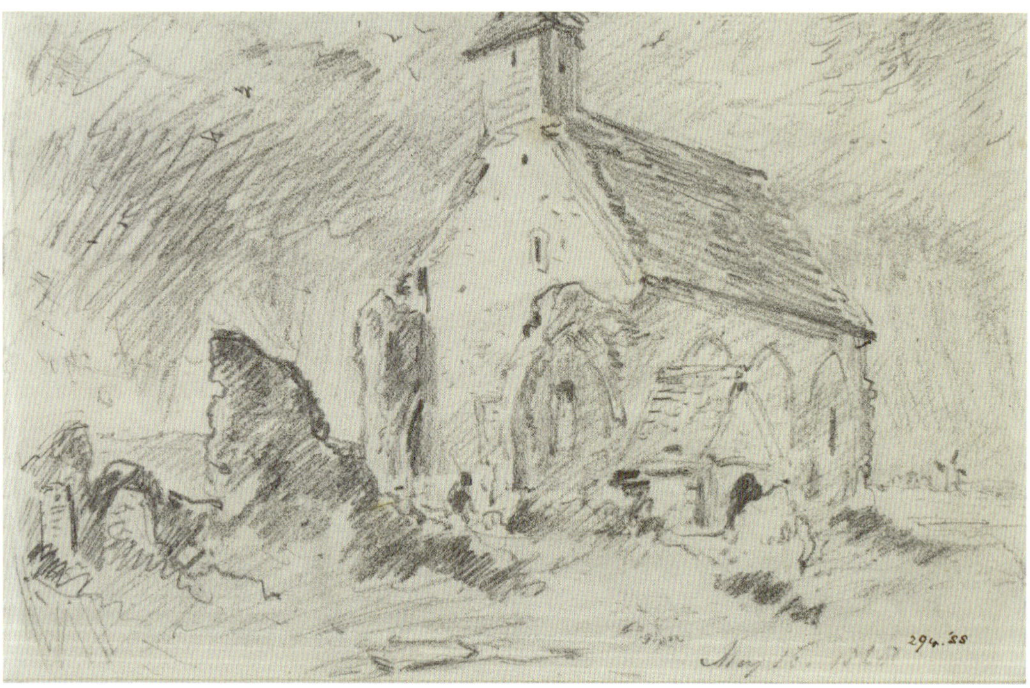

Fig. 107
Shoreham Bay
22 May 1828
Oil on paper, 20 × 24.8 cm
R.28.7
Victoria and Albert Museum, London

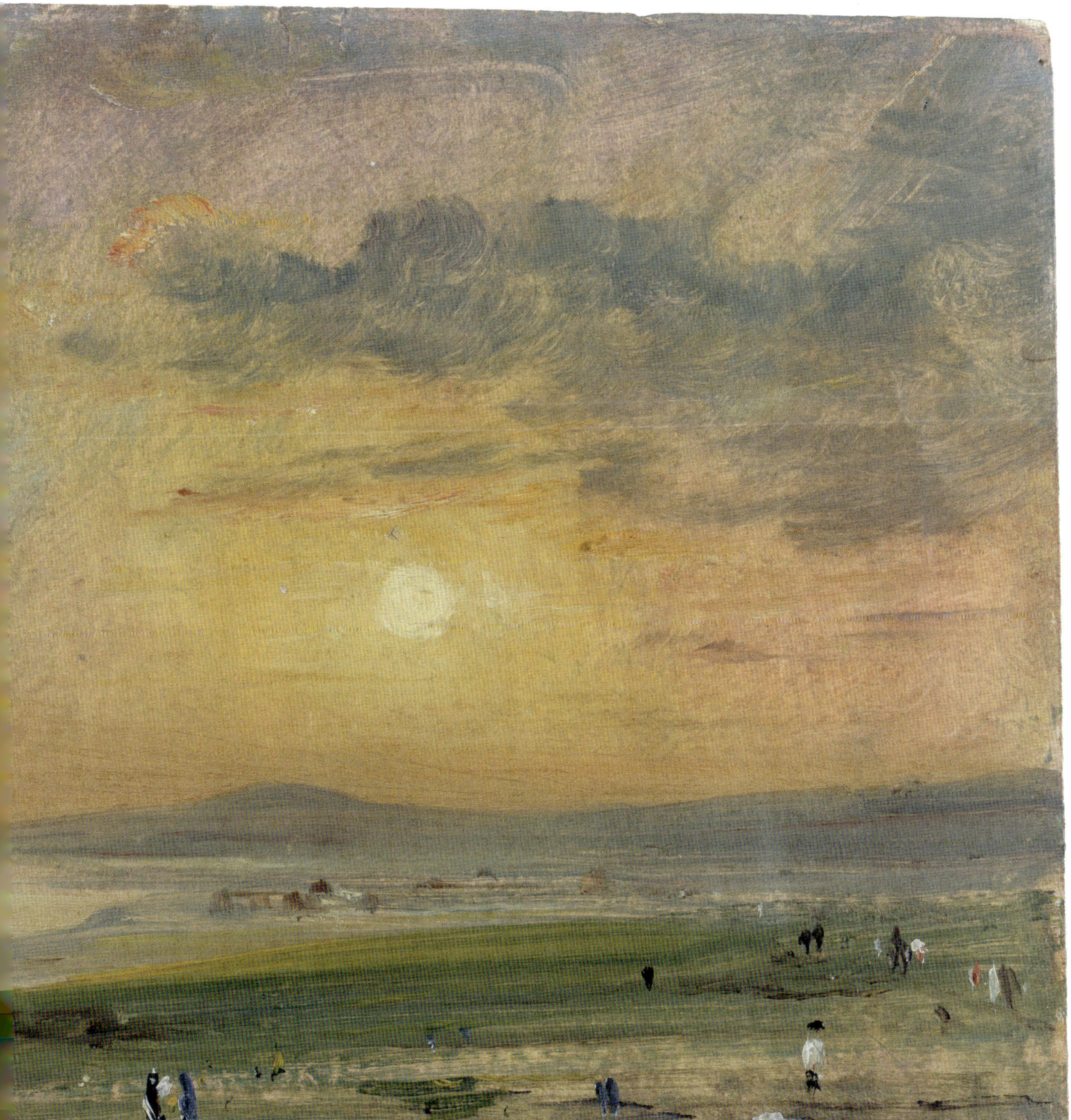

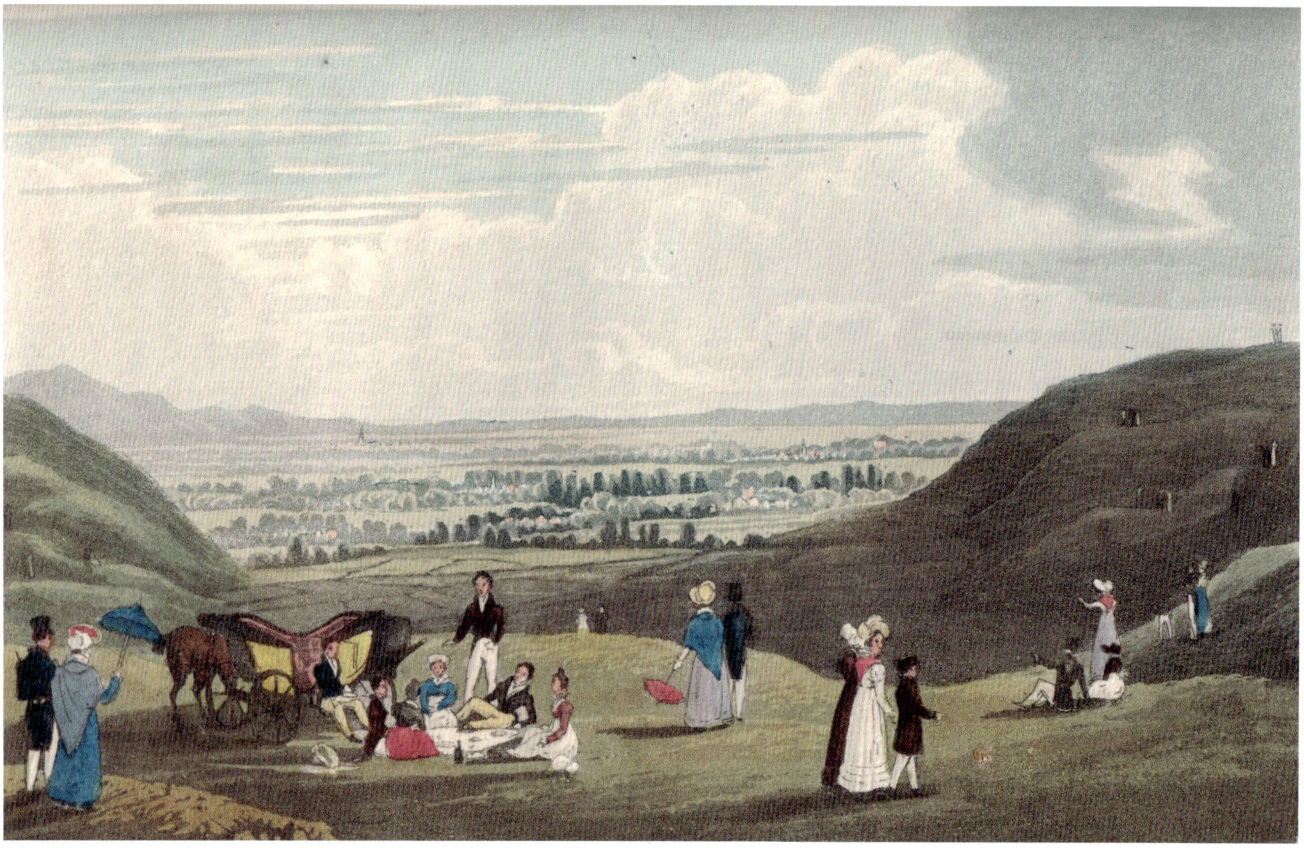

2. The Downs and Devil's Dyke

'there is nothing more interesting than the flying shadows across the downs' [23]

Above the noise and bustle of the resort Constable found fields of grain and extensive open pastures on the South Downs captured in his print published by Lucas (see fig. 61).

Heading up on to the Downs north and north-west of the resort, Constable ignored buildings such as the workhouse and perhaps more surprisingly, local beauty spots as well. This very selective approach is reflected in his observations about the Devil's Dyke (fig. 108). In recalling the trip he made there with the family on 24 August 1824, he observed that it was 'the most grand & affecting landscape in the world – and consequently a scene the most unfit for a picture. It is the business of a painter not to contend with nature & put this scene (a valley filled with imagery 50 miles long) on a canvas of a few inches, but to make something out of nothing, in attempting which he must almost of necessity become poetical.'[24]

Constable preferred to interpret nature, not just to represent it. He left that job to the able printmakers who produced some interesting vistas of this popular destination, to which visitors were attracted by the views of the sea to the south, the lower-lying and wooded Weald of Sussex and Surrey to the north, and the inland scarp of the downs curving east and west. So the deep valley called 'The Devil's Dyke' was but part of the attraction of the area.

The small country houses close to Brighton, such as Patcham Place or Preston Place, with their neat grounds and small neighbouring woodlands, and the remains of sixteenth-century Hangleton Place, long used as a farmhouse, were among the many features of the rural landscape that attracted other artists.[25] Constable too may have sketched there (see p. 135 and fig. 135), but of much greater interest to him were the windmills just up on the

Fig. 108
Robert Havell Jr
(1793–1878)
Devil's Dyke
1825
Print
Private collection

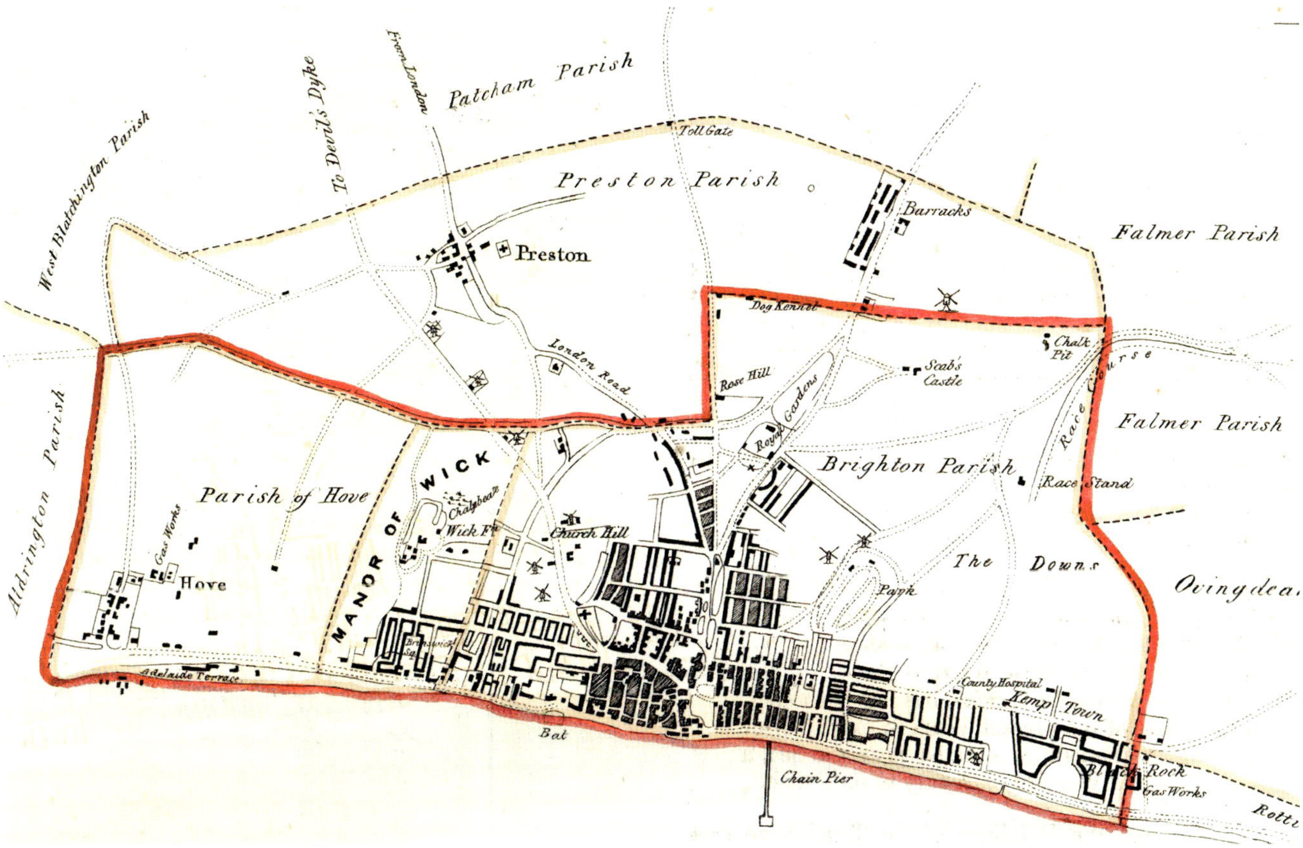

Fig. 109
Colonel Robert K. Dawson RE (1798–1861)
Brighthelmstone, from the *Ordnance Survey* 1831
Map
Private collection

Downs to the north of the town closest to his accommodation (fig. 109). On one excursion in November 1825, for example, Constable walked to West Blatchington, north of Hove, to make his only sketch of the windmill (fig. 105).

It is not easy to identify windmills with certainty, unless the artist provides an accurate name or description of the location or it appears in other pictures, correctly labelled. Windmills were moved or demolished, and the parts recycled. The timber-built post mill on Belle Vue field (where Regency Square is today) was towed to a new site on the Dyke Road in 1794 by 36 yoke of oxen and became Streeter's Mill.[26]

Relocating in that way could not be done with mills built on brick bases, such as Hodson's Mill (which stood off Dyke Road). Inevitably, as the town grew, these were demolished, mainly during the later nineteenth century, and Hodson's met this fate in 1866. Constable particularly liked this smock mill, with a distinctive domed top and fantail. He may have been attracted by its shape too: such mills were tapered, the tower clad in weatherboard and usually octagonal, but Hodson's was exceptional, a rare case of a smock mill with twelve sides (fig. 113).[27]

Peter Harrap comments that Constable had a very methodical approach to painting Hodson's Mill. By locating and articulating a single point of motif within a landscape and rotating in an incremental way, Constable builds up his knowledge of this particular windmill, recording and assimilating as much experience as possible and distilling his knowledge into a sequence of images, for potential further use on perhaps a larger canvas.

The post mill Constable sketched on 27 July 1824 is intriguing (fig. 110). The reddish hues of the soil suggest that it is somewhere on the coastal plain, but the only post mills that survived locally in the mid-1820s were Vine's Mill (after which a twitten – walkway – is named just north of Clifton Terrace), Port Hall and Trusslers, on the way over the top of the Downs. Later paintings of this mill confirm that it is Vine's.[28]

The presence of the tower of St Nicholas, the parish church, peeping over the horizon in the lower-right corner of *A Windmill Near*

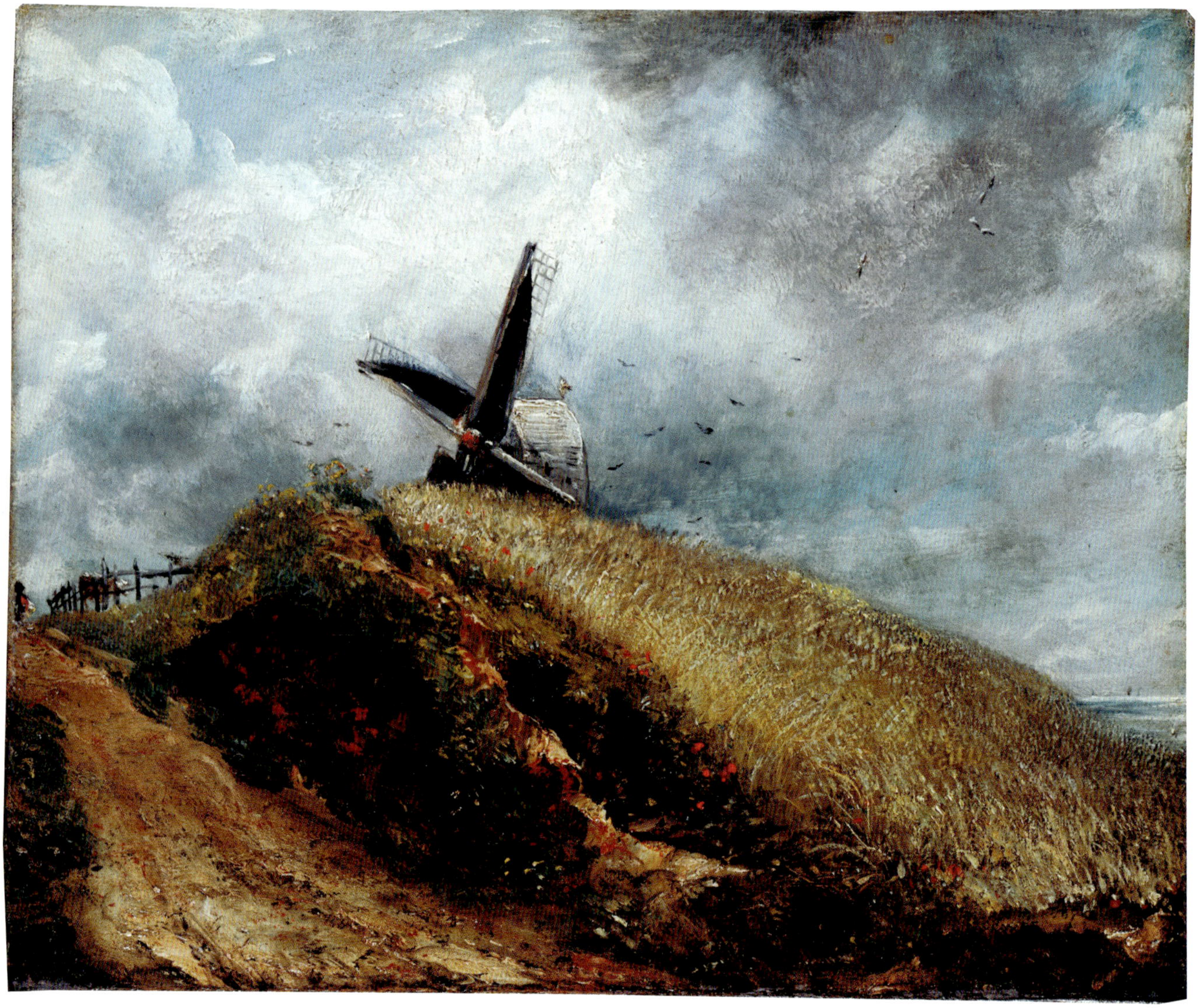

Brighton (fig. 111) suggests that the subject of this painting is also Vine's Mill, but without its buildings in sight. But the other paintings are harder to place. Both Port Hall Mill, a slim white post mill, and Streeter's Mill were only just north of Hodson's, so we cannot assume that Constable always painted the same post mill (fig. 109).[29]

In the sketch *A Windmill and Gleaners at Brighton* (fig. 112) Constable shows the bareness of the arable areas close to the resort. For this work he chose a viewpoint to the south-west of Vine's Mill, slightly below the hilltop, so that only the sails of the windmill are visible on the left. The other mill is not Clifton Gardens Mill, as some think, but Hodson's. The angle of the painting could be misleading.[30]

Peter Harrap suggests that, on one of his tramps across the Downs, Constable painted his celebrated study of an elm tree at Preston Place (see fig. 135). More usually associated with Constable's work in Hampstead, recent research has revealed that elms were a feature of the country house gardens surrounding Brighton. The dense foliage of various other trees in the background of the picture and the glimpse of another building suggest that the study could indeed have been made in one of the small parks adjoining Preston or Patcham Place, or on Mr Roe's landscape *orné* at Withdean. Here Roe kept the existing trees and planted more, as a hobby, recording his work as he did so. He began in the late 1790s, and by 1808 his new clump and hedgerow planting was largely completed. It was a long-term

Fig. 110
A Windmill Near Brighton
27 July 1824
Oil on canvas,
20.2 × 25.1 cm
R.24.15
Tate, London

Fig. 111
A Windmill Near Brighton
20 August 1824
Oil on paper, 15.7 × 24.4 cm
R.24.21
Victoria and Albert Museum, London

Fig. 112
A Windmill and Gleaners at Brighton
1824
Oil on paper laid on canvas, 15.9 × 30.2 cm
R.24.20
Tate, London

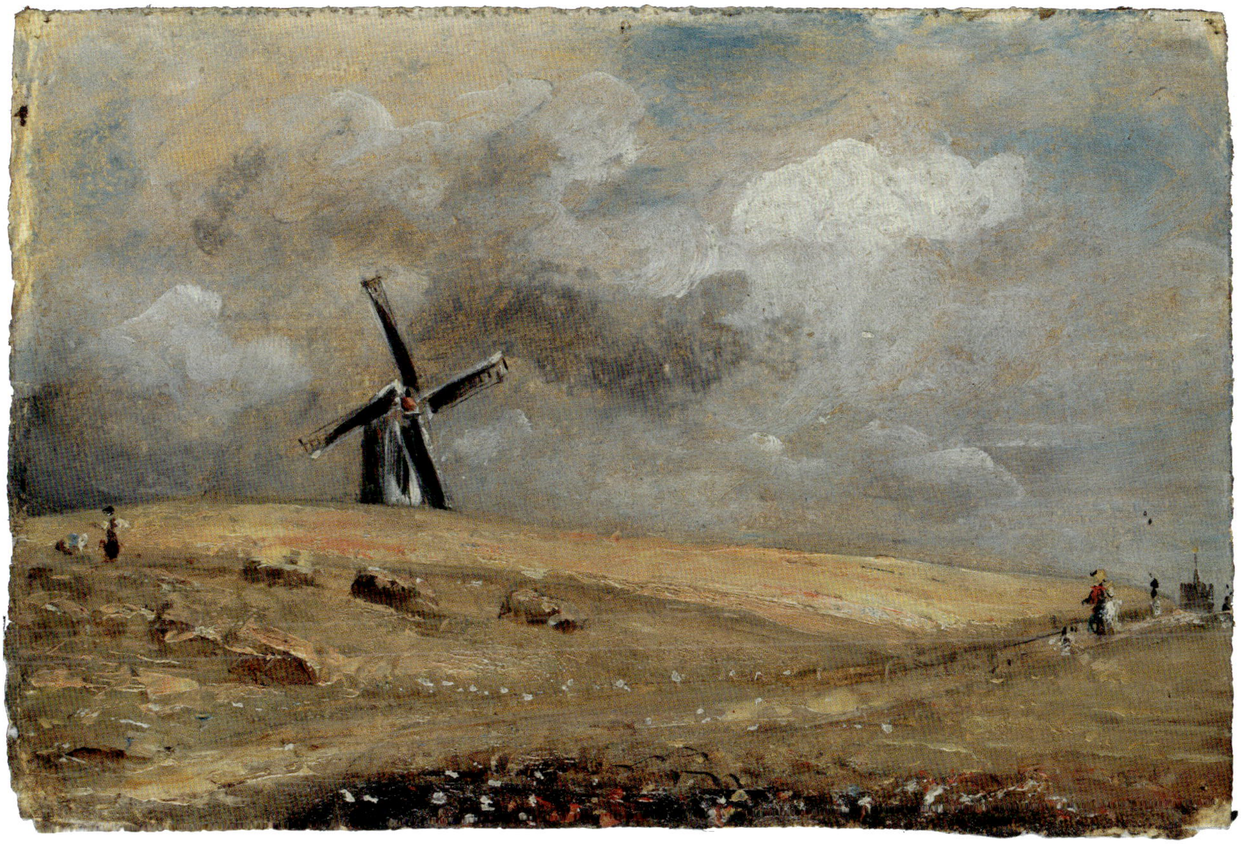

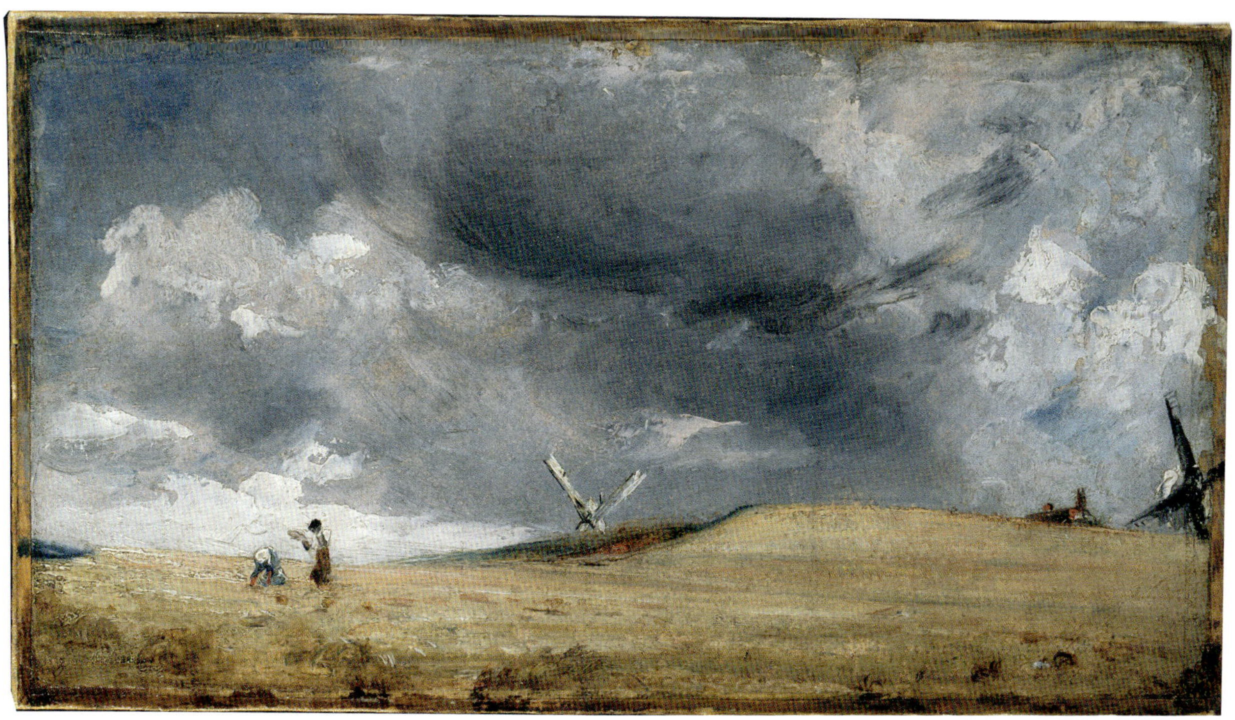

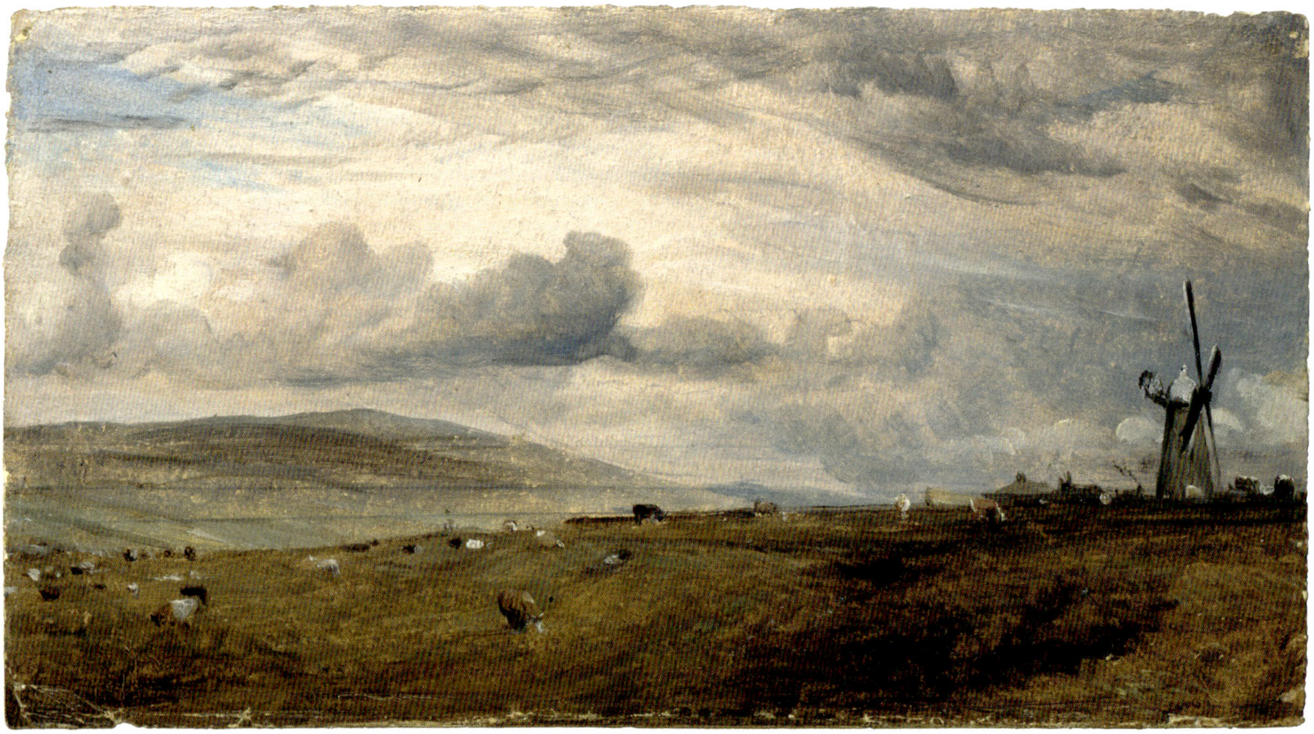

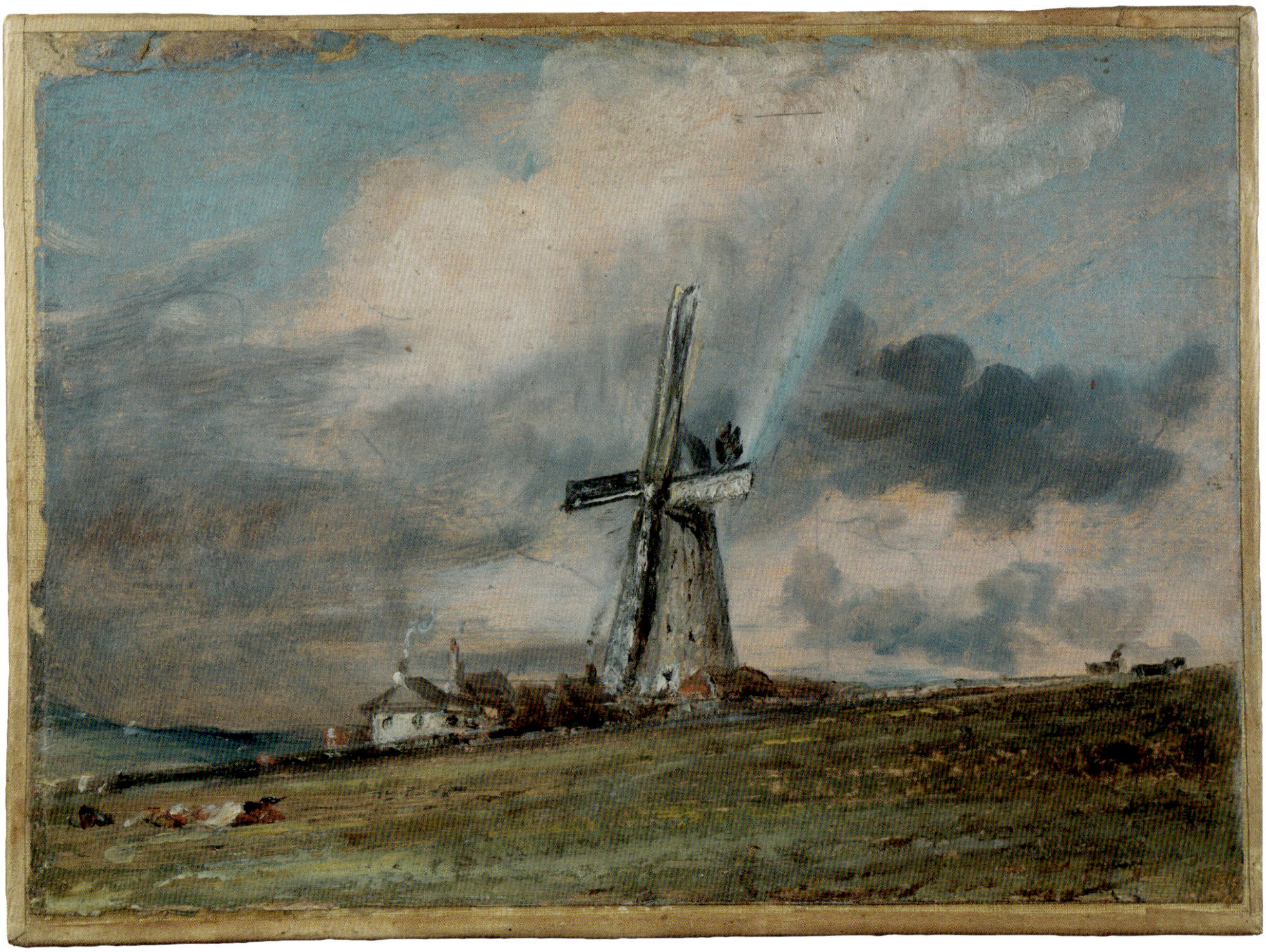

Fig. 113
A Windmill Near Brighton
3 August 1824
Oil on paper,
16.2 × 30.8 cm
R 24.17
Victoria and Albert Museum, London

Fig. 114
A Windmill on the Downs Near Brighton
1824
Oil on paper laid on canvas,
21 × 30.4 cm
R.24.73
Victoria and Albert Museum, London

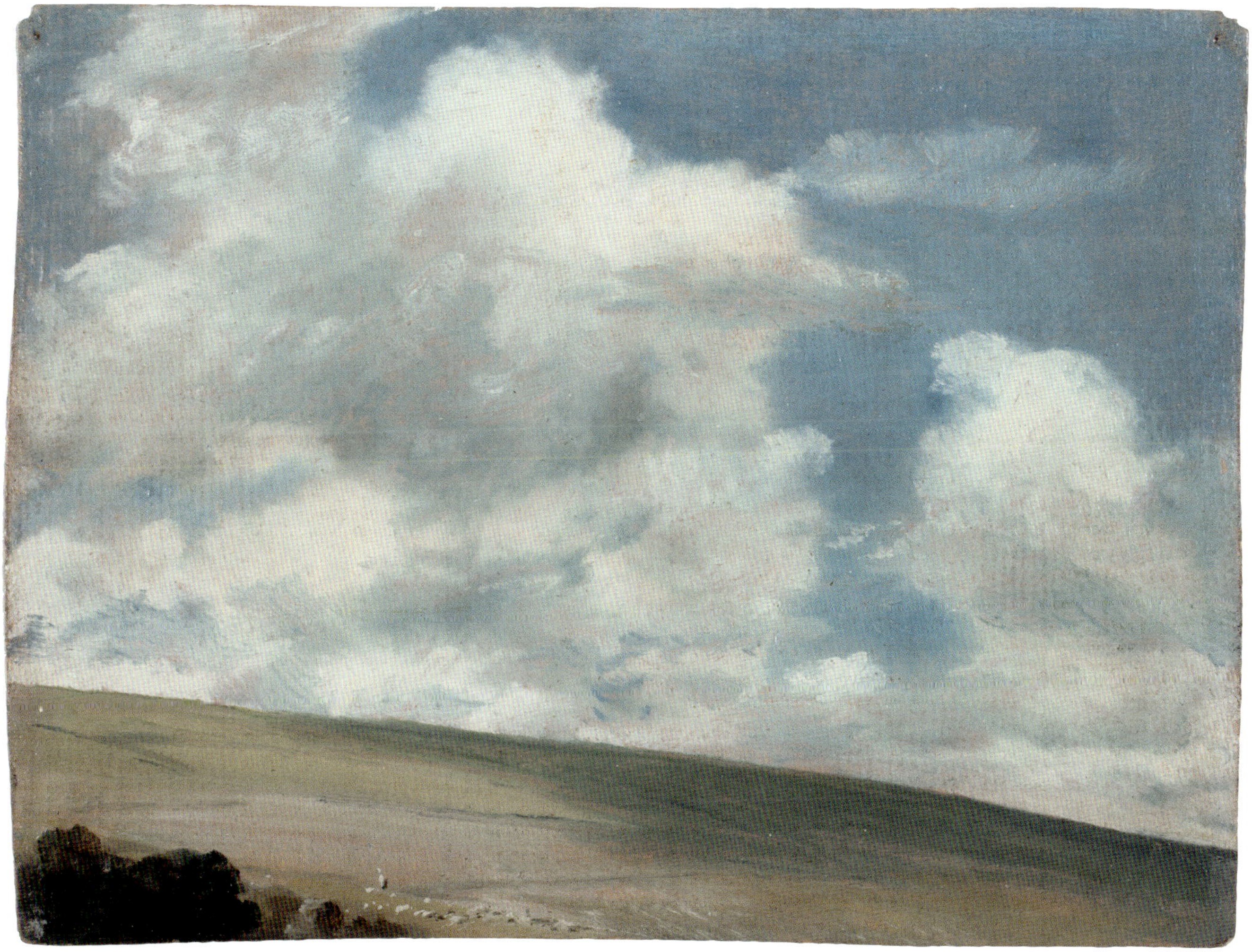

Fig. 115
Scene on the Downs Near Brighton
c.1825
Oil on card,
11.5 × 16 cm
R.24.77
Private collection

project, and the attractive results were not fully apparent until a map of the area was done in 1842. Why he did this is not clear, but perhaps it was to pass the time while his wife and daughters were enjoying Brighton.[31]

But the Downs appealed chiefly to Constable for their limitless vistas, which were ideal for making studies of clouds. From his position above the town he could watch the patterns made by shadows of clouds scudding by, capturing the effect that Maria drew to his attention in a letter in June 1824: 'There is nothing more interesting than the flying shadows across the downs'.[32] In the tiny oil sketch he made on a piece of card it is easy to miss his simple depiction of the shepherd and part of a flock of sheep in the left corner (fig. 115). The closely grazed pastures indicated in this painting fed Southdown sheep, valued for the flavour of their mutton, for which the Downs were famous.

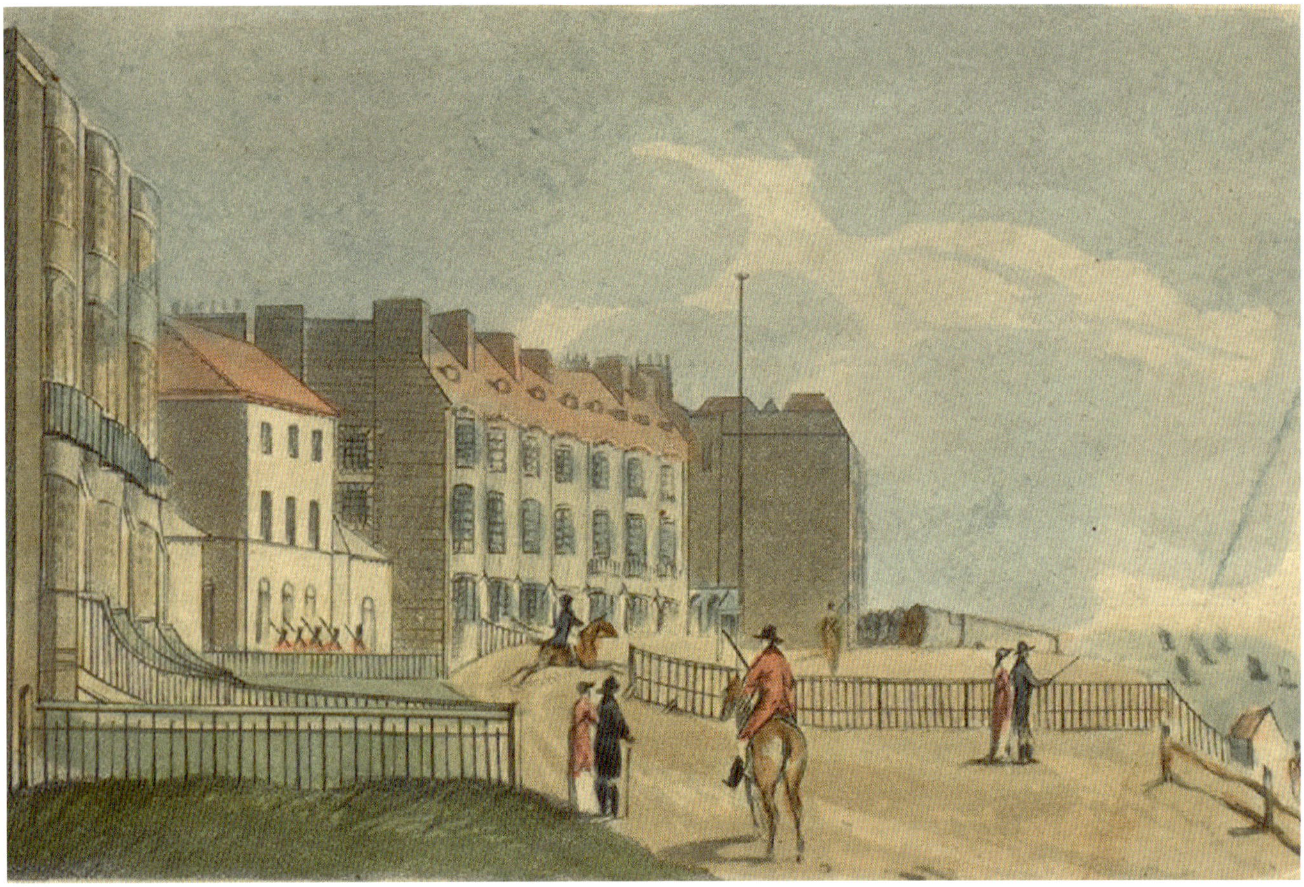

Fig. 116
Edward Fox (1788–1875)
West Battery
c.1827
Engraving
Private collection

3. Brighton Seafront

'the beach is only Piccadilly – by the sea-side'

Confronted with the animation at the heart of Brighton's seafront, Constable had more specific details to engage with, and so his sketches of this area are different in character from the more abstract approach he used for many of the paintings looking west from Hove.

He concentrated on the fishing boats but also painted coal colliers (see figs 45 and 63). These brought coal from Newcastle, a trade that was established by the later sixteenth century. The smaller boats could beach by running onto the shore at high tide and then settling in to the shingle as the tide receded and float off with the next tide. But the bigger ones which were becoming more common because they were cheaper to run, could not be beached and unloaded so easily. By the mid-1820s Shoreham was about to be developed as a proper harbour to accomodate them.

Constable continued to make detailed sketches of the two types of inshore fishing boat he saw – the double bowsprit lugger and the hogboat (the latter longer and wider, and with a prow and stern). Both were designed to be pulled up onto the beach, often with the help of capstans, which he also drew. He spotted that nets were sometimes hung from the mast to dry and air. The catch was sold on the beach at the Fish Market (see fig. 33).

By 1824 the Grand Junction Road had been constructed, providing for the first time a road along the seafront. It can be seen in Havell's superb panorama of 1824 (see fig. 8). But, typically, although Constable crossed it to get to the beach, he ignored it in his sketches. Occasionally he did delineate the seafront buildings just enough for us to identify where he

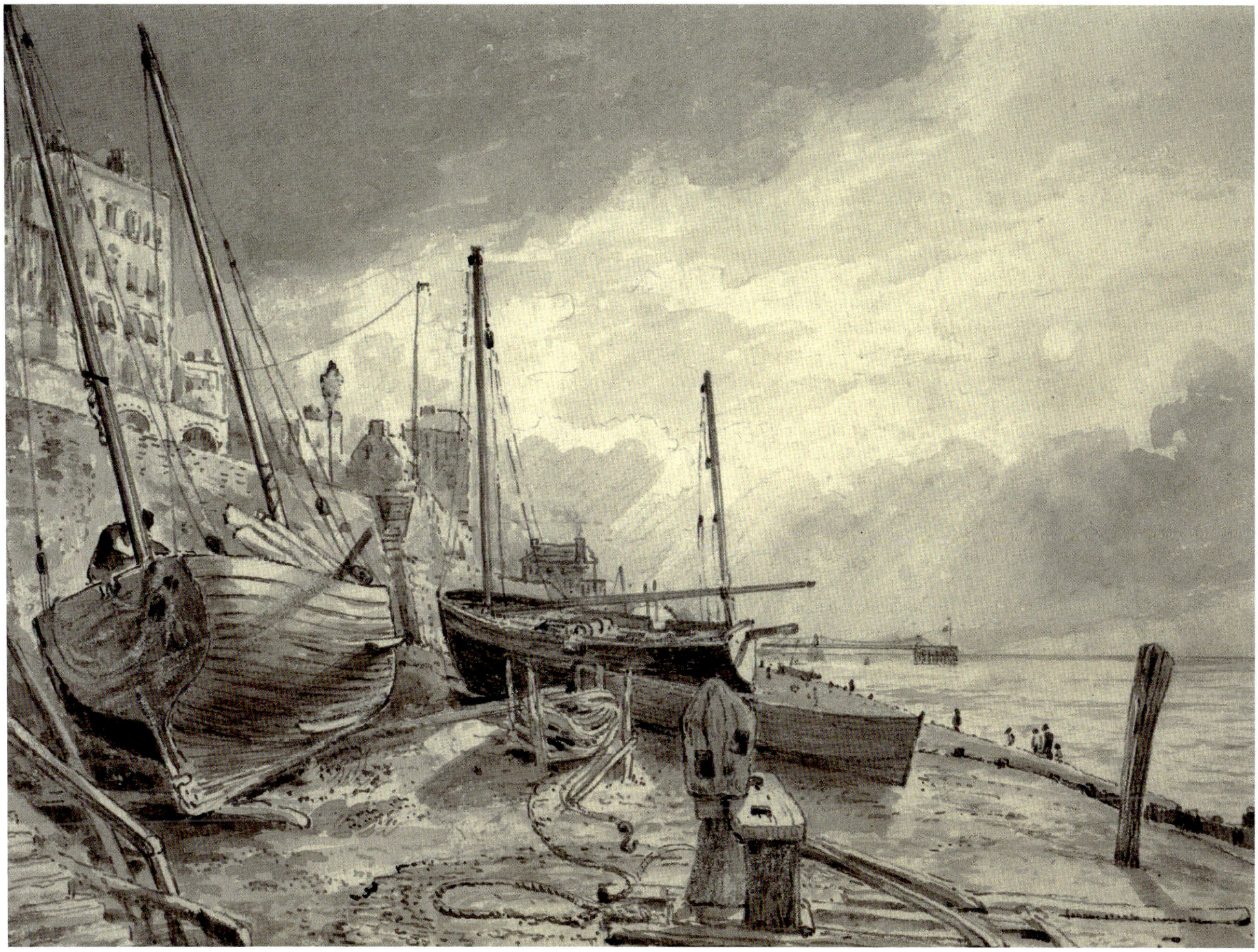

Fig. 117
Brighton Beach, Early Morning after a Wet Night
c.1824
Ink (grey wash) on paper, 17.9 × 26 cm
R.24.35
Royal Pavilion & Museums, Brighton

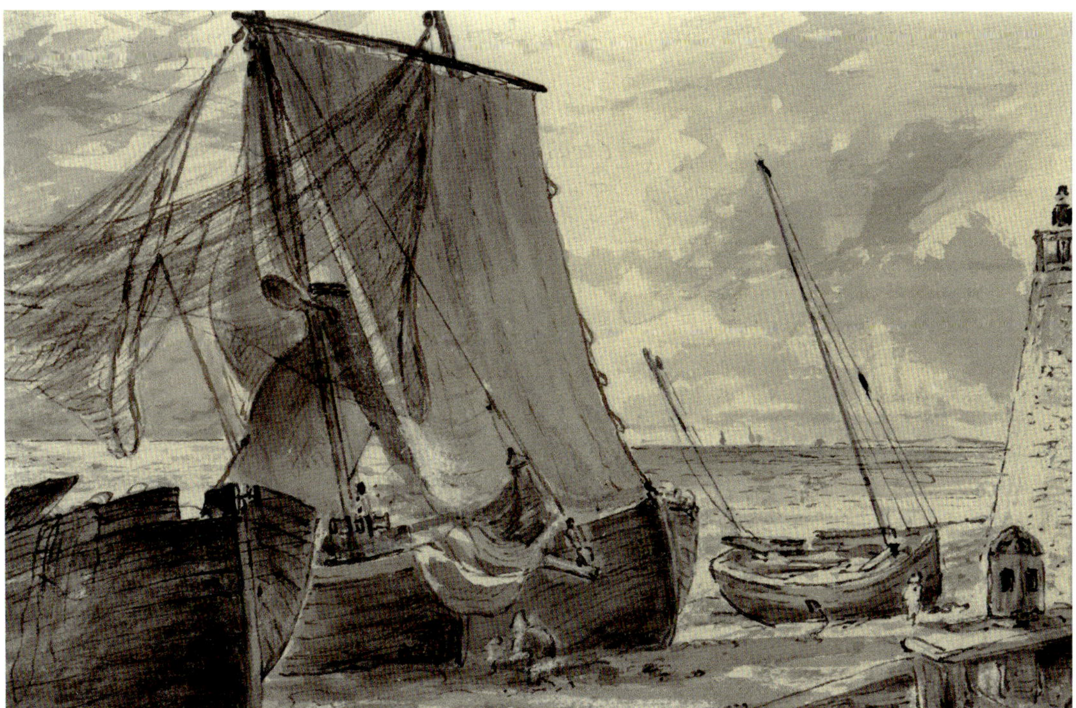

Fig. 118
Brighton Beach, Rainy Weather
c.1824
Ink (grey wash) on paper, 10.2 × 18.4 cm
R.25.41
Royal Pavilion & Museums, Brighton

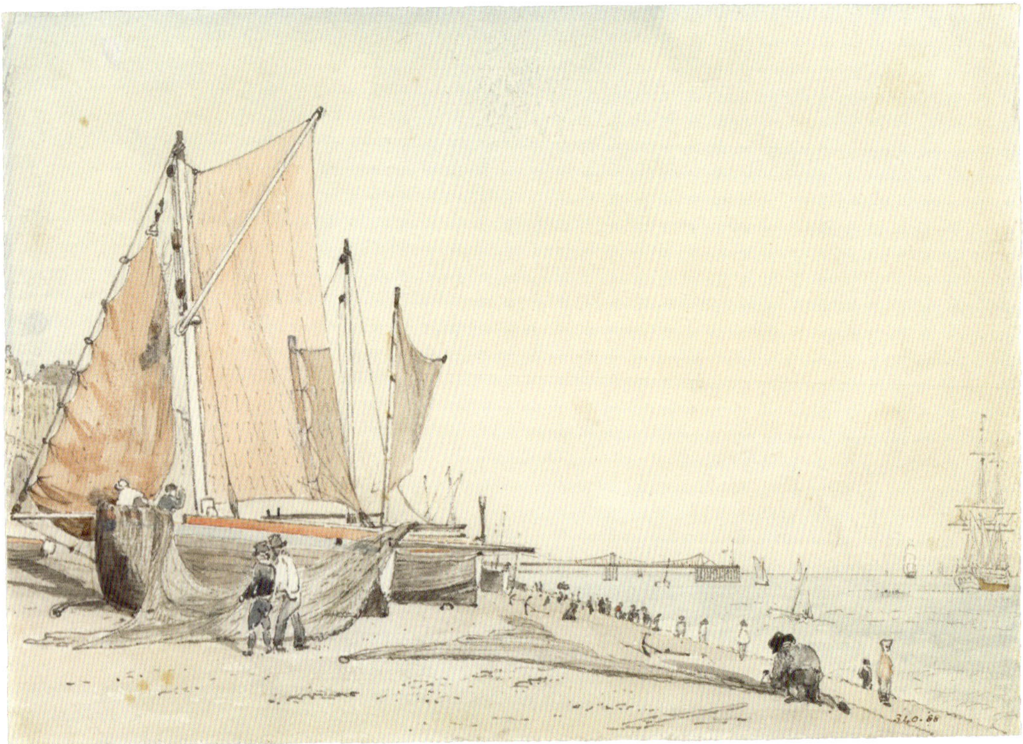

Fig. 119
Brighton Beach with Fishing Boats and the Chain Pier
c.1824
Pen, pencil and watercolour,
17.8 × 26 cm
R. 24. 41
Victoria and Albert Museum, London

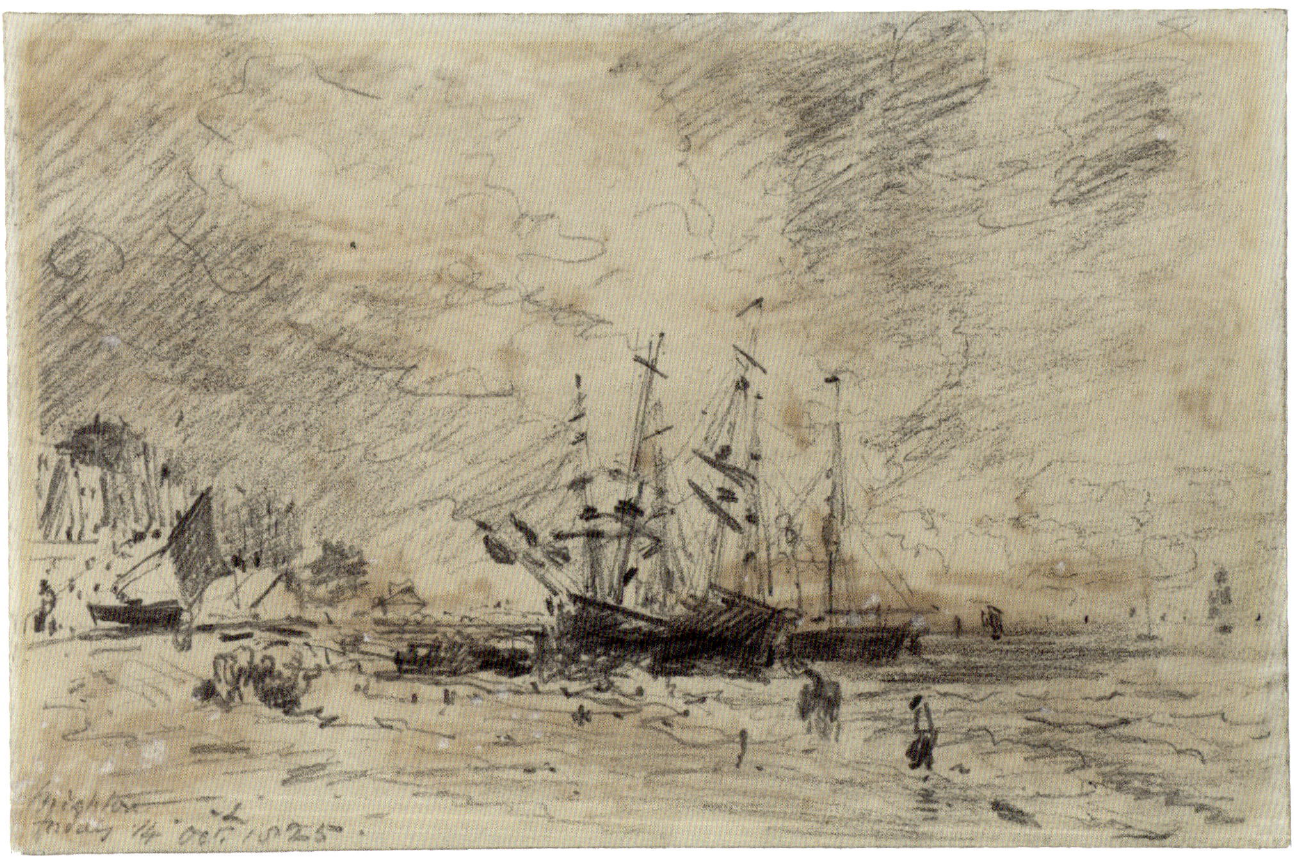

Fig. 120
Colliers on the Beach at Brighton
14 October 1825
Pencil, 11.5 × 18.5 cm
R.25.20
The Courtauld Gallery, London

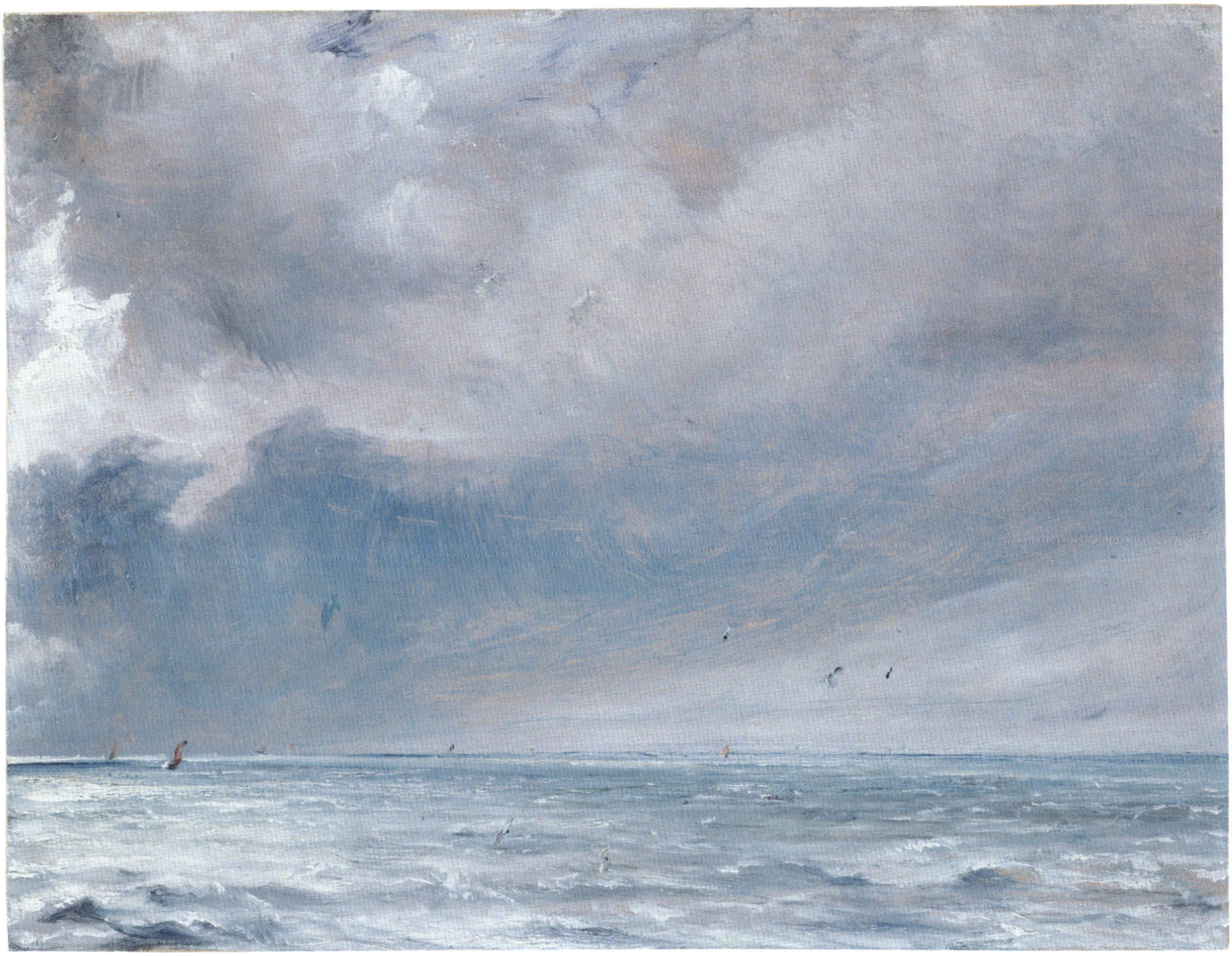

Fig. 121
The Sea Near Brighton
1826
Oil on paper laid on card,
17.3 × 23.9 cm
R.26.5
Tate, London

was; similarly, he sometimes picked out the sea wall of the West Battery, where the road in front of the Grand Hotel now runs.

The 1824 watercolour of *Brighton Beach, with a Rainbow: Colliers Unloading* (Oldham Art Gallery) shows the distinctive low cliff in front of central Brighton, a mixture of raised beach and chalk, and the white cliffs of east Brighton in the distance. These landscape features can also be seen in the sequence of sketches Constable made a year later, where he once again recorded the colliers below the seafront townhouses (fig. 120).

As Constable moved east along the beach, his view was dominated by the Chain Pier. It is clear that some of his small sketches and paintings contributed to the composition of his famous oil painting: for example, his sketches of fishermen's equipment (fig. 124).

Constable made some detailed sketches and watercolours of the busier beach in front of Brighton; they share the theme of vessels beached or close to shore, capstans and sometimes the prow half of old vessels upended as stores, a motif used by E. W. Cooke, R. H. Nibbs and other artists who worked here (see fig. 126).

His eye for detail is reflected in two of the monochrome drawings of 1824, which look as if they were done in sequence, although different in scale. *Brighton Beach: Early Morning after a Wet Night*, dated 1824 (fig. 117), was painted facing east and sitting on the beach in front of the town centre. It is at first glance simply a small inshore fishing craft typical of the town, with the top of a timber groyne becoming buried in shingle running up the beach behind the craft, and a rather decrepit capstan for hauling vessels up the beach. But closer inspection reveals that Constable was interested in the broader setting. In the distance he sketched in the Chain Pier and, in front of it, people trudging up the shingle.

Fig. 122
Sea Off Brighton
1824
Oil on paper laid on canvas,
12.7 × 21.6 cm
R.24.69
Daniel Katz Family Trust

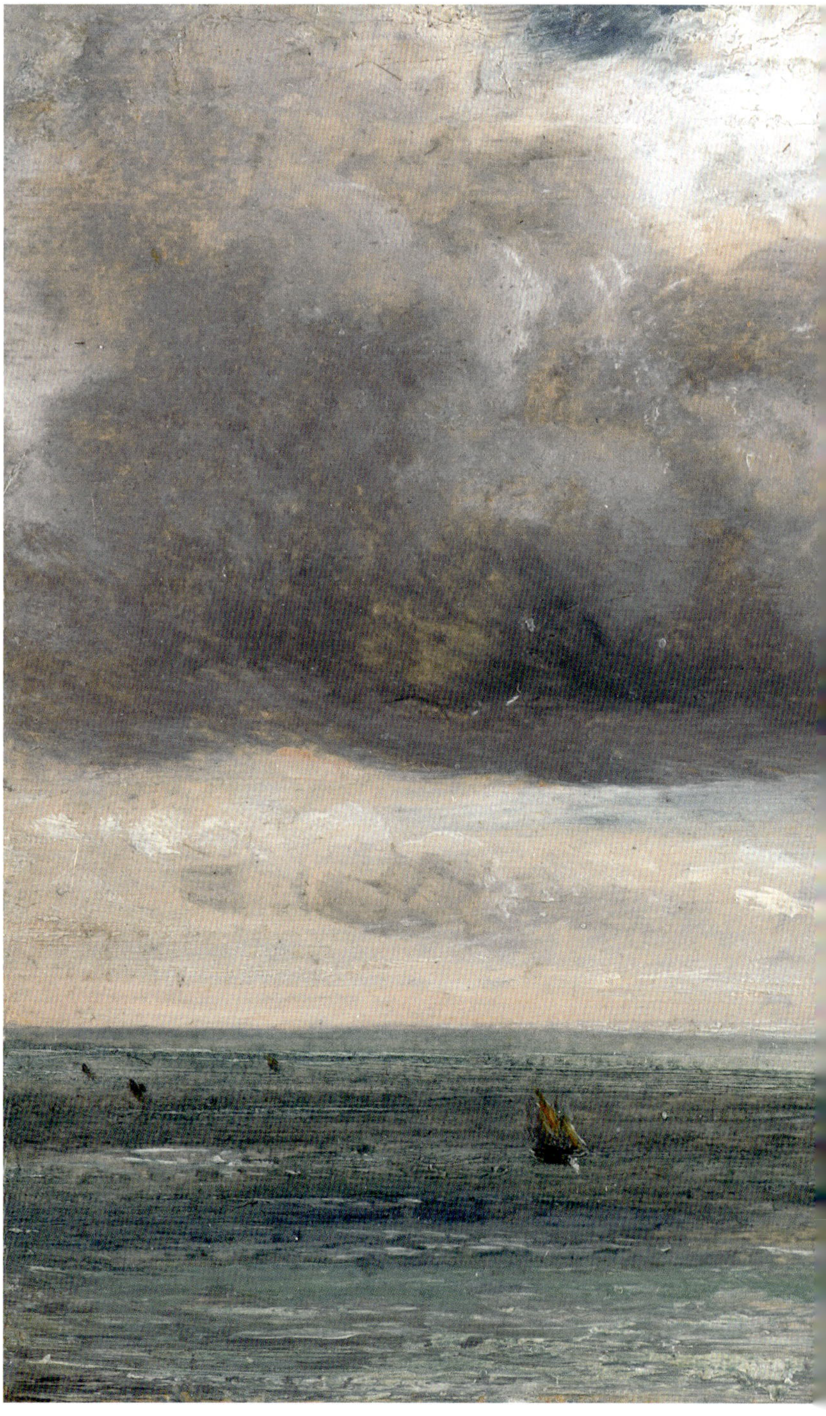

Above the sea defences built to protect the new road he added a few of the buildings on the front of the eastern end of the old town. The cluster of buildings around the gas light were at the bottom end of East Street, an area that was close to that depicted in his famous painting of the Chain Pier.

Constable then turned to a fresh view, and *Brighton Beach: Rainy Weather* (fig. 118) was the result. The capstan resembles the one in the drawing we have just considered (fig. 117), seen from the east side. Constable is now facing west. In the distance, around the curving coastline, is the outline of Worthing, the view he repeatedly painted in oils from further along the seafront in Hove. Two people look down from the cliff-top, and this may be the edge of the old West Battery, built in the late eighteenth century. The nearer fishing vessel has nets blowing about in the breeze.

Wherever he was on the seafront, Constable could not resist dramatic effects out at sea, caused by the passage of light onto the water through the shifting masses of rain cloud. He vividly captured some of these in works such as the little oil sketch catalogued as *The Sea Near Brighton* (fig. 121).

Peter Harrap comments that *The Sea Near Brighton* is a fresh, yet brooding painting, showing the dancing light through the clouds. Constable uses the pink ground and the blue and green-grey paint brushed over the surface to reveal the underlying warm half-tone, presenting an irresistible description of an atmospheric pooling of light on the water.

In fig. 122 Constable's interest was in coastal light and moods again. And he has the boat's sails angled to show a gentle onshore breeze – even in the little dabs indicating boats on the left of the picture. He used the sea to reflect the clouds

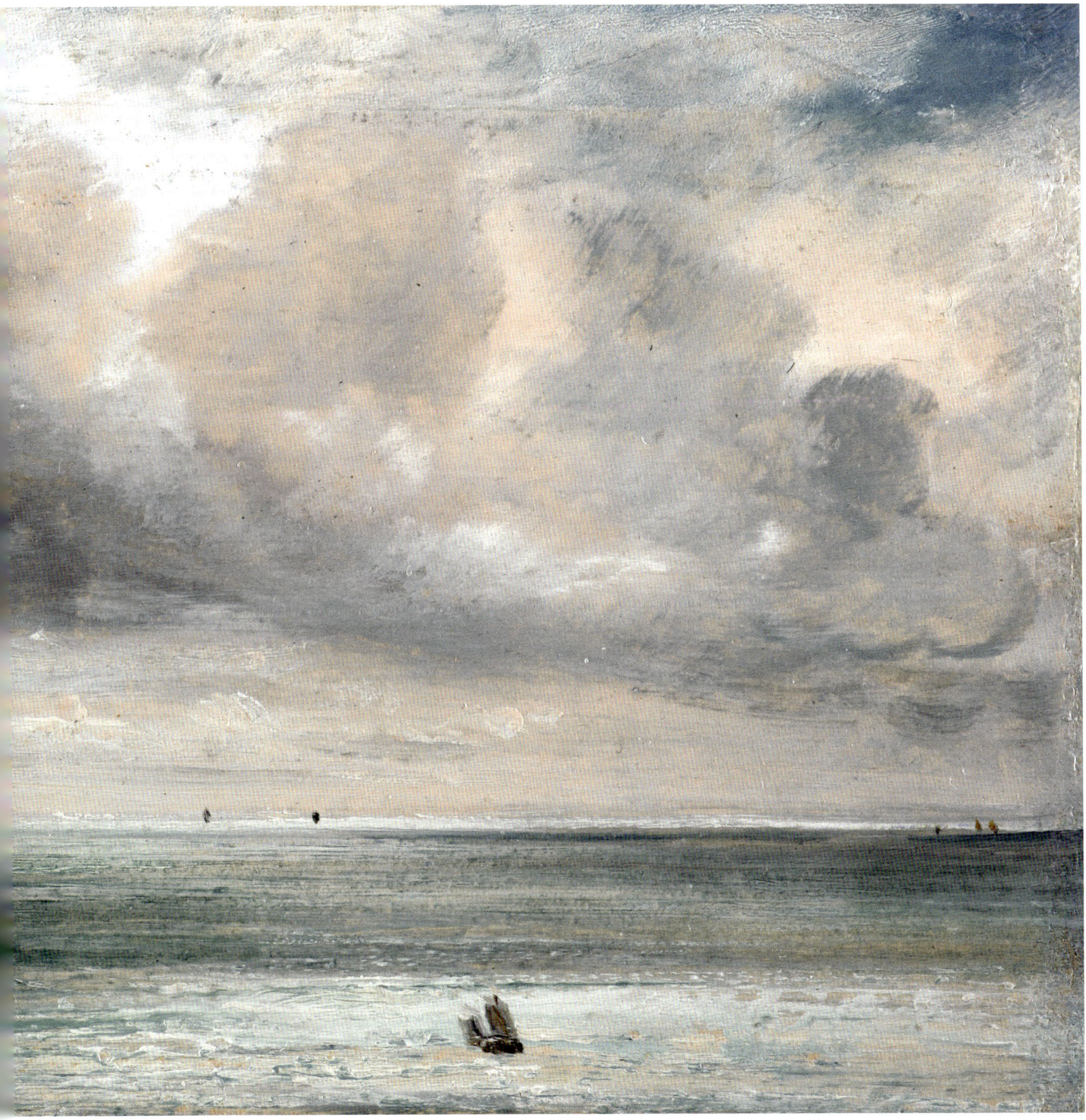

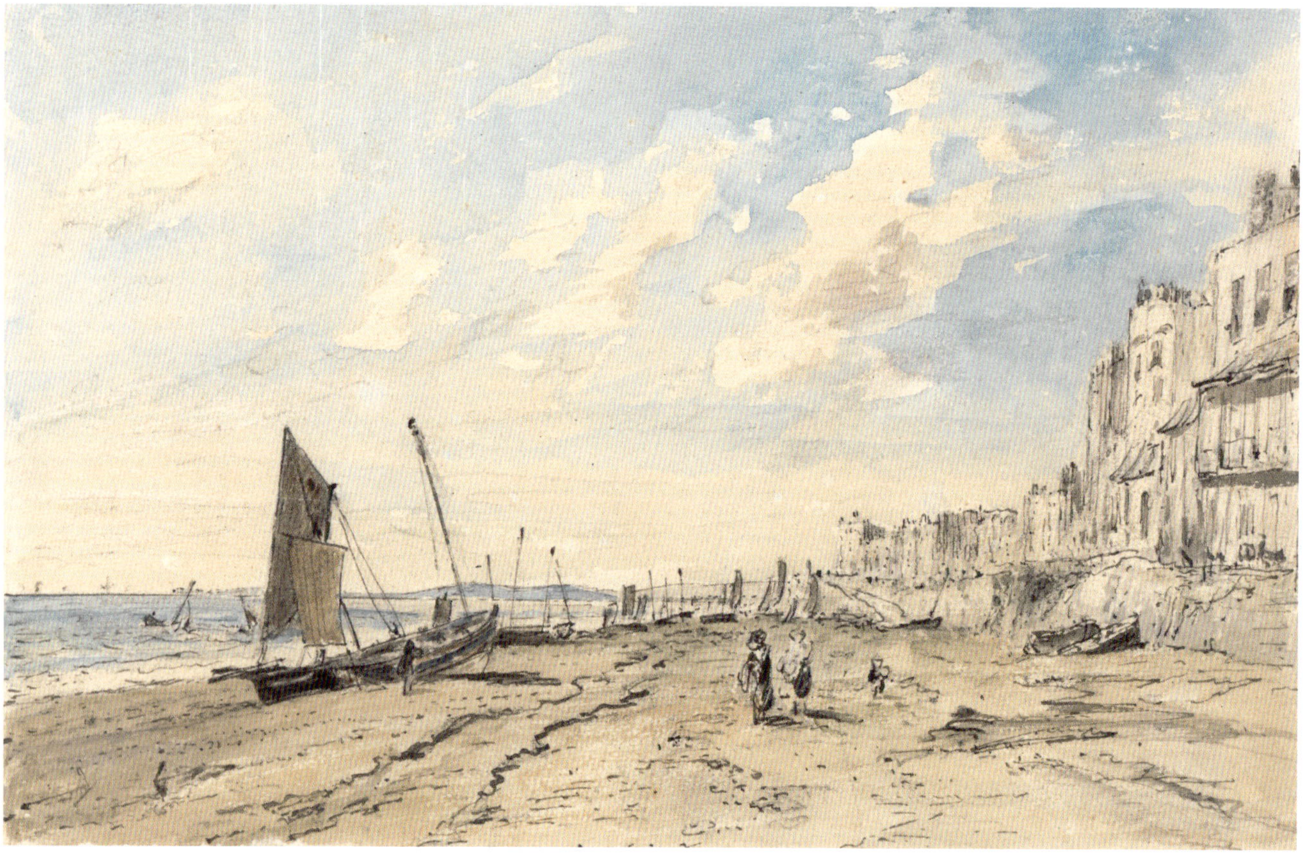

building up in the foreground. During his stay in 1824, when he hoped to impress Lord Egremont (see Ch. 4), Constable took a greater interest in the prospect over the eastern end of the town, producing a sketch from near the Fish Market, within sight of the Albion Hotel, looking towards Marine Parade on the East Cliff and the Chain Pier (see fig. 127). The sketch shows the irregular heights of the houses on the East Cliff clearly, and also the small area of beach in front of the pier favoured by fishing vessels because beaching was easy. This looks like the idea for his big oil starting to develop. Close examination of this masterpiece (pp. 124–5) shows that he used some of the work he had done on his visits, such as the studies of the fishing gear (fig. 124), in order to complete it. His work does not reveal any interest in depicting the pier during one of the storms that did so much damage to it, a theme popular in prints (fig. 125).

Peter Harrap observes that *The Marine Parade and Chain Pier, Brighton* (fig. 127) is a highly topographical study of the seafront looking towards Kemp Town; it serves as a guide for Constable's *Chain Pier, Brighton* (see fig. 48). The dotted ink foreground may imply some sort of transfer method, possibly tracing through glass, in order to achieve an accurate transcription of the foreground. The Pump House is reworked into the final painting in the mid-ground, behind a boat.

In spite of his inclusion of the Chain Pier and other changes along the coast that resulted from tourism, such as the development of the

ABOVE: **Fig. 123**
Brighton Beach Looking West
c.1824
Graphite, pen and black ink and watercolour on cream wove paper,
11.4 × 18.1 cm
Yale Center for British Art, New Haven, CT

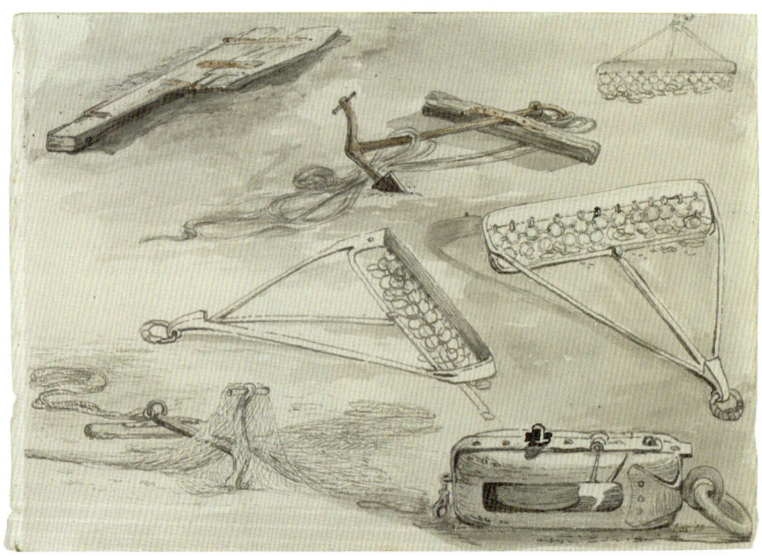

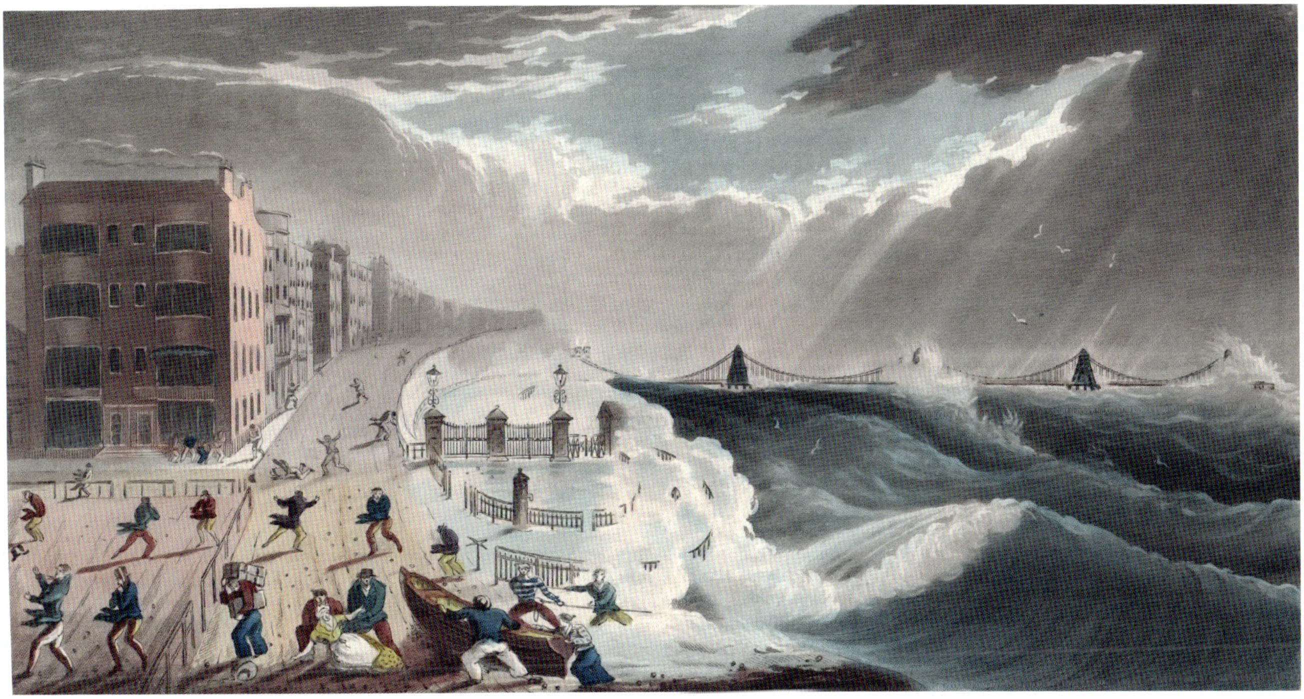

OPPOSITE BELOW: **Fig. 124**
Studies of Tackle on Brighton Beach
c.1824
Pencil, pen and grey wash,
18.1 × 26.4 cm
R.24.36
Victoria and Albert Museum, London

ABOVE: **Fig. 125**
J. BRUCE (active 1820s)
Chain Pier Tempest ... the Situation of the Chain Pier at Brighton during the Late Tempest ... Novr 23 1824
Aquatint print
Private collection

houses on the East Cliff, Constable's tendency to seek and depict the picturesque resulted in his ignoring some of the changes in the town. However, he did not entirely ignore the sea defences in front of the town centre, as can be seen in *A Sea Beach, Brighton* (see fig. 57), where a groyne runs down to the sea. Elsewhere, however, as in fig. 123, he shows the seafront

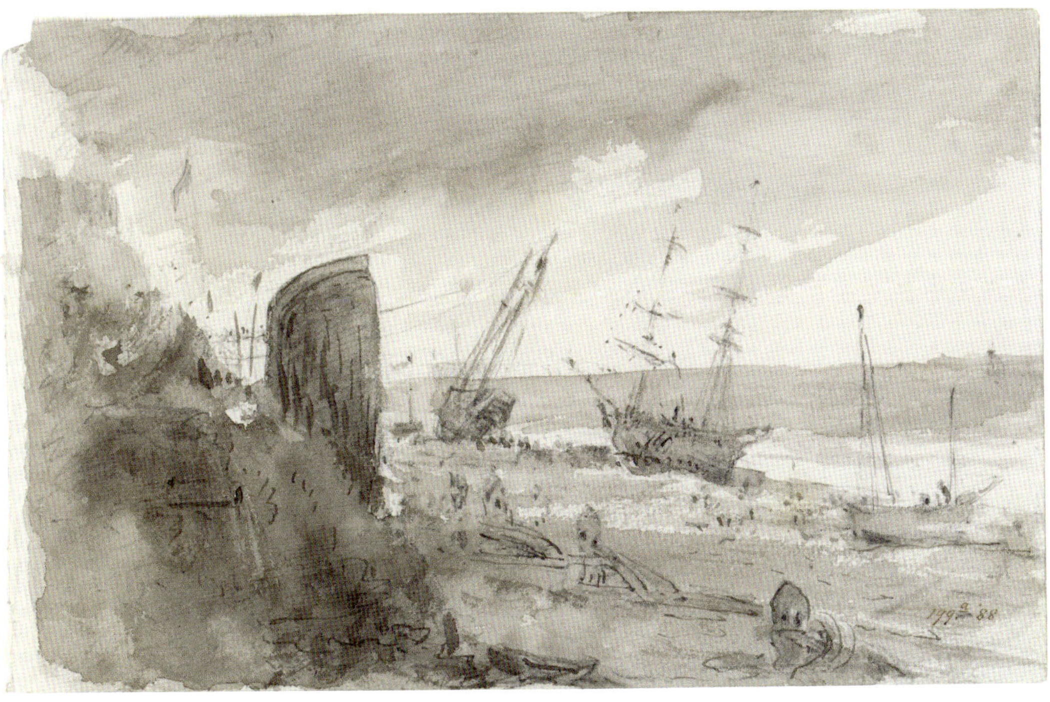

RIGHT: **Fig. 126**
A Coast Scene with Vessels on the Beach at Brighton
30 May 1828
Pencil, pen , ink and grey wash,
11.5 × 18.6 cm
R 28.10
Victoria and Albert Museum, London

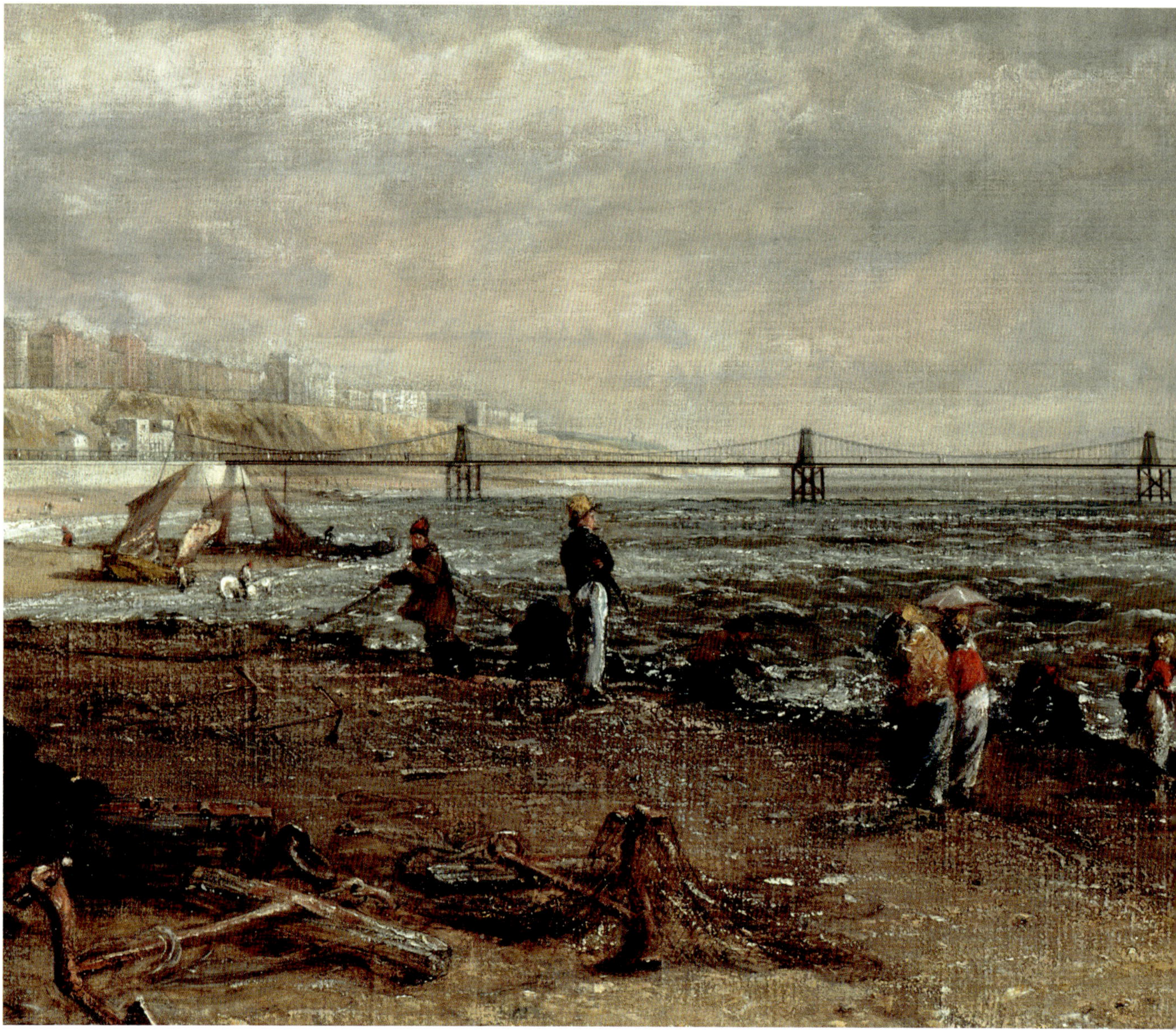

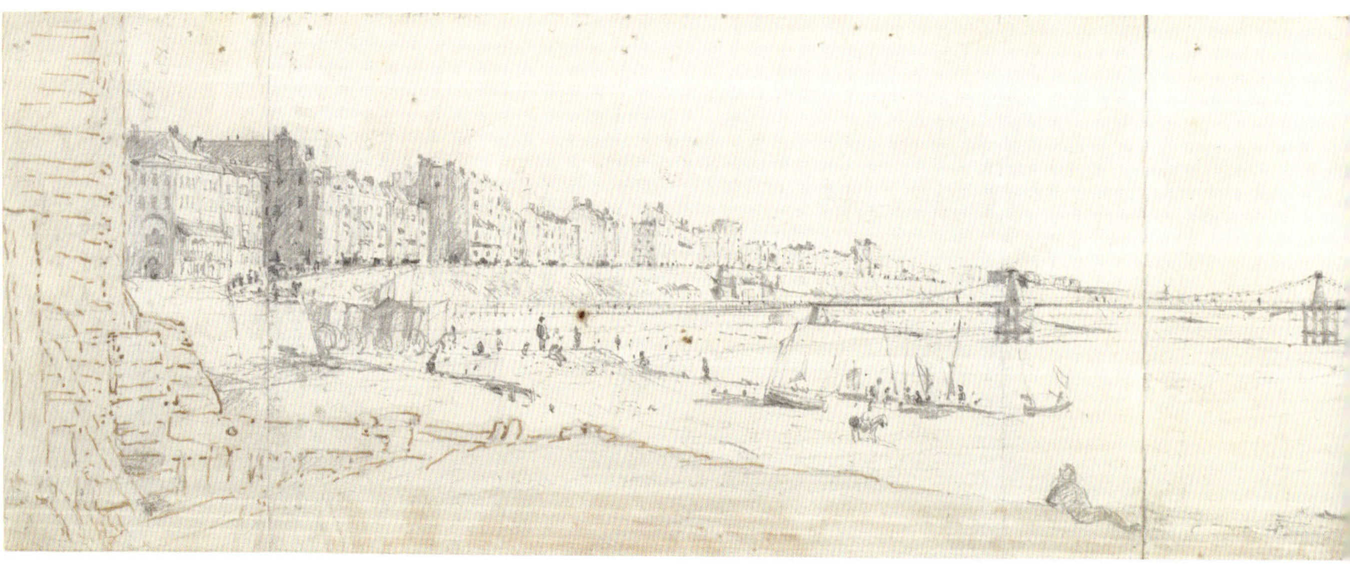

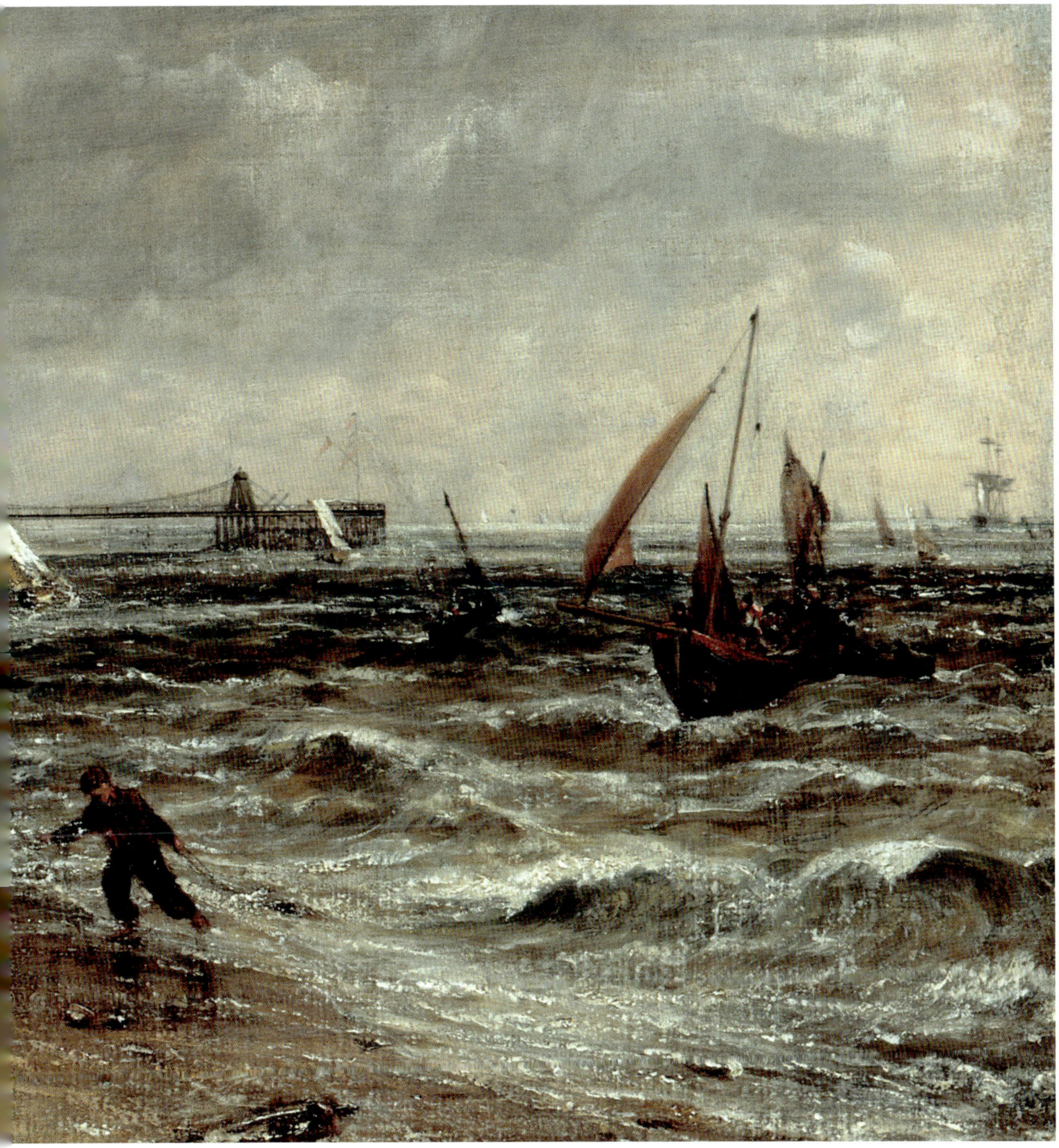

Detail of fig. 48

BELOW:
Fig. 127
The Marine Parade and Chain Pier, Brighton
*c.*1824
Pencil with pen additions,
11.1 × 42.5 cm
R.27.2
Victoria and Albert Museum, London

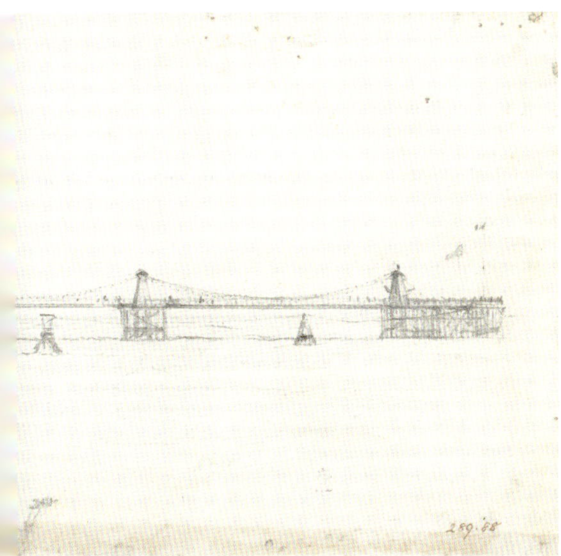

buildings standing as if still close to the edge of the low cliff of the old town and without defences. The fishing craft are very lightly sketched in.

Constable's view of the resort and its surrounds is inevitably selective. He worked in the areas where he felt more at ease and with the type of subjects he enjoyed most. His wanderings to the west and north of the resort and along its seafront capture them at a point around 20 years before they were to change dramatically. From the mid-1840s rapid urban expansion and developments along the seafront began the transformation of all these areas into a landscape more familiar to us than it would have been to him and other artists working during the 1820s.

OVERLEAF:
Fig. 128
Stormy Sea, Brighton
*c.*1828
Oil on paper laid on canvas,
16.5 × 26.7 cm
R28.13
Yale Center For British Art, New Haven, CT

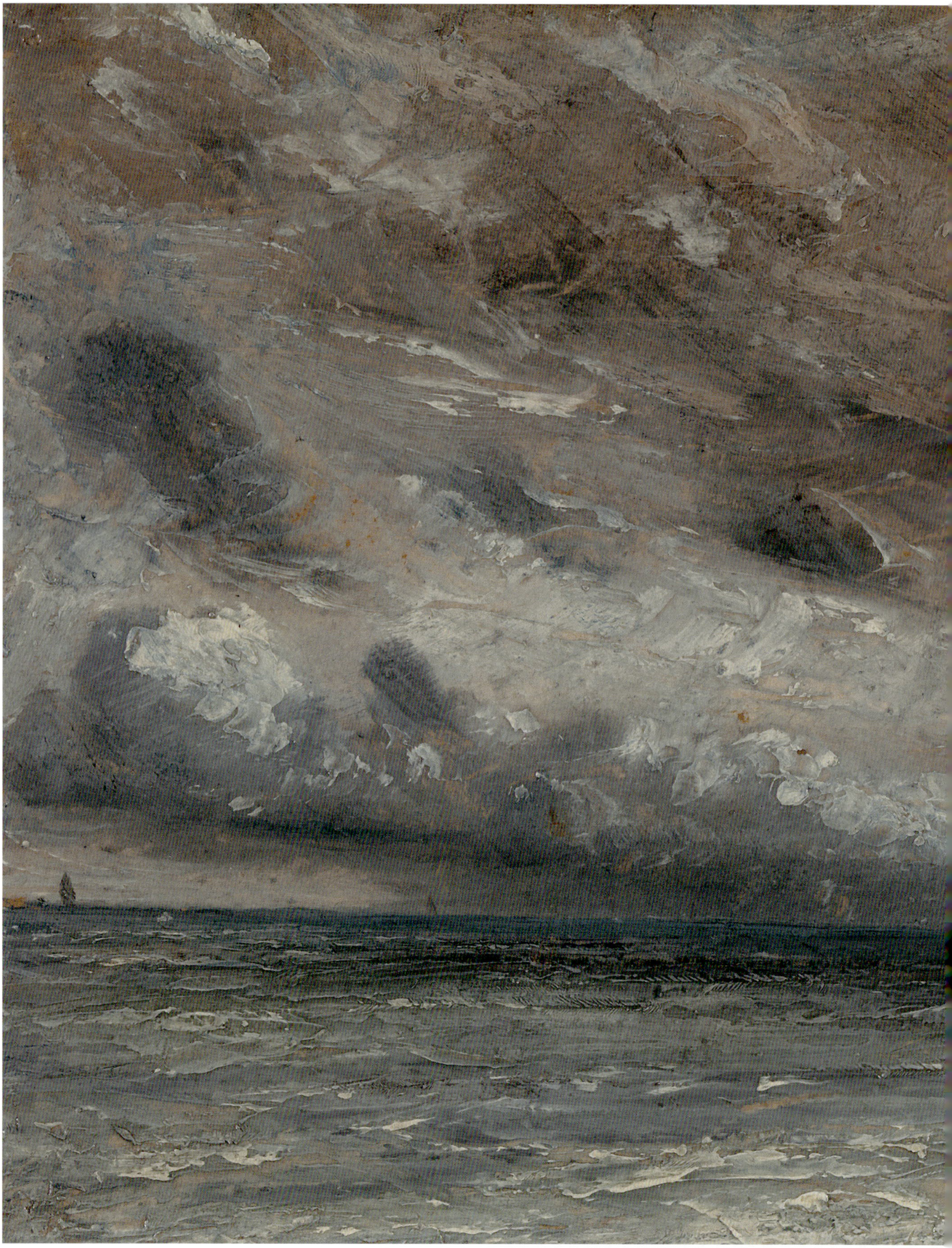

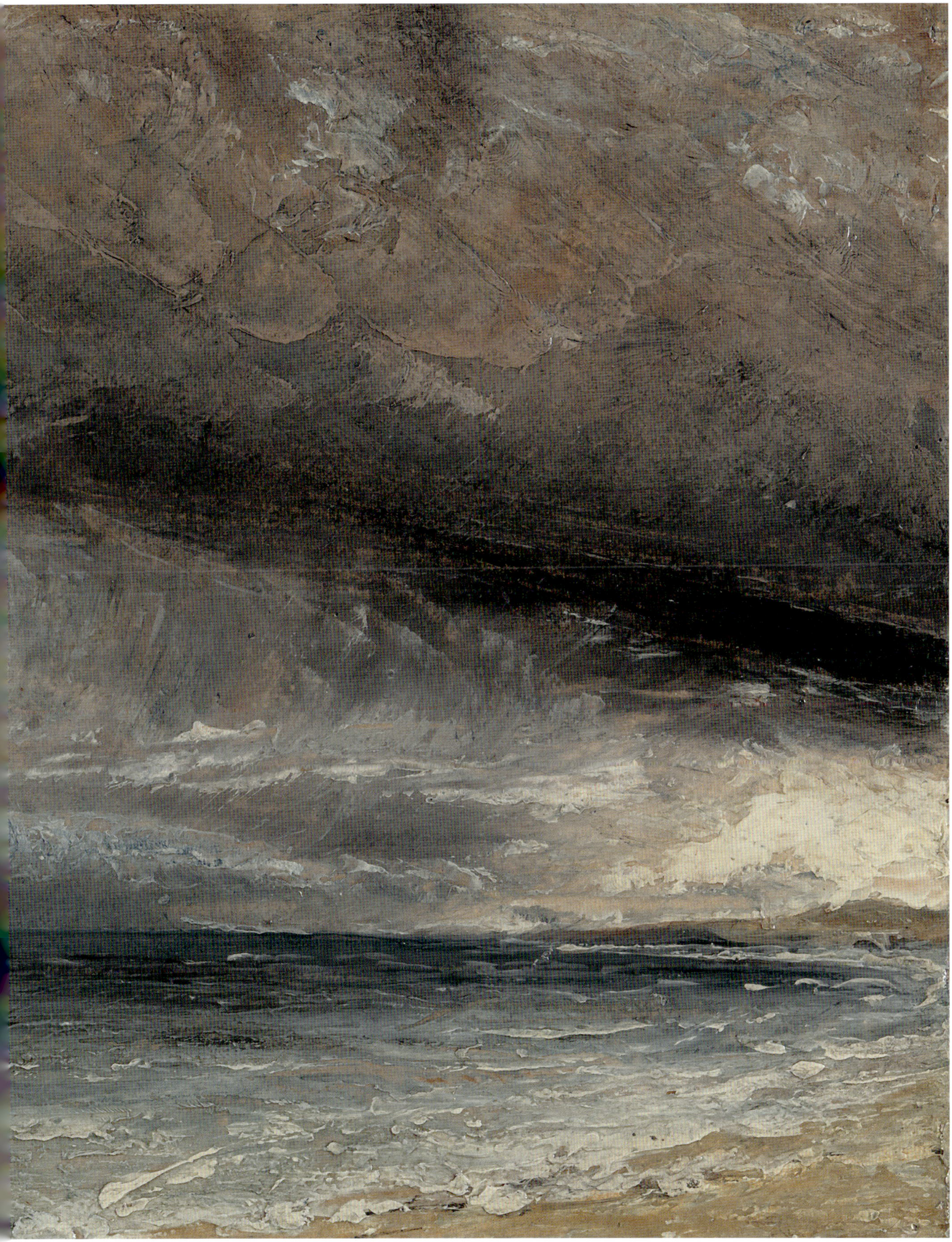

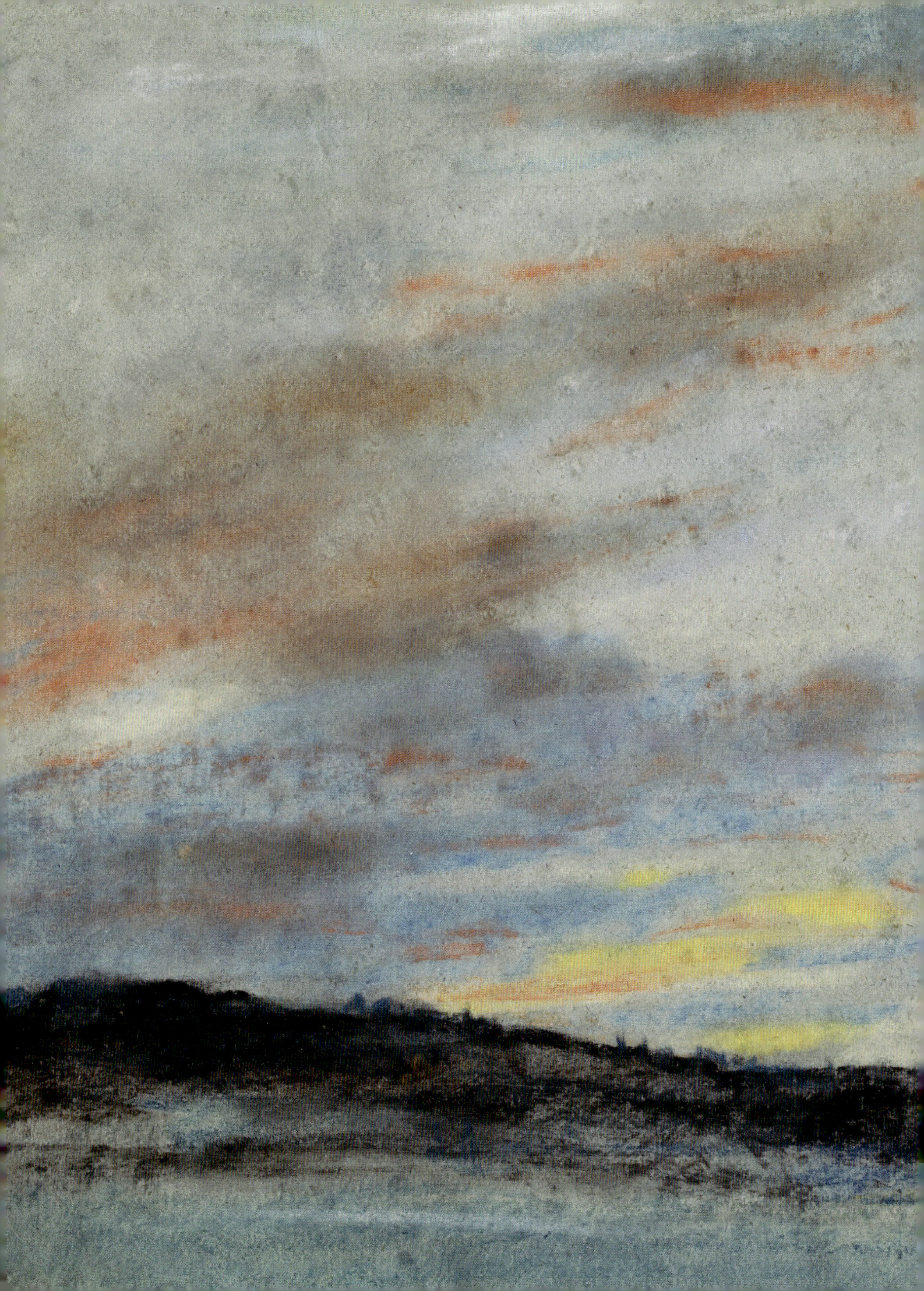

7 An Interview with Peter Harrap, Artist and Curator

'something out of nothing'[1]

MARK SHEERIN

'NEITHER SKY NOR SEA IS BLUE on the August day I meet Peter Harrap at his Brighton home. But the plaque outside his home in the city centre is a luminous shade of azure. Cloud-white letters, the colour of the weather today, tell us that, in 1824 and then 1828, John Constable lived and worked here. In one of those literary fictions in which houses are granted psychology, you would say that this terraced property appears proud of its new fixture from the City of Brighton and Hove. For the painter and curator who welcomes me into the modern interior, it is a matter of both professional kinship and happy coincidence.

Harrap and his partner, Natasha Kissell, moved here in 2010, the day after the opening of *No New Thing under the Sun*, a show for which he was the assistant curator at the Royal Academy of Arts. A key work in his selection was an evocative and unlikely painting by Constable, a brooding seascape rather than a landscape. Harrap was to discover that *Rainstorm over the Sea* (see fig. 95) was painted when Constable had a studio at the back of his new home. Again, it's more like a literary device than a real-life coincidence, and to this day Harrap describes the event as 'really bizarre, literally a hairs-on-the-back-of-your-neck event'.

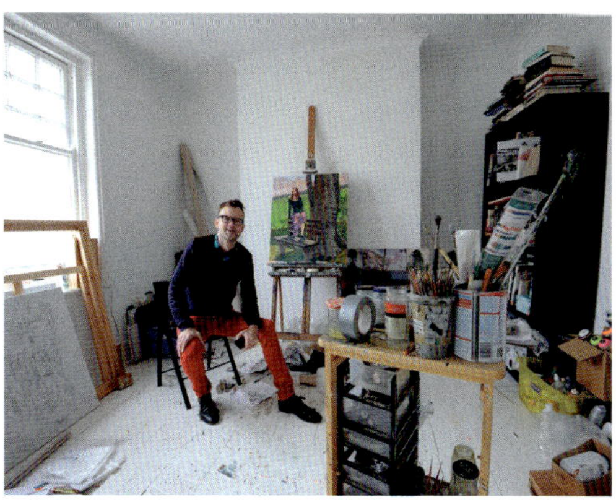

Detail of fig. 131

Fig. 129
Peter Harrap in his studio at 9 Sober's Gardens
2013
The Argus, Brighton

So while already an admirer of Britain's greatest landscape painter, the artist–curator was soon to become obsessed by the Brighton chapter of the earlier artist's life. Together with former journalist and local history expert Shân Lancaster, he tracked down letters that confirm the tenancy on Sillwood Road. Then, by turning left outside his front door, Harrap took a series of walks down to the sea in order to fix geographically certain of the small, but well-turned-out paintings that Constable executed during one of the most tumultuous and productive episodes of his life: productive because he executed 150 paintings; tumultuous because his wife, Maria, was dying of consumption.

No matter how much formalists will counsel you against the use of biographical details in order to read paintings, it is hard not to see in his brooding skies of East Sussex a certain melancholy on the part of Constable. Certainly when one compares two paintings such as the featured

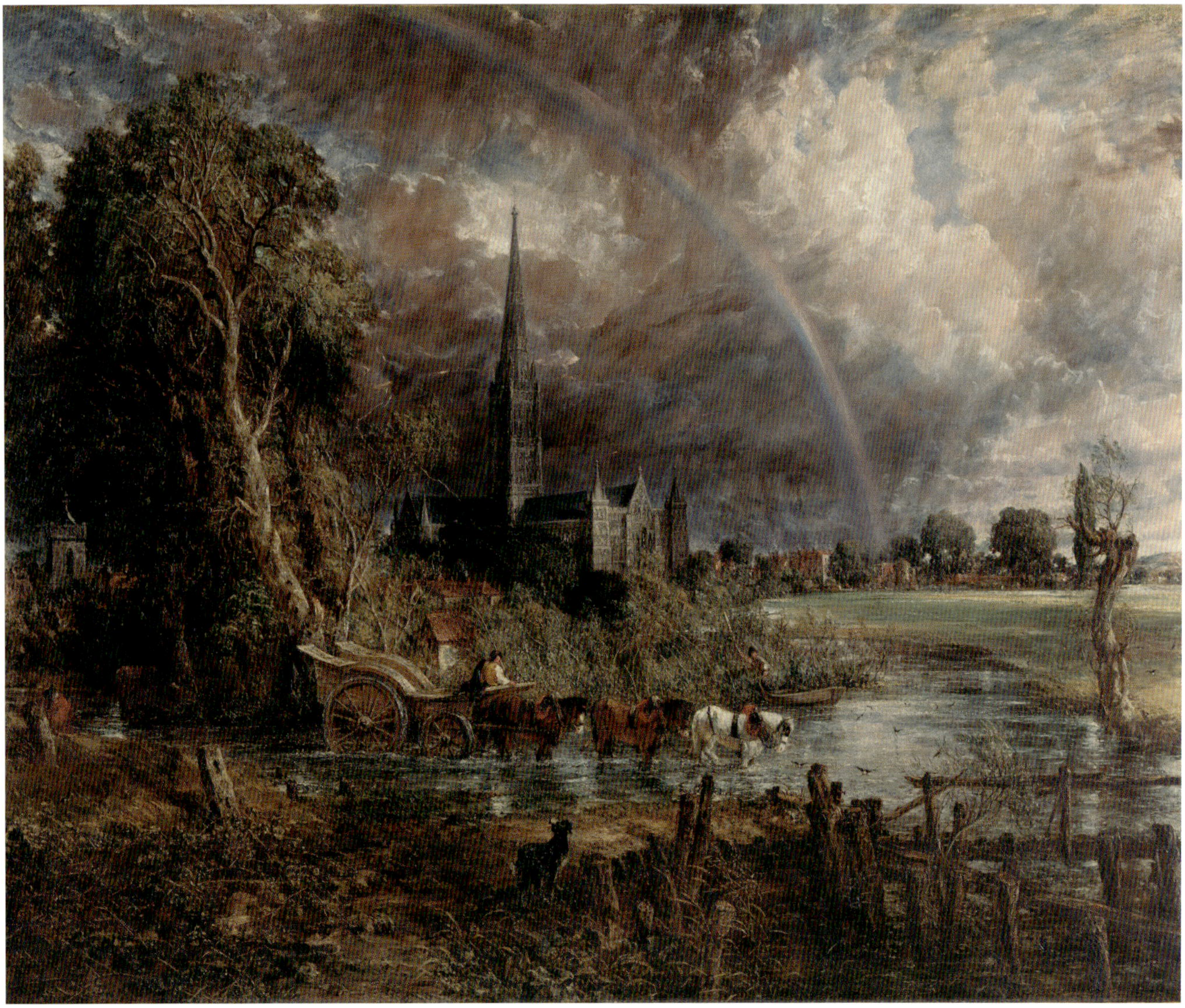

Fig. 130
Salisbury Cathedral from the Meadows
1831
Oil on canvas,
151.8 × 189.9 cm
R.31.1
Tate, London

views of Salisbury Cathedral, one sees that stormy forces have captured his imagination. This cathedral is one of Constable's best-known motifs, and so it is a telling scene. In 1823 (see fig. 16) he paints what you might expect from the maker of *The Hay Wain*. Harrap describes it as a 'highly topographical, sensitively drawn out but essentially pastoral view'. One might add 'pleasant' and 'English' to that. But in 1831 (fig. 130) he returns to the theme with a dark energy that holds land and sky in unholy tension. According to Harrap, 'It has the very dramatic use of the darks and the lights and the storms moving across the landscape and that is something that he was looking at particularly in Brighton. So much so that the master starts to paint in a more abstract plastic way, so that the emotion is conveyed not so much by topography as by texture, movement and colour.'

Had Brighton changed the way Constable responded to the elements? Or had life events, given that the couple only moved to Brighton so that Maria might recover, shaped the views the painter saw before his eyes? Both are conjecture, but not wild conjecture. More intriguing, and of greater interest to a painter such as Harrap, is the expanded range of marks and brushstrokes that one encounters after 1824, together with Constable's prolonged engagement with the English Channel. Harrap comments: 'There's just a massive shift in terms of the way the paint

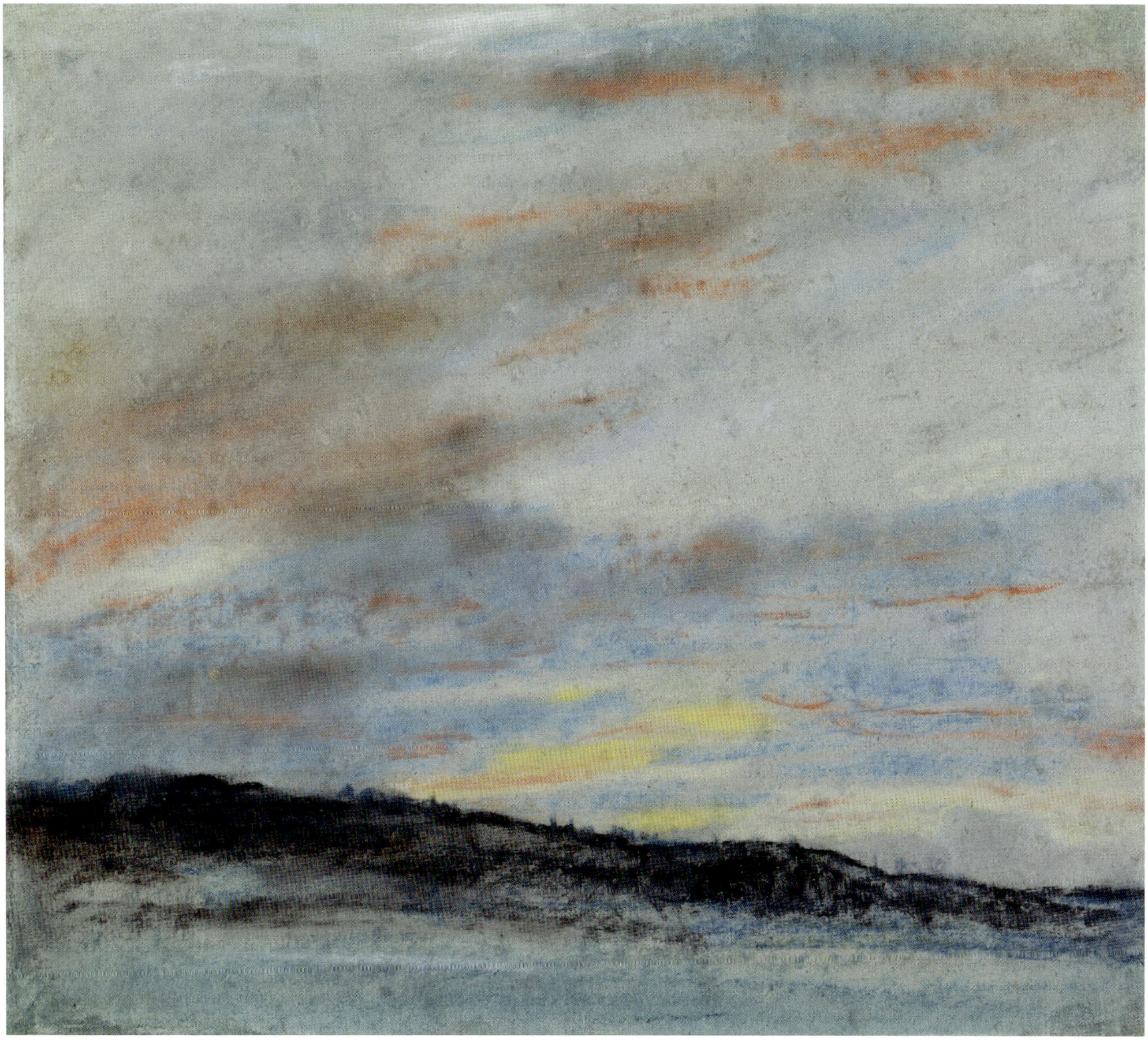

Fig. 131
Eugène Delacroix
(1798–1863)
Study of the Sky at Sunset
c.1849
Pastel on blue paper,
22.8 × 26.8 cm
British Museum, London

is handled; it's scraped, it's impasto, it's scratched back, it has an infinitely bigger range of visual language.' It is always interesting to observe a sea change in an artist's approach, but Harrap does still advise caution. Technically, scientifically, he's using the same blacks and umbers. But 'you can see from his handling he's more versatile, from experience', the younger painter says, with clear appreciation of the master's art.

Given that he painted the same place of worship in such contrasting ways, one wonders whether the demise of his wife provoked a loss of faith. But Harrap rejects this idea, based on his extensive reading of Constable's correspondence. 'I think that the cathedral is an object to paint in the landscape', he says, comparing the church to the windmills that Constable came to study on the South Downs, those deceptively steep round hills which close in on Brighton and Hove from the north. Since the Suffolk painter was apt to circle his quarry, in order to prepare studies from all angles, we might come to expect him to move around the cathedral, stylistically, emotionally, psychologically, as well as literally. Harrap talks about his subject's 360° approach as 'radial expansion', to which we might add 'dramatic expansion'; his second view of Salisbury has more depth in every sense.

When Harrap shows an illustration of Constable's *The Leaping Horse*, from 1825

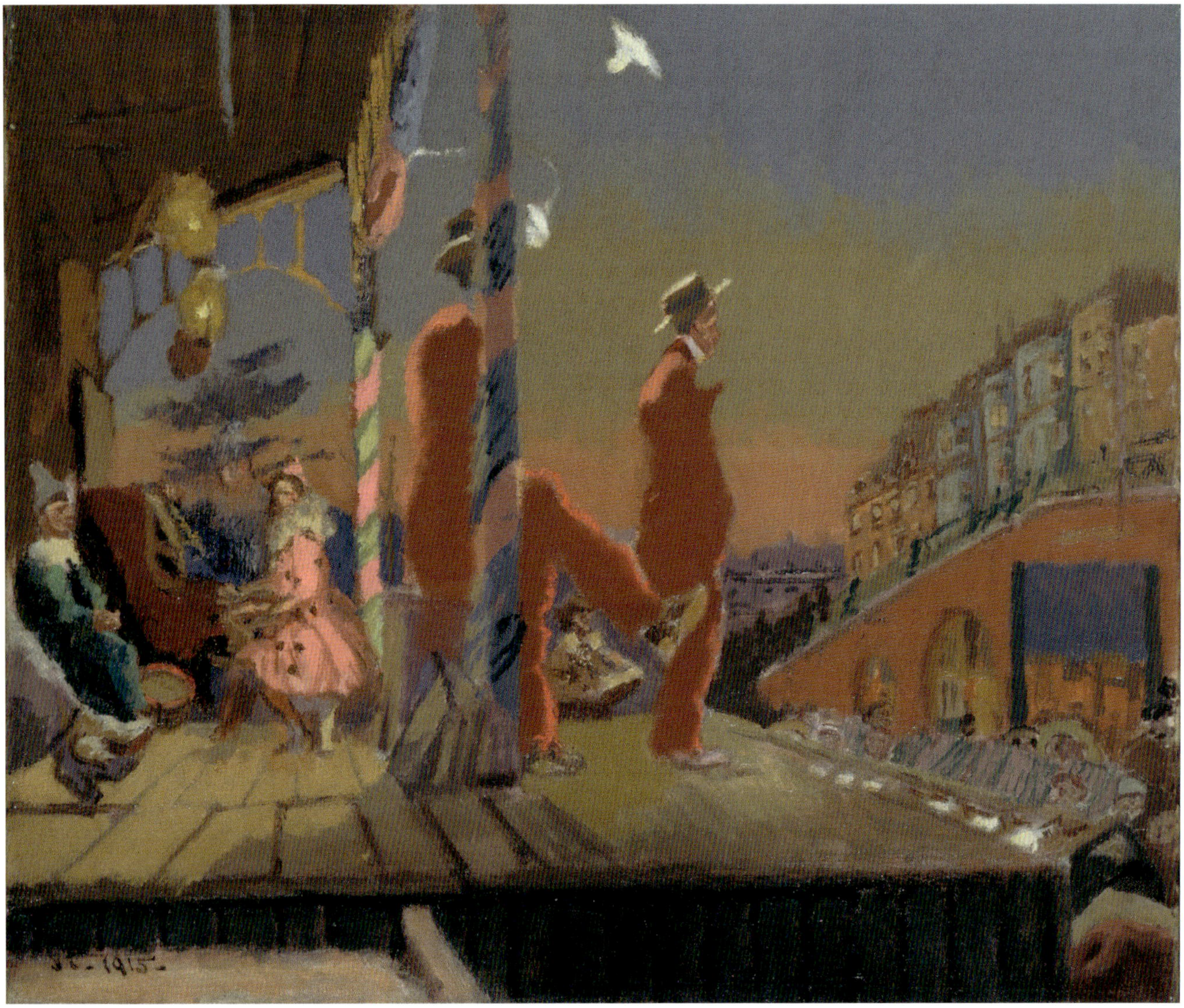

(see fig. 4), one may well reflect upon the leap the nineteenth-century painter was in the process of making. It's a jump we might broadly describe as one from the illustrative towards a greater appreciation of the sublime. So this is no tame horse, and one sees the inclement weather approaching in energetic waves, as it still does along Brighton beach, from the west, whatever the time of year. If Delacroix, who painted horses with equal drama, had seen this steed, he might have noted that the influential English painter was going beyond the Arcadian past of landscape art in England in one bound. We know that in 1825 he even paid a visit to Constable's studio at Charlotte Street in the English capital.[2]

Delacroix was also a great writer and so, in terms of influence, we have a good quote to go by: 'Constable says that the superiority of his green in his meadows is due to the fact that it is composed of a multitude of different greens ... What he says about the green of his grasslands can be applied to all other tones.'[3] In other words, he didn't make up a universal green; he instead worked out a complementary system for his greens, using the idea that to make a painting vibrant you might oppose two complementary colours, for example yellow and violet (fig. 131).[4] The French artist certainly understood you can apply this musical chord-like approach to all colour.[5] Delacroix was already central to the emergence of colour theory in the eighteenth century, as noted by John Gage.[6] And with him in the vanguard of this intellectual development is a commonsensical corn merchant's son.

Fig. 132
W. R. Sickert (1860–1942)
Brighton Pierrots
1915
Oil on canvas,
63.5 × 76.2 cm
Tate, London

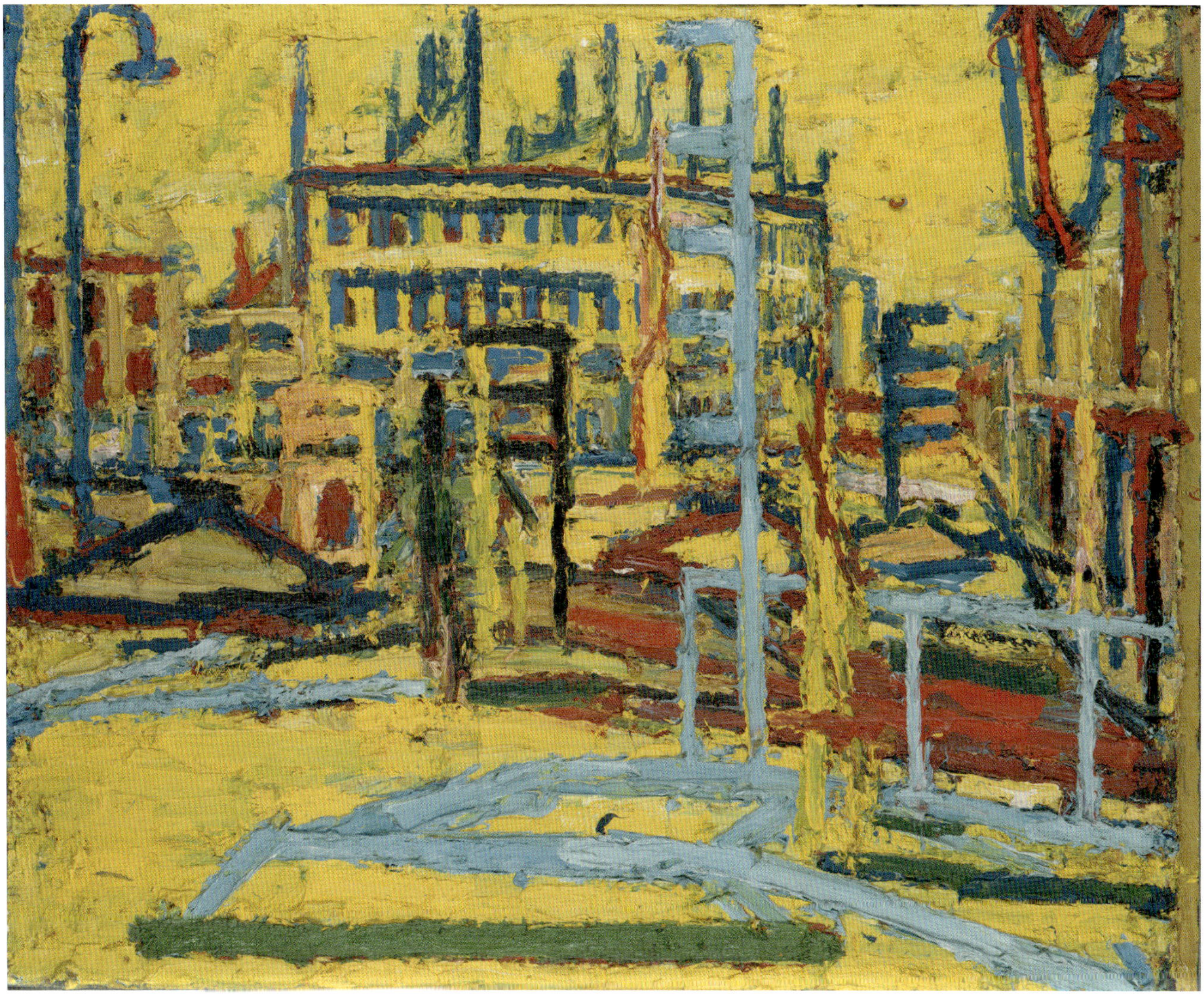

Fig. 133
FRANK AUERBACH (b. 1931)
Mornington Crescent with Statue of Sickert's Father-in-Law III, Summer Morning
1966
Oil on board,
121.3 × 152.4 cm
Private collection, courtesy of Marlborough Fine Art

That said, it would have had little to do with Constable's aspirations; he was no modernist. Rather, Constable's work has been described as 'the most profound expression' of an imaginative project begun by the home-grown landscape artists John Sell Cotman, David Cox and John Varley.[7] Perhaps that is why, despite the high regard in which he was held by the French, Constable stubbornly refused to visit France, even though Brighton–Dieppe was the main point of crossing. Boats would sail from a picturesque chain link pier, but the Suffolk-born painter's interest in this fragile-looking departure point was purely architectural. It fell to an equally prickly character to import the latest developments in colour theory back to England, even if, at various points during his time in Dieppe, it looked as if Walter Sickert (who married a local fisherwoman[8]) was never likely to return at all. He did, however, spend time in Brighton. Once there, he soon came across pierrots, sombre clowns who in his painting seem to be lost on their way to a *fête galante* (fig. 132). Pierrots are long gone from the seafront, needless to say. But the pallid green of the entertainers' flesh may be as derived from theories of colour separation.

Sickert, certainly, shared an analytical cast of mind with Constable. As many times as the earlier artist would choose a vantage point from which to rotate and recalibrate, Sickert would stalk his pictorial prey, making for example dozens of meditative paintings from all angles of Dieppe's church of St Jacques. As

Fig. 134
Claude Gellée, le Lorrain
(c.1604/5–1682)
Trees in Vigna Madama; A Large Oak Tree Overgrown with Ivy, Others Beyond
c.1638–40
Black chalk with brown ink and grey-brown wash,
33 × 22.4 cm
British Museum, London

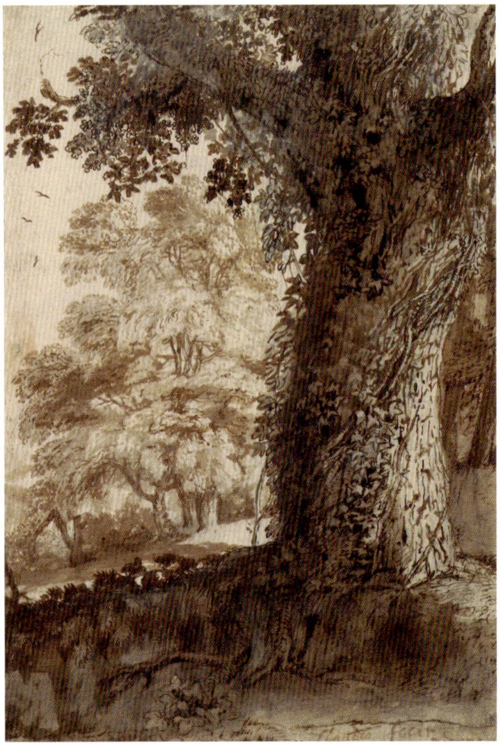

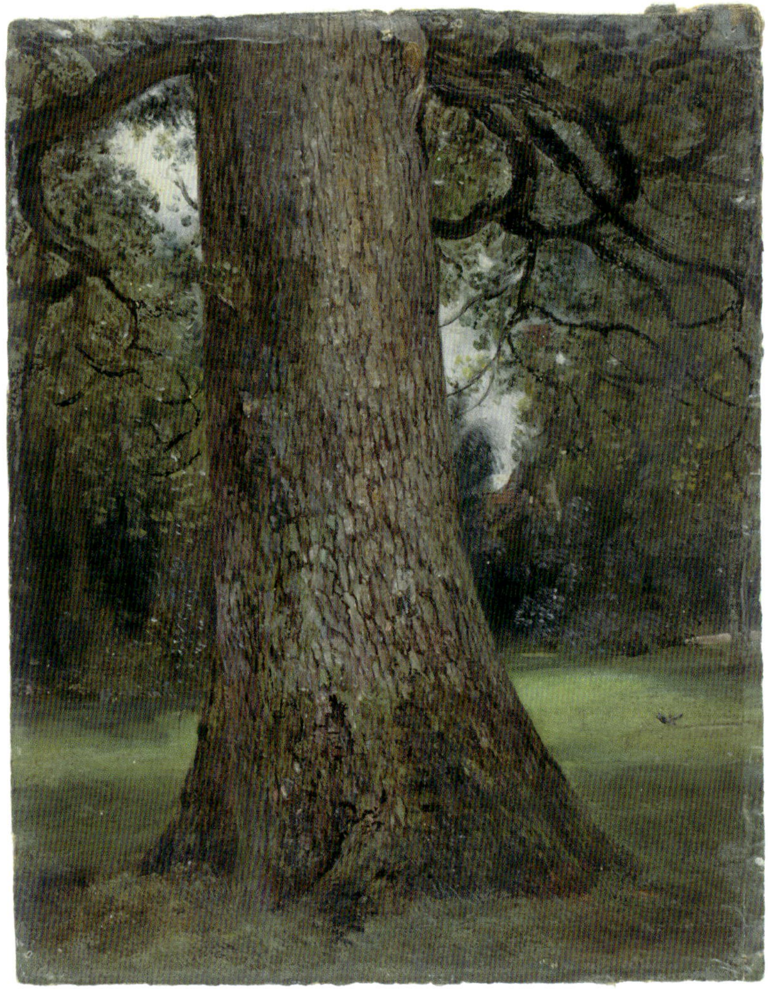

Fig. 135
Study of a Trunk of an Elm Tree
c.1824
Oil on paper,
30.6 × 24.8 cm
R.21.113
Victoria and Albert Museum, London

an encounter between one great painter and another, Harrap delights in this comparison. He reiterates the way in which Constable used small studies to work up larger paintings like patchwork. Often relying on working grid layouts, Sickert did the same. The notorious painter of Camden Town may have come from a world far removed from the rural outlook of Constable, but the similarities are there. 'We're moving from working in series, and then sequence, and in parallel', the curator tells me, with clear enthusiasm for the connections he has discovered.

More recently Frank Auerbach took his holiday for one day every year on the Palace Pier in Brighton.[9] If Constable began exploiting materials and working more swiftly when he was in Brighton, Auerbach, with his claustrophobic, impasto handling of paint, is perhaps taking up the Romantic approach to brushwork. Harrap also tells me that 'Auerbach is intrigued by both Sickert and Constable together with their routines and sequences of drawings'.[10] Auerbach shares a few of Sickert's London haunts, and the painting *Mornington Crescent* (fig. 133), with the inclusion of a statue of one of Sickert's three fathers-in-law (the statesman Richard Cobden), is another intriguing connection.

Here we find another parallel across time. Just as Constable once did, Auerbach loves to walk, and walks daily round north London in

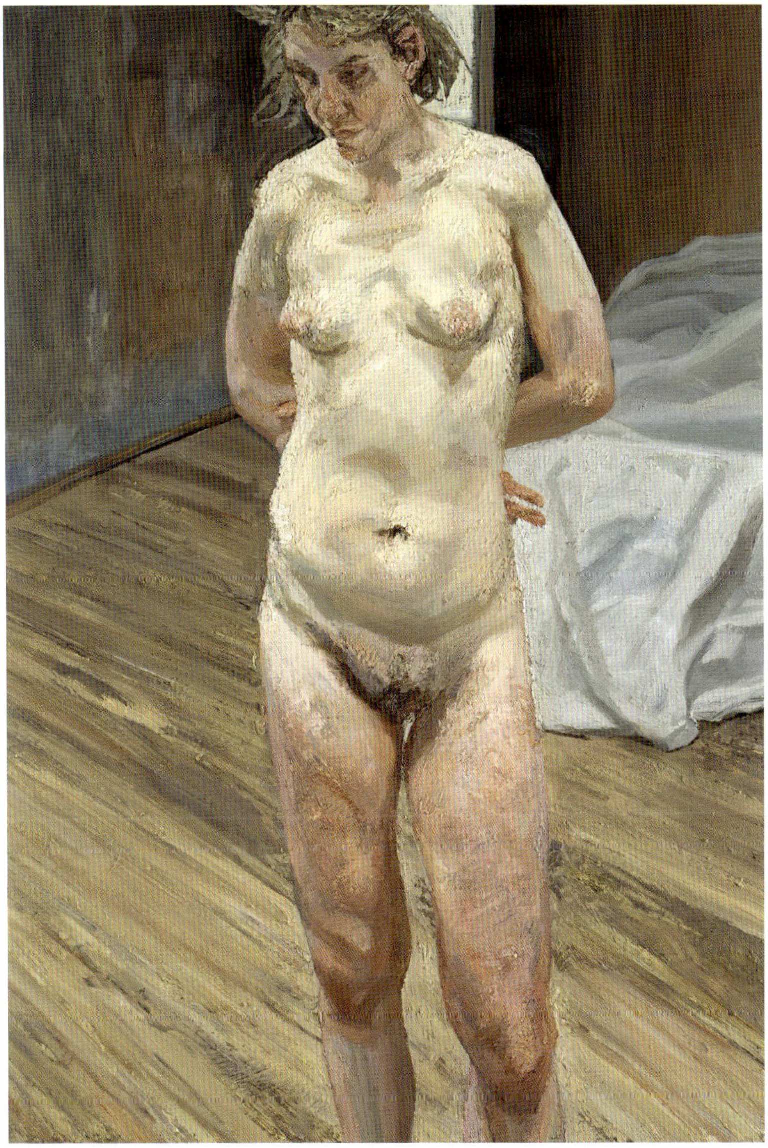

Fig. 136
LUCIAN FREUD (1922–2011)
Naked Portrait Standing
1999–2000
Oil on canvas,
109.2 × 77.5 cm
Private collection

search of his subject-matter.[11] Constable's walks form the skeleton of the exhibition. They were neither evidence of flâneurism nor experiments in psychogeography. They were simply searches for the best scenes and a way of understanding the landscape in a physical way. But this peripatetic cast of mind can still be found in later generations of land artists, as opposed to landscape painters. Perhaps Richard Long, who gained notoriety by wearing a path across a field as art, had Constable in mind when he said, 'Nature has always been recorded by artists, from prehistoric cave paintings to twentieth-century landscape photography. I too wanted to make nature the subject of my work, but in new ways.'[12]

In another parallel that resonates through time, Harrap has chosen to explore a set of tree studies that 'branch out' from a quite personable elm (fig. 135). He believes that Constable found the tree near Preston Manor, to the north of Brighton, and in painting it he drew inspiration from a Claude (fig. 134), which he saw in January 1824,[13] three months before the family came to Brighton for the first time.[14] The remarkable and exquisitely detailed work Constable made has previously been attributed to Hampstead and dated to around 1821. Harrap's view of the location of the elm chimes with the findings of Mark Evans,[15] who examined the work in the light of the most recent technical findings and concluded that it was made almost certainly after the summer of 1823 and very probably in 1824.[16] Harrap endorses Evans's conclusions and builds upon them to suggest that the painting is a Brighton work, pointing out that it shows the tree in the full leaf of summer, and that as Constable did not visit Hampstead at all in 1824, Brighton now seems to be the most likely location. Indeed, 1824 afforded the artist a rare leisurely summer when he had both the opportunity and the free time to paint freely, and the elm seems to connect naturally into the theme of experimentation and exploration we have already seen developing here.

Anthropomorphism cannot be ignored. As if to make this point, our near-contemporary Lucian Freud has embraced this tree, even as Constable's tree appears to embrace the viewer. As a portrait specialist, Freud had little trouble relating the trunk of this gentle tree to the trunk of a woman of young middle age (fig. 136). Look closer and you'll see there is more to it than lexical slippage between parts of trees and parts of bodies. Freud twists the woman's arms

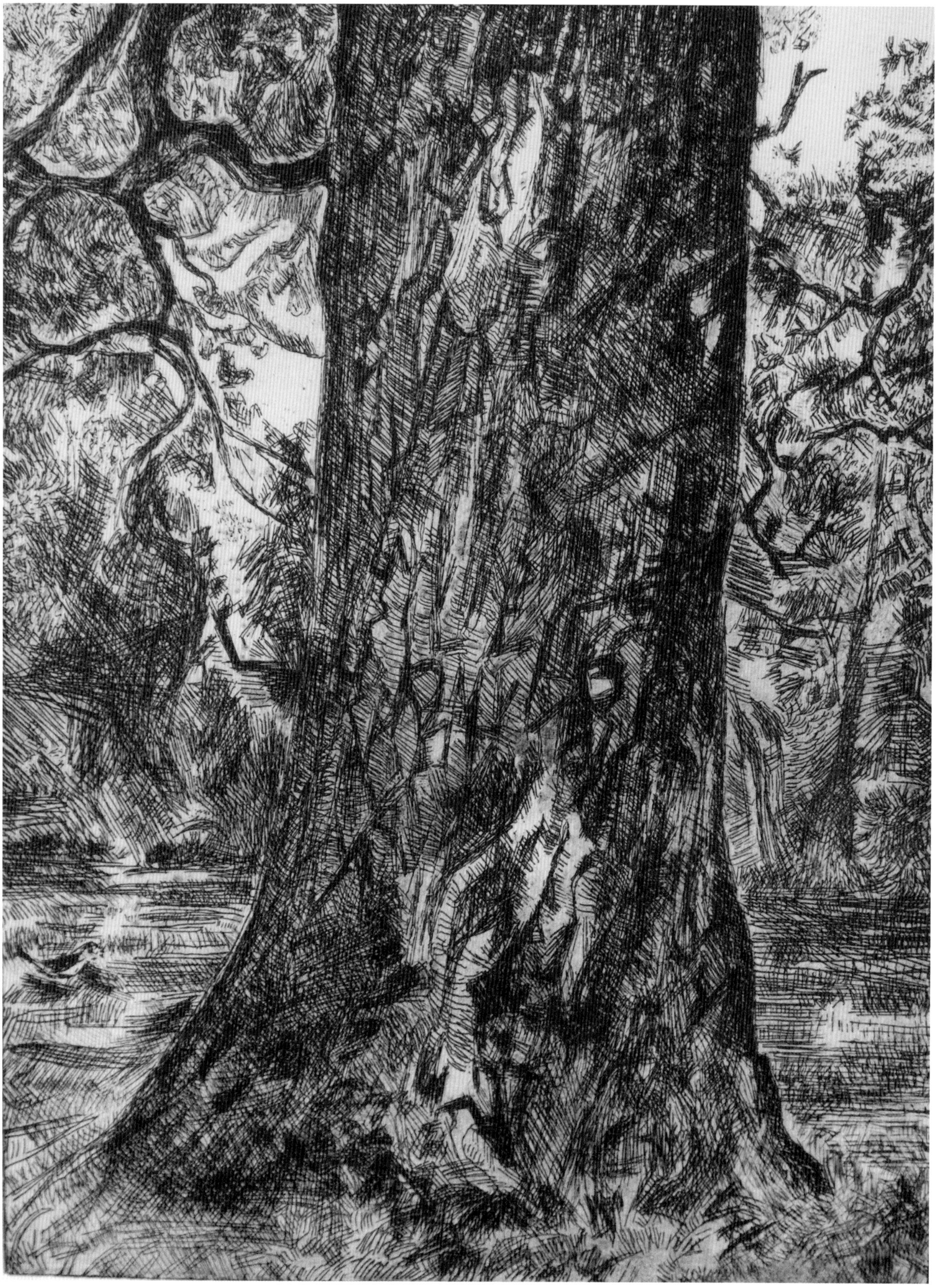

Fig. 137
Peter Harrap (b. 1975)
Proof after Freud after Constable
2016
Etching on paper,
31 × 24 cm
Collection of the artist

Fig. 138
Peter Harrap (b. 1975)
Body in the Trunk
2016
Oil on paper, 50 × 39 cm
Collection of the artist

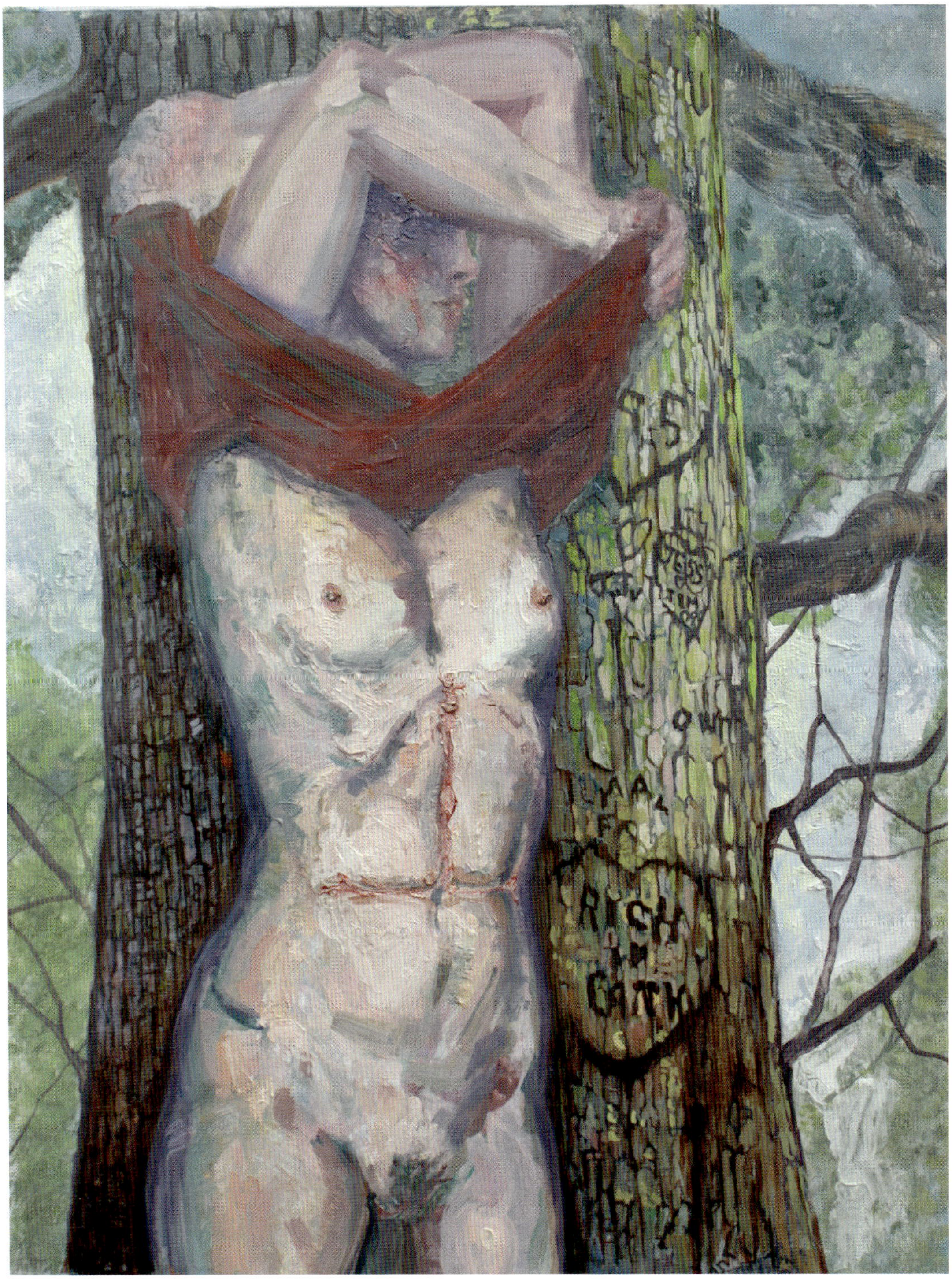

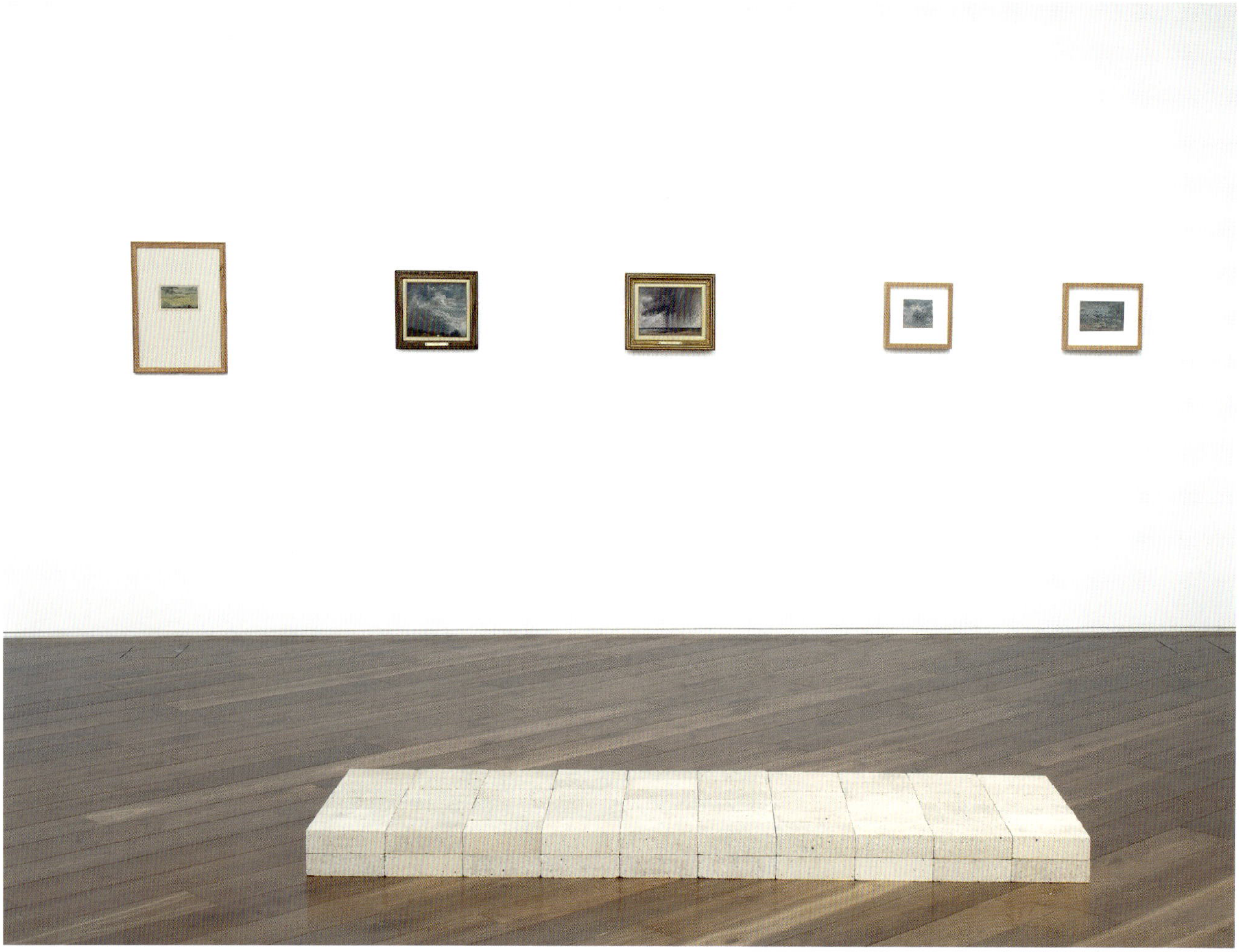

behind her back like the limbs of his arboreal model.

Harrap himself has been fascinated by this sequence, which enjoyed pride of place at *Constable: le choix de Lucian Freud*, an exhibition at the Grand Palais, Paris, in 2002. With his long-standing interest in people and psychology, Freud has paid careful attention to the bark. Harrap further interprets the hard-etched lines as written carvings, scarring the trunk (fig. 137). And it is these arborglyphs, these collisions of nature and culture, that connect language and painting. This may be what led Harrap to paint over Constable's trunk with the trunk of a female friend (fig. 138); her body is scarred from an automobile accident. Scars speak volumes, even to those who cannot read.

We must return to language, specifically English, to consider a further sequence of works, usefully put together at Firstsite, Colchester, by

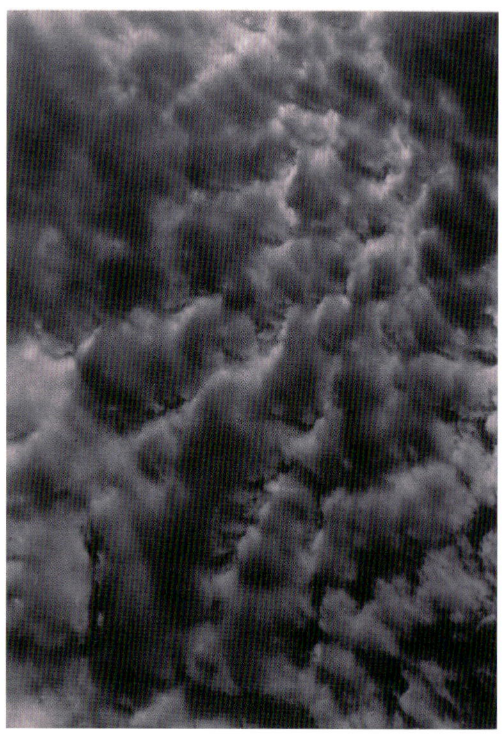

Fig. 139
Carl Andre (b. 1935)
Equivalents
1966
Firebricks,
12.7 × 68.6 × 229.2 cm
Tate, London
Installation view at Firstsite, Colchester, 2012, curated by Stephen Claydon

Fig. 140
Alfred Stieglitz (1864–1946)
Equivalent VIII
1929
Gelatin silver print,
11.7 × 9.2 cm
Phillips Collection, Washington, DC

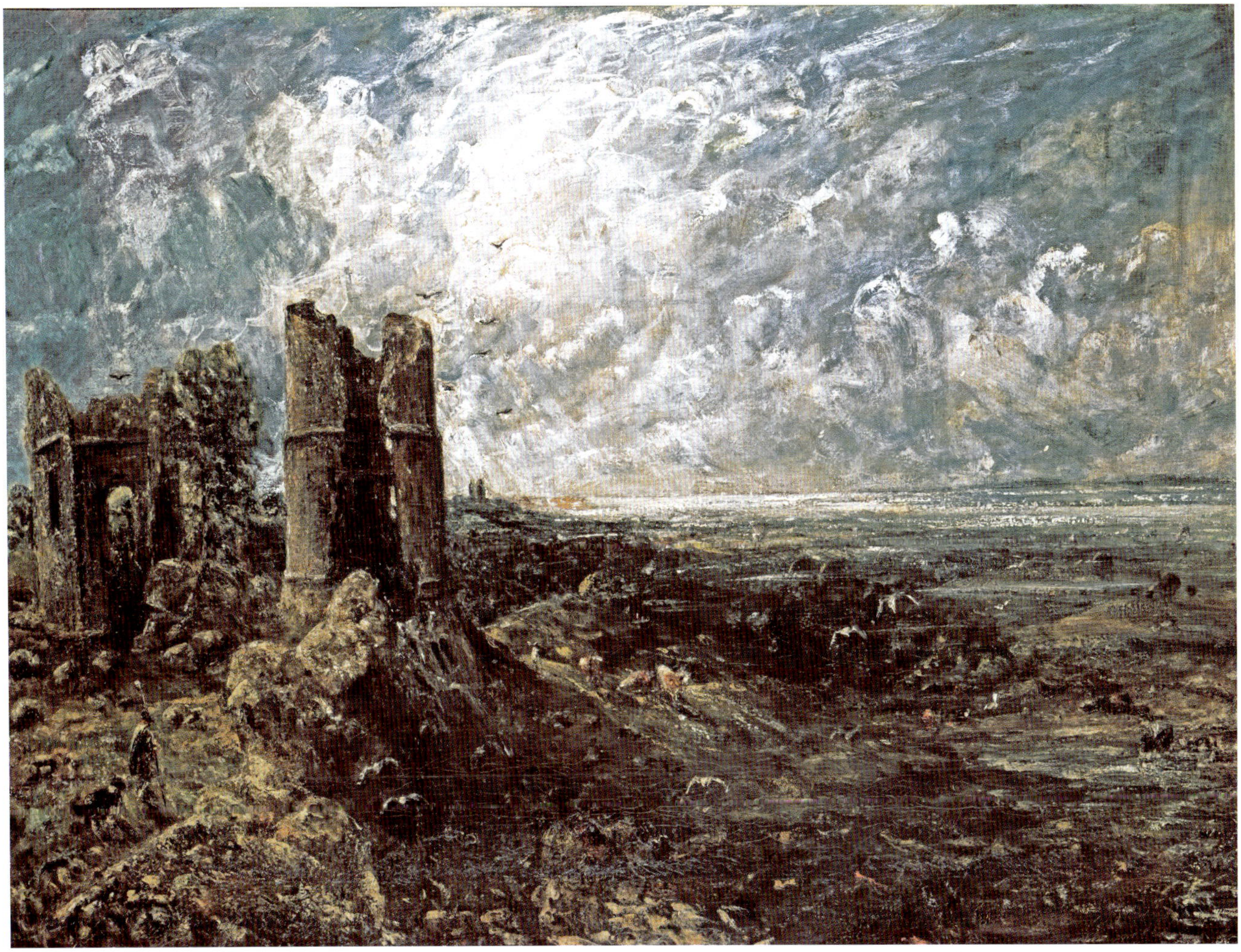

Fig. 141
Sketch for 'Hadleigh Castle',
c.1828–9
Oil on canvas,
122.6 × 167.3 cm
R.29.2
Tate, London

the artist Stephen Claydon (fig. 139). Harrap unveils the three works in question with excitement, telling me we are moving beyond the 'serial' and the 'sequential' into the realm of 'equivalence'. And it can be seen at once that we've now reached one of those artistic full stops that characterised the twentieth century and which still seem impossible to follow: Carl Andre's *Equivalent* series, otherwise known as the 'pile of bricks' from the Tate.

The missing link between this work and the Constable seascape mentioned at the start of this chapter is another cloud study, by Alfred Stieglitz (fig. 140), which the American photographer named *Equivalent VIII*. The trio have the satisfying correspondence of a Mensa puzzle. The former's painting conceals hours of preparatory work, just as Andre's piece is built on screeds of hidden theory. Harrap also reminds me that, in their day, both these artists took their share of flack from press and public alike. And finally both the non-photographic works enjoy some independence from the empirical world, creating 'something out of nothing', as Constable famously proclaimed he set out to do. But whereas Andre works with the simplest of building materials, Constable is drawn to the sight of their decay. Both *Equivalent VIII* and this stirring, foreboding *Sketch for Hadleigh Castle* (fig. 141) represent a 'pile', which is another of those lexical slippages. But like any historic castle, this one is imbued with mystery, rather than systemic thinking. This is the Constable work that most inspires Natasha Kissell. Harrap's partner (and thus the other resident of their Sillwood Road home), Kissell habitually places iconic modernist buildings in sublime landscape settings. In so doing, here (fig. 142) she confronts Bauhaus with Romantic excess, and uses each

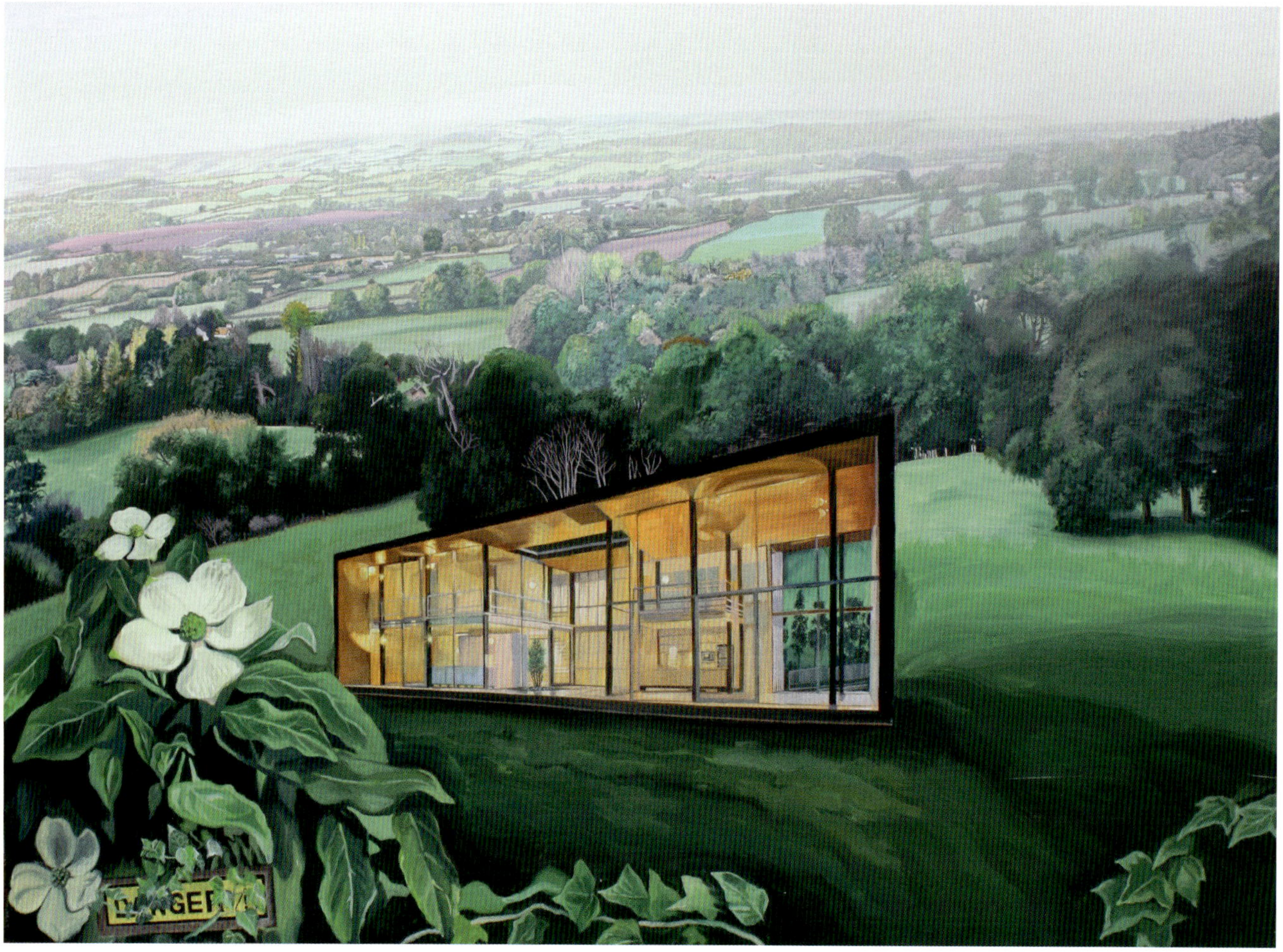

Fig. 142
NATASHA KISSELL (b. 1978)
English Idyll
2012
Oil on canvas,
122 × 163 cm
Private collection

approach to problematise the other, making a space for doubt. Doubt, as we learn from the poet Keats and his Romantic theory of negative capability, can be radical.

You also have to suspend belief to read the paintings of Alexander Cozens and their early embrace of chance operations. Cozens's *modus operandi* was to take his paper, screw it into a ball, coat the ball in ink and then flatten this alphabet of blots. He then painted the landscape that imposed itself upon his mind (fig. 143). It was a kind of Rorschach test for the nature-loving visionary. According to Harrap, Constable was looking closely at Cozens in November 1823; he admired his liberated approach to the study of trees and clouds.

Coincidence may be neat, but the concluding painting here is also a void. Charlotte Verity painted *The Gap* (fig. 144) in response to Constable's own response to Cozens. It is a void because in the copious fields of white space we have the 'nothing' from which Constable always hoped to produce 'something'. But we have also come full circle, because Verity's calligraphic monochrome was painted in East Anglia. The region is, of course, where any contemporary landscape painter can return to the source of the English agricultural sublime. 'It's the middle distance of a Constable', Harrap explains, a space in which one can easily lose oneself. Without Constable's time in Brighton there would not be nothing but, in terms of landscape art, there would be a lot less.

Fig. 143
Alexander Cozens
(1717–1786)
Plate 6
c.1785
Aquatint on paper,
24 × 31.5 cm
Tate, London

Fig. 144
Charlotte Verity (b. 1954)
The Gap, the Middle Distance
2015
Sepia and grey watercolour on paper,
41 × 52 cm
Private collection

OVERLEAF: Fig. 145
Christopher (1786–1855) and John (*fl.* 1821–1840) Greenwood
The Sussex Hundreds
1824–25
Print
Andy Garth, BrightonStuff

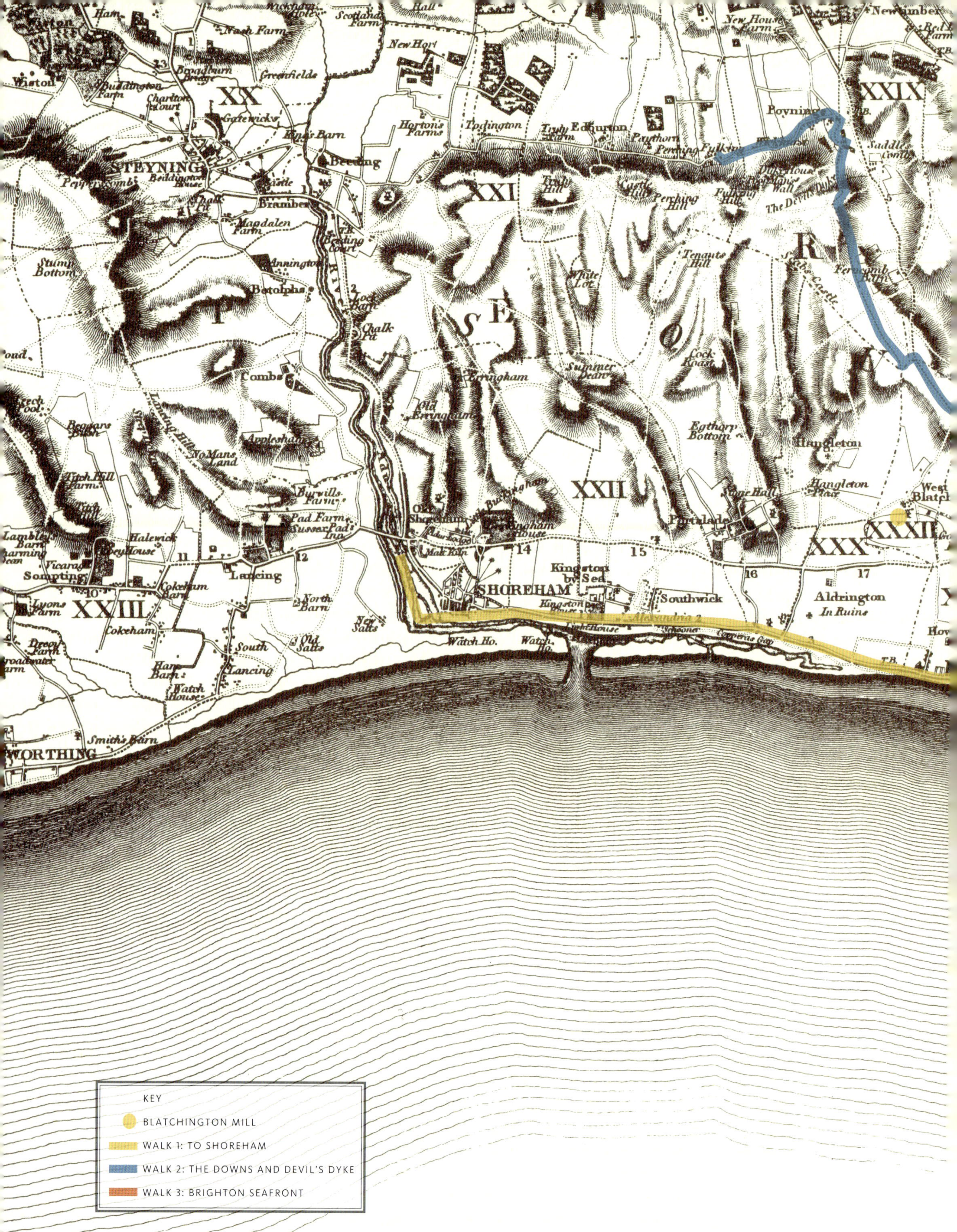
KEY
BLATCHINGTON MILL
WALK 1: TO SHOREHAM
WALK 2: THE DOWNS AND DEVIL'S DYKE
WALK 3: BRIGHTON SEAFRONT
STEYNING
SHOREHAM
WORTHING
Lancing
Sompting
Southwick
Aldrington
Portslade
Hangleton
Poynings
Bramber
Beeding
Botolphs
Kingston by Sea
Edburton
Truly Hill
Tenants Hill
Summer Down
Cock Roast
Erringham
Old Erringham
Applesham
Combs
Coombes
North Barn
South Lancing
Smith's Barn
Watch Ho.
Nash Farm
Greenfields
Buddington Farm
Wiston
The Devil's Dyke
Perching Hill
Fulking Hill
Castle Hill
Egthorp Bottom
Hangleton Place
Aldrington In Ruins
West Blatch
Newtimber
New House Farm
Tottington
XX
XXI
XXII
XXIII
XXIX
XXX
XXXII

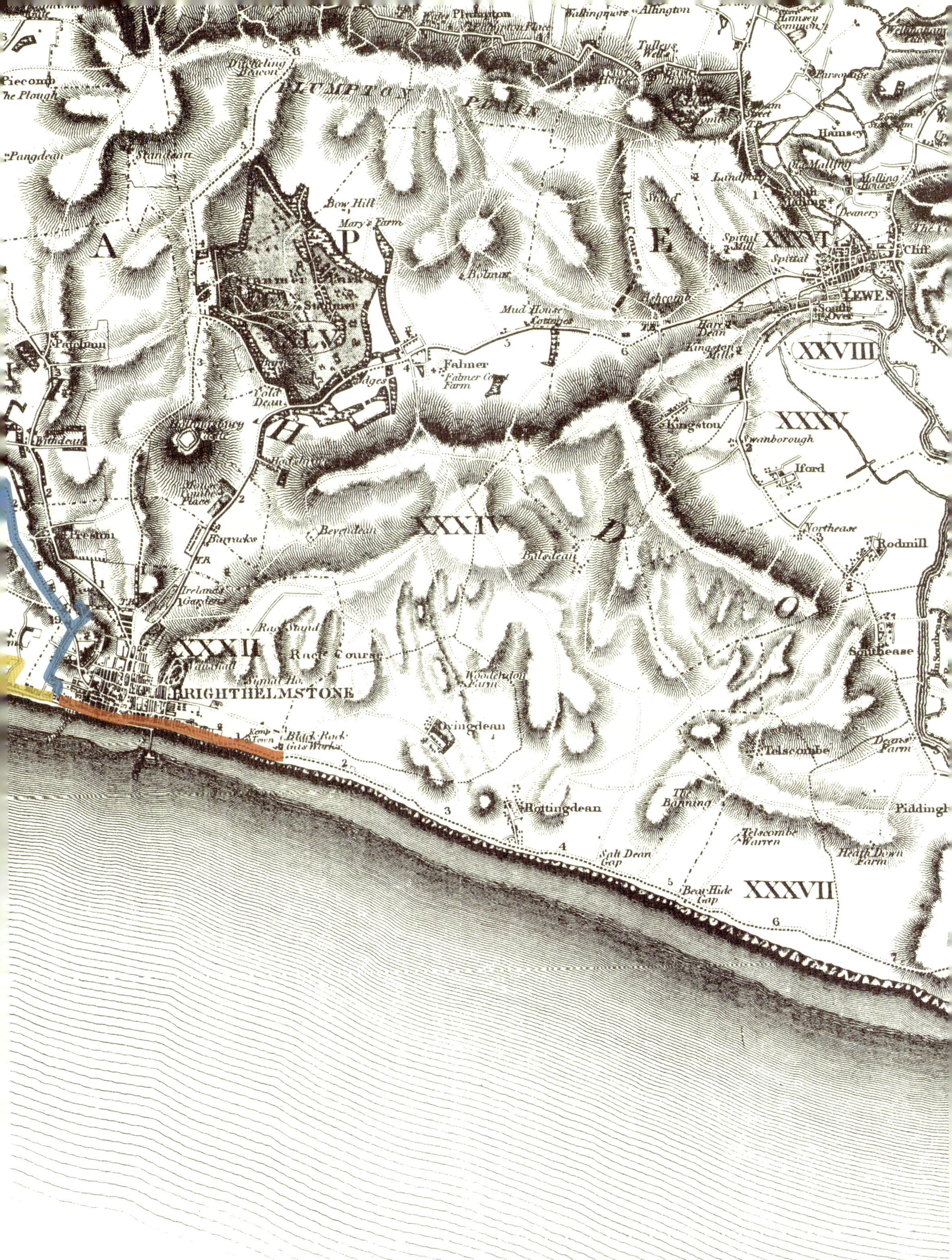
Plumpton
Wallingpore
Allington
Hamsey Common
Ditcheling Beacon
Piecomb
The Plough
PLUMPTON
PLAIN
Tulleys Wells
Parsonage
Hamsey
Pangdean
Standean
Bow Hill
Mary's Farm
Landport
South Malling
Malling House
Deanery
A
P
E
Spittal Mill
Spittal
XXVI
Cliff
Botney
LEWES
South Over
Mud House Cottages
Ashcomb
Hare Dean
Kingston Mills
XXVIII
Patcham
Falmer
Falmer Court Farm
Lodges
Cold Dean
XLV
Kingston
XXXV
Swanborough
Iford
Hollingbury Castle
H
Withdean
Preston
Barracks
Bevendean
XXXIV
Northease
Rodmill
D
Balsdean
Irelands Gardens
O
Race Stand
XXXII
Race Course
Southease
Woodendon Farm
BRIGHTHELMSTONE
Signal Ho.
Kemp Town
Black Rock
Gas Works
Ovingdean
Telscombe
Deans Farm
Rottingdean
The Banning
Piddingh
Telscombe Warren
Heath Down Farm
Salt Dean Gap
Bear Hide Gap
XXXVII

Timeline

1776

John Constable born at East Bergholt House, Suffolk, fourth of six children of prosperous mill owner and corn merchant Golding Constable (1739–1816) and Ann Constable (1748–1815).

- America publishes Declaration of Independence.
- Adam Smith's *The Wealth of Nations*, the founding text of modern economics, is published.

1778

- Death of Voltaire and Rousseau.
- James Cook establishes first British colony in Australia.

1779

- William Blake enrols as student at the Royal Academy

1780

- The 'Gordon Riots': violent anti-Catholic demonstrations in London.

1781

- A mysterious disease now believed to be porphyria causes George III to suffer several attacks of mental trauma in the early 1780s.

1783

- Britain recognises the independence of United States of America.

1785

- First edition of the *Daily Universal Register*, soon renamed *The Times*.

1788

- Birth of Byron.
- George III becomes more deranged.

1789

At school in Dedham, destined to take over the family business but showing early interest in art.

- Storming of the Bastille; start of the French Revolution.
- Mutiny on *HMS Bounty*.
- Turner admitted to Royal Academy as a student, aged 14.

1791

- Death of Mozart.
- Turner exhibits two watercolours at the RA.

1792

Employed in his father's mills to learn the business at first hand. Known locally as 'the handsome miller'.

Privately copying the engravings of Raphael.

- Mary Wollstonecraft writes *A Vindication of the Rights of Woman*.

1793

- France declares war on Britain. Louis XVI and Marie Antoinette executed by guillotine.
- Louvre in Paris opens to the public as an art museum, with 537 paintings mostly confiscated from the Church and the French royal family.

1795

Meets Sir George Beaumont, sees his paintings by Claude Lorrain. Smitten by the handling of landscape.

1796

Working, very unwillingly, as a clerk in his father's office.

- Turner exhibits his first oil painting and ten watercolours at the Royal Academy.

1799

Leaves East Bergholt for London to try his fortune as an artist. Admitted to the Royal Academy Schools.

- Discovery of Rosetta Stone.
- Birth of Balzac and of Pushkin.
- Turner elected Associate of the Royal Academy.

1800

Becomes full student at RA.

- Beethoven conducts first performance of *Symphony No. 1*.

1801

Father tells him he is 'Persuing a shadow' and wishes to see him employed

A sketching tour of the Peak District, Derbyshire.

- Act of Union establishes the United Kingdom of Great Britain and Ireland.
- Discovery of ultraviolet radiation.

1802

He infuriates his father by refusing post of drawing master at Military Academy, Great Marlow, Buckinghamshire.

For the first time he has a picture– *A Landscape* – accepted for the RA Exhibition.

- Marie Tussaud, who made death masks of the victims of the guillotine in Paris, opens waxworks in London.
- Turner is elected RA (Royal Academician).

1803

- Napoleonic Wars disrupt European grain markets until 1815.
- Grain prices in Britain rise sharply, benefiting grain merchants such as Golding Constable but causing suffering for the poor.

1805

- Nelson victorious over the French at the Battle of Trafalgar, but fatally wounded.

1806

Tour of the Lake District.

1807

- Britain abolishes the slave trade within its empire.

1809

Declares his love for Maria Bicknell, daughter of Charles Bicknell (1751–1828), solicitor to the Admiralty. His mother writes to him, 'Dear John, How much do I wish your profession proved more lucrative.'

- Birth of Charles Darwin, Abraham Lincoln and Edgar Allan Poe.

1810

On list of candidates for election Associate of Royal Academy. No votes.

Sells first landscape, for 30 guineas.

- Goethe: *Theory of Colours*.
- The first Indian restaurant opens in London: *the Hindoostanee Coffee House*.

1811

Maria warns that her father is unlikely to ever consent to their marriage because of his 'objection on the score of that necessary article, cash'.

- George, Prince of Wales, made Prince Regent on 5 February as King George III is now entirely mad.

1812

Working hard at 'wretched portraits' to make money. Father tells him to forget courtship 'till prospects improve'.

Exhibits four landscapes, including a view of Salisbury, at the Royal Academy.

- British Prime Minister, Spencer Perceval, assassinated.
- Napoleon's armies invade Russia.

1813

- Jane Austen: *Pride and Prejudice*.

1814

Tells his uncle: 'I have not yet in a single instance realised my ideas of art.'

Paints *Boat Building near Flatford Mill* entirely from nature (V&A).

- Napoleon exiled to Elba.

1815

- Napoleon escapes from Elba, defeated at the Battle of Waterloo and exiled to St Helena.
- Louis XVIII crowned King of France.

1816

Marries Maria at St Martin-in-the-Fields.

- On a wet summer holiday Byron, Percy and Mary Shelley and John Polidori write ghostly tales to amuse one another. Mary wrote the first draft of *Frankenstein* and Polidori of *The Vampyre*. Both became international best sellers.

1817

Moves to 1 Keppel Street, Bloomsbury. Birth of first child, John Charles, on 4 December.

1818

On list of candidates for election as Associate of the Royal Academy. Receives one vote.

1819

Birth of second child, Maria Louisa, 'Minna', on 19 July. Elected Associate of the Royal Academy.

Exhibits *The White Horse* (fig. 12), his first six-foot-wide landscape, at Royal Academy.

- The Peterloo Massacre in Manchester leaves 11 dead after rally for votes for working men is brutally broken up.

1820

Exhibits second six-footer, *Stratford Mill* (fig. 15).

- George III dies on 29 January.
- End of the Regency as George IV, builder of Brighton Pavilion, is crowned.

1821

Birth of third child, Charles Golding, on 29 March.

Exhibits third six-footer, *The Hay Wain* (fig. 25). Much admired by visiting French artists.

1822

Unsuccessful in election as full Academician. Moves to 35 Charlotte Street. Birth of fourth child, Isabel, on 23 August.

Exhibits fourth six-footer, *View on the Stour Near Dedham* (fig. 13)

- Charles Babbage presents a paper on his 'Difference Engine' – the earliest form of computer.

1823

Unsuccessful in election as full Academician.

Exhibits *Salisbury Cathedral from the Bishop's Grounds* (fig. 16).

1824

Unsuccessful in election as full Academician. Spends much of summer and autumn with Maria and children in Brighton.

Exhibits fifth six-footer, *The Lock* (fig. 9). *The Hay Wain* (fig. 25) and *View on the Stour Near Dedham* (fig. 13) at Paris Salon to great acclaim. Awarded a Gold Medal by Charles X of France (fig. 31).

- Stock market boom which began after the end of Napoleonic Wars is at its height.
- Execution of Henry Fauntleroy, last banker to be hanged for fraud in England, on 30 November.

1825

Birth of fifth child, Emily, on 29 March. Takes Maria and children to Brighton from August until January 1826.

Exhibits sixth six-footer, *The Leaping Horse*.

1826

Unsuccessful in election as full Academician. Birth of sixth child, Alfred Abram, on 14 November.

- More than 10 per cent of British banks fail.

1827

Leases 40 Well Walk, Hampstead, last in a series of Hampstead lodgings, a retreat for the rest of his life.

Exhibits *Chain Pier, Brighton* (fig. 48), his next big picture.

1828

Birth of seventh child, Lionel, on 2 January. Maria in Brighton, May–August. Death of Maria on 23 November in Hampstead, where she is buried.

1829

Elected Royal Academician by one vote.

Begins a series of 20 mezzotints after his paintings called *Various Subjects of Landscape Characteristic of English Scenery* (later known just as *English Landscape*), engraved by David Lucas under his supervision.

1830

- Death of George IV.
- William IV crowned.

1831

Exhibits *Salisbury Cathedral from the Meadows* (fig. 130).

1832

- Birth of Charles Lutwidge Dodgson (Lewis Carroll).

1833

Lectures on landscape painting in Hampstead

1834

Exhibits *Old Sarum* (V&A).

1835

- Henry Fox Talbot creates first photographic negatives.
- Charles Darwin visits Galapagos Islands on the Beagle.

1836

Exhibits *Stonehenge* (V&A). Lectures at the Royal Institution, London.

- Battle of the Alamo.

1837

Dies at home in Charlotte Street on 31 March. Buried beside Maria in Hampstead.

- William IV dies.
- Queen Victoria is crowned.

Notes

All volumes published in London unless stated otherwise.

JOHN CONSTABLE'S LETTER FROM BRIGHTON

1 *JCC* VI, p. 171 . Supplemented by annotations on typescript in Tate archives.

INTRODUCTION

1 *JCC* II, p. 319 (Constable in London writing to his wife, Maria, in Brighton, 28 May 1824).
2 Peter Harrap and Shân Lancaster, *The Burlington Magazine*, April 2013, pp. 250–51.
3 *JCC* VI, p. 171. In the Pigot Directory of 1828 the address appears as 'Sober's Garden', but it was also referred to either as 'Mrs Sober's Garden' or 'Mrs Sober's Gardens'. Nineteenth-century naming policy for street names was not as fixed as ours today, and therefore there was no 'correct' address.
4 'Plan of the Western Part of the Parish and Town of Brighton Shewing the Magnificent Building Arrangements Now in Rapid Progress in the Adjoining Parish of Hove, 1825', C. Busby, Architect, Waterloo Place, Brighton; East Sussex Records Office.
5 *JCC* VI, p. 172.
6 S. Berry, 'Thomas Read Kemp and the Shaping of Regency Brighton', *Journal of the Georgian Group*, XVII, 2009, pp. 125–40.
7 *Hereford Journal*, 9 October 1816.
8 *JCC* VI, p. 171.
9 *JCC* VI, p. 183.
10 *JCC* VI, p. 175.
11 *Oxford Dictionary of National Biography*, Oxford, 2004.
12 *Morning Post*, 16 October 1824.
13 *JCC* II, p. 433.

CHAPTER 1

1 *JCC* VI, pp. 156–58.
2 A. Lyles, 'Soliciting Attention: Constable, the Royal Academy and the Critics', in Lyles 2006, p. 37; see also Solkin 2001.
3 *JCC* VI, pp. 87–88 (letter to Fisher, 13 April 1822).
4 Ibid.
5 *JCC* VI, p. 91 (letter to Fisher, 17 April 1822). ('I shall not let the Frenchman have my picture. It is too bad to allow myself to be knocked down by a French man.')
6 *JCC* VI, p. 149 (letter to Fisher, 17 January 1824). Fisher's agreement to relinquish his interest in the picture was given in a letter the following day (*JCC* VI, p. 151).
7 *JCC* VI, p. 156 (letter to Fisher 15 April 1824). Constable painted three versions of the *Yarmouth Jetty* composition. The version generally regarded as the first (R.22.36) is the one that is signed, and this is generally also thought to be the one which Constable exhibited at the British Institution in 1823 and which Arrowsmith came to own. The other versions (R.22.37–38) were probably made with the assistance of John Dunthorne, and it is one of these – R.22.38, in the Tate – that is reproduced here as fig. 14.
8 On 15 April 1824 Constable had written to Fisher that 'I shall not let [my pictures] go out of my hands 'til paid for' (*JCC* VI, p. 156).
9 *JCC* VI, p. 157.
10 *JCC* VI, p. 204 (letter to Fisher, 10 September 1825).
11 For sketches of Constable's studio at 76 (formerly 35) Charlotte Street, made from memory by Claude Rogers and William Coldstream, see Cove 2006, p. 53.
12 *JCC* II, p. 314; in a letter of late May 1824 (*JCC* VI, p. 160) Constable told Fisher that the case containing the *Hay Wain* and *View on the Stour near Dedham* 'contained 3 others which i had ready', and assuming one of these was the *Yarmouth Jetty* he had already agreed to let Arrowsmith have, that leaves two more pictures which, from the context of the letter, it appears he had sold to him for an additional £50.
13 *JCC* II, p. 314.
14 *JCC* II, p. 316; it is from a letter Constable wrote to Fisher around 27 May 1824, when he summarises the various commissions that he is engaged on for Schroth and Arrowsmith, that we can deduce the sizes of the four small pictures commissioned by the latter in his second order (see *JCC* VI, p. 160, and R. B. Beckett's helpful summary in *JCC* IV, p. 181).
15 'However small ... the picture itself must be perfect, & the subject as good as one on a six foot canvas', Constable told Fisher on 18 July, when discussing his small commissions (*JCC* VI, p. 167).
16 For example, on 16 June 1824 Constable wrote in his journal that Monsieur le Vicomte de Thullusson ordered 'a little picture' (*JCC* II, p. 330).
17 Most of these commissions for, or demands on his time from, English clients are recorded in the journal Constable kept in 1824, between 31 May and 16 July (see *JCC* II, pp. 320–64, *passim*).
18 *JCC* IV, p. 99 (24 August 1825).
19 *JCC* II, p. 335 (18 June 1824).
20 These various episodes are recorded in Constable's journal of 1824, between 6 June and 4 July (see *JCC* II, pp. 326–56, *passim*).
21 *JCC* II, p. 327 (journal, 7 June 1824); the 'painting box' in question may well be the small wooden one that survives today in the family collection and which Constable is thought to have used in Brighton (discussed by Cove in Parris and Fleming-Williams 1991, pp. 501 and 514). However, the reference here could apply to any type of painting box, even a larger one perhaps holding bulkier painting materials when in transit. Another painting box owned by Constable, this one in metal, is in the collection of the Clark Art Institute, Williamstown, MA, and is discussed by Cove in Lyles 2006, pp. 194–96.
22 *JCC* II, p. 336 (letter from Maria Constable to John Constable, 19 June 1824).
23 The other possibility is that Constable used as his painting room the larger room at the top of the house, but this would have been less suitable as it faces west, and the light would surely have been too bright and variable. Furthermore, if that room had been used as a painting room, it would have deprived the family of a capacious room to accommodate most of the children and perhaps the nurse as well.
24 See note 22 above.
25 *JCC* II, p. 110 (letter to Maria, 30 June 1813).
26 Although no very early deeds exist for 11 Sillwood Road, Shân Lancaster and Sue Berry think it most likely that in 1824 Mrs Sober still owned the house. Not only had it just been built, but she also owned what are now numbers 8 and 14 Sillwood Road; she was in due course to move into the former property herself, and the latter she leased out until the 1830s, when she sold it.
27 *JCC* II, p. 363 (journal, 16 July 1824).
28 *JCC* II, pp. 363–64.
29 *JCC* VI, pp. 167 and 171 (18 July and 29 August 1824 respectively).
30 See note 27 above.
31 The wooden paint box which Constable is thought to have used in Brighton is referred to in note 21. It measures 9 ¼ × 12 inches. The

lid contains a removable wooden panel on which the artist would lean (or pin) his support (usually paper) for making his *plein-air* sketches in oils. The sketches would then be stacked inside the lid of the box behind the wooden panel for carrying home (Cove in Parris and Fleming-Williams, 1991, pp. 501 and 514).

32 See note 27 above.

33 *JCC* VI, p. 65 (letter to Fisher, 1 April 1821), and see Cove 2006, p. 52.

34 For example, there are references to him working at Charlotte Street on *The Leaping Horse* in 1824 (*JCC* VI, pp. 181 and 187) and to *The Cornfield* in 1826 (*JCC* V, p. 80).

35 *JCC* IV, p. 155 (letter to Dominic Colnaghi, 6 April 1827, written from Downshire Hill, Hampstead).

36 *JCC* II, p. 397 (journal, 1 October 1825, when Constable records how he had heard of an offer made in Paris for one of the two Hampstead subjects 'which i did at Brighton').

37 As suggested in Reynolds 1984, under R.25.12.

38 There are compositional similarities between the two; and indeed Reynolds (R.22.14) suggests that *A View at Hampstead* may show the vista across Branch Hill Pond.

39 R.25.7 and 25.8, *for Branch Hill Pond, Hampstead* (Oskar Reinhart Foundation) and *Child's Hill* (Private Collection) respectively. The original commission from Schroth was for two Hampstead views measuring 21 × 30 inches, which conforms to the size of other Hampstead views that Constable had painted before that date. In the event, however, he delivered paintings measuring around 24 × 30 inches. See also note 41 for the picture in the Dick Institute.

40 R.25.5 and 25.6.

41 The third pair, which entered the Dick Institute in 1943 from the estate of Dr John McGregor (died 1938), are not catalogued in Reynolds 1984. For the version in Ayrshire, see note 39 above. The version in Bury Art Gallery is R.25.11. Related to the composition of *Branch Hill Pond, Hampstead*, and no doubt used in the process of making the replicas, is a tracing of a detail of the carts and carters from the right-hand foreground (Reynolds 1996, 'Additions to the Later Paintings and Drawings of John Constable', R.25.5A) as well as a similar study of the same detail, in oils, and incised, which passed through Bonham's on 9 December 2012.

42 See Reynolds 1984, p. 159 (R.25.9), which records the inscription on the verso stating that the buyer, William Purton, is said to have been so satisfied with the picture in its unfinished state that he requested Constable did no further work to it. This is not necessarily inconsistent, however, with its being a near same-size compositional sketch for *Branch Hill Pond, Hampstead*; and indeed, Reynolds notes the observation of a former scholar that its dimensions tally with those Constable gave for the original (slightly smaller) version of the composition he was engaged to paint for Schroth.

43 *JCC* IV, pp. 186–88 (letters from Schroth to Constable, 13 July and 20 July 1824).

44 *JCC* IV, pp. 188–89 (4 August 1824).

45 *JCC* IV, p. 171.

46 Ibid.

47 He would, instead, surely have made the replicas at his Charlotte Street studio with the help of Johnny Dunthorne, who presumably prepared the two tracings for *Branch Hill Pond, Hampstead* cited in note 41 in the course of transferring that part of the design onto a fresh canvas. Furthermore, Constable does not refer to having copied the Hampstead pictures until 17 December (*JCC* VI, p. 187), some two months after his return to London, and in the interim he made a number of references in his letters to Dunthorne's usefulness in the studio, particularly in copying his paintings.

48 *JCC* II, p. 341.

49 *JCC* II, p. 338 (journal, 21 June 1824). As Beckett points out (*JCC* IV, p.183), 'Cum Paul's' seems to have been a family nickname for St Paul's Cathedral, the dome of which often forms a feature in the distance of Constable's Hampstead Heath subjects.

50 *JCC* II, p. 335 ('I was at work & had been so all day – on the little Osmington coast'). Two labels on the back of this picture indicate that it was painted for Arrowsmith in 1824 (see Reynolds 1984, pp. 135–36, R.24.5). The *Osmington Bay* composition exists in two further versions by Constable, which have slight differences (R.24.6 and 24.7).

51 *JCC* IV, p. 171.

CHAPTER 2

1 *JCC* II, p. 340.

2 *JCC* IV, pp. 183–84 (19 June 1824).

3 See note 1 above.

4 Beckett in *JCC* IV, p. 179; and M. Florisoone, 'Constable and the *Massacres de Scio* by Delacroix', *Journal of the Warburg and Courtauld Institutes*, no. 20, 1957, p. 181, citing Delacroix's letter to T. Silvestre about Géricault's reaction on seeing *The Hay Wain* in London in 1821. Florisoone suggests that it may have been on Gericault's recommendation (as, presumably, passed on to Arrowsmith) that the painting was taken to France.

5 As Judy Ivy points out, Nodier's *Promenade* was published in France in 1821 (Ivy 1991, p. 91). An English translation appeared the following year, published in Edinburgh, from which Ivy gives an extract (Ivy 22.8, p. 93) and also a review of the book (in *The New Monthly Magazine*, Ivy 22.9, p.94).

6 Whiteley 2002, p. 48.

7 *JCC* VI, pp. 87–88.

8 See L. Whiteley, 'John Arrowsmith', Grove Art Online/Oxford Art Online, Oxford, 2007–15; for more about the Diorama, see Pieter van der Merwe, 'Diorama', Grove Art/Oxford Art Online. (Van der Merwe points out that the patent for the Diorama in London was taken out in John Arrowsmith's name.)

9 *JCC* VI, p. 134 (letter to Fisher, 30 Sept 1823).

10 *JCC* VI, p. 156.

11 Whiteley 2002 (p. 48) points out that Régnier's painting by Constable was the first one we hear of by the English artist in France, and argues that he probably acquired it on a visit to England, bearing in mind that he (Régnier) was to include English views among the subjects he sent to the Paris Salon in 1824.

12 Whiteley 2002, citing the source in Delacroix's journal for November 1823. This was the second time Delacroix had seen the painting, which he refers to mistakenly as a sketch, owing no doubt to the brushwork being more spontaneous than he was used to seeing in a 'finished' picture.

13 Beckett in *JCC* IV, pp. 182–83 (citing Delacroix's journal entry for 19 June: 'Un Cogniet et le tableau de Géricault. Vu les *Constable*. C'était trop de choses dans un jour. Ce Constable me fait un grand bien').

14 Schroth was established as a dealer in Paris by 1820, and was an early supporter of Bonington. His shop was under the patronage of the Duchesse de Berry (see L. Whiteley, 'Claude Schroth', Grove Art Online/Oxford Art Online).

15 See *JCC* III, p. 126 (letter to C. R. Leslie, 21 June 1835), for the comment about David's pictures being 'loathsome'; and *JCD*, pp. 59–60, for his lecture draft ('the French Taste') in which he mentions the rigidity of David's figures. He also referred to David's *Crowning of Bonaparte* as 'below notice as a work of execution' (*JCC* VI, p. 107).

16 For a discussion of the post-Waterloo phase of Anglomania in France, see R. B. Beckett, 'Constable and France', *Connoisseur*, vol. CXXXVII, 1956, pp. 249–55, and D. Sutton, 'The Dawn of the Entente Cordiale', *Apollo*, Jan 1985, pp. 48–54.

17 Whiteley, 2002, p. 12, who cites Nodier's comment on the English artists' liking for their own places ('c'est comme dans la nature, et chacun affectionne les richesses de son pays').

18 C. J. Holmes, *Constable and His Influence on Landscape Painting*, London, 1902, p. 184.

19 *JCC* VI, p. 167.

20 See Cove 2006, pp. 62–63, who points out (citing Ivy 1991, pp. 85–86) that English critics had often found fault with Constable's work at this date for its 'want of finish'. She cites, for example, their response to his *Stratford Mill* of 1820, commenting on its 'scattered appearance' or its 'busy and flickered' brushwork.

21 Delacroix, journal, 23 Sept 1846, cited in Gage 2002, p.38. Gage also cites a similar observation by Claude-Joseph Vernet, in a letter published in 1817, long after the artist's death.

22 See note 2 above.

23 P. Noon, 'Art on View: Expositions, Exhibitions and Salons', in Noon et al. 2003, p. 94.

24 For a list of works shown by British artists at the Paris Salon, see Basil S. Long, 'The Salon of 1824', *Connoisseur*, vol. LXVIII, Feb 1924, pp. 66–76. The Bonington *French Coast*, although dated on the Tate website to *c.*1825, is now thought to have been one of Bonington's exhibits at the Paris Salon in 1824. It was subsequently shown in London, at the British Institution, in 1826 and purchased by the Countess de Grey (D. B. Brown, with S. Skinner and I. Warrell, *Coasting: Turner, Bonington and Some Contemporaries on the Shores of the Channel*, exh. cat., Nottingham Castle Museum and other venues, 2009, p. 27).

25 Works exhibited by these artists at the Paris Salon in 1824 are given in Basil S. Long, The Salon of 1824', see note 24. Four of Copley Fielding's watercolours were owned by Claude Schroth. Copley Fielding's address was given in the Salon catalogue – as was that of Gastineau, Harding, Varley and Wilde – as 25 Quai des Grands-Augustins, an address associated with the publisher J. F. d'Ostervald (and D. F. d'Ostervald, known as Ostervald Jr), with whom these artists had links through the latter's various illustrated publications, such as *Excursions sur les côtes et dans les ports de France*, 1823 (see Pointon 1985, p. 83, and Noon et al. 2003, pp. 235 and 239–40).

26 Beckett in *JCC* IV, pp. 179, 190; and Whiteley 2002, p. 47.

27 Whiteley 2002, p. 49.

28 *JCC* VI, p. 185 (letter to Fisher, 17 Dec 1824); Whiteley 2002 (p. 49) also cites comments from Delécluze, Stendhal, Coupin de la Couperie and Charles Nodier.

29 For the fullest discussion of this, see M. Florisoone, 'Constable and the *Massacres de Scios* by Delacroix', n. 4, who notes that the whole issue is complicated by the fact that Delacroix reworked the picture again in 1847, and because some time after that the picture was also cleaned – thus making it more difficult to judge which passages may have been retouched in 1824. Nevertheless, he suggests that Delacroix's retouchings in 1824 were probably made to some of the figures in the foreground, where one can decipher an intensification of some of the white touches and of the highlights, in an attempt by the artist to render these areas more luminous.

30 *JCC* IV, p. 195 (undated letter from Arrowsmith, which arrived in London 20 Jan 1825).

31 Pointon 1985, p. 81, cites the Comte de Forbin approaching David Wilkie by letter to invite him officially to show work at the 1824 Salon (which Wilkie declined), and also mentions the fact that d'Ostervald had gathered around him a group of English artists in the early 1820s (see also note 25 above). Furthermore, Arrowsmith, in negotiating to buy *The Hay Wain* and *View on the Stour* from Constable, had promised him that the two paintings would form a feature at the 1824 Salon exhibition (see Ch. 1, n. 6, and also note 2 above). So although Arrowsmith requested Constable to write a formal letter requesting that his pictures 'might be admitted if such was the opinion of the directors' (*JCC* II, p. 347, journal entry, 30 June), it would seem that submitting his works to the Salon jury – if this happened at all – would presumably only have been a formality.

32 *JCC* VI, p. 185.

33 See Beckett in *JCC* II, pp. 367–68, and *JCC* IV pp. 190–91 (letter from Arrowsmith, 5 Oct 1824, in which the latter told Constable that 'there has been a room made ready for you since two months at least').

CHAPTER 3

1 *JCC* VI, p. 171.

2 See Wilcox 2011 and Ian Warrell, *Turner's Wessex: Architecture and Ambition*, London, 2015.

3 Warrell 1995b, p. 33. It is proposed there that the artist may have been the 'Mr Turner' listed as staying at the New Steine Hotel on 3 June.

4 See Riding and Johns 2013, pp. 108–10, 116, 123.

5 In fact, Turner's presence in London can be documented for the evening of 25 May, when he attended the annual dinner at the Artists' Benevolent Institution. Constable occasionally attended events at the Institution, but it is not known whether he was also present on this date.

6 Ford 1981, pp. 86 and 669. See also the view by Louis Francia, engraved by W. B. Cooke in 1827, which may well date from somewhat earlier (Ford 1981, no. 83).

7 See Beddoe 1995.

8 Edward Wedlake Brayley, *Topographical Sketches of Brighthelmston, and Its Neighbourhood*, 1825, pp. 11–12 and 18–19.

9 Corbin 1994, p. 80.

10 Brayley, *Topographical Sketches*, p. 12. In addition to Brayley, other contemporary guidebooks include: John Evans, *An Excursion to Brighton, with an account of the Royal Pavilion*, 1822; John Baxter, *The Stranger in Brighton and Directory*, 1822; Richard Sicklemore Jr, *History of Brighton and Picture of the Roads*, 1823; John Bruce, *Select Views of Brighton*, 1824; C. and R. Sicklemore, *Descriptive Views of Brighton*, 1824; Jonathan Whittemore, *An Historical and Topographical Picture of Brighton and Its*

Environs, 1825; Edward Mogg, *Pocket Itinerary*, 1826; James Taylor, *The Royal Brighton Guide*, 1826; Jonathan Whittemore, *Royal Brighton Guide for 1826*; Edward Wallis, *Brighton Townsman and Visitor's Directory*, 1826; John Baxter, *Select Sketches in Brighton, Lewes and their Environs*, 1827; John Bruce, *History of Brighton*, 1827; and Edward Wallis, *Brighton As It Is*, 1828.

11 John Gore (ed.), *Creevey's Life and Times*, 1934, p. 115. Similar comments occur in C. M. Westmacott's *The English Spy*, 1825, p. 346. The issue of awkward social interaction at Brighton is extensively discussed in Hemingway 1992, pp. 157–58.

12 Mary Shelley, 'A Visit to Brighton', *London Magazine*, ser. 2, vol. 7, December 1826, p. 466.

13 Ford 1981, pp. 41–54, and 381–577.

14 Brighton and Arundel sketchbook, TB CCX; Tate Britain

15 For a summary of recent thinking, see Nicholas Mirzoef, *How to See the World*, 2015, Ch. 2, especially pp. 86–87.

16 Brayley, *Topographical Sketches*, p. 22.

17 See the Brighton and Arundel sketchbook (Tate Britain, TB CCX, fol. 20a [Brunswick Terrace, continued on fol. 21 as a panoramic view towards central Brighton and the Chain Pier] and fol. 23 [Arundel Terrace, with Lewes Crescent; continued on fol. 22a as a panoramic view westwards towards the pier]). See also fols 25a–26, sketches of Lewes Crescent and Sussex Square.

18 Musgrave 1981, pp. 181 ff.

19 Ford 1981, nos 33, 1042, 1049.

20 Ford 1981, pp. 65–74 and nos 163–334.

21 See Tate: TB CCX fols 14a, 17a, 20, 21, 22, 22a, 27, 28, 33, 34a, 35a.

22 Tate: TB CCX, fol. 30 (the seafront looking west up to the Albion hotel, with the church and windmills), fol. 29a (from the Steine and the donkey wheel, with the domes of the Royal Pavilion), fol. 31 (the last pylon of the Chain Pier, with a lifeboat and the sundial on the seaward platform; the New Steine on the right) and fol. 30a (Marine Parade east of the New Steine).

23 As well as pirate editions, such as that by 'Hunt', the image was utilised in other formats, such as the filigree porcelain basket made by Worcester in the collection of Brighton Museum. The design was also a source for amateur artists: see the rather basic version in the Yale Center for British Art, New Haven, CT (B1974.12.1092).

24 Ford 1981, pp. 21–24 and p. 21; see also Hemingway 1992, p. 166.

25 See Warrell 2013.

26 J. J. L. Whiteley, *Claude Lorrain: Drawings from the Collections of the British Museum and the Ashmolean Museum*, London, 1998, p. 12, and see p. 84, no. 38 (repr. p. 86). For Constable's apparent distaste for the drawings, or the amount of money spent on them, see *JCC* VI, pp.149–50. See also the note in Turner's Brighton and Arundel sketchbook of 1824, which appears to read 'Claude morning' (TB CCX 10a).

27 *Somerset House Gazette and Literary Museum*, vol. II, no. XXXIX, 3 July 1824, pp. 189–90. The other English artists named are Callcott and James Ward.

28 See the following in the Reynolds catalogue: nos 24.26–24.41, 24.45–24.50 (but for 24.49 see note 50, below), 24.91–24.93, 24.26A and 24.31A. See also Fleming-Williams 1990, pp. 208–9, who describes the outline on the back of an oil sketch, *The Battery on the West Cliff* (V&A; R.24.22), faintly dated '20 August', as a precursor to the series.

29 See the *Sussex Weekly Advertiser* for 30 August, and 6 and 13 September. The report in the latter notes the exceptional temperature of 80 degrees in the shade on 10 September, but that peak was broken by rain before the 13th.

30 See R.24.44. Furthermore, the sketch on the other side (R.24.43) records Hodson's mill, which Constable painted in oils the following day (R.24.17; V&A).

31 Both ideas are set out in more detail on a sheet of paper at the Rhode Island School of Design (RISD), of much the same dimensions as several oil sketches (see R.24.89 and 24.90). Reynolds noted that the paper was prepared with size on one side, and proposed that Constable possibly 'had intended to use it for an oil sketch', but he did not connect the compositions with those on the Horne Foundation sheet. It is worth speculating that the graphite outlines on the RISD sheet (as well as on a similar doubled-sided sheet at the V&A: R.24.21 and 24.22) perhaps suggest that Constable worked over similar preliminary designs on other occasions, even where it has been the general assumption that he was working purely in oils in front of the motif.

32 Sue Berry, 'Myth and Reality in the Representation of Resorts: Brighton and the Emergence of the "Prince and Fishing Village" Myth 1770–1824', *Sussex Archaeological Collections*, 140, 2002, pp. 97–112.

33 *JCC* VI, p. 171.

34 See Payne 2007, pp. 176–180; Solkin 2008, pp. 55–61.

35 *JCC* VI, p. 191.

36 Fleming-Williams 1990, p. 209.

37 See R.24.39. See also *Beached Fishing Boats*, formerly owned by Victor Rienaecker, lent to the Burlington Fine Arts Club in 1929 (no. 8; photo in the Witt Library). Another pencil sketch (its lines strengthened in pen and ink), probably on a fragment of one of the sketchbook leaves (like R.24.50), was recently sold at Cheffins Auction House, 15/16 June 2016, lot 755 (with a note by Anne Lyles).

38 See also *Brighton Beach, with a Rainbow; Colliers Unloading* (Oldham Art Gallery; R.24.34) and the works in the Huntington (R.24.27) and the Fogg Art Museum (R.24.33).

39 *JCC* VI, pp. 184. It has sometimes been claimed that this letter specified that the engravings would be made by Reynolds, but the reference to him is actually concerned with his work on the Salon exhibits.

40 *JCC* VI, p. 182.

41 *JCC* VI, p. 184.

42 See *JCC* II, pp. 205–9; *JCC* VI, pp. 208–9. There is a subsequent reference in Constable 's journal on 14 September 1825 to a request from Miss Drew, who sought to borrow the Brighton sketchbook (*JCC* II, p. 393).

43 See R.24.93 (private collection), fig. 118 and fig. 42. Also note that the drawing catalogued by Reynolds as 24.49, now at the Museum of Fine Arts, Houston (see note 51).

44 *Brighton Beach: Fishing Boats by a Breakwater* (British Museum; R.24.46) and *Beach Scene, Brighton* (private collection; R.24.26A). The third drawing, *Brighton Beach: A Fishing Boat with a Net* (V&A; R 24.40), is an elaboration of an idea set out more simply on another page of the book (V&A; R 24.37).

45 *Brighton Beach, with Boats and Fishermen* (V&A; R.24.45); and *Coal Brigs on Brighton Beach* (V&A; R.24.48).

46 There is an obvious relationship between R.24.48 and *Coal Brigs on Brighton Beach* (fig. 45). In the case of R.24.45 there are three works that seem to be connected. The most

obvious link is with the pencil sketch *Fishing Boats on Brighton Beach* (private collection; R.24.50), showing the same group of three boats in more or less the same configuration. The two boats on the left would also appear to be those in *A Lugger and Hog-Boat at Brighton* (not Constable's title; Oldham Art Gallery; R.24.28), which was dated by Constable on 11 September 1824. Finally, a lost drawing, bearing the same date, shows the sterns of three boats, which may well depict the vessels in the other drawings (R.24.29).

47 See R.24.51–24.56, all in the V&A. Of the boat drawings, R.24.56 is closest to those in the Brighton sketchbook series, and perhaps features the stucco façades of the seafront on the far right. On its verso is a faint sketch of a mother and child, which may represent Maria and her daughter Isabel, who was two on 23 August 1824.

48 Robert C. Leslie, *A Waterbiography*, London, 1894, p. 57.

49 *Brighton Beach, with Capstan* (private collection; R.24.26).

50 Fig. 44 was sold at Christie's, 4 March 1975, lot 20, as *A Beach Scene, with a Fisherman Unfurling a Sail, and Beached Boats*. It is apparently on Whatman paper. In addition to this work, not listed by Reynolds, the sale catalogue commentary mentions another drawing that does not seem to be part of the current corpus: 'dated 3rd Sept, 1824, in the Johnson Collection, Philadelphia'.

51 The coal brigs feature in an apparent sequence of four drawings: three boats can be seen in the twilight view at the Higgins, Bedford (fig. 45); there are two in the drawing with a rainbow at Oldham Art Gallery (R.24.34); and one of the V&A drawings shows a re-floated brig departing towards the pier (R.24.41). The last two of these drawings are closely related stylistically. In between the Bedford and Oldham sheets Constable seems to have used half a page of the sketchbook for a pencil sketch, now at the Museum of Fine Arts, Houston (R.24.49, where the dimensions are wrongly given; they are 13.5 × 17.7 cm).

52 But a sketch by Turner in a notebook of 1828 (Tate: TB CCXXXVII 4, D21858) is directly comparable with fig. 43 (R.24.30), demonstrating that the fishing quarter at the Battery appealed to other artists.

53 Two younger children play at the edge of R.24.40 (V&A).

54 *Sailing Boat, Brighton Beach*, 10.6 × 14.8 cm, formerly Constable family collection (not in Reynolds). I am grateful to Anne Lyles for bringing this to my attention.

55 *Worthing Beach* (private collection; R.24.31); see also Fleming-Williams 1990, pp. 203–9.

56 Advertisements for the sale appeared in the local and national newspapers; see Warrell 1995a, p. 30. It is possible he attended the auction with Henry Phillips, who had worked as a banker in Worthing. For Constable's own collection, see Evans 2014, pp. 81–91.

57 *Sussex Weekly Advertiser*, 18 October 1824.

58 See also *Shipping on the Beach, with a Stormy Sea* (private collection; R.24.92); *Shipping in a Stormy Sea at Brighton* (private collection; R.24.91); and *Brighton Beach, with a Horse turning a Capstan* (R.24.33), Fogg Art Museum.

CHAPTER 4

1 *JCC* VI, p. 171

2 R.27.2; Reynolds's dating was revised in Parris and Fleming-Williams 1991, p. 281.

3 On 10 July *The Morning Post* records his departure two days earlier, after a very short stay; Egremont's presence in August was announced on the 15th, but he may not have stayed long, since his horses ran at Goodwood on 20 August. He is next documented as heading back to Brighton on 26 October (see also *JCC* II, p. 370).

4 *Morning Post*, issue 16724, 27 July 1824.

5 *JCC* VI, p. 161.

6 *JCC* VI, p. 171.

7 See C. H. Collins-Baker, *Catalogue of the Petworth Collection of Pictures in the Possession of Lord Leconfield*, London, 1920. See also Loukes 2014, pp. 2–6 and p. 14.

8 The most recent summary of this is in Eric Shanes, *Young Mr Turner: The First Forty Years: 1775–1815*, New Haven, CT, and London, 2016, pp. 436–41.

9 *Morning Post*, issue 16711, 12 July 1824.

10 *Brighthelmston Suspension Pier Company Register of Shareholders*, The Keep, Brighton.

11 Lyles 2006, p. 185.

12 The removal of the fishermen from the Steine was very recent, coming into force after the publication of John Evans's *Excursion to Brighton*, 1822 (p. 52). Their banishment was certainly complete by 1824, when Edward Wedlake Brayley compiled his *Topographical Sketches of Brighthelmston, and Its Neighbourhood*, 1825, p. 27.

13 Sue Boulton, 'Church under a Cloud: Constable and Salisbury', *Turner Studies*, vol. 3, no. 2, Winter 1984, pp. 29–44.

14 Hemingway 1992, p. 188.

15 *The Sun*, 8 May 1827; see Ivy 1991, pp. 119–26, for other reviews.

16 *The Times*, 11 May 1827.

17 *JCC* VI, p. 231.

18 Reproduced in Riding and Johns 2013, pp. 144–45. He also bought B. R. Haydon's *Alexander the Great Taming Bucephalus*, which was also included in the 1827 exhibition; the penurious Haydon was perhaps a more urgent cause than Constable.

19 *'Now for the Painter' (Rope) – Passengers Going on Board* (Manchester City Galleries) and *Port Ruysdael* (Yale Center for British Art, New Haven, CT).

20 *JCC* VI, p. 220.

21 See Christopher Rowell, Ian Warrell and David Blayney Brown, *Turner at Petworth*, London, 2002, for the most recent detailed discussion of these works.

22 See Lyles 2006, pp. 128–61.

23 See the image of it in situ by C. R. Leslie in Rowell, Warrell and Brown, *Turner at Petworth*, p. 127. The sketches of the pier in the *Arundel and Shoreham* sketchbook (Tate, TB CCXLV) must date from 1829 onwards, and suggest that the artist returned to Brighton to refresh his memory of the buildings lining the seafront prior to resolving this part of the Petworth canvas.

24 See Martin Butlin, Mollie Luther and Ian Warrell, *Turner at Petworth: Painter & Patron*, London, 1989, pp. 120–21, 276–79, pls 126–29. A report from Brighton on 28 October gave notice that 'Lord Egremont is expected to return to East Lodge in a few days' (*Morning Post*, issue 17746, 30 October 1827).

25 For the full range of the friction between the two artists, see Leslie Parris in Evelyn Joll, Martin Butlin and Luke Herrmann (eds), *The Oxford Companion to J. M. W. Turner*, Oxford, 2001, pp. 60–61, and Lyles 2013.

26 See the *Morning Post*, 16 May 1824, for a report of the first voyage of the *Rapid*.

27 This striking, and somewhat unnerving, detail also occurs in some of his earlier paintings of the Thames estuary, where echoes of the Nore mutiny must have continued to resonate; see, for example, *Sheerness as Seen from the Nore* (1808; Museum of Fine Arts, Houston, TX).
28 See Martin Butlin and Evelyn Joll, *The Paintings of J. M. W. Turner*, New Haven, CT, and London, 1984, p.168 69.
29 See: Hill 1985; Parris and Fleming-Williams 1991, pp. 319–57; and Stephen Calloway in Evans 2014, pp. 183–207.
30 See Warrell 1995b, p. 37.

CHAPTER 5

1 *JCC* VI, p. 191 (23 January 1825).
2 *JCC* VI, p. 181 (17 November 1824).
3 The exception was the *Valley Farm* (R.35.1), bought by the collector Robert Vernon two months before it was sent to the Academy exhibition in 1835.
4 For the negative review in *The London Magazine*, see Ivy 1991, pp. 115-16, and see Ivy elsewhere for other reviews of Constable's work around this date.
5 Ivy, 1991, 28.7, p. 126 (again *The London Magazine*).
6 On 1 October 1825, Constable reported in his journal that 'Mr Woodburn' (probably Samuel Woodburn, the picture dealer) had overheard a collector in Paris offer Claude Schroth £100 for one of his Hampstead paintings; and on 4 October he wrote that 'Mr Allnutt of Clapham [the collector John Allnutt, a wine merchant] ... had been in France – & was quite excited with the accounts of me in Paris' (*JCC* II, pp. 397–98).
7 Beckett in *JCC* II, p. 377, and *JCC* IV, p. 211 (where Beckett gives a useful summary of all the works by Constable that seem to have gone to France around this time).
8 In a letter to Fisher of 8 April 1825, Constable writes that 'I am fulfilling many orders in small for Paris – Mr Schroth 3 more – M.Didot (the great printer) 3 – Mr Arrowsmith 2– ...' (*JCC* VI, p. 198). It is not clear from this whether the two works listed here for Arrowsmith were paintings not yet completed from a previous order or new commissions from a third transaction with the dealer.
9 For the introduction from Arrowsmith, see letter from the latter to Constable, 20 March 1825 (*JCC* IV, p. 198) and for Didot's order, see n. 8 above.
10 *JCC* IV, pp. 199–200 (17 May 1825).
11 As Gage points out (Paris 2002, p. 38), all that is known for certain is that the letter from Schroth was delivered by Delacroix, given that it survived in the family papers. Gage further mentions that Delacroix's reference (in his journal, 1846) to having heard that Constable said ('Constable dit ...') that the superiority of the green in his meadows was owing to the fact that it was made up of a multitude of different greens might simply mean that Delacroix is referring here to something he read in a newspaper or magazine article as yet untraced (see also Gage in Paris 2002, p. 45, n. 31).
12 The sketchbook, in the Louvre, measures 3¼ × 4½ inches (8.3 × 11.5 cm) and was later used by Delacroix. The pages contained in the book that are thought to have been drawn on by Constable in Brighton in 1824 and 1825 are catalogued by Reynolds, 1984 (24.80). However, some of the latter have been coloured in a way that is not characteristic of Constable (although it has been suggested, somewhat unconvincingly, that the colouring may have been added by another hand). Furthermore, in reviewing Reynolds's 1984 catalogue of Constable's *Later Paintings and Drawings*, Leslie Parris and Ian Fleming-Williams queried the quality of some of the drawings in this sketchbook attributed to Constable (*Burlington Magazine*, CXXVII, March 1985, p.168).
13 For example, on 6 September 1825, Constable noted in his journal that he 'worked on Mr Schroth's pictures' (*JCC* II, p. 385); and on 6 December he wrote 'Got my picture for Mr Didot forward' (ibid., p. 416).
14 *JCC* IV, p. 194 (19 December 1824).
15 *JCC* IV, p. 198 (20 March 1825).
16 Catalogued by Robert Hoozee (*L'Opera completa di Constable*, Milan, 1979, no. 653) as a work of doubtful attribution, and not included in Graham Reynolds's 1984 catalogue. De-accessioned by the Museum of Fine Arts, Boston, sold Sotheby's 6 April 1993, lot 69 (as attributed to John Constable); sent to auction at Bonham's, *Old Master Paintings*, 9 July 2014, lot 28, with a full Constable attribution but remained unsold.
17 S. Cove, '*The Seabeach*, Technical Examination Report', 2013. Cove also notes that Constable marked up the proportions of a squaring-up grid over the pink priming, which implies that the design was enlarged from another, earlier study by the artist, almost certainly the smaller oil sketch in the Detroit Art Institute (see n. 18 below). The *Fake or Fortune* episode in which the painting featured was first broadcast on 26 January 2014, series 3.
18 The engraving of this subject, entitled 'A Sea Beach, Brighton, Heavy Surf – Windy Noon', appeared in part 2 of *English Landscape*, December 1830 (Hill 1985, no. 10, p. 103); for the oil sketch in Detroit, see Reynolds 1984 (R.24.79).
19 In a letter to Fisher of 10 September 1825 (*JCC* VI, p. 204), Constable says John Charles's health was already improving and 'he is now fond of bathing'.
20 *JCC* VI, p. 212 (letter to Fisher, 14 January 1826).
21 Ibid. and *JCC* VI, p. 206, in which Fisher writes to Constable (September 1825) that the mill had now 'burnt to the ground, and exists only on your canvas'. Constable referred in his letter of 14 January 1826 to Mrs Hand being 'a friend of the Chancellor', which has been interpreted as the Chancellor of the Diocese of Salisbury, although Parris and Fleming-Williams (1991, p. 263) doubt Mrs Hand had any Salisbury connections. Meanwhile, Wilcox (2011, p. 76) suggests the commission from Mrs Hand for this picture of *Gillingham Mill* would more likely have been made through Constable's friend and Hampstead neighbour William Collins.
22 See n. 20. The publication came out in 1824, in French, a language in which Maria was proficient.
23 For a full discussion of the quarrel and Arrowsmith's pending insolvency, see Beckett in *JCC* IV, pp. 204–7.
24 *JCC* IV, pp. 207–8 (letter from Schroth to Constable, 13 July 1826).
25 *JCC* VI, p. 172 (letter to Fisher, 29 August 1824), in which Constable refers to Phillips's 'instructive and entertaining botanical publications' and makes a resolution to buy them. He did indeed acquire a copy of Phillips's 'history of trees', as a copy of this book (*Sylva Florifera, or the Shrubbery, Historically and Botanically Treated*, 1823) survives in the Constable family library (*FDC* 1975, p. 45).
26 Phillips's various schemes for public gardens in

Brighton are discussed by Beckett, *JCC* V, pp. 80–82.

27 *JCC* II, p. 403 (journal, 22 October 1825).

28 Reynolds 1984 (p. 87, under R.26.7).

29 Reynolds (ibid.) also mentions that the album from which the drawing was extracted originally contained another drawing of the butter burr by Constable, dated 2 January 1826, whose whereabouts are currently unknown. It thus seems likely that the *Butter Burr in Flower* was made on the same occasion, perhaps from an illustration.

30 *JCC* V, p. 80 (1 March 1826). Phillips was also interested in plants for their medicinal qualities; in 1828 he sent Constable some arrowroot when Maria's health was especially poor (*FDC* 1975, p.123).

31 Beckett in *JCC* V, p. 79.

32 *JCC* VI, p. 230 (letter to Fisher, 26 August 1827).

33 The first reference to Evans in the family correspondence dates from early October 1827, when Maria records the doctor visiting the house at Well Walk when Constable was away in Suffolk. She refers to Evans 'being pleased with the frame' (*JCC* II, pp. 440–41, letter of 5 and 6 October), to which Constable's reply was that the frame was 'optional' (ibid, p. 442), all this implying that Evans had been given one of the artist's paintings, in lieu of a cash payment, for medical services rendered.

34 *JCC* IV, p. 139 (letter to James Carpenter, 23 July 1828, in which Constable refers to having taken an easel with him). See also Bailey 2006, pp. 185–86.

35 Fleming-Williams 1990, p. 215.

36 Reynolds 1984 (R.28.13), inscribed on the verso (by a hand transcribing Constable's original inscription) 'Brighton – Sunday evening July 20 1828'.

37 *JCC* IV, p. 139 (23 July 1828).

38 The two plant studies in the British Museum (R.28.14 and 28.15) are inscribed with their dates, 24 and 25 July 1828 respectively, the former also with the additional word 'Brighton'. The one in the V & A (R. 28.24), although not dated, is usually associated with the other two, and thus assumed to have been painted in Brighton. However Constable is known often to have often collected plants, lichen and mosses, and to have made sketches of them indoors, especially in later life (see under R.28.24, pp. 195–96).

39 Leslie 1951, p. 171.

40 Ibid, p. 173.

41 Beckett (*JCC* III, p. 11) notes that Phillips had been appreciative of Constable's work before the latter's election as an Associate Academician in 1819, but then a few years later seemed to think that Constable had been showing disrespect for the Academy by seeking fame abroad. Then, when Constable was standing for election as a full member in February 1828, Phillips apparently harangued the former in a conversation, extolling the 'higher walks of art', shortly after which Constable felt compelled to write to Phillips to justify his own ambitions as a landscape painter and asking to be considered fairly by him in the forthcoming voting for new members (*JCC* IV, pp. 279–81). Whether Phillips supported him that year or not, it took Constable another year to become a full Academician.

42 Loukes 2014, pp. 27–30.

43 *JCC* V, pp. 125–26, and *JCC* III, pp.32–33(letter to Leslie, 12 November 1830, in which Constable speaks of visiting John Charles in Brighton).

44 The invitation to exhibit at Lille came via the French painter Auguste Hervieu, who had settled in London in Newman Street, close to where Constable lived, in Charlotte Sreett. Hervieu was a member of the Society of Fine Arts at Lille, and was asked by the Society to approach leading artists in London to exhibit at the Lille Salon in 1825 following the success of the Paris Salon the previous year (*JCC* IV, pp. 270–74).

45 Colnaghi's, an art-dealing as well as a print-selling and publishing business, had been founded by the Italian émigré Paul Colnaghi in the late eighteenth century. Constable visited their premises in Pall Mall East on a regular basis, being a keen print collector (see Evans 2014, pp. 88–105). It was Paul Colnaghi who had originally vouched for the respectability and creditworthiness of Arrowsmith at the time when Constable was negotiating with the latter over the sale of *The Hay Wain* and *View on the Stour near Dedham* (see Ch. 1, and *JCC* VI, p. 156). Arrowsmith had arranged the transport of Constable's pictures to Paris at that time. By 1827, however, Arrowsmith had gone out of business, so Constable decided to use Colnaghi's as his agent when sending *The Cornfield* to the Paris Salon that year, by now generally liaising with Paul Colnaghi's son Dominic (*JCC* IV, pp. 153–56).

46 Beckett in *JCC* IV, p. 209.

47 Ibid. (recording a comment made by the artist Thomas Uwins).

48 In a letter of 17 May 1825, Schroth had told Constable that the two Hampstead paintings had met with an even more favourable reception than those shown at the Paris Salon the year before (*JCC* IV, pp. 199–200).

49 Hoozee 1985, p. 41 and n. 31, draws attention to the general influence of Constable on this picture; and indeed it seems especially close to the two Hampstead pictures owned by Schroth, *Branch Hill Pond* and *Child's Hill*, especially in the way Huet uses a receding path in the foreground and the way he shows the landscape receding with its distinct intersecting planes into the far distance, the latter then picked out by bright sunlight under an expansive, cloudy sky.

50 Hoozee, ibid., and I. Fleming-Williams and L. Parris, *The Discovery of Constable*, London, 1984, p. 53.

51 Ibid.

52 Huet's son René-Paul attempted to deny that his father's art was strongly influenced by Constable (or indeed by Turner or Bonington). But Huet himself admitted that 'the appearance of Constable's works was a major event in the history of modern painting' (*Paul Huet d'après ses notes, sa correspondance, ses contemporains*, ed. R. P. Huet, Paris 1911, p. 95, cited in Hoozee 1985, pp. 39–40). He also admitted that it was English painting that first demonstrated to him how he might merge his own naturalistic vision with the poetry of the Old Masters (P. Noon, *Richard Parkes Bonington: On the Pleasure of Painting*, exh cat., Yale Center of British Art, New Haven, CT, 1991, p. 158).

53 Hoozee, ibid., p. 40.

CHAPTER 6

1 *JCC* VI, p. 189.

2 Ford 1981.

3 *JCC* VI p. 128.

4 Berry 2005, pp. 46–62.

5 British Library (BL) Add. MS 69246 fols 107–174; *Morning Post*, 19 Sept 1819, 19 July

1820; *Morning Chronicle*, 5 Nov 1823; *Brighton Gazette* 29 Jan 1824, 19 Feb and 18 Mar 1824, 27 May 1825; *Brighton Herald* 9 Apr 1834.

6 East Sussex Record Office (ESRO) SAS-BRI 27, SAS-DD 620.

7 Berry 2015, pp. 213–29.

8 ESRO AMS 6545/1; ACC 5310/271; ACC 5316/271.

9 *Morning Chronicle*, 7 Mar 1842; C. Wright, *The Brighton Ambulator*, 1818, p. 66; *London Gazette*, 30 Nov 1821; *Brighton Gazette*, 19 Jan 1826.

10 Berry 2009, pp. 125–40.

11 S. Berry, 'The Castle Inn Assembly Room, Brighton, and John Crunden', *Journal of the Georgian Group (JGG)*, 2013, pp. 212–16; *Caledonian Mercury*, 11 Mar 1822; M. Ray, 'Domestic Service in Superior Suburbs; Brunswick Town, Hove', *Sussex Archaeological Collections*, 131, 1993; residential listings in street directories from 1824; Berry 2012, pp.162–83; *Brighton Gazette*, 8 Sept 1825; *Morning Post*, 30 June 1826; *Morning Advertiser*, 14 Oct 1829.

12 Berry 2015, pp. 213–29.

13 S. Berry, 'Royal Crescent Brighton (built c.1796–1805) – an early seaside crescent', *Journal of the Georgian Group* XXV, 2017 (forthcoming).

14 *JCC* II, p. 388, letter from John Constable to Maria on 9 September 1825, says 'Place' not 'Square', and they should not be confused. Russell Place is the north side of Russell Square, and has smaller houses. *JCC* II p. 395; *JCC* II p. 433; *JCC* V, p.199.

15 *JCC* II p. 404.

16 *JCC* II, p. 416, and Constable family letters seen by Shân Lancaster.

17 *JCC* II, pp. 432–33. *JCC* V, p. 199.

18 *JCC* VI, p. 237; *JCC* II, p. 448.

19 Fauntleroy was a London banker who was found guilty of stealing his customers' deposits and was hanged outside Newgate Prison in November 1824. *Times*, 20 Sept 1824; *Chester Chronicle*, 7 July 1825.

20 *Part of Old Shoreham Church* (Louvre 6234 p.105), is most likely to have been drawn around 22 May 1828, when Constable was actually in Shoreham Bay rather than viewing it from a distance.

21 *JCC* VI, pp. 170–71.

22 Ibid.

23 *JCC* II, p. 336 (Maria Constable to John).

24 *JCC* VI, p. 172.

25 Preston Place became 'Manor' in the later nineteenth century, a Victorian fashion. S. Farrant, 'William Roe of Withdean: The Purchase & Management of a Small Estate on the South Downs 1794 to 1808 & Its Consequences for the Modern Landscape', *SAC*, 119, 1981, pp. 173–79. S, Berry, 'Patcham Place', *SAC*, 153, 2015, pp. 210–13, includes plan of landscape showing wooded area. See S. Berry, 'Suburban Development on the Stanford Estate in Brighton and Hove in Sussex . c.1869-1939', *SAC*, 152, 2014, pp. 117–38, for an image from the 1820s.

26 A painting of the mill being moved is in Preston Manor Museum, Brighton.

27 Hodson's is clearly marked just off Dyke Road on the Pigott-Smith map; http://www.sussexmillsgroup.org.uk/smockmill.htm (accessed 8 September 2016) and http://regencysociety-jamesgray.com/volume31/source/jg_31_025.html (accessed 10 September 2016).

28 www.WilliamVine.net.

29 Catalogue.millsarchive.org. regencysociety-jamesgray.com.

30 http://www.cmpcaonline.org.uk/page_id_219.aspx (accessed 1 Sept 2016), on which is Steve Myall, 'The Gleaners 1824'.

31 ESRO BH/G/2/7000/1, Withdean Map 1808, TDE/46/2 Map 1842.

32 *JCC* II, p. 336 (Maria Constable to John, 19 June 1824).

CHAPTER 7

1 *JCC* VI, pp. 170–71. 'It is the business of a painter not to contend with nature [...] but to make something out of nothing, in attempting which, he must almost of necessity become poetical.'

2 *JCC* IV, pp. 199–201.

3 Andrei Joubin (ed.), *Eugene Delacroix 1822–1863*, Paris, 1981; supplement, entry dated 23 September 1846, p. 881.

4 'Catalogue raisonné des dessins de Delacroix' (Sérullaz et al, 1984 II) RF6234, F046 verso.

5 Hubert Wellington (ed.), *The Journal of Eugene Delacroix, A Selection*, trans. Lucy Norton, London, 1951, p. 138. After an evening walk with his friend Villot, the French master writes in his journal about a sunset and how complementary colour works within it: 'It was sunset, the chrome and lake tones were most brilliant on the side where it was light and the shadows were extraordinarily blue and cold ... the grey clouds ... were verging on blue. It would seem that the warmer the lighter tones, the more nature exaggerates the contrasting grey ... What made appear so vivid in the landscape was precisely this law of contrast.'

6 John Gage, *The Big Picture*, from Lyles 2006, p. 24; the original observation was from P. Conisbee, 'Pre-Romantic Plein Air Painting', *Art History*, vol. 2, no. 4, 1979, pp. 413–28; it is worth remembering that *plein-air* painting was especially cultivated by younger artists in Rome, and had been in Italy since Rubens's day.

7 Ann Bermingham, *Landscape and Power, English Landscape Drawing around 1795*, London, 2002, p. 97.

8 Katy Norris, *Sickert in Dieppe*, exh. cat., Pallant House Gallery, Chichester, 2015.

9 Catherine Lampert, *Frank Auerbach Speaking and Painting*, London, Thames and Hudson, 2015, p. 114.

10 Lampert, *Frank Auerbach Speaking and Painting*, p. 32.

11 Christopher Riopelle, 'Constable/Frank Auerbach', *Encounters*, London, National Gallery, 2000, pp. 32–43.

12 Nicholas Alfrey, Joy Sleeman and Ben Tufnell, *Uncommon Ground: Land Art in Britain 1966–79*, exh. Cat. London, Hayward Gallery, 2013.

13 *JCC* VI p.150.

14 *JCC* VI, p. 150.

15 Mark Evans with Nicola Costaras and Clare Richardson, *John Constable. Oil Sketches from the Victoria and Albert Museum*, London, 2011.

16 Ibid p.155.

Selected Bibliography

Place of publication London, unless otherwise specified.

Anthony Bailey, *John Constable: A Kingdom of His Own*, 2006

Stella Beddoe, '"Hung Like a Fairy Fabric O'er the Sea ...": The Brighton Chain Suspension Pier 1823–1896', in Beevers 1995, pp. 40–43

David Beevers (ed.), *Brighton Revealed through Artists' Eyes c.1760–c.1960*, exh.cat., Royal Pavilion, Art Gallery and Museums, Brighton, 1995

Sue Berry, *Georgian Brighton*, Chichester, 2005

Sue Berry, 'Thomas Read Kemp and the Shaping of Regency Brighton', *Journal of the Georgian Group (JGG)*, XVII, 2009

Sue Berry, 'The Georgian Chapels of the City of Brighton and Hove *c.*1700–1840', *JGG*, XVIIII, 2011

Sue Berry, 'The Impact of the Georgians and the Victorians on the Early Churches of the City of Brighton and Hove', *Sussex Archaeological Collections*, 149, 2011

Sue Berry, 'Amon and Amon Henry Wilds of Lewes and Brighton: Provincial Builders and Architects *c.*1790–1850', *Sussex Archaeological Collections*, 150, 2012

Sue Berry, 'East Lodge, the Brighton Home of George O'Brien Wyndham, 3rd Earl of Egremont', *Sussex Archaeological Collections*, 152, 2014

Sue Berry, 'A Resort Town Transformed: Brighton, *c.*1815-1840', *JGG*, XXIII, 2015

Alain Corbin, *The Lure of the Sea: The Discovery of the Seaside, 1750–1840*, Place of publication? 1994

Sarah Cove, 'The Painting Techniques of Constable's "Six-Footers"', in Lyles 2006, pp. 52–67

Mark Evans, with Nicola Costaras and Clare Richardson, *John Constable: Oil Sketches from the Victoria and Albert Museum*, 2011

Mark Evans, with Stephen Calloway and Susan Owens, *John Constable: The Making of a Master*, exh.cat., Victoria and Albert Museum, London, 2014

J. H. Farrant and **S. P. Farrant**, 'Brighton 1520–1820: From Tudor Town to Regency Resort', *Sussex Archaeological Collections*, 118, 1980

S. P. Farrant, 'William Roe of Withdean: The Purchase and Management of a Small Estate on the South Downs 1794 to 1808 and Its Consequences for the Modern Landscape', *Sussex Archaeological Collections*, 119, 1981

FDC 1975
Leslie Parris, Conal Shields and Ian Fleming-Williams (ed.), *John Constable: Further Documents and Correspondence*, London and Ipswich, 1975

Ian Fleming-Williams, *Constable and His Drawings*, Place of publication? 1990

John and Jill Ford, *Images of Brighton*, Richmond upon Thames, 1981

John Gage, 'Le Paysage est ma maîtresse', Paris 2002, pp. 35–45

Peter Harrap and Shân Lancaster, 'John Constable's House in Brighton', *The Burlington Magazine*, CLV (April 2013), pp. 250–51

Andrew Hemingway, *Landscape Imagery and Urban Culture in Early Nineteenth-Century Britain*, Cambridge, 1992

David Hill, *Constable's English Landscape Scenery*, 1985

Robert Hoozee, 'Constable and English Landscape Art', in Jan Sillevis and Hans Kraan, *The Barbizon School*, exh. cat., Gemeentemuseum, The Hague, 1985, pp. 35–44

Judy Ivy, *Constable and the Critics, 1802–1837*, Woodbridge, 1991

***JCC* I**
R. B. Beckett (ed.), *John Constable's Correspondence*, I, Ipswich, 1962

***JCC* II**
R. B. Beckett (ed.), *John Constable's Correspondence*, II, Ipswich, 1964

***JCC* III**
R. B. Beckett (ed.), *John Constable's Correspondence*, III, Ipswich, 1965

***JCC* IV**
R. B. Beckett (ed.), *John Constable's Correspondence*, IV: *Patrons, Dealers and Fellow Artists*, Ipswich, 1966

***JCC* V**
R. B. Beckett (ed.), *John Constable's Correspondence*, V: *Various Friends, with Charles Boner and the Artist's Children*, Ipswich, 1967

***JCC* VI**
R. B. Beckett (ed.), *John Constable's Correspondence*, VI: *The Fishers*, Ipswich, 1968

JCD
R. B. Beckett (ed.), *John Constable's Discourses*, Ipswich, 1970

Charles Robert Leslie, *Memoirs of the Life of John Constable (1843/1845)*, ed. Jonathan Mayne, 1951

Andrew Loukes, *Constable at Petworth*, exh.cat., Petworth House, Sussex, 2014

Anne Lyles (ed.), with Sarah Cove, John Gage, Charles Rhyne, Franklin Kelly, *Constable: The Great Landscapes*, exh.cat., Tate Britain, 2006

Anne Lyles, '"Turner, Calcott and Collins will not like it": Constable, Brighton and the Sea', in Riding and Johns 2013, pp. 158–61

Clifford Musgrave, *Life in Brighton*, Place of publication? 1981

Steve Myall, *The Victorian Development of the Clifton, Montpelier and Powis Estates of Brighton*, Lewes, 2008

Patrick Noon (ed.), with Stephen Bann, David Blayney Brown, Rachel Meredith, Christine Riding and Marie Watteau, *Constable to Delacroix: British Art and the French Romantics*, exh.cat., Tate Britain, Minneapolis Institute of Arts and Metropolitan Museum of Art, New York, 2003–4

Paris 2002
Constable: le choix de Lucian Freud, exh.cat., with contributions by W. Feaver, J. Gage, A. Lyles, O. Meslay, L. Whiteley and R. Ur, Grand Palais, Paris, 2002

Leslie Parris and Ian Fleming-Williams, with Sarah Cove, *Constable*, exh. cat., Tate Gallery, 1991

Christiana Payne, *Where the Sea Meets the Land: Artists on the Coast in Nineteenth-Century Britain*, Bristol, 2007

Marcia Pointon, *The Bonington Circle: English Watercolour and Anglo-French Landscape, 1790–1855*, Brighton 1985

Graham Reynolds, *The Later Paintings and Drawings of John Constable*, 2 vols, New Haven, CT, and London, 1984

Graham Reynolds, *The Early Paintings and Drawings of John Constable*, 2 vols, New Haven, CT, and London, 1996

Christine Riding and Richard Johns (eds.), *Turner and the Sea*, exh.cat., National Maritime Museum, Greenwich, 2013

David Solkin (ed.), *Art on the Line: The Royal Academy Exhibitions at Somerset House, 1780–1836*, Place of publication? 2001

David Solkin, *Painting Out of the Ordinary: Modernity and the Art of Everyday Life in Early Nineteenth-Century Britain*, New Haven, CT, and London, 2008

Ian Warrell, '"Piccadilly by the Seaside": John Constable at Brighton', in Beevers 1995a, pp. 17–31, and pp. 70-83, nos 31–50

Ian Warrell, 'J. M. W. Turner in Brighton', in Beevers 1995b, pp. 32–39, and pp. 61–69, nos 19–30

Ian Warrell, *Turner in Brighton*, exh. brochure, Royal Pavilion, Brighton, 2013

Linda Whiteley, 'Constable et le Salon de 1824', in Paris 2002, pp. 47–51

Timothy Wilcox (ed.), *The Romantic Windmill: The Windmill in British Art from Gainsborough to David Cox, 1750–1850*, exh. cat., Hove Museum and Art Gallery, 1993

Timothy Wilcox, *Constable and Salisbury: The Soul of Landscape*, London, 2011

Author Biographies

Dr Sue Berry FSA, formerly a Principal Lecturer in Tourism Management, has developed her love of landscape history. Her many articles in journals and books cover a range of topics, such as resorts (mostly in the eighteenth century), architects, agriculture, country houses and urban development; she also lectures on these subjects. She is now revising and extending *Georgian Brighton*, Chichester (2005).

Peter Harrap is the curator of *Constable and Brighton* at Brighton Museum. He studied at Camberwell College of Art (1993) and Winchester School of Art (1994–97). He was elected a Royal Academy of Arts schools graduate in 2004 as director of Young RAS. In 2010/11 Harrap was an assistant curator of, and exhibited in, *No New Thing under the Sun* at the Royal Academy. He also curated *Radical Art* (2005) at the Jerwood Space in London, and *Play*, featuring Jake and Dinos Chapman (2007). He lives and works in the former 9 Sober's Gardens.

Shân Lancaster is a writer, editor and researcher. As a freelance journalist she has worked for most national newspaper titles, and as a researcher she has collaborated on numerous book developments and television and film scripts, including the BBC Four television documentary *Constable: A Country Rebel*, first shown in 2014. Her research originally identified the exact location of Constable's lodgings at 9 Sober's Gardens, now 11 Sillwood Road, Brighton, and marked with a Brighton & Hove City Council Blue Plaque.

Anne Lyles is an art historian and curator specialising in late eighteenth- and early nineteenth-century British landscape painting. She worked at Tate Britain for twenty-five years, initially on J.M.W. Turner and British watercolour painters, and then on John Constable. She has co-curated (or contributed to the catalogues of) many exhibitions about the work of these artists: for example *The Great Age of British Watercolours, 1750–1880* (Royal Academy of Arts, London, 1993), *Constable's Clouds* (Liverpool and Edinburgh, 2000), the *Constable* exhibition in Paris in 2002 selected by Lucian Freud, *Constable: the Great Landscapes* (Tate Britain and other venues, 2006–7) and *Constable Portraits* (National Portrait Gallery and Compton Verney, 2009).

Mark Sheerin has specialised in contemporary art since training as a journalist in 2009. His work appears in Hyperallergic, Culture24, Artdependence and the Arts Desk. He maintains a long-standing art blog at www.criticismism.com and has been fortunate enough to interview many artists, including Georg Baselitz, Glenn Ligon, Jake Chapman, Jeremy Deller and Martin Creed. He holds an MA in Critical Theory from Sussex, which he draws on sparingly.

Ian Warrell is an independent curator specialising in nineteenth-century British art and photography. Formerly a curator at Tate Britain, he is currently Senior Visiting Scholar for Collections Research at the Yale Center for British Art, where he is cataloguing the paintings and watercolours by J.M.W. Turner. His many publications on the artist include, most recently, *Turner's Wessex* (Scala, 2015) and *Turner et la Couleur* (Hazan, 2016).

Acknowledgements

This book accompanies the exhibition *Constable and Brighton* at Brighton Museum and Art Gallery, 8 April–8 October 2017. Many individuals and institutions have helped bring both book and exhibition to fruition, but we must begin with special thanks to Mr James Stunt. Without his very generous donation there would be no book at all.

We must also particularly thank Anne Lyles, whose guidance has been invaluable, both as advisory specialist to the exhibition and as an author, and her fellow authors Ian Warrell, Dr Sue Berry and Mark Sheerin. Their commitment to, and enrichment of, this project has really been remarkable. Christopher Le Brun, President of the Royal Academy of Arts, was not only immensely supportive of the exhibition but also wrote the elegant Foreword, which draws on his personal experience of seeing Brighton through an artist's eyes.

At Scala publishing we are very grateful to Esme West, Nigel Soper and Matthew Taylor. Research into the Constable family's visits to Brighton was hugely assisted by the following: Adrian Glew from the Tate Archive, Pippa Parris, Andy Garth, Jill Clisby, Tim Clayton. Other research was assisted by Nicola Christie, Mark Evans, Lowell Libson and Andrew Loukes, as well as the staff of the London Library and the Witt Library.

Sarah Cove, who has recently re-examined many of the Brighton oil sketches and hopes to write up her findings in the near future, has been a source of generous and fascinating advice and encouragement. As curators of the exhibition, we are indebted to: the British Museum, London; Bury Art Gallery and Museum, Lancashire; the Castle Museum, Norwich, the Courtauld Institute, London; the Daniel Katz Family Trust; the Dick Institute, East Ayrshire; the Evans family; the Fitzwilliam Museum, Cambridge; the Hatvany family and Agnes Peresztegi; the Hugh Lane Gallery, Dublin; Colin Wiggins and Dr Susanna Avery-Quash at the National Gallery, London; the National Portrait Gallery, London; the Royal Academy of Arts, London; the Royal Pavilion and Museums, Brighton and Hove; Tate Britain, London; and David Thomson, Conal Shields, David Franklin, Michelle Wilson, Mr Tom Toppin, David Dallas, Cassandra Albinson, Catherine Hess, Ming Aguilar and the Victoria and Albert Museum, London, for their generous loans and for images they have supplied for this book.

Frank Auerbach and Geoffrey Parton of Marlborough Fine Art, David Dawson of the Freud Estate, Natasha Kissell, Steven Claydon and Charlotte Verity allowed us to reproduce their works in the final chapter. We have also received assistance in obtaining images from Louisa Dare (Courtauld Institute), Lynda Clark (the Fitzwilliam Museum, Cambridge), Anna Sheppard and Patricia Perez (Victoria and Albert Museum), Chris Sutherns (Tate, London), Louise Green, Jenny Liddle and Lauren Taylor (Felbrigg Hall, National Trust), Daragh Kenny (National Gallery, London), Iain Calderwood and Parveen Sodhi (British Museum), Caroline Doyle and Victoria Partridge (The Higgins, Bedford), Karen Lawson and Shruti Patel (Royal Collection Trust), Nikki Braunton (Museum of London), Katherine McClung-Oakes (Bury Art Gallery), Fiona Ford (Norfolk Museums), Teresa O'Toole (Sterling and Francine Clark Art Institute), Genevieve Webb (Dunedin Art Gallery), Andrew Bennett and Jenny Geering (East Sussex Records Office), Allan Hutchings (Brighton Argus), Romy Arm and Verena Schmidt (Oskar Reinhart Museum, Winterthur), Sian Phillips (Bridgeman Images), Finn Hopson and Mark Heathcote.

Ewan Clayton's calligraphy brought a new dimension to the design of this book.

We must also extend our warmest thanks to the Director and staff at the Royal Pavilion and Museums, Brighton and Hove, for their work on the development of the exhibition over the past five years. At Brighton Museum we particularly thank Janita Bagshawe, David Beevers, Nicola Coleby, Helen Grundy, Fiona Redford, Alexandra Loske, Jenny Lund, Jo Nightingale and Krystyna Pickering.

Finally, personal thanks are due to Natasha Kissell, Tessa James, Roger Bamber and Pat Berry.

Index

John Constable is referred to as JC. Illustrations are denoted by the use of *italics*. All places are in Brighton unless otherwise stated.

DEDICATION

This book is a tribute to the life of Richard Constable, the great-great-grandson of John Constable and a talented artist himself. Richard was hugely knowledgeable about his ancestor, and he and his wife, Val, were extraordinarily generous and supportive from the first moment we approached them to ask if we could hunt for Brighton connections in their family archives. Richard and Val came to Brighton to unveil the City of Brighton and Hove Blue Plaque on the front of 9 Sober's Gardens in 2013, but unfortunately Richard died in 2015, before final plans for the exhibition and book took shape. *Constable and Brighton* is dedicated to his memory.

Peter Harrap and Shân Lancaster, March 2017

First published in 2017 by
Scala Arts & Heritage Publishers Ltd
10 Lion Yard, Tremadoc Road
London SW4 7NQ, UK
www.scalapublishers.com

ISBN 978-1-78551- 069-4

Project managed by Esme West
Edited by Matthew Taylor
Designed by Nigel Soper
Calligraphy by Ewan Clayton

Printed and bound in Spain by Ganboa

10 9 8 7 6 5 4 3 2 1

FRONT COVER: detail of fig. 104
BACK COVER: detail of fig. 101
INSIDE FRONT COVER: detail of fig. 128
INSIDE BACK COVER: detail of fig. 122
PAGES 2–3: detail of fig. 93
PAGES 4–5: detail of fig. 121

Within some captions in this publication, an 'R' number indicates the listing of the work in the catalogue raisonné of Constable's work compiled by Graham Reynolds in 1984 and 1996 (see bibliography)